A PENGUIN SPECIAL

SICK CITIES

Mitchell Gordon

SICK CITIES

PENGUIN BOOKS
BALTIMORE · MARYLAND

Penguin Books Inc.
7110 Ambassador Road
Baltimore, Maryland 21207

This edition first published 1965 by arrangement with
The Macmillan Company, New York

Reprinted 1966, 1967, 1969, 1970

Set in Linotype Times Roman
Printed in the United States of America

To my mother and my Uncle Phil
. . . in memory

Contents

Acknowledgments

A SPECIAL note of thanks for a variety of assistance, from the gathering of primary information to suggestions on the reading of chapters in manuscript, is extended particularly to Dr. Victor D. Brannon, Director of the Governmental Research Institute in St. Louis; Boris Laiming, writer and consultant on fire problems, now retired in California; Professor Roger S. Freeman of Stanford University in Stanford, California, former Research Director for President Eisenhower's Education Committee of the Commission on Intergovernmental Relations; and to Arthur G. Will, County-City Coordinator for the Chief Administrative Officer of the County of Los Angeles.

The author is also indebted for assistance to such persons as Dr. Vern O. Knudsen, former Chancellor of the University of California at Los Angeles and a physicist specializing in the problems of noise; Eleanor O. Ferguson, Executive Secretary of the Public Library Association of the American Library Association in Chicago; Donal E. J. MacNamara, President of the New York Institute of Criminology; Bruce Smith, police consultant, Norfolk, Virginia; Murray Brown, Managing Editor of *Western City* magazine; Frank R. Bowerman, Assistant Chief Engineer of the Sanitation Districts of the County of Los Angeles; Chief S. Smith Griswold and his staff at the Los Angeles Air Pollution Control District; Eric F. Johnson, Publications Director of the American Water Works Association in New York; Murray Stein, Chief of the Enforcement Branch of the Division of Water Supply and Pollution Control in the

Acknowledgments

United States Public Health Service; John R. Kerstetter, Associate Director of the American Municipal Association, a leading authority on annexation; James P. Economos, Director of the Traffic Court Program of the American Bar Association in Chicago; and George Hjelte, retired head of the Department of Recreation and Parks for the city of Los Angeles.

Expression of gratitude is due also to many individuals in such organizations and agencies as the United States Department of Health, Education, and Welfare (and particularly to Dr. B. Harold Williams in the Office of Education and Patricia Foley in the Public Health Service), the Housing and Home Finance Agency (especially Wayne Phillips, Special Assistant to the Administrator), the International City Managers Association in Chicago, which made detailed confidential studies available to the author over a broad range of subjects (and to such individuals as David Arnold and, formerly, Robert L. Brunton, who provided this and other help), the National Education Association (particularly Drs. L. G. Derthick and Richard I. Miller), the American Transit Association and the National Recreation Association in New York, the Metropolitan Transit Authority in Los Angeles, the National Fire Protection Association in Boston, the National Safety Council and the Municipal Finance Officers Association in Chicago, the Bureau of Governmental Research at the University of California in Los Angeles, and others too numerous to mention.

One organization, I believe, deserves special recognition, and that is *The Wall Street Journal*, in whose employ I have been for the past thirteen years. Its publisher, Bernard Kilgore, and its editors, William F. Kerby, Buren H. McCormack, Robert Bottorff, and Vermont C. Royster, and, in the past, William H. Grimes and Henry Gemmill as well, have consistently placed a premium upon and provided spirited encouragement to comprehensiveness in re-

Acknowledgments

porting, research, and analysis that is uncommon even on much less perishable publications than newspapers. The expenditure of time and money was never an object if it gave the reader a better product. For their roles in helping to bring this work more specifically into being, I particularly wish to thank Charles Stabler, Managing Editor of the San Francisco edition, who fired an originally lethargic interest in the problems of local government, and to News Editor Ed Cony and Managing Editor Warren Phillips. Neither they nor any other individuals on this newspaper, however, are responsible for opinions expressed herein; nor, for that matter, have they seen any portion of manuscript prior to publication.

To Peter Ritner, Senior Editor of The Macmillan Company, goes the credit – or blame – for conceiving of this volume, inspiring its fulfillment, and patiently enduring the pains of its accomplishment. And, beyond all others, to Rhoda White, who endured the labors of typing and retyping and reading and rereading manuscript, no expression of gratitude can be sufficient.

San Pedro, California
June, 1962

CHAPTER ONE

By Way of Introduction: A Few Stepping-Stones to a Preface

H E N R Y Ford once said, "We shall solve the city problem by leaving the city" – and promptly provided the means to do so. The vehicle, however, was capable of coming back. Otherwise what follows might not have been.

*

A California citizens' group describes the urbanism created by the automobile as neither suburb nor city. Its word is "slurb." Its definition: "sloppy, sleazy, slovenly, slipshod semi-cities."

*

Author Carey McWilliams in the early 1920's described Los Angeles as "a collection of suburbs in search of a city." Los Angeles began taking to the suburbs too early in its urban life ever to have firmly rooted an urban center. Older metropolises sprouted suburbs around long-established hubs and then proceeded to choke their hubs with their automobiles.

As the architect and city planner Victor Gruen put it: "We turned our cities into doughnuts, with all the dough around the center and nothing in the middle."

*

One reason, perhaps, sprawl was considered peculiar to Los Angeles for so long may be found in the fact that the automobile appeared on the scene while the city was still in swaddling clothes. As late as 1880, Los Angeles had only

10,000 inhabitants. It grew phenomenally the following decade; even so, it had only 50,000 inhabitants by 1890. The automobile was thus able to fashion the city in fledgling form. It was also able to do this at high speed because of the compatibility of the early automobile with Southern California's climate. The vehicle's worst detractors at the time – cold weather and mud – were minimal in an area that enjoyed a long dry season and basked in warm sun. The speed of the ensuing courtship did not make it any easier to read as a portent of things to come. But there is no longer any doubt that that is what it was for many cities in the world.

In the first half of the twentieth century, Los Angeles swelled 13 times as fast as the average of the nation's 57 largest cities. Their populations rose 160 percent in that period while Los Angeles rocketed 2,199 percent.

*

Like so many concepts of the present age, from the size of the federal budget to the speed of spacecraft, the rate of urban growth is an exceedingly difficult one to grasp in anything like its full import. Its dimensions, like those of an elephant viewed by a mouse, begin to be seen only on examination from many different angles. Consider some:

"The Athens of Pericles' day," Professor James Marston Fitch notes in an article in the *Columbia University Forum,* "was never larger than Yonkers. Renaissance Florence was smaller than New Haven. Chicago is three times the size of Imperial Rome."

The Population Reference Bureau, a nonprofit organization of biologists and other professionals who think the alert should be sounded on man's prolificacy, figures one out of every twenty-five people who ever walked the earth from the time Homo sapiens supposedly made his debut on the planet, more than 600,000 years ago, is doing his walking today. It calculates total human births since that date at approximately 77 billion. The global population in 1962 was close to 3 billion.

14

By Way of Introduction

It took sixteen and a half centuries for the population of the world to double, from approximately 250 million at the time of Christ to an estimated 500 million when Cromwell was ascending to the rule of Britain in the mid-seventeenth century. It took only two centuries to double again; the total came to one billion in 1850. The next doubling took but eighty years; the figure was two billion by 1930. It will take half that time – some forty years – to double the 1962 figure; population prognosticators place the total at six billion around A.D. 2000.

The United States is expected to grow at about the average global rate; the 180 million people it had at the time of the 1960 census should exceed 360 million by the year 2000. Some states, of course, will surge ahead even more rapidly. California will have to make room by 1980 for as many people again as it had in 1960, though it was already the most populous state in the nation by 1963.

The population density of the thirteen former colonies in 1790 was 4.5 persons per square mile. That same territory today contains close to 700 persons per square mile.

If present population trends continue, the day will come when there is "standing room only" in America. In 800 years, an average of only one square foot of space would be available for each person in the nation.

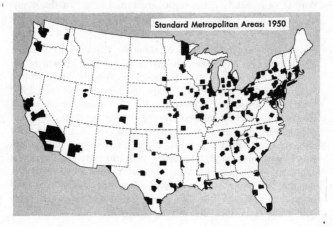

Standard Metropolitan Areas: 1950

Sick Cities

Children born after 1956 who live out their normal life expectancies can expect to see the United States a nation of 400 million people. The country had just under 100 million people as recently as 1915.

Metropolitan New York gives birth to a city roughly the size of Norfolk, Virginia, every year. New York City and its bedroom communities in northeastern New Jersey counted 300,000 births in 1960. Norfolk, with just under 305,000 people in 1960, was the 41st largest city in the United States at the time – bigger than Miami, Omaha, or Akron.

By 1980, over 90 percent of the American people will be living in urban areas. The figure in 1920 was exactly 51.2 percent. In 1962 it was just under 70 percent.

Five metropolitan areas accounted for 20 percent of the nation's total population in 1960. One out of every five Americans then lived in either greater New York, Chicago, Los Angeles, Philadelphia, or Detroit.

At the time of the first United States census, in 1790, the largest city in the land, Philadelphia, had but 44,000 persons. New York was the new nation's second largest city with 33,000 inhabitants. Boston, which ranked third, had only 18,000. Levittown, New York, which didn't exist before World War II, was nearly 50 percent larger in 1960 than the country's biggest city was in 1790. Levittown had over 65,000 inhabitants at the time of the 1960 census.

Despite the many detractors of suburban life and the massive effort to renew city cores, the nation's speediest growth is expected to continue to take place in the suburbs. The United States suburban population is expected to triple between 1960 and 1980 while the population for the nation as a whole climbs less than 50 percent. In the decade to 1960, suburban populations increased 56 percent while the nation's largest cities rose less than 5 percent. Chicago's suburban population, which was only slightly smaller than the city's in 1960, is expected to be nearly twice as great as the city's in 1990. Among the nation's three largest cities, only New York will be entering the 1970's with most of its daytime work force still resident within its city limits.

By Way of Introduction

URBANIZATION

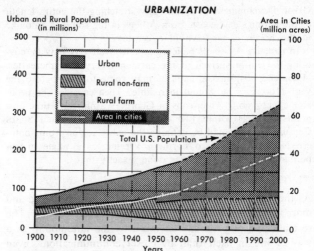

Urban and Rural Population (in millions) — Area in Cities (million acres)

Legend:
- Urban
- Rural non-farm
- Rural farm
- Area in cities

Total U.S. Population →

Years

Note: The change in the urban-rural definition in 1950 resulted in an increase in the urban population of 7.5 million.

Source: Census Reports.

The nation's major metropolises thus are turning into urban dinosaurs. They may prove just as ungainly.

The surge to the city will be even greater in some of the world's underdeveloped countries than in the United States. Urban-growth rates in parts of Asia in the early 1960's were running 400 percent higher than those in the West, and the movement to cities on that great land mass obviously has only just begun.

Only ten cities in the world had populations in excess of one million persons in 1900. More than 60 did in 1962.

Athens is finding congestion almost as formidable a foe as Sparta was. The Greek architect and city planner, Dr. Constantine A. Doxiadis, is an expert in that country who believes the crush of cars and population is making the city untenable as the nation's capital. A number of alternative sites have been suggested, including Pella in northern Greece, a city that served as the capital of Macedon in the time of Alexander the

17

Great. Development of a solid city stretching the entire length of the nation's east coast, from Athens in the south to Salonika in the north, is seen within a century.

In fact, Dr. Doxiadis believes a "universal" city may be covering the entire surface of the earth not very long thereafter. "Ecumenopolis," as he calls it, may come to pass before the year 2100, says he. Sound incredible? Then consider the probable effect among Americans of George Washington's time of a prediction that within two hundred years the United States Census Bureau would be defining the entire region from southern New Hampshire to northern Virginia as a single metropolitan area. In 1960 it was doing exactly that.

*

As they burgeon, foreign cities are likely to look more and more like American cities, particularly Los Angeles. The resemblance may be caused more by the automobile as a way of life in itself than by closer communications, even with the growing influence of television, the internationalization of the cinema, and the commuter touch that jet airliners give global travel. Cities shaped by the automobile, which both requires space and makes more space accessible, are bound to look increasingly alike whether the chisel bears a Volkswagen or a Buick brand. The Germans already have a word for their sprawl: *Randgemeinden*.

*

The diseases of sprawl, similarly, are likely to grow more universal. Dr. Luther Gulick, Chairman of the Institute of Public Administration, defines them thusly:

    Clogged streets
    Dying public transit
    Spreading blight
    Increasing air and water pollution
    Growing lawlessness
    Diverging educational opportunities
    Neglect of park space and other community facilities, such
      as libraries

By Way of Introduction

A sorely felt lack of comprehensive governmental institutions necessary for mustering fiscal and political support for the community's "most elemental" requirements.

They are the table of contents for this book.

*

Or are cities themselves the disease? Lewis Mumford, in *The Culture of Cities,* indicated a good many seemed to be. He saw the metropolis as an accumulation of people accommodating themselves "to an environment without adequate natural or cultural resources: people who do without pure air, who do without sound sleep, who do without a cheerful garden or playing space, who do without the very sight of the sky and the sunlight, who do without free motion, spontaneous play, or a robust sexual life. The so-called blighted areas of the metropolis," says he, "are essentially '*do without*' areas. If you wish the sight of urban beauty while living in these areas, you must ride in a bus a couple of miles (nowadays a car, for many more miles); if you wish a touch of nature, you must travel in a crowded train to the outskirts of the city. Lacking the means to get out, you succumb; chronic starvation produces lack of appetite. Eventually," he warns, "you may live and die without even recognizing the loss."

*

"Men come together in cities," said Aristotle, "in order to live. They remain together in order to live the good life."

In many cities today, men come together principally to earn a living – and get out of it as quickly as they can, tortuously if necessary, in order to enjoy the pleasures that Aristotle might easily have taken for granted in his day: clean air, refuge from noise and crowds, a patch of earth and a glimpse of sky.

*

Cost of living trends, to be meaningful, are adjusted for inflationary factors. Trends in living standards, to be meaningful in an urban environment, must similarly be adjusted for "congestionary" factors. The difference between the Model T Ford and the modern automobile does not consist in physical differences alone but in their abilities to accomplish what their owners expect them to accomplish. The fact that the penalties of congestion do not readily lend themselves to computation does not make them any less real. Progress against congestion may thus be regarded in the same light as the development of a new engine with greater power and gas economy. It accomplishes the same thing and something more.

*

The *Saturday Evening Post* in an editorial in 1961 called sprawl "perhaps our cruelest misuse of land since our soil mining days. Urban sprawl," it went on to state, "is not the growth of cities. Instead, the cities are disintegrating and spreading the pieces over miles and miles of countryside."

Robert Moses, responsible for so many of Gotham's public achievements in the present century, takes the opposite point of view in an article in the *Atlantic Monthly:* "The prosperous suburbanite," says he, "is as proud of his ranch home as the owner of the most gracious villa of Tuscany. The little identical suburban boxes of average people, which differ only in color and planting, represent a measure of success unheard of by hundreds of millions on other continents."

Sprawl in itself is perhaps not the evil any more than the automobile, in itself, is.

*

In 1959, on the occasion of its twenty-fifth anniversary, the National Planning Association, a nonprofit group with a wide range of interests in business and government, mapped a program of essential urban projects it felt should be carried out over a five-year period. The cost of its program averaged $60 billion a year – considerably above the $46 billion then being spent per annum by the federal government on national security programs of all types. The N.P.A. figured $100 billion would be needed in that five-year period for slum clearance, $75 billion to alleviate traffic congestion and make roads safer, $60 billion for cleaning up and conserving the nation's water resources, $35 billion for hospital and health needs, and at least $30 billion for improving educational facilities, reducing delinquency, and a host of other purposes.

Those concerned with the idleness that global disarmament might impose have only to contemplate those figures.

*

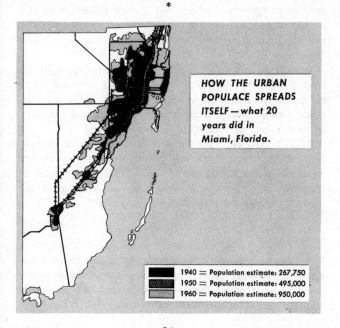

HOW THE URBAN POPULACE SPREADS ITSELF *— what 20 years did in Miami, Florida.*

1940 = Population estimate: 267,750
1950 = Population estimate: 495,000
1960 = Population estimate: 950,000

Sick Cities

With all but 10 percent of the nation's population headed for city living within the foreseeable future, efforts to improve the nation's urban environment become highly pertinent in the peacetime competition between the free and the Communist world. The way Americans live at home inevitably will affect the nation's prestige abroad. In addition, the nation's economic efficiency is bound up in its urban condition. Unless nuclear war brings wholesale destruction first, the city cannot help but serve as the proving ground for rival ways of life.

John Kenneth Galbraith, the brilliant Harvard economist and author who became United States Ambassador to India in the Kennedy Administration, puts it this way in his book *The Liberal Hour:* "There are three weaknesses of our society which are gravely damaging to our reputation and prestige at large and which cast a dark reflection on the quality of our society. The first of these," says he, "is the unhinged and disorderly quality of our urban society and the consequent squalor, delinquency and crime."

Senator Joseph Clark, Pennsylvania Democrat, told the United States Senate in 1960 that the cities "are our greatest source of economic strength. In many ways, our national welfare is dependent upon their continued efficiency as instruments of production in our economy."

Says Dr. Gulick in the *National Civic Review* of December, 1960: "Our strength, our culture, our self-respect, our influence in the world, can never rise above our achievements here in the United States; we cannot win in the world on the foundation of defeats at home."

*

This volume is primarily an attempt to stimulate the interest of the average general reader in some of the principal problems confronting the city in which he lives – or shortly will live even if he does no more than stay put. It has, then,

By Way of Introduction

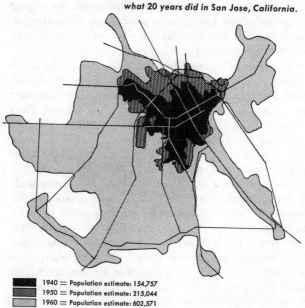

1940 = Population estimate: 154,757
1950 = Population estimate: 215,044
1960 = Population estimate: 602,571

one principal purpose: to light up some of the darker corners of city housekeeping.

No attempt is made to deal with every city problem. The present effort would be unmanageable if such an attempt were made. Some of the problems that have not been treated at length, such as the growth of racial dichotomies in northern and western cities in the thick of urban sprawl, are perhaps more properly treated in tomes of their own; they are dealt with here mainly as they affect the performance of such government functions as urban renewal, the provision of police protection, and education.

The focus, therefore, is on functions. They range from the services of safety (police, fire, traffic) to those for the use

of leisure time (recreation, libraries), and from menaces to
health (air and water pollution) to the means for coping
with metropolitan problems in general (by minimizing financial burdens and arresting the waste of too many governments, for instance).

It is a premise of this effort that while day-to-day developments in areas of local government often receive considerable attention in communities immediately involved, their
implications are seldom set forth for the layman on a
broader basis. It is also a premise of this volume that there
is sufficient similarity in urban problems, not only among
cities of the nation but also among cities of the world, for
the experiences and experiments of one to be of considerable use to others if they would only take the time to study
and extract them. The shibboleths so often sounded, sometimes for political reasons and sometimes in all sincerity,
which hold that "peculiar local conditions" or "special situations" make the solutions or approaches of one region
totally inapplicable in any other, are rarely more than
shibboleths. It is true, of course, that circumstances vary
among localities, but the experience is rare, as urban history is proving more and more, which does not contain
some highly pertinent instruction for those who pay attention to it.

The accent in any effort such as this must inescapably be
placed on simplicity and even, where possible, on drama-
tization for the sake of arresting and detaining average
reader interest. Any volume aimed these days at a general
audience can hardly afford to do otherwise against competition, not always unworthy, from the motorcar, the
television screen, the movie house, and a host of other
sources. Business spends many millions of dollars yearly
for a fleeting focus on much lesser complexities in advertising messages; it is hardly possible, therefore, to overesti-
mate the importance of packaging and presentation of
issues of public importance. This volume is perhaps more

validly open to criticism for failure to realize those objectives of simplicity and interest than for making that attempt.

If extremes have been used to further these purposes, they have been selected as extremes only in degree, and not in basic nature; lesser examples may have been used only with lesser effect. There is, nevertheless, ample use throughout this work of the typical where the typical is deemed more appropriate for the purpose.

Though it is hoped the specialist, whether he be a police executive or a school administrator, will find this volume both informative and sound, the intent is essentially one of stimulating the lay person into further inquiry in subject areas that too often appear forbidding. If the reader at the end of this work is furnished with a kit of questions to make any further encounter with his servants in local government more stimulating and educational, the purpose of this work will have been served. It has no greater ambition.

Certainly there is no shortage of materials or opportunities for those desiring to probe beyond the ambitions of this volume. One state agency in California, in fact, recently paid a private research firm $47,000 simply to suggest a way for pulling together all the information in its own field, water pollution. The same might have been done in almost any other area of local government.

One brief word is perhaps appropriate to any volume that endeavors, in however limited a fashion, to contribute toward the alleviation of the problems of modern society and particularly of urban life: unless this earthly species succeeds in finding some way of controlling lawlessness among the planet's growing community of nuclear nations, each with well-rooted historic hatreds and very real present-day rivalries, what follows herein must properly and in all humility be placed in the category of doily-arranging inside a blazing building. The citizen who walks down a dark city

25

street in fear of molestation is in no greater danger than a world that must depend indefinitely for its safety on the fine balances of many mutual terrors subject to disturbance by any of a wide variety of possible accidents or human shortcomings, temporary or otherwise.

CHAPTER TWO

Traffic Jam: The Concrete Spread

AUTOSCLEROSIS

I T once advertised itself, immodestly but with good reason, as "the greatest electric railway system on earth." At the peak of its glory in the early 1920's it provided service on more than 150 routes. A thousand trains glided daily over its 1,100 miles of track fanning as far as 70 miles from downtown Los Angeles eastward to Redlands in Riverside County, southward 44 miles to scenic Balboa, 17 miles westward to the shores of Santa Monica, and 28 miles northward into a then sparsely settled San Fernando Valley. As recently as 1945, it hauled as many as 103 million passengers between some 50 cities in four Southern California counties at speeds up to 55 miles an hour. The system served not only existing communities but reached out to meet others still being spawned.

"No other area of the country ever had such an intensive network of lines," declared George W. Hilton and John F. Due in a scholarly volume published by the Stanford University Press in 1960 and entitled *The Electric Interurban Railways in America.*

Today the celebrated system no longer exists. Except for a few fragments reserved solely for boxcar service to nearby plants and warehouses, even its rights of way – so tantalizing to transit planners of today – are gone, having long since reverted to the local municipalities or private individuals who owned them. To resurrect only a skeletonized 75-mile version of the former network, the Metropolitan Transit Authority of Los Angeles is contemplating the expenditure of over $500 million – more than five times what the entire system had originally cost. Yet, the area was the fastest-growing in the nation: back in 1899, when its commuting network was just coming into being, Los Angeles had a population of just over 100,000. At the time of the 1960 census, the figure was nearly 2.5 million – and the increase in suburban populations, particularly in San Fernando Valley and Orange County, had been greater still.

The system was known to its patrons as "the Pacific Electric." It was, and in its freight-carrying capacity still is, owned by the Southern Pacific Railroad Company. But if the Southern Pacific could have kept it running, it would have. The company, of course, is in business to make a profit. And for a good long while, the P.E. was doing exactly that. It was said, in fact, to have been the most profitable intercity electric railway in the world at one time. Some routes, however, began to become unprofitable as early as the mid-1920's, and more did so in the 1930's, but World War II gave the P.E. a lease on life. Shortly after the end of the war, the decline set in again. By 1950 the operation was costing the Southern Pacific over $3 million a year, despite considerable trimming of its routes. By 1953 the P.E. was already being described by those with short memories and even shorter foresight as "the ancient lemon." In 1961 service ceased on the last remaining passenger line, a 21-mile segment between downtown Los Angeles and the harbor of Long Beach.

The story of the P.E. may be of special interest to Angelenos, but it bears also on the commuting headaches, past, present, and future, of residents of practically every major metropolis in the world, with the possible lone exception of idyllic, aquatic Venice. For one reason: the killer of the P.E. is still on the prowl. It is, of course, the automobile – and all the sprawl and congestion that vehicle brings with it wherever it goes.

In France, where the automobile has worked a revolution

even in that culinary nation's eating habits by bringing the sale of sandwiches to gasoline stations, the highway death rate is already so high – two and a half times that of the United States – that the equivalent of a city the size of Lille (150,000) stands to be completely wiped out on the roadways by the time France completes the fifteen-year highway modernization program it announced in mid-1961. In an effort to relieve its road congestion, the Communist Yugoslav government recently ordered ox-, horse-, and man-drawn carts off the streets of Belgrade. Bonn, the "temporary" capital of West Germany, has planned skyscraper garages in the heart of the city to accommodate vehicles that keep its parking lots in a continuous state of overflow. In Argentina, the city of Buenos Aires recently put sixteen tow trucks to work clearing illegally parked vehicles off cluttered downtown streets so moving vehicles could get through.

Since the end of World War II, the automobile has laid public transit systems to rest in over 150 American towns and cities. Others that couldn't survive in private ownership were purchased by public agencies, to be subsidized in one way or another by tax revenues.

The way the automobile laid the P.E. low is the way it has been laying mass transit low practically everywhere. First and foremost, it has made it possible for millions of families to live practically anywhere they wish instead of having to remain close to transit stations. By scattering population, the automobile has robbed transit systems of the heavy population densities needed to nourish those systems. Population densities of at least 10,000 persons per square mile are needed to support rail transit systems, according to Northwestern University's Transportation Center. Sprawling subdivisions fall considerably below that minimum. Women, children, and others who may have used public transit are forced to turn to second cars and personal chauffeuring instead; the loss of their patronage is particularly difficult for transit systems to take since these are the people who tended to use their facilities when they were most in need of use, during the offpeak weekday hours and on weekends.

The worst loss of all, however, is the loss of transit's bread-and-butter riders, the working men and women who apparently prefer the door-to-door convenience, the relief from waiting, and the seat-assured, radioed comfort of their own cars to the dubious privilege of jousting for a seat inside a stuffy, noisy, overcrowded vehicle. Many prefer to fight the waiting battle in their own quiet, upholstered environment, consoled in the knowledge their mechanical servant will be waiting for them at any hour they chose to leave, for whatever destination they wish to reach.

The automobile has also tightened the noose around public transit through sheer numbers. It has slowed the journey of buses on city streets and clogged crossings of surface rail systems, such as the P.E. Automotive congestion has been blamed for slowing by as much as 50 percent the average speed of the Los Angeles rail system between the 1920's and the late 1940's. The steady loss in patronage to the automobile, from sprawl, curtailed service and other causes ultimately brought the systems' demise.

The passing of the P.E. as a passenger carrier in Los Angeles would perhaps be less lamentable – and its lesson for folks elsewhere a good deal less ominous – if the automobile actually did provide the comforts and convenience it promised. But, like the legendary Lorelei who lured Rhine fishermen to rocky self-destruction, the automobile is threatening commuting experiences much worse than the walk to the station, the waiting for trains, and the crowded ride into town ever brought. Urban planners almost without exception agree the nation's proliferating automotive population, which doubled in the 15 years between 1940 and 1955 and promises to double again by 1976 to some 113 million vehicle registrations, will produce even worse paralysis on city streets and urban highways despite unprecedented expenditures that almost certainly will be incurred for its accommodation in the years ahead.

Three-quarters of the nation's adult population are now licensed drivers. On January 1, 1960, they were driving over 87 million vehicles – 74 million of them automobiles, each registering an average of 10,000 miles a year. Part of the increase in vehicle numbers comes from population growth – and part from the fact that automobiles are hauling fewer and fewer people on each journey. In California, for instance, there were 310 cars for 1,000 people in 1940; by 1958 the figure had risen to 353, and it is expected to climb to 420 by 1980.

Today's modern motorcars are making slower progress on some downtown streets than horse and buggies made decades ago. The Automobile Club of Southern California in 1938 found modern motorcars moving from First to Tenth Street on Broadway in Los Angeles were taking as much as 14 minutes and 12 seconds for the journey compared with 10 minutes and 21 seconds once recorded for horse-and-buggy travel over the same route, and the journey has not been sharply hastened since.

The rate of progress in Gotham, according to another survey, has been slashed from approximately 11.5 miles an hour in 1907 to as little as six miles an hour at present. The contrast will be even more startling in the future, when supersonic transports are whisking passengers from New York to Los Angeles in a scant one hour and 46 minutes, making the transcontinental trip quicker than the journey to and from airports. "We know more about how to get to the moon than how to get to the airport," says Carlton Green, Manager of the Stanford Research Institute's Southern California Laboratories.

Besides spreading congestion, the vehicular horde, like the locust of the Middle East, threatens to cut ever-wider swaths through the works of man and nature. In the proc-

31

ess, fiscally desperate cities are losing valuable properties which once yielded handsome tax revenues only to be covered over with concrete carpeting laid out to accommodate the automobile.

The auto's appetite for space is horrendous. The 41,000-mile interstate highway system born with the passage of congressional legislation in 1956 will occupy more land than the entire state of Rhode Island when it is completed in 1972. The fact that 90 percent of the facility's $40 billion cost is being borne by the federal government, and only 10 percent by state governments, is only meager consolation for municipalities spared the construction burden but not the tax loss. Two-thirds of Los Angeles' entire downtown area is already given over to the automobile – approximately 33 percent of it to parking lots and garages and the rest to roads and highways. Each one of the city's interchanges, linking one freeway to another, consumes approximately 80 acres of real estate; every mile of freeway, 24. By 1980 the city is expected to have 34 square miles of land devoted to its freeway system – about the size of the entire city of Miami.

The average standard-sized automobile with a driver but no passengers takes up more than nine times as much space per person in motion than a public conveyance. At rest, it needs as much space as the average downtown office devotes to each employee. "Highways are the greediest consumers of real estate we have," declares William N. Casella, Senior Associate of the National Municipal League in New York.

Cars don't pay property taxes – but buildings do. When autos take over, revenues are lost. A three-mile stretch of freeway through Cleveland removed an estimated $20 million worth of assessed property from that city's tax rolls. Parking space for 20,000 cars provided in downtown Los Angeles in the decade to 1961, nearly twice as many as the 11,000 spaces the area had previously, chucked an estimated $10 million worth of assessments from that city's revenue potential. However, businessmen claim property depreciation would have been greater still if such provision were not made for the accommodation of vehicles. The county, which has more autos than all but five states of the nation (California, Illinois, New York, Pennsylvania, and Ohio), had 2.8 million vehicles registered on December 31, 1960, nearly 65 percent more than it had only a decade earlier.

The cost of failing to accommodate vehicles also runs high. An official of *McCall's* magazine estimates traffic delays cost that publication an estimated $50,000 a year in extra driver wages, gasoline, and equipment. The Russell Sage Foundation in New York, after a detailed study, figured traffic congestion was already running New Yorkers at least $350 million a year as far back as 1931. A *New York Times* survey of business and automotive executives recently estimated the national loss, inclusive of executive time lost in taxicabs, delays in freight deliveries, and other waste, at close to $5 billion a year. Bus systems are among the biggest sufferers: Milwaukee, just to cite one example, figures it has 45 more buses in its fleet just to make up for delays due to traffic congestion. That's approximately $750,-000 worth of buses, to say nothing of the expense of operating them.

Many of the costs of congestion, of course, cannot be calculated. How, for instance, does one estimate the cost of strained nerves, frayed tempers, and depression in experiencing or even in only contemplating the traffic ordeal? What might the manhours total which are poured into the massive vehicular two-step that has Manhattan motorists scrounging daily for adequate curb space on alternate sides of the street to make way for street cleaning operations? Anxious Angelenos, desperate for word of road conditions ahead, have turned helicopter-borne radio announcers into areawide celebrities; one Los Angeles radio station finds enough demand for the service to keep two whirlybirds hovering over the sprawling area's freeways seven days a week throughout the year from 6:30 to 9:30 in the morning and again from 3:30 in the afternoon to dusk for broadcasting travel conditions.

The Mayor of Philadelphia painted this picture of traffic in the City of Brotherly Love not so long ago: "We have 2,400 miles of very old streets, the average width of which is not more than 20 to 25 feet. In many of our built-up sections we have no garage or parking facilities and at night cars are left indiscriminately on sidewalks. In some of the very congested sections, you would not be able to get a fire engine through."

Lyle Fitch, First Deputy City Director of New York and President of the Institute of Public Administration, describes a typical hot-weather metropolitan weekend scene in that city: "Every summer weekend a vast horde of pleasure-seeking passenger automobiles pour out of the city like bats leaving Carlsbad Cavern at sunset. Not being able to operate in three dimensions, they put up with conditions which no bat has to tolerate."

Lewis Mumford describes the weekday commuting process in major metropolitan areas as "an exchange of urban jam for suburban jelly."

It should not take long, however, for the suburban jelly to take on the consistency of urban jam. The plight of Los Angeles, again, may be more than a little enlightening in this respect.

Los Angeles is the freeway-buildingest metropolis in the world. By the end of 1960, it had poured over $900 million into 310 miles of freeways and expressways reaching into Orange and Ventura counties. Los Angeles' rush-hour congestion, however, is worse than it has ever been. And, with the number of automobiles increasing even faster than population, it may grow more intolerable still. The area's highway officials figure they'll need over 1,500 miles of freeways to accommodate vehicles that will be on the road by 1980. By that time the metropolis will have over $5 billion invested in its freeway system. S. S. Taylor, General Manager of Los Angeles' Traffic Department, recently told a gathering of highway officials in San Francisco that traffic conditions in Los Angeles might well be worse in 1980 than they are today despite such construction. By that time, he said, Los Angeles may have as much traffic on its city streets as it had in 1960 on freeways and streets combined.

In Atlanta, the Metropolitan Planning Commission estimated it already had enough traffic on one six-lane portion of expressway in 1958 to justify 16 lanes during peak rush hours; by 1970, it said, the need would soar to 36 lanes. In Florida, a Dade County Commissioner recalls the opening of a second freeway in the Miami area in the summer of 1961: "Traffic engineers told us it would be saturated the day it opened and that we would immediately need two additional lanes on each side which would cost another $100 million over its 16-mile length." Robert O. Bonnell, Chairman of the Maryland State Roads Commission, foresees the development of "almost insurmountable traffic problems" for the Baltimore-Washington metropolitan area in the years ahead.

Statistics tell this poignant tale: In the decade from 1947 to 1957, the nation as a whole constructed 53,000 miles of highway lanes while Detroit was stamping out enough automobiles to cover 200,000 miles of highway lanes bumper-to-bumper. And the worst is still to come, not only in the Los Angeles, Atlanta, and Washington areas but throughout the nation.

Urban Land Institute President Boyd Barnard warns: "The expected increase of automobiles in the next decade will mean bumper to bumper traffic not only on all our present roads, turnpikes and expressways, but all those that are in the planning stage as well." The automobile, says he, "has created problems which appear almost insolvable."

Sick Cities

"Every metropolitan area in the United States," said Wilfred Owen in *The Metropolitan Transportation Problem* published by the Brookings Institution in 1956, "is now confronted by a transportation problem that seems destined to become aggravated in the years ahead. Growth of population and expansion of the urban area, combined with rising national product and higher incomes are continually increasing the volume of passengers and freight movement."

Expressways, at the same time, are growing costlier and costlier to construct. Los Angeles' first freeway, the six-lane Arroya Seco that stretched eight miles between downtown Los Angeles and Pasadena, cost just under $1.5 million to build, inclusive of acquisition costs for the right-of-way, in the late 1930's. Today, freeway costs of $10 million a mile are not considered at all unusual. And in some eastern cities, the cost of hacking through well-developed areas has recently run as high as $30 million and more per mile. One newly constructed Los Angeles freeway interchange, linking the Santa Monica and Harbor freeways near downtown Los Angeles, set highway builders back $19 million with the cost almost equally divided between construction and expenditures for the acquisition of some 200 parcels of private property.

Mounting criticism of elevated expressways and their effect on city appearance threatens to make urban freeways costlier still. Incensed by what elevated expressways were doing to their waterfront, and particularly by the defacement of the historic view down Market Street to the city's venerated Ferry Building, aroused residents of San Francisco brought that construction to a thudding halt in January, 1959, pending the study of alternative solutions. Despite the prospective cost, the handwriting is on the wall: more and more cities will be putting the squeeze on their state governments, and on Uncle Sam as well where federal highways are involved, to run their roadways beneath city street levels rather than above them. Such pressure recently tacked $13 million on to the cost of a 7.3-mile stretch of freeway in New Jersey – increasing its originally projected cost by approximately 50 percent.

Some cities are resisting the routing of freeways, depressed or otherwise, through their urban hearts. Highway authorities are thus forced to turn to longer, circuitous routes. The state of California stirred a nest of opposition in its own state capital in 1962 when it proposed running a freeway through the center of Sacramento. Irate citizens claimed the route would destroy no less than 31 historic buildings, including the original western terminal of the Pony Express constructed in 1861. In the somewhat newer community of Malibu, down the coast, the cry was over the prospective loss of more than 25 percent of built-up area to a projected eight-lane freeway. In nearby Santa Monica, the same projected roadway stirred fiercer opposition still: neither one of the state's two original alternative routes satisfied residents, one because it threatened to slice the compact 8.5 square-mile community clean in two and the other because it threatened to consume half the city's beach acreage. Santa Monica's own preference, which the state may yet be compelled to accept, calls for the construction of some six miles of causeway about half a mile offshore on concrete pilings 60 feet high in order to permit 30-foot boat clearances beneath it at mean low water. The causeway would cost about $16 million a mile, considerably more than a dry-land route.

In Washington, D.C., a $2 billion, 20-year freeway construction plan was set aside for further study late in 1961 when fears were voiced over the capital's disfigurement. The area has been as much a victim of urban sprawl as almost any in the land, having experienced a 40 percent increase in its population in the decade to 1960 alone.

Arguing against the vast road network, the American Institute of Architects told a joint congressional committee on Washington metropolitan problems in July, 1960, that wholesale submission to the automobile would necessitate "such vast changes in the form of freeways, underpasses, cloverleafs and automobile parking areas that much of the charm of the present city will be lost. In the last half of the 19th century," the AIA declared, "we nearly spoiled the plan of Washington by the reckless use of railroads; we are now in danger of spoiling the city by an almost equally reckless use of automobiles."

The automobile has proved particularly lethal, of course, in its effect on downtown areas. Not only has it strangled them with crisscrossing roadways and expansive interchanges, but it has also yanked entire structures from the remaining core for its parking needs. The effect, of course, is to tear away the attractions which might otherwise move pedestrians effortlessly in a continuum of commerce. Lodestones of interest which pull humans through the bazaars of Baghdad and the piazzas of Italy lose their magnetism in the auto-mismated metropolis.

The impact on downtown can be read in the statistics on retail sales: Los Angeles' downtown merchants accounted for only 20 percent of the metropolitan area's total sales in 1960 compared with 88 percent in 1930.

Practically all prescriptions for dealing with the auto-sclerosis of cities call for the revival of public transit. And, despite their financial destitution, more and more cities are attempting to fill these prescriptions lest future burdens of accommodating the automobile become more intolerable still. The devices cities are using to nurture transit systems back to life will be discussed shortly. There is no shortage of suggestions, however, for dealing with the automobile itself.

The most extreme of these, and possibly the inevitable solution for many highly congested areas, calls for banning vehicular traffic altogether from the heart of downtown areas except for emergency vehicles, specially authorized freight vans, and possibly a modicum of public transit. Motorists would be expected to leave their autos in strategically located garages on the periphery of the core area and walk or ride to their close-in destinations on public vehicles. The garages would also be served by taxis and light merchandise trucks for delivering purchases to the shopper's vehicle or some convenient pickup point. Whenever the public conveyances produced too much congestion, they would be replaced by moving sidewalks or "carveyors" designed to provide continuous public transit.

A small number of cities are already moving toward this ideal. City planner Victor Gruen's now famous proposal for Fort Worth, which never got much beyond the blueprint stage, was based on the development of a downtown core free of automotive congestion with rest rooms, benches and other facilities for the pedestrian. Oxford, the famed university city of the dreaming spires in England, has likewise considered the banning of cars from the center of town and the closing of its Magdalen Bridge to automotive traffic. If it were to accommodate the greater flow of automotive traffic, it would have had to widen its streets and rip out many historic buildings in the process. A community which has been spared motormania all these years, Fire Island, which lies off the southern shore of Long Island in New York, has repeatedly resisted efforts of municipal officials to construct roads that would usher in the automotive horde. Another, which has similarly been spared this fate by the facts of topography, Venice, has been somewhat less wise: it took a veto from Rome recently to prevent the city from building vehicular bridges that would have brought automotive traffic to within a mile of St. Mark's Square, at the city's heart.

Less extreme remedies would seem even more difficult to effect, and a good deal less capable of accomplishing the desired result. For example, various means have been suggested for getting motorists to take on riders and thus cut down on the number of cars on the road. S. S. Taylor, General Manager of the Los Angeles City Traffic Department, would like to see concessions made on motor vehicle license fees for automobiles customarily used in car pools; he would employ a system of notarized affidavits containing the signatures of riders to document that fact. Dr. Fritz Zwicky, a California Institute of Technology Professor of Astrophysics with earthly as well as heavenly problems on his mind, wants to use the stick rather than the carrot: he would charge motorists a dollar apiece for entering congested areas with no one else in their vehicles, though attempts to collect the charge would present other problems.

Some cities, notably St. Louis on its Mark Twain Expressway and Chicago, have experimented with convertible lanes—lanes that can be converted to travel in either direction, according to varying morning and evening loads. An installation made some years ago in Chicago, consisting of low steel barriers that rose a couple of feet above the ground, however, was rendered inoperative at times by ice and snow. St. Louis' system of convertible lanes, which went into operation in the summer of 1962, consists of five 336-foot long "zipper" trains that open or close a dual lane of freeway sandwiched between three-lane strips moving in either direction so they can provide five lanes one way when necessary. The "zippers" are closed off at one end or the other of the five-mile long dual strip by police who flush traffic out ahead of them and operate the necessary switches accordingly. The system set St. Louis back $350,000 − but it spared the construction of two lanes of highway that otherwise would have been required over the route in each direction.

Improved laws and stricter enforcement of those already in effect undoubtedly could relieve traffic problems in many cities. New York, at least until recently, had been notorious for its failure to clamp down on double-parkers on streets that should not have permitted parking at all, even beside the curb. The city has had authority since 1952 to impose a $5 monthly fee for overnight parking on public streets but has never attempted to impose it, though at least two American cities have done so with considerable success – Milwaukee and Monterey Park, California. Milwaukee's $4 monthly fee, which still does not liberate motorists from having to park on alternate sides of the street each day, produced enough revenue in the first decade following its imposition in 1950 to enable the city to purchase and pave four offstreet parking lots. Its $500,000 annual income from this source pales next to New York's potential, however: it is estimated Gotham could garner $40 million or more yearly from such a levy.

Offstreet loading facilities for commercial vehicles and stiff penalties for using city streets for the loading and unloading of freight must likewise be more vigorously employed if the city's essential arteries are to be kept open. Some cities have already gone a good deal further than this. Tokyo since early 1962 has banned outright the entry of large trucks into the city between the hours of 8:00 A.M. and 8:00 P.M. during weekdays. There is nothing new about such discrimination against goods vehicles. Julius Caesar prohibited the entry of freight carts into Imperial Rome during daytime hours to permit pedestrians freer movement, much to the consternation of residents who had to put up with the noise at night.

One device for the purpose of controlling traffic flow which generally gets a good bit of attention, the so-called electronic or automated highway, may reduce road capacities if safe operation is to be ensured. At least that is the view of the United States Bureau of Public Roads, which hopes to build a 50- or 100-mile test strip shortly. The system would permit motorists to sleep, play cards, or otherwise forget the driving chore while vehicles were guided safely and steadily along at speeds of up to 100 miles an hour. The scheme raises one knotty legal problem, however: who bears responsibility if something goes wrong with the apparatus, resulting in a mishap?

The question may prove an even bigger stickler than price. Some authorities believe electronic highways can be provided today at a cost of only $30,000 to $150,000 more per mile than conventional roadways. Necessary attachments for the auto itself might run another $300 per vehicle, they figure.

Some authorities would prefer to put electronics to work first as a means of billing motorists for highway use. Champions of the idea argue that the nation is already spending more on personal transportation than on housing and that individuals doing the driving should be prepared to pick up the tab instead of foisting it off on the general taxpayer. No one, however, has come up with an inexpensive way of making the tally. Columbia University Professor William Vickrey thinks it can be done through the use of roadside electronic viewing apparatus which would pass the essential details on to processing centers for later billing. The scheme, needless to say, is perhaps less feasible politically than technically.

TRANSITANEMIA

EXCEPT for subway and elevated lines, whose patronage has hovered at its 1958 nadir for some years now, there was not a single variety of public conveyance that went through the 1950's without showing consecutive year-to-year losses in paying passengers. Surface rail lines carried only one-eighth as many passengers in 1960 as they did in 1950. For every three people riding buses in 1950, only two did so in 1960.

A 1962 Census Bureau survey showed nearly two-thirds of American workers were getting to their jobs in private automobiles and that more were walking than were taking either buses, streetcars, railroad, subway, or elevated trains. Some 86 percent of the more than $50 billion Americans

Traffic Jam: The Concrete Spread

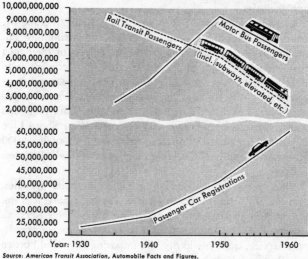

Source: American Transit Association, Automobile Facts and Figures.

spent on all kinds of transportation in 1960, from transit to jet travel, went for automobiles and whatever was necessary to make them go.

While public transit has been losing passengers, its costs have been soaring. Commuter railroads figure their costs rose 250 percent in the 1933-1960 period while fares rose only 116 percent.

The attitude of the general public toward mass transit, as reflected in the unwillingness of regulatory bodies to grant fare increases and of riders to tolerate them, has pulled a cord on transit revenues. The Long Island Railroad, the most heavily traveled commuting facility of its kind in America, went twenty-nine years – from 1918 to 1948 – without a single fare increase. But the piper had to be paid eventually, and he was – in two disasters that tragically demonstrated the state of neglect of the road's equipment and facilities.

In addition to finding fare increases difficult to come by, commuter lines have been prevented from trimming unprofitable services and taking other measures for their own survival where such efforts have come into conflict with public convenience. Public policies of this type can be exceedingly costly to mass carriers. New York Central President Alfred Perlman noted that in the five years that road sought permission to cease service on its West Shore Line it lost $15 million – enough to buy every one of its 4,000 patrons a brand-new Chevrolet, complete with all the latest gadgets.

Since many transit-regulating bodies are state agencies, and therefore rurally dominated for the most part, it is not uncommon to find efforts at paring unprofitable services thwarted. Transit bodies forced to maintain such unprofitable service, quite obviously, are imposing an added burden on all users which is usually reflected in the fares they pay or in the additional subsidies they require from tax bodies. "Too often in public transit," says Mayor Ben West of Nashville, Tennessee, "it is a case of the people inside the city subsidizing those outside it." Nashville's situation was eased somewhat in the mid-1950's when the state turned over to the city its authority to regulate Nashville's privately-owned but city-subsidized transit network up to seven miles beyond the city's boundaries. The city, of course, is much more sympathetic toward allowing the discontinuance or reduction of unprofitable outlying transit service than the state was.

At the same time that they have found it harder to hike fares and pare unprofitable routes, public carriers have also been saddled increasingly with welfare tasks, such as the transport of oldsters and schoolchildren free or at reduced rates. In some instances – New York is one – the cities themselves are making up the differences where the carrier cannot carry the load, but many cities inflict it upon the carrier.

Oldsters invariably are the carriers' wards. In Los Angeles, for instance, the Metropolitan Transit Authority, a public agency whose operation is nevertheless supposed to be self-sustaining, put a "senior citizen" discount plan into operation in mid-1961. It provided 10-cent discounts from the usual 25-cent fare for men over 65 and women over 62, if their incomes didn't exceed $1,200 a year. Laminated identification cards with the bearer's photograph tell drivers who is eligible for the reduced rates, which apply to all but rush-hour riding (good weekdays from 10:00 A.M to 3:00 P.M and after 7:00 P.M. and anytime on weekends).

Since the practice may spread to other cities as the population of oldsters increases, the philosophy behind the concession may be enunciated with some frequency. It was stated not so long ago by Jean M. Maxwell, staff consultant for the National Committee on Aging: "Old persons isolated in sprawling suburbs without cars or other transportation," she told a group in White Plains, New York, "are inclined to be exceptionally lonely." Cheaper mobility for old folks who have to watch their pennies, she suggested, might help save them from that prospect. Transit authorities argue that such assistance, if it is going to be provided at all, should come from welfare, not from public transit funds, lest the transit industry be rendered even less capable of coping with its problems.

For years, the inability of politically-bound public transit to meet its economic problems was nowhere better read than in New York's subway system. In 1904, when the first section of what has since become a 237-mile system was opened, the subway known as the IRT (for Interborough Rapid Transit) was one of the wonders of the modern world: it moved passengers at a breathless 40 miles an hour from the lower end of Manhattan Island to 145th Street at the other end in comfort and with rare delay.

Today, with 6 million people packing its trains and platforms daily, the system affords an ordeal unique in the nation for physical discomfort (screeching noise and dangerous jostling), degradation (grime, dilapidation and crime) and undependability. Gilbert Burck in a *Fortune* article in May, 1961, called a ride on New York's subway "one of civilization's most degrading experiences." There's little doubt about it: were the devil an engineer, his pride and joy would almost certainly have been the largest public transit system in the largest city of the richest nation on earth.

Early in 1962, officials of the underground network proudly proclaimed they had drastically reduced the number of fires in their transportation system in 1961 to just 1,650! The system also averages one suicide or fatal "fall" every day – nearly 400 a year. The city, in fact, has more police underground – in its subway force – than all but two dozen cities have above ground. It had some 950 in 1962 – 30 more than Denver, which had the 24th largest corps in the nation going into 1962, including non-uniformed personnel.

Fiscally, the system has been in bad shape for years. Despite the fact that it enjoys the highest population density in the country and has been blessed with rising revenues since 1958, the New York City Transit Authority simply cannot make ends meet. Operating losses were officially estimated at close to $6 million in 1962, and some sources believe it may exceed $200 million a year if depreciation is taken into account. The Transit Authority, however, has long since been relieved of the necessity of paying for its rolling equipment, station improvements, and system extensions. The city itself picks up the tab for these items. It entered 1962, for example, with the prospect of having to spend over $200 million replacing cars over 40 years old; by way of contrast, the city paid $317 million for the entire IRT and BMT (Brooklyn-Manhattan Transit) systems when it purchased them in 1940. Only 2,000 of the system's 7,000 cars were less than 15 years old in the beginning of 1962.

Though New York City officials have repeatedly insisted the 15-cent fare is sacred, it is obviously only a question of time – possibly very little time at that – before it is hiked again. It is ironic, perhaps, but it was the city's insistence on maintenance of the 5-cent fare that forced the Interborough Rapid Transit system into bankruptcy and brought municipal ownership in the first place.

Another major commuting facility, the New Haven Railroad, one of the eight commuter lines that haul suburbanites into Manhattan to work, recently ended up in the bankruptcy courts despite forgiveness of more than $6 million yearly in taxes by the four states it serves. Notwithstanding some well-heralded progress in recent years, still another important commuting facility, the Long Island Railroad, said to be the biggest passenger hauler in the world, was so short of funds in the spring of 1961 that it was unable to meet its weekly payroll until it sold off a piece of real estate for $400,000.

Even the railroads which rack up the highest passenger revenues in the nation – the Pennsylvania and the New York Central – are chronic conveyors of mounting commuter losses.

New York's and Los Angeles' transit afflictions are widespread. At the moment, the largest cities in the nation, including Chicago, Philadelphia, and Boston, are struggling desperately to keep their commuter operations going. A good many smaller cities are in even more dire straits.

More than a dozen railroads have quit the passenger business completely since 1950. Other transit systems, bus and rail alike, have cut their services substantially, drastically altering modes of life. Residents of Piermont, New York, for instance, recently found themselves without bus service from New York City after 11:15 at night where they had been accustomed to service up to 1:15 in the morning.

The neglected state of the transit plant causes commuters other hardships. Recently, when a fire broke out on a New Haven train, the railroad thoughtfully broadcasted a spot announcement to waiting housewives that their husbands would be delivered two hours late, and then proceeded to deliver them seven hours late.

The American Municipal Association, in a study entitled *The Collapse of Commuter Service,* found that 75 percent of all commuter railroad cars in use in the United States in 1959 were over 40 years old. It placed equipment needs of the country's commuter roads and transit lines at the time at close to $1.3 billion.

Recognizing their plight and their vital public function, municipalities increasingly are forgiving transit systems from paying stiff franchise fees, property taxes, and other levies, including fuel taxes. More than 300 such tax amnesties were extended to public transit systems in the 14 years to 1961, according to E. C. Houghton, President of the American Transit Association.

Where tax forgiveness isn't sufficient, subsidies – local, state, and federal – are becoming more common. Public bodies justify such assistance to transit systems as necessary to prevent their fading into oblivion. The continued existence of public transit, it is reasoned, spares vast expenditures on roads that would otherwise be needed to accommodate the same number of people in automobiles. The argument further runs that automobiles destroy city property values, while transit improvements enhance them, thus returning the subsidy many times over.

One of the more widely acclaimed new subway systems in the world is Toronto's Yonge Street subway. Its first link, consisting of 4.6 miles, was opened in 1954. Property values along its route rose 37 percent between 1954 and 1958 while property values in the rest of the city improved an average of 20 percent. The subway's contribution to property values was estimated to be producing some $4 million a year in revenues to the city. The system was financed principally from funds accumulated during World War II, but the $4 million annual contribution would have been more than enough to liquidate, with interest, any debt that might have been incurred to cover its $50.5 million construction cost.

The system is credited with keeping an estimated 10,000 automobiles daily out of Toronto's most congested area. It has proved so successful that another 10-mile segment, the so-called Bloor-University line, is being added at a cost of $200 million.

Approximately 60 percent of the cost of a new subway in Melbourne, Australia, is expected to be returned from enhanced property values in its first decade of operation. Local property owners in areas served by the subway are to help pay for the system by annually turning over to the city one fourth of the increase in assessed valuation during the first ten years the subway is in operation.

Philadelphia has possibly gone as far as any community along the subsidy road, short of outright public ownership. Its specially formed nonprofit Passenger Service Improvement Corporation began contracting for the purchase of commuter service with privately owned roads in 1958. PSIC contracts with the carriers to offset losses from low fares and unprofitable services that would otherwise be pared or eliminated. The program, which the city figures has succeeded in putting some 8,600 motorists weekly into public transit, cost Philadelphia approximately $1.5 million in 1961. The city is said to be spending in excess of $4 million a year on various direct efforts to keep transit healthy and in private hands.

The International City Managers Association figures Boston-area municipalities pay about $20 million a year in subsidies to systems serving that region. The Boston subsidies are raised by direct assessment against 14 cities and towns served by the Boston Metropolitan Transit Authority, a state agency.

The federal government started subsidizing public transit with the passage of the Housing Act of 1961. The initial kitty, which was to be made available in the form of loans and "demonstration grants" in the year to June 30, 1962, totaled $42.5 million. But before the program was six months old, requests were in for more than eight times that amount. And many of the biggest programs had yet to come in.

A federal transit bill under consideration at the time of this writing would have provided another $500 million for aid to local transit systems over a three-year period. The bill would have provided up to $2 in federal aid for every $1 produced in local funds for efforts designed to make commuting faster, easier, cheaper, or more comfortable.

One of the earliest transit experiments proposed under the demonstration grant program came from Ithaca, New York (population 29,000). It brought the public's transit thinking to the ultimate, proposing that maybe the way to make a transit system pay was to charge no fares at all. People would then spend more money inside the city of Ithaca, the argument ran, and the returns would be realized through higher sales tax revenues and enhanced property values.

The Wall Street Journal, in an editorial on December 8, 1961, suggested carrying the Ithaca proposal one step further. "What causes traffic jams?" it asked. "Basically, it's not too many cars or inadequate trains. It's too many people. The solution," it suggested, "is simple: Let the Federal Government pay people to stay home. Surely that's no more illogical than paying the farmer not to grow crops."

Privately-owned transit systems, however, are nowhere near so disdainful of Uncle Sam's help as all that. Nine out of ten transit companies responding to an American

Transit Association survey early in 1962 said they needed and wanted federal help. In all, some 287 systems spoke up for the dole, 265 of them privately owned.

The biggest demands for federal assistance promised to come from systems not yet built and from older, publicly-owned ones. Los Angeles, for instance, was looking to the federal government in 1962 for guarantees that would enable it to sell some $200 million worth of bonds to get a 23-mile combination subway-surface rail system built between Beverly Hills in the western part of the county and El Monte in the east. The system was described as a "bare backbone" route for a projected $500 million, 75-mile rail network.

Washington, D.C., itself had blueprints at the time for a 33-mile rapid transit system that would cost an estimated $400 million.

The Regional Plan Association, a nonprofit group promoting governmental cooperation in the metropolitan New York area, told the United States Senate in 1961 a capital outlay of between $650 million and $800 million "might serve" as a "first step" toward preventing "further deterioration" of mass transit in the New York metropolitan region.

The most ambitious transit project of all, however, is that of the San Francisco Bay Area. It involves the construction of a 75-mile system whose 70-mile-an-hour trains are to link the three counties of San Francisco, Alameda and Contra Costa at a cost of more than $1 billion by the time it is completed in 1971. A $792 million bond issue to help finance the system squeezed by voters in November, 1962, by a scant 0.7 percent above the required 60 percent majority. The issue would not have carried if it hadn't received strong support from San Franciscans, whose city, of course, will be at the hub of the system; they gave the measure a 65.9 percent approval compared with 59.5 percent in Alameda County where Oakland is located, and just 54.4 percent in Contra Costa. Two other counties, San

Mateo and Marin, pulled out of the original plan, partly, at least, because no final determination had been made on the ability of the Golden Gate Bridge, which links the two counties, to accommodate commuter trains.

The system is to consist of 31 miles of aerial structure, 24 miles of surface track and 20 miles of undersurface line, including four miles of tunnel under San Francisco Bay which will cut the present 35-to-45-minute rush-hour trip between Oakland and San Francisco down to eight minutes for a projected fare of 35 cents. The longest trip, 30 miles between Daly City south of San Francisco to Concord in Contra Costra, a 75-minute rush-hour journey by car, would be reduced to 45 minutes for a fare of 95 cents. By agreeing to the system, which will sink a subway beneath San Francisco's Market Street, voters consented to tacking on 67 cents a year to their annual property tax rate for every $100 worth of assessed valuation they own. In addition, motorists using the overburdened San Francisco Bay Bridge will finance the $133 million Trans-Bay transit tube through the payment of tolls; presumably, they will one day be rewarded for those payments by less congestion on the bridge – or the opportunity to go speedily and effortlessly on the public conveyance instead.

A good many rapid-transit plans being readied and ballyhooed by desperate municipalities may, of course, be years in getting started. The *Los Angeles Times* in 1961 reported city planners in that metropolis had "little hope that any form of mass transportation will make up for the added automobiles that will converge on the Civic Center in the next 20 years." Indeed, city officials as far back as 1912 were busily studying the merits of a proposed six-mile, $12 million subway system which was to make it possible for Los Angeles to "spread over a vast territory." Los Angeles did the spreading, all right – without the subway system. Now it is trying to decide whether it can afford one with which to pull itself together.

Traffic Jam: The Concrete Spread

Whether or not they ever mean to do anything, one thing is clear: officials in a good many municipalities are not going to lack for studies. Los Angeles may be particularly notorious in this respect. It has paid for "30 to 40 studies in as many years," confesses a spokesman for the MTA. The city, in fact, is almost never without a transit study. It spent close to $1 million on no less than a dozen surveys between 1953 and 1960. By the time one study is complete another is outdated. Says a top official of the city's Chamber of Commerce: "The metropolitan area's rapid transit potential has been overstudied and oversurveyed."

No one yet has come up with a panacea to the nation's transit headache. A good many planners, particularly in cities suffering from sprawl such as Los Angeles, believe no single treatment or medication is going to cure the disease. Many efforts must be made together – starting with zoning itself to create lines of high-density population capable of feeding transit systems. The task of rezoning developed areas in this manner, however, could prove still more formidable than slicing rights-of-way for a new automobile route and probably a good deal more difficult where several cities must coordinate their zoning practices to make the attempt effective.

Chicago has come up with one promising answer to the transit puzzle: it involves the use of existing expressway routes as rights-of-way for transit operations. At a cost of $13 million a mile, two strips of transit track have been run down the center of the city's eight-lane Congress Street Expressway. The solution has proved so successful that Chicago is planning to build at least four more center-transit expressways, and other cities are considering similar measures. One sign of the success of the Congress Street approach: even though it is operating at only about a fourth of capacity, the transit system is carrying 50 percent more passengers than all auto lanes on either side. It can thus accommodate substantial increases in usage without the congestion or the outlay involved in greater auto use. Angelenos could have been similarly blessed had they not allowed their Pacific Electric routes to wither in the first blush of the automotive age.

The newly established Metropolitan Washington Area Transit Commission, serving the District of Columbia and parts of two states around it, Maryland and Virginia, had some $200,000 in the till in mid-1962 earmarked for the acquisition of median strips in future interstate highways for exclusive use at first by buses and later, when passenger volume warrants it, for a rail system. For the most part, however, municipalities contemplating the measure are cooled by prospective costs. Former trial lawyer Jerome P. Cavanagh, Mayor of Detroit, says his city "contemplated the use of a center area for rapid transit when we first started our freeway system but it was turned down because of cost. Besides," says he, "people are not ready to switch from cars to buses, at least not in this city."

The facts of transportation efficiency are something else again. A single track of express subway or elevated train is capable of accommodating up to twenty times as many people as a single lane of express highway, according to the American Transit Association. The ATA figures that even buses traveling ordinary city streets can haul three times as many persons per hour past a given point than can automobiles on express highways.

What, short of physical coercion, is going to get motorists to switch to public transit or at least prevent transit passengers from further feeding the exodus to the automobile?

The challenge is a mighty one. Even the highly lauded new transit systems of Chicago, the rail operation down the center of the Congress Street Expressway, and Toronto, with its expanding subway, have been unable to make sizable dents in automotive travel. Recent surveys showed only 12 percent of Chicago's Congress Street transit passengers and only 10 percent of Toronto's were persons who traded motoring for transit. Over 88 percent of the patrons of the two facilities, in other words, had not been driving to their destinations anyway.

A survey of more than 1,000 motorists in Los Angeles and San Francisco showed resistance to public transit was based largely on three concepts: that it was "too expensive," "too crowded," and provided "poor service." The last two reasons may have a certain amount of validity, but the first, despite the persistence of the belief, is rarely true. The cost of gasoline, tire wear, and other operating expenses, plus the price of parking, is almost invariably greater than the price of a bus or train ticket. But transit is at a disadvantage in this respect because its patrons are constantly reminded of the price of public transit where they are seldom aware of the true total cost of driving their automobiles to work. And even if they were, many of them, more than likely, would continue driving for reasons of comfort and convenience.

Convinced commuters would flock to the Chicago and North Western Railroad if they were assured "safety, reliability, comfort, and speed," Board Chairman Ben Heineman in recent years has replaced his entire commuter fleet with new double-decked, air-conditioned cars. Despite the fact that he hiked fares 26 percent to meet the expenditure, Mr. Heineman succeeded in bringing the road's commuter operation from red to black ink. Though it is still not as profitable as it should be to attract new investment in commuter transportation, the road has demonstrated the public's willingness to pay for a better ride.

The provision of parking facilities at transit stations has helped lure motorists back to commuter transportation in some areas. "Park 'n' Ride" facilities, as they are called, are credited with helping double commuter volume between the city of Cleveland and the wealthy suburb of Shaker Heights. The Shaker Heights station achieved fame with its so-called "kissing loops" as well, where housewives could drive their husbands to the station and linger long enough to kiss them goodbye without setting a bevy of horns off, but the system's most effective selling point is not to be found in lingering: it achieves a relatively fast 30-miles-an-hour average speed over the entire system by making relatively few stops. Its fourteen stations average more than a mile between them.

The provision of parking facilities at transit stops is not in itself a guarantee of use. The New York Transit Authority tried leasing two parking lots to private businessmen to operate such facilities in 1959. One of the parking lots was located in the Upper Bronx and the other in the Canarsie section of Brooklyn. Motorists were permitted to leave their vehicles at the lots and ride free into town for only 75 cents a day. Two subway tokens worth 15 cents apiece, good for the round trip, were handed to each motorist as he parked. But the system, quite possibly for lack of promotion, drew disappointing patronage. The Bronx lot, as a result, was shut down after only six months of operation while the Canarsie operation hobbled along well under capacity usage.

The privately-owned Dallas Transit Company in 1955 located new bus stops at sixty gasoline stations which agreed to let motorists park on their property in hopes they would then buy gas and service at the station. The plan fizzled out after mutual disillusionment: the transit company got very few new passengers and the gas stations even fewer new customers. The "ride" apparently is at least as important as the "park"; where motorists stand to benefit significantly from the switch, as they did on the speedy Shaker Heights run, the provision of parking may contribute importantly to the switch to public transit.

Amenities may similarly summon passengers back to public transportation. The Long Island Railroad early in 1961 began offering "quickie breakfasts" on its 5:39 A.M. train from Port Jefferson. It also broke tradition with its

127-year past, by launching bar service on its late-afternoon trains, as the New Haven had been doing for some years. A champagne cart, with a white-jacketed steward to keep the sparkling wine moving and flowing, is featured on de luxe buses chartered out to private dinner-theater parties by the Carey Transportation Company of New York.

It may seem somewhat paradoxical, but the same lines that have the toughest time with riders over a nickel increase in fares have no difficulty at all peddling the same ride with more comfort and luxury at well above the usual rate. The Long Island Railroad, for instance, rarely has trouble selling out its parlor-car service at $1.50 more per seat. Its private compartments, which cost up to $18.82 for the three-hour journey to Montauk, are traditionally among the first to sell out, though the passenger cannot board them until the Jamaica stop is reached, about twenty minutes out of Manhattan. A "club class" bus service that provided patrons with reserved seats and front-door delivery in the evening on any one of three buses has little difficulty garnering added charges in Cincinnati. The paradox, of course, is simply explained: a little bit of imagination in the way of providing something more than just "a ride" can go a long way in the transit business as in any other.

Some bus lines are running special midday shopping expresses to step up off-peak patronage by providing speedier, well-advertised downtown service. The ride is sometimes provided free of charge or at cut rates with merchants making up the difference. Sometimes the bus company itself provides the free ride – to acquaint the public with its new air-conditioned equipment, for example. Some bus systems have permanent arrangements with merchants to pick up the passenger's fare, through a refund or validation procedure, whenever his purchases total over a given sum. The practice is probably more in the retailer's own best long-term interests than that of validating motorists' parking tickets, and rarely costs him more. Its adoption, however, is often resisted by merchants who doubt that bus passengers are good customers, on the theory that they do not have the financial means to buy nor the physical means to haul away their purchases.

Transit systems could do worse in their merchandising endeavors than to tear a page from the book of the Municipal Bus Lines of Santa Monica, California, the most consistently successful local bus operation in the nation. The Santa Monica line scored its seventh consecutive year of increased patronage in 1961 during a period when transit lines around the country have been losing passengers with fearful consistency. The city-owned system also scored its seventh consecutive year of profits in 1961. Never once in that time has it failed to return an after-tax profit of at least 7 percent, not a bad record for a publicly-owned transit company under any circumstances. The profit achievement, furthermore, had been scored without a single hike in the bus line's 15-cent fare since 1952 despite higher wages and costlier equipment.

William F. Farell, superintendent of the Santa Monica line, insists the answer to better transit operations cannot be found in short-lived campaigns or in the institution of one or two techniques, no matter how well received they may be. A former bus-line owner himself, and a consultant to other ailing systems, Mr. Farell maintains it takes "a host of efforts applied persistently over the years" to get people back to buses. Those efforts, says he, must be directed toward "raising the prestige of the line to where it is no longer a social error to be seen on a bus."

Among the methods Mr. Farell uses to achieve this objective: personal delivery of bus schedules and maps by uniformed supervisors whenever a telephone operator or dispatcher catches one of the line's three supervisory radio cars in reasonable range of the caller, the return of lost articles to their owners in the same manner, the trusting of patrons to pay a double fare next time they are on the bus if they have bills the driver cannot change, the elimination of such signs as "please have proper fare ready," "exit to the rear," and others deemed too regimentive of passengers, help extended to mothers bringing strollers on board though many bus lines prohibit them altogether, and generally providing a more cheerful atmosphere both inside and outside the bus through the use of gay two-tone pastels that escape the depressing effects of commonly employed bus decor.

Much of the Santa Monica bus line's success lies, too, in its awareness of the value of publicity and the imaginative, energetic cultivation of those opportunities. To begin with, the line advertises regularly in the local press. Ads, written by Mr. Farell himself and aimed at improving the prestige image of the bus line, contain such exhortations as "Step Up To The Big Blue Bus." Rarely is an opportunity missed for plastering the operation across newspaper pages free of charge in the more widely read news columns themselves. The receipt of new buses not long ago occasioned a 45-minute parade staged by the line consisting of some 12 different types of transit vehicles borrowed from various sources in the area. Hostesses enlisted from local women's groups show passers-by through new vehicles, which are parked at strategic downtown locations for the purpose just before they are put into service. Downtown department stores occasionally contribute the use of a window for a week or two at a stretch so the bus line can make a pitch for public transit through displays of miniature bus models and other items.

Celebrities, especially top civic officials and business leaders, are urged to ride the buses to set an example for the general public and are invariably photographed in the process for the local press. Certain community events have occasioned the use of a bus, with the driver dressed in a tux affording excellent background for other newsworthy "shots." The line got its longest run on local news pages some years back when it sent its drivers to Detroit to pick up a fleet of new buses and then had them stage various civic banquets at points en route. Their progress and reception were fully reported, with photographs, of course, for the folks back home.

The line could not get anywhere with its publicity efforts, however, unless its bus-operating practices were themselves genuine, foresighted, and vigorous. There is no doubt but that they are. A Santa Monica housewife tells of the time she phoned the bus company to find out when she could catch the bus nearest her shortly after noon on a Saturday for Beverly Hills. An employee told her there would be one at her particular corner at 12:20 P.M. She was at the corner at 12:10 when a uniformed bus-line employee pulled up in a car, asked her if she was waiting for the bus, and then told her the employee had made a mistake. He was there, he stated, to take her wherever she wanted to go – at no charge to her. Drivers who fail to comply with the company's courtesy rules, which include the honoring of an expired bus transfer when the passenger insists he just got it, are severed from their jobs. Fortunately, the bus line has the full cooperation of the union.

Though he had not had to use it by the time of this writing, Mr. Farell feels the technique of hiking transit fares is also important in keeping passengers and public support when such action has to be taken. He is an ardent advocate of raising fares "only in small increments at a time, preferably by only a couple of pennies, and doing it as often as it may be necessary." Mr. Farell figures too many transit operators wait too long to increase their fares and then have to make up for the delay by raising fares so sharply as to antagonize the general public and cause previous passengers to consider alternative modes of transportation, such as the motorcar. A fare policy of this nature, or any other for that matter, requires cooperation from the rate-setting authority, of course, for its success.

Traffic Jam: The Concrete Spread

Transit operators may be able to reduce the frequency of their trips to rate authorities, however, and retain more of their passengers in the process, if they would look to their operations for economies to make ends meet. Transit systems, whether they are privately or publicly owned, rail or bus, often can cut their costs substantially by hacking away at their deadwood. Transit operations in many cities, for example, are notoriously overstaffed. One authority says he knows of a major western metropolis which could save $4 million a year if it reduced its payroll only to the American Transit Association standards of no more than two employees for every bus on the road, drivers and office staff included. Many cities, says he, have as many as three employees per bus. A California municipality that bought out its private operator in 1961 and promptly cut his staff from five employees to two, began showing a profit almost immediately.

Subway authorities in Paris are catering to both passenger comfort and speedier service by equipping their trains with rubber tires and replacing their steel rails with wooden ones; the switch was designed to make the city's subway almost silent and, by better braking, permit 20 percent faster speeds between stations. Faster speeds have an appeal not only for passengers but also for carriers, since they permit the accommodation of greater numbers of customers at little, if any, added cost over the same period of time.

The community itself can take steps to put public transit on a paying basis, besides simply doling out subsidies, providing tax forgiveness and, important as it is, creating a favorable climate of rate regulation. One of the more promising efforts it can extend is to make streets, which the public has paid for anyway, more useful to modes of transport that use them the most efficiently. That objective is served, for example, by reserving curbside lanes on down-/town streets exclusively for the use of buses at least during rush hours. Chicago, Baltimore, Dallas and a growing number of other cities are finding the system highly effective in cutting the operating costs of public transit while improving service, and attracting passengers, at the same time. Entry by autos into the bus lanes is precluded by conspicuous markings on the roadway itself and on signs above it, constantly repeating: "Do Not Enter, Buses Only." The message is reinforced by ticket-issuing traffic police. Bus operators say the system has enabled them to slice as much as 30 percent off their transit time in certain periods of the day over their most highly traveled routes. Nashville, which has had the plan in operation since 1956, claims it can provide the same rush-hour service with 17 buses as the 19 it needed before the system was in use.

To the extent that curb parking is permitted on downtown streets, the provision of lanes exclusively for bus use is impossible except on the broadest of boulevards. Even when the operation of buses is not the issue, curb parking cuts down road use. One reason curb parking is still permitted in many areas where it should have been abolished long ago is that local merchants generally oppose the prohibition for fear of losing customers. A recent survey conducted in the city of San Diego, however, would indicate such fears are ill-founded. Of 4,533 persons interviewed outside a bank, a jewelry store, and a hotel, only 51, or 1.1 percent of the total, were found to have entered any of these establishments; the others went elsewhere. "The parker at the curb," said William G. Austin, Manager of the Merchants Association of Kansas City, long before that survey was conducted, "is not a shopper." Merchants who insist on curb parking on busy commercial streets are thus extracting a public subsidy that is perhaps more dubious still than any which might be provided to public transit.

Municipal authorities have still another reason, besides ensuring proper use of the taxpayer's street dollar, for eliminating curb parking on busy downtown streets: their safety hazard, as will shortly be detailed at greater length. Allowing curb parking on busy thoroughfares is highway robbery in terms of human life and public cost.

In addition to making travel simpler for buses on downtown streets, concessions may have to be made to buses or expressways as well. Eventually, this may require the reservation of rush-hour bus lanes on expressways as well as on downtown streets, but there are other devices for giving the buses a helping hand short of this extreme. Chicago, for example, permits faster speeds for buses than for other vehicles on some of its expressways. Buses are allowed to travel at up to 60 miles an hour, compared with 55 miles an hour for automobiles and 50 miles an hour for trucks.

Public authorities could provide transit operators with a big assist in their attempts to make ends meet by helping to iron out peak traffic loads through the encouragement of staggered work hours. One reason transit is so costly is that it is, for all practical purposes, only working a 20-hour week though its costs go on round-the-clock. Furthermore, the peaks are getting sharper; Toronto's Yonge Street Subway, to cite a single instance, was getting 10,000 more people in its peak hours several years after the system went into operation, though there was little increase in total daily traffic. Many transit systems haul 50 percent of their passengers in two two-hour periods, between seven and nine o'clock in the morning and four and six o'clock in the evening, a commission on metropolitan area problems reported to California's Governor Brown in 1962. Efforts to get private firms to stagger their working hours have so far proved almost futile. Public bodies, however, can set an example. In Los Angeles, the State Division of Highways, which is particularly sensitive to the need, recently placed some 1,400 of its employees on 7:30 A.M. to 4:15 P.M. workweeks to help flatten the load on freeways and transit lines. Many other government bodies, however, have yet to take such measures, including those in the transportation field themselves.

Another device for putting the costly transit plant to greater use consists in finding other jobs for it to do in idle hours, such as hauling different types of freight. A Los Angeles business consultant not long ago suggested that the city's transit authority make provision for hauling garbage at night on its projected rail transit system. The consultant, J. Jamison Moore, claimed the city could also cut its garbage-hauling costs by as much as a third, since the rail system would be cheaper than trucks.

There are other ways of cashing in on the transit plant, particularly in a rail operation where valuable real estate is involved. The New York Transit Authority, for example, penned an agreement in 1961 with the Subway Bowling Corporation, a private undertaking, calling for the installation of 76 lanes of bowling alley in three stations of its Independent (IND) system at an estimated total cost of $1.5 million. The Transit Authority was to get 12 percent of the yearly gross from the alleys, which would be accessible to riders and nonriders alike, or a minimum of $650 a year from each alley rising to at least $850 a year if the State Liquor Authority permitted the sale of beer on the premises. The New Haven and New York Central railroads are attempting to turn the same trick with the air space over a waiting room they jointly operate on the Forty-second Street side of Grand Central Terminal: a tentative agreement with the Vanderbilt Bowling Corporation would produce $92,500 in yearly lease income from a bowling alley VBC would construct beneath the structure's high ceilings. Complete buildings over railway rights-of-way, such as the massive Pan Am Building near the same famous terminal, are similarly being used more heavily to supplement railway company income. There is even some talk of the device being used by municipalities, to get apartment houses built over expressway routes so what those roadways take away in the form of taxable properties may be returned, at least in part, in rental income; restaurants straddling state highways are increasingly serving as a source of supplemental income to public bodies.

The pressure of population growth is bound to produce many more such opportunities in the years ahead. It may also help transit systems that can benefit most from population densities, such as subways, to pull themselves out of the mire in which transit finds itself so deeply embedded at present. In recent years, new subway systems have begun construction or operation in such far-flung places as Stockholm and Caracas, Haifa and Winnipeg, Rome and Rotterdam, and Leningrad and Lisbon, as well as in Melbourne and Toronto. London, of course, has long been served by underground transport; built in 1863, it is the oldest of all subway systems. Paris' "Metro" began operating in 1900. Both of these systems are considerably more tolerable than New York's, though they are almost as densely used. Paris' 210 miles of track hauls just under 1.2 million persons yearly compared with almost 1.4 million carried on New York's 237-mile system.

Practically all rail systems, above and below ground, are feeling the crush of swelling rush hour populations. In Tokyo, commuter roads have resorted to hiring university students as "pushers" to help pack as many passengers as possible into their trains during that city's rush hour. On one particularly zealous day, 85 persons were hospitalized in the process.

Public transit is largely a financial headache today. To the extent that self-correcting economic forces are not allowed to operate, or fail to do so, it will be primarily a political headache tomorrow. The sequence is already visibly in motion in a good many cities. Those that can still avoid it, and wish to do so, must obviously quit tossing roadblocks in the way: instead of saddling still-healthy transit operations with welfare burdens or unprofitable

service, they must see that these extra-transit services, if the
community chooses to provide them, are amply compen-
sated and that, wherever necessary, the system is further
bolstered by efforts to clear lanes for speedier service and
lighten financial burdens through tax-forgiveness or other
devices. Such measures are likely to prove cheaper and
more satisfactory in the long run than a publicly-owned
operation that is fully and helplessly exposed to political
pressures for this and that service at the lowest conceivable
fares.

For their part, transit operators, whether publicly or
privately directed, must be capable of making better use of
their economic opportunities and adjusting to changing
situations even if that means breaking with time-honored
traditions, whether the tradition stems from a social myopia
that precludes experiments with multiclass transit service
(it has worked in theaters and elsewhere for years without
insulting the democratic process) or from psychological
resistance to the promotional merchandising that has become absolutely vital in so many other lines of competitive
endeavor.

THE HUMAN TOLL ROADS

THE nation suffered more than three times as many casualties on its streets and highways in the period from December 7, 1941, to August 14, 1945, than it did in battle during
World War II, which covered that span. United States war
casualties, including missing, totaled just over one million
(1,070,524 to be exact) compared with 3.3 million on the
road, according to the Institute of Traffic Engineers. The
holocaust took more lives – approximately 292,000 in actual combat compared with 94,000 claimed by vehicles –
but lifetime disabilities from motor accidents usually run
higher than the two-to-one wounded-to-killed war ratio.
Worse, the highways never cease to exact their human toll
from one year to the next or from hour to hour.

Traffic Jam: The Concrete Spread

The United States between 1919 and 1941 lost twice as many lives in motor-vehicle accidents, in fact, as it did in battle during all the wars it fought to 1941. And the yearly death toll continues at a high level. Motor vehicles are presently taking an average of one life every 14 minutes, or more than 100 a day. There were only five days in one recent 10-year span, in fact, in which fewer than 100 persons were killed in the United States in automotive mishaps.

The sixth biggest killer in the nation, and the largest by far of persons from five to thirty-one years old, motor vehicles in 1961 claimed 38,000 lives, according to the National Safety Council. The total, which had been climbing at breakneck speed through the early postwar years, was arrested for a short time in 1957 and 1958 but has since resumed its upward climb. By 1975 the annual toll is expected to top 45,000.

The cost of highway accidents to the nation by 1975 is expected to approximate $9.5 billion a year, nearly twice the 1958 figure and almost twenty times that of 1920. Even Americans who are not involved in highway accidents help pay the bill – in higher insurance rates, added police and other public costs and, to some extent, in increased prices for the goods they buy since carriers must similarly meet these added burdens.

It is true, of course, that there are many more vehicles about. Computed on the basis of miles traveled, the motor journey would appear to have become much safer than it used to be: the death rate on this basis amounted to just 5.2 per 100 million miles traveled by a single vehicle in 1961 compared with 11.4 in 1940 and 28.2 in 1920 – and it is expected to fall further, to 4.4 or less in 1975. In terms of population, however, the likelihood of death by automobile is just about as great as it has ever been, despite dramatic advances in automotive engineering (improved door latches and the all-steel body, for instance), highway construction (through the elimination of intersections and other dangerous accesses by freeway and expressway projects), and notable medical progress in saving lives of the injured (new drugs, mainly). The automotive death rate worked out to 21.8 persons per 100,000 population in 1927; in 1961 it was still 20.8, a scant 5 percent below the figure 34 years earlier. And it hasn't changed substantially since 1957, though it got as high as 24.3 in 1952 and was greater still in the reckless thirties.

Traffic congestion may worsen survival chances in the future. "It's getting to be a real problem to get ambulances or police to the scene of a highway accident where cars may be backed up for miles," notes one traffic authority.

Los Angeles, for one, is considering the use of helicopters as emergency ambulances, though prospective costs and risks have inhibited their adoption for these purposes up to now. French police are experimenting with closed-circuit TV for transmitting the condition of a patient to physicians in hospitals so policemen on the scene can render proper care until medical help arrives. The provision of broader "shoulders" or wider center strips for emergency access is, unfortunately, growing more and more prohibitive in cost.

In an effort to keep accident rates down, authorities are turning more toward the use of such devices as center barriers for highways and safety belts in automobiles. Center barriers, opposed at first by many highway engineers who argued they would promote rather than prevent accidents and cut capacity by veering drivers away from center lanes, are proving highly effective. A five-mile strip of cable-reinforced safety fencing has been credited with reducing deaths on one 15-mile length of Los Angeles freeway from 17 the year before its installation to only 7 the year following.

Replacing damaged fences, of course, is costly business. The California State Division of Highways figures it may have to replace as much as one-third of its chain-link divider fences yearly on some of its more heavily traveled freeways. Since such repairs cost about as much as the original installation – $3.50 or so per foot – the rate of repair is equivalent to installing a new fence every three years. In the overall Los Angeles metropolitan area, so-called District VIII, the division budgeted over half a million dollars in its 1962-1963 fiscal year for the replacement of an estimated 30 miles of chain-link fencing on the slightly more than 100 miles it had installed. The amount was expected to increase substantially a year later when 470 miles of freeway were to have been fenced down the center.

Seat belts, though they proved their value long ago, were many years in gaining any kind of general acceptance, and even then they needed the help of government bodies to do it. At approximately $15 a pair installed in front seats, they should have seemed a bargain in the light of safety findings. Cornell University's Automotive Crash Injury Research Center some years back showed that persons thrown from automobiles were five times as likely to be killed as those who remained inside; the standard 5,000 block-pound seat belt is designed to hold the wearer in his seat even on impacts that would completely demolish the front half of the vehicle and destroy the driver anyway, such as a head-on collision with each vehicle traveling at 50 miles an hour. The National Safety Council figures seat belts could save one in every eight lives currently lost in highway accidents. Notwithstanding such findings, seat belts were offered to the motoring public as optional equipment on 1949 Nashes and on other makes not long thereafter, but fewer than 5 percent of the vehicles on the road by 1962 were equipped with them.

It was not until New York State in 1962 followed the example set earlier by Wisconsin, in requiring their installation, that the automobile industry moved to make them standard equipment on all makes of cars by 1964. But the

automakers, who admittedly might have spent more to promote the use of safety devices, such as the seat belts, have
not been entirely disinterested in the survival of their customers. They have attempted repeatedly, in fact, to make
their vehicles safer, in the process of which they have only
succeeded in proving that safety is not often a product the
public is willing to buy. The Ford Motor Company in 1956
offered a "safety package" consisting of padded visors
(recognizing the tendency to move up and forward on the
impact of collision), padded dashboards with recessed
knobs, safety belts, and steering wheels with recessed columns at a price well under the cost of a set of white walls
and wheel covers. It sold fewer than 5 percent of its customers on the package the first year. Shortly thereafter,
when it began offering the items individually, the one most
often bought was neither the biggest contributor to automotive safety nor the cheapest, but the one with most eye
appeal, the padded dash.

Safety features which do not add excessively to cost, and
therefore impair the competitiveness of one make of auto
against another, have been added by automakers without
consulting the general public. Improved door latches on
cars of 1956 model vintages resulted in 40 percent fewer
ejections than those experienced in collisions involving
1940 to 1955 model cars, according to a recent study.

The American motoring public seems no more favorably
disposed toward tougher safety laws than to the spending
of nominal sums for improving chances of highway survival. A study of motoring accidents in Connecticut in
1959 revealed that nearly half of all fatalities recorded that
year involved a drinking driver or a drinking pedestrian;
two out of five of the drivers and a much larger proportion
of adult pedestrians involved in the fatalities were found to
have been drinking. In Maryland, where the Department
of Post Mortem Examiners analyzes the blood of drivers
and pedestrians who die within six hours of an accident,

three of four drivers and three of every five pedestrians who died in 1959 were found to have had at least some trace of alcohol in their blood. Medical research has demonstrated that the driving ability of most individuals is affected in some degree after just two or three drinks, enough to produce a 0.05 percent blood-alcohol concentration on an empty stomach. Most states, however, don't consider a man guilty of drunk driving unless his blood-alcohol concentration exceeds 0.15 percent. It takes eight drinks in the span of just an hour to produce that concentration in a two-hundred pounder, provided he does not take any solid food in the interim of just prior to drinking.

John C. Hall, Director of the Western District of the National Safety Council who served seventeen years on the police force of Pasadena, California, and became that department's court-qualified expert on alcoholism, says that in none of the 1,500 humans he examined had he ever seen an individual with a 0.15 blood alcohol content who had downed less than a pint of whisky. Deeming the 0.15 rule altogether too lenient, New York is one of the few states in the nation that puts the onus of proving sobriety on the driver if his blood-alcohol content exceeds 0.10. Some 19 states, including California, did not have even the 0.15 rule at the time of this writing, which means police officers had to establish some other test of sobriety, with the possibility of added doubt being raised in any court case the motorist might choose to fight. As it is, no state compels a motorist to submit to a blood test establishing the level of his blood-alcohol content, though a few states permit the test to be made where the motorist has lost consciousness and there is reason to believe he had been drinking.

The likelihood of fatality, not surprisingly, grows with every drink. According to one study, a driver increases his chance of getting into an accident by 50 percent with his first three or four drinks. If he has eight or more, he has nearly ten times as much chance of a wreck than if he had only one or two.

The fact that holiday driving is on the average 25 percent more dangerous than nonholiday driving is likewise attributed to alcohol.

Drinking, as well as fatigue, is believed to play a role in making wee morning hours more dangerous than other periods of the day. Fatality rates on some highways have been found to run twice as high between two and four o'clock in the morning as between nine and eleven o'clock at night.

Senator Abraham Ribicoff tried getting tough with drunk drivers while he was Governor of Connecticut, from 1955 to 1961. Those convicted of drunk driving were to lose their licenses for one year under a law that was already on the books but seldom enforced. Persons convicted of speeding were to have their licenses suspended for 30 days on the first offense, 60 days on the second, and indefinitely on the third. Judges who failed to invoke these penalties risked their reappointment. Neither police officers nor the judges, however, proved capable of executing the Governor's wishes for very long. Though the state is still noteworthy today for its relatively strict treatment of traffic offenders, enforcement is nowhere near as severe as prescribed by law. "The public just won't take it, and elected officials aren't about to buck them," explains one traffic authority.

Far stricter drinking-driver laws, however, prevail in such countries as Sweden and Finland – and get enforced. In Finland, for example, any sign of alcohol whatsoever in the bloodstream of a driver, whether he is involved in an accident or not, is enough to get him three months' forced labor – and there are no exceptions. Helsinki's main airport is said to have been constructed almost entirely with labor from this source – including some top executives of some of the country's biggest business firms. A Finn who plans to drink customarily makes arrangements for his rides long in advance of the occasion, or relies on taxis. It is standard practice in Sweden for drinking drivers to request – and receive – rides home from the police.

The National Safety Council believes speed was a contributing factor in at least 35 percent of 1960's fatal accidents, with the proportion being considerably greater in rural (40 percent) than in urban areas (27 percent), possibly because of longer stretches of open road.

The Commerce Department, in a study published in 1959 entitled *The Federal Role in Highway Safety,* suggests slow speed may be as dangerous as relatively high speed – at least on main rural roads. It finds the statistics suggesting "that relatively high-speed driving is, on the average, safer than either low-speed or excessively high-speed driving on main rural highways where good design and other features are adequate to accommodate it." The daytime accident involvement rate, it holds, is actually lowest for speeds between 55 and 70 miles an hour. Drivers in rural areas, the report states, were found to have been involved in accidents at speeds below 40 miles an hour "at a rate several times higher than that of drivers traveling at faster speeds."

Of course, the greater speeds produce the worst accidents. Only 31 of 100 persons involved in crashes at speeds under 40 mph were counted as casualties, compared with 86 in 100 involved in accidents of vehicles going faster than 70 mph, according to the Commerce Department report.

Does drinking tend to make motorists drive faster or slower? Is too much horsepower a menace to some and not others? How can dozing drivers be alerted and how much of a handmaiden is weariness to death? How often are highway manslaughterers repeat killers? When do aged drivers begin to get in trouble and what determines it? How much more dangerous is riding in small cars compared with big ones? Do trucks take a human toll out of proportion to their number? And what, if anything, can be done about such findings?

These and many other questions remain to be answered if the nation's highways are ever to be made substantially safer and the wealth they waste notably reduced. Financial and human resources for such studies, relatively speaking, are not lacking. The federal government and other public bodies have been pouring funds into studies on highway safety for some years now under a system of research contracts and grants-in-aid for those already under way. The studies, however, are often highly academic and, at best, only indirectly useful while the seemingly most pertinent questions of a practical nature are largely neglected. The United States Bureau of Public Roads, for instance, has been financing a relatively costly and continuing study for some years now on the elements that go into "the driving task," but an official admits the agency has only the most cursory knowledge of what color might do to keep motorists from driving the wrong way on off-ramps, for instance, or the value of median barriers on freeways and the respective merits of different types of barriers or even of the various safety devices offered for sale on the open market for such purposes as alerting drowsy drivers. An official of the agency privately apologizes for the "sad state" of federally-aided highway safety research with the only partially true explanation that "we can only choose among the projects that are offered us, we can't initiate anything ourselves." In practice, of course, the agency could "inspire" the kind of research it might deem desirable but it either does not know what that might be or does not choose to do so, or possibly both.

Until highway safety research, privately or publicly sponsored, is more productive, however, communities will go on pursuing sharply divergent practices while conceivably neglecting some of the most vitally needed action to ensure the public safety. Some time ago, for example, the

Traffic Jam: The Concrete Spread

Commerce Department found that "large dimensional differences" between truck and automobile bumpers were resulting in unduly serious damage involving collisions between the two, but the finding never was considered conclusive enough to justify remedial action by federal, state, or municipal authorities; large trucks continue to sport bumpers posing serious dangers to small and compact cars on the slightest mishap. The truck itself is a subject of considerable schizophrenia, largely for lack of convincing evidence in any direction. Pasadena, for example, bans heavy freight vehicles on its freeways, but the National Safety Council finds they get involved in fatal accidents not disproportionate to their number in relation to the total number of vehicle registrations.

Regardless of the detailed findings that have yet to be made, it is obvious that much can still be done to make highways safer besides clamping down on drinkers, snapping on the seat belts, and tightening up laws. Among the more obvious of these measures is a closer screening of drivers and vehicles. Only one state, Pennsylvania, bothered to give applicants for drivers' licenses a physical examination in 1962. Some 39 states never again even take the trouble to test an applicant after he has once passed a written exam. Kansas Highway Safety Director Claude McCamment not long ago found 10 percent of those receiving state aid for the blind had drivers' licenses – which would suggest that the state was being taken for a ride either on its welfare or on its driver-licensing program.

Hawaii is one of several states which still issue lifetime licenses, which are good until revoked. The island of Kauai at one time had over 32,000 valid drivers' licenses in effect when its total population stood at only 28,000 – not just the adult population, but its *entire* population.

Only 17 states in 1962 required yearly inspections of motor vehicles they licensed. Very few even bother to inspect vehicles involved in fatal accidents to learn what role mechanical failure may have played in the tragedy. A team of scientists who are doing about as thorough a job of investigating highway accidents as has ever been performed, even to the extent of getting out of bed and to the scene of an accident in the wee hours of blustery winter mornings, believe the oversight is a serious one. Members of Harvard University's Medical School whose work summoned forth a grant of $809,820 from the United States Public Health Service for five years of continued labors, they hold that every highway fatality should be investigated as thoroughly as a murder, if for no other reason than to add to the body of knowledge that might someday help reduce the carnage. Writing in the Spring, 1962, issue of *Harvard Today,* a campus quarterly, Alfred L. Moseley, Chief Investigator on the research project, maintained that the use of automobiles for deliberate death – suicide and murder – may be second only to poisoning as a method for lifetaking and far more likely to go undetected.

Besides Mr. Moseley, the Harvard investigating team is made up of several medical specialists, a sociologist who probes the driver-victim's background to determine what steps may have led up to the accident, a lawyer, a psychiatrist, and even a minister.

Whether for policing or for other safety reasons, more thorough and systematic investigations into the causes of highway fatalities must certainly be among the first prerequisites of any scientific attack on the phantoms of highway death. One of the biggest handicaps facing researchers in this endeavor are the often unskilled and inadequate reports filed by police or other authorities at the scene, with no effort made at a follow-up. Reporting forms may themselves be inadequate. A prospectively rich body of data and lots of valuable time are being lost, highway researchers contend, by allowing the potential lessons from today's accidents to slip away through unconcern.

According to the United States Commerce Department,

youths under 20 years of age account for two and a half times as many accidents, and those between 20 and 24 twice as many, as the average driver of all ages based on the number of miles driven. Statistics show servicemen get involved in twice as many accidents as other drivers in their age group. The possibility of more closely supervising servicemen, youngsters, and others involved in a disproportionate number of accidents would also seem worthy of greater attention than it has been given.

Municipalities themselves tolerate altogether too many unsafe practices. Notable among these is curb parking, and especially angle parking. Curb parking is a squanderer of vital roadway, as already noted, but it is also a noteworthy contributor to the urban accident rate: 15 percent of all accidents in urban areas were attributed by a recent study to curb parking, 12 percent to parked cars at rest, and 3 percent to cars leaving parked positions. Angular parking is especially hazardous; the substitution of parallel for angular parking has reduced accident rates involving parked vehicles by as much as 50 percent in some instances. "The economic losses stemming from accidents and congestion due to curb parking would more than pay for equivalent space in offstreet parking facilities," the Commerce Department declared in a published statement recently.

Owners as well as drivers must be held responsible for the condition of their vehicles, and some courts have started doing exactly that. The principle, of course, has greater application to commercial than to private vehicles, where drivers and owners are generally identical. In 1962 a United States District Court in Denver meted out a suspended six-month sentence to the owner of a truck whose driver testified that prior to a fatal accident involving mechanical failure, he had warned the owner of faulty air brakes, a malfunctioning hand brake, and a defective horn.

Whether or not public school systems should be providing driver education, the value of teaching emergency behavior and instilling such response in drivers is vital if impulse is to be prevented from misleading drivers to the morgue. Experience is not a satisfactory teacher for this purpose; the penalty for miscue is altogether too high. Few driver-education courses, however, effectively train students in emergency behavior.

The encouragement and provision of facilities – sometimes at considerable public expense – for speed-happy youths to test out their vehicles in drag races is another area in need of closer scrutiny. Such strips, Pennsylvania Commissioner of Traffic Safety O. D. Shipley stated in an article in the *Saturday Evening Post* in May, 1962, "spew forth upon our crowded highways a class of young people trained to drive as rashly, as belligerently, as competitively as possible."

The use of unmarked highway patrol cars, likewise, bears further investigation, despite the opposition of motorists who claim it is "unsporting" (which it unquestionably is, if hunting humans on highways is to be considered a sport). The state of Connecticut turned all its patrol cars into unmarked vehicles by 1962, after experimenting with the system for three years. Observing that fact, the California Traffic Safety Foundation noted recently that "studies indicate the distance over which a marked patrol car will influence traffic behavior is often less than a mile in each direction. If drivers know unmarked cars are being used," it added, "there is an element of uncertainty. Drivers do not know whether or not they are being observed" – and, consequently don't take the chances they are often tempted to take when they feel reasonably sure there isn't a traffic officer around.

One objection to the unmarked car that is often voiced is the opportunity it may afford molesters, particularly at night. The objection, however, can generally be met at least in some significant degree by having police officers in such vehicles in uniform at all times and by making sparing use of such vehicles at night, when marked cars are not so easily spotted anyway.

The use of tachometers or tachographs, devices which record engine revolutions and thereby indicate speeds at a given time, has proven highly effective in preventing truck drivers from pushing their vehicles to excessive speeds. Some road safety experts think the day may come when inexpensive tachographs may be installed at inaccessible places in all motorcars and kept under seal for removal only by police authorities. Such a device, they believe, might have psychological as well as investigative value in inhibiting motorists from reckless driving. School buses would seem to be particularly good candidates among vehicles on which the device might first be required.

One thing that is not going to work in making highways safer is bluff. Ingenious as the trick may be, its staying power is seldom notable, and its effects, quite often, are opposite of what is intended. Once motorists on the New York Thruway some time back discovered the patrol cars they spotted in conspicuous positions ahead were nothing but junkyard relics painted to deceive, the tendency was to ignore the real thing as well; the half-dozen or so wrecks were finally put back in the junkyard where they belonged. The state of Washington was taught a similar lesson after it planted approximately a hundred phony boxes along its roadways to simulate radar sets. More often than not, such practices tend to turn highway safety into a game with the winner being the one who believes himself to have done the most outwitting – until someone comes along to scoop up his remains.

Traffic safety experts agree that one of the most essential elements in any attack on the automobile accident rate, as in so many other human endeavors, lies in alerting the public itself to prospective dangers and the means for coping with them or avoiding them altogether. The greatest opportunity for sounding such an alert, quite obviously, and one of the least expensive, lies in the news value of an accident itself, when it occurs. It is the rare newspaper, however, which reports the essential details of even the most newsworthy traffic accidents, partly because of the natural handicaps involved in speedily reporting the event before essential elements are known (they are no longer considered news after the event) and partly because of factors over which they do have some control but choose not to exercise it such as stating the make of an automobile crushed beneath a truck. The problem of getting vehicular accidents across to an interested public in more meaningful fashion may similarly be worthy of investigation.

THE JAM IN JUSTICE

THE swelling horde of automobiles produces traffic jams not only on concrete roadways but in the courtrooms as well. Justice is invariably the victim, maimed by delay as if it were some aged pedestrian struck down by a youthful speeder.

"Before World War II," notes James P. Economos, Director of the Traffic Court Program of the American Bar Association since 1943, "a year's delay on a civil suit would have been a long wait even in Chicago or New York. Today, thanks largely to the pile-up of personal injury cases, delays of two to three years are not at all unusual for a trial case. It gets as long as four to five years in New York and Chicago."

Though New York has a special calendar for personal-injury cases so other civil suits do not have to line up behind them, many courts elsewhere continue to lump all their civil actions together. And even those that separate them, like New York, cannot help suffering from the heavier burden of traffic and personal-injury cases resulting from highway accidents.

Authorities figure that close to 90 percent of all currently backlogged civil cases in metropolitan-area courts are personal-injury litigations arising from traffic mishaps. The courts, unfortunately for those who equate delayed justice with no justice at all, have proved pathetically incapable of keeping up with the rising load. And there is little to prevent the gap from widening.

"We recommended 27 judicial officials for traffic cases alone for Chicago's Municipal Court but we have only nine," observed Mr. Economos in mid-1961. In Los Angeles, Judge Louis H. Burke, just before his appointment as chief judge of a new division of the State Court of Appeals in the fall of 1961, asked for 24 new judges to tackle a case backlog that had grown from 14 months to over 17 months in the course of just one year; he got 18. Though legal authorities figure justice's rule-of-thumb ratio at one judge to every 50,000 inhabitants, only Florida, among the fifty states in the Union, requires that ratio to be maintained. And exceedingly few communities manage it without such strictures.

The pile-up in civil and traffic courtrooms produces assembly-line justice with few opportunities on the part of the courts for appropriate remedial action. "In the five years between 1955 and 1960 alone," notes Mr. Economos, "the number of traffic summonses issued in the United States rose 50 percent, from approximately 20 million to approximately 30 million a year. Five million of the 1960 summonses for moving violations ended up in court, but five million more, also for moving violations, were processed by violation bureaus, when they should have gone to court."

Safety authorities have long contended that the engineering of better safety into motor vehicles probably is not capable of reducing highway accidents by more than 5 percent to 10 percent. They have given the same percentage to highway improvements. The "human factor" is thus held responsible in one way or another for 80 to 90 percent of highway fatalities. And one of the greatest opportunities for coping with that factor, safety authorities agree, may be in the courtroom itself, where physical, mental, and other defects afford unusual opportunities for detection, and ailing drivers can be handled accordingly. They may be barred by the court from getting behind the wheel; they can be assigned to special traffic schools for the teaching of rules and skills; and those who simply will not obey the law can be punished to the point of having their licenses revoked.

Highway utilization, as well as highway safety, suffers from courtroom congestion. "When the courtroom is full, the tendency is to avoid handing out summonses to slow drivers or hoggers of outer lanes," says one legal authority, "but enforcement activities should be directed against these people as well as the speedsters for failing to use the highways for the speeds intended."

Congestion in the civil courts and assembly-line justice may be having a detrimental effect on attitudes toward justice in general, especially among youth. Los Angeles Superior Court Judge Ralph H. Nutter argues that if traffic courts cannot give individual attention to each defendant, the requirement of a court appearance "might just as well be abolished. Defendants," says he, "should not get the impression that the purpose of the appearance in traffic court is to shepherd them in lines to the cashier's window."

William J. Gottlieb, President of the Automobile Club of New York, charged in 1962 that that city's traffic courts were being operated "as a profitable business" rather than as a means of "dispensing justice and educating the offender." He figured New York's traffic courts produced an $8 million profit in 1961, after deducting $5 million worth of expenses from $13 million in collected fines.

Many persons, of course, plead guilty rather than lose the time that may be involved in a second court appearance. The cynicism toward justice often nourished by such defeatism is only too frequently carried over into nonauto-motive cases as well. Businessmen and others who face severe financial hardship through interminable court delay, however, cannot help but seek to settle their cases out of court. Justice, often, is the bigger loser.

Warns Chief Justice Earl Warren: "Interminable and unjustified delays in our courts are compromising the basic legal rights of countless thousands of Americans and, im-perceptibly, corroding the very foundation of constitutional government."

"If we're going to restore respect for the law," adds Mr. Economos, "we had best start in the traffic courts because this is where more people see the courts in action than do so in all other courts combined. For a great many people, the traffic court is an introduction to the law and to justice."

What might be done to speed the wheels of justice and restore the waning faith? A larger corps of judges, obvi-ously, is needed in many communities – but numbers alone are not the answer. Further encouragement can be lent to formal arbitration in personal-injury, commercial, and other civil cases. The submission of disputes to one or more indi-viduals for hearing and decision, binding on both parties by prior agreement, has already proved highly useful in such cases. Two organizations of insurance firms, the Asso-ciation of Casualty Surety companies and the National Asso-ciation of Mutual Casualty companies, arranged in 1960 for the arbitration of over 19,000 auto-insurance claims compared with only 247 in 1955 when the procedure was in a more rudimentary stage.

Much can still be done in the courts themselves. Wider tenure in posts of authority and the delegation of adminis-trative duties to civil servants are among reforms most generally urged. Others call for removing judgeships from political appointment or election, with nominations coming instead from professional groups, such as the local bar association.

A more unified court system to permit the shifting of cases from badly overloaded dockets to lighter ones wins wide support in the profession and just about as much opposition from local politicians who don't like losing control of any function capable of discretionary use. As one candid critic puts it: "They squawk about home rule, but what many of them are really objecting to is losing the right to pin up to 90 percent of their traffic violations on out-of-towners – or forgiving a local wheel his indiscretions."

Another target for would-be court reformers: the abuse by lawyers of the contingency-fee system. Barristers have been accused of clogging the legal calendar with suits that never should have been brought in the first place on the off chance they may win a settlement and collect a third or more of the final award themselves. Of $220 million worth of accident-case awards made to 160,000 persons in New York City in one recent year, more than $75 million, it is estimated, went to lawyers. The American Judicature Society figures contingency fees paid lawyers may be running as high as $700 million or more per annum. Efforts to limit such fees to 20 or even 33⅓ percent have been roundly defeated by bar associations in practically every state of the Union, though some courts have taken it upon themselves to limit the lawyer's take.

Commenting on lawyer abuses of the contingency-fee system, Louis Banks, writing in the December, 1961, issue of *Fortune,* states: "Such high stakes, contingent on plenty of litigation and confusion, inspire special-interest legal groups to a performance that would raise the curls on a British barrister's wig." He notes further: "Some lawyers' lobbies use their considerable influence with state legislatures and city councils to kill changes in the law that might cut into the volume of legal business." Mr. Banks cites the case of New York City's chronic submission to approximately $4 million a year in personal-injury suits allegedly due to defective sidewalks. A simple change in the law that would have brought the city's liability in line with that of most other municipalities and saved it millions of dollars, says he, "was defeated by a lobby of plaintiffs' lawyers."

But the guilt doesn't belong entirely on one side. Defense counsels themselves occasionally delay settling even the most obviously meritorious suits until they are faced with the necessity of a court appearance.

Whatever the shortcomings of the municipalities' judicial machinery and the profession that uses it, one prospect is certain: the shortcomings of municipal justice will be magnified many times over as the automotive population increases in the years to come. Communities lamenting the rise in local lawlessness can hardly swing the spotlight on their own judicial shortcomings too soon.

CHAPTER THREE

Beware of the Air

FOR four years, from 1952 to 1956, while he was Associate Professor of Pathology at the School of Medicine at the University of Southern California, Dr. Paul Kotin conducted an interesting series of experiments involving several hundred mice and some painstakingly collected particles of Los Angeles smog. His findings hold some frightening implications for urban humans.

Large blowers located next to Los Angeles County Hospital and on a portable rig parked near the city's four-level downtown freeway interchange drew in foul air. Tiny particles and gases in the air were caught in filter paper. Solutions were then made from the particles and painted on the skins of some 100 mice as often as 3 times a week over a period of 14 months.

By the end of that time, 75 percent of the mice had developed skin cancers.

Dr. Kotin admits his experiments do not prove smog causes cancer in humans. The cancers produced on the mice, he concedes, may have been due to an unusual concentration of regularly applied pollutants not necessarily dangerous to humans in the highly diluted, airy forms in which they make highly irregular appearances.

"Nevertheless," Dr. Kotin states, "the experiments do prove there are chemical carcinogens (agents capable of producing cancer) in Los Angeles smog. Solutions made from washed and filtered air produced no cancers on test mice painted just as frequently over the same period of time. Furthermore, we know that what is capable of producing cancer in one mammal is generally capable of producing it in another.

"We know also," he said, "that the state in which these agents exist makes them capable of being breathed by humans and deposited on the lining of the lung where they can survive long enough to do damage."

Dr. Kotin and his colleagues at the University of Southern California are pushing their cancer studies further under long-term grants from the United States Public Health Service. In 1962 they placed some 3,000 rats, mice, hamsters, guinea pigs, and rabbits at four different sites in Los Angeles County, one of them in a broad open area between the inbound and outbound lanes of the heavily traveled Hollywood Freeway. Another 3,000 animals were kept in rooms supplied by filtered air. Their detailed studies were expected to shed further light on the relationship of air pollution to cancer.

In South Africa, Japan, and other lands being showered with an influx of automobiles and a surge of industry, concern over air pollution is likewise growing. In 1960 Dr. Geoffrey Dean, of the Union of South Africa's Eastern Cape Provincial Hospital, told a medical conference, "There seems to be very strong evidence that lung cancer results from environmental factors and that it has not been primarily genetically determined, that it results, in fact, from the air we breathe."

In Japan, where mortality rates from lung cancer quadrupled in the years from 1948 to 1960, belief is rising that some of the contributory causes, at least, may be found in polluted air, particularly from the rapid growth in vehicular traffic.

One of the most emphatic statements of all comes from former Surgeon General, Dr. LeRoy E. Burney. "There is a very definite association between community air pollution," says he, "and high mortality rates due to cancer of the respiratory tract, cancer of the stomach, esophagus and arteriosclerotic heart disease."

Consider some of the evidence.

Not long ago, Dr. David F. Eastcott, of New Zealand, found that lung cancer among Britons who emigrated to the down-under isles after they were thirty years old was 75 percent more common than among natives who had lived in New Zealand all their lives, though New Zealanders are known to be among the heaviest smokers in the world. New Zealand's air is nowhere near as badly polluted as Britain's, though it is getting fouler and fouler as additional autos and factories dot its scenic landscape. The theory, of course, is that polluted air breathed in Britain may have started a physiological sequence in the émigrés which the native-born, inhaling cleaner air, escaped.

Studies of cancer victims in England and Wales revealed a doubling of mortality from lung cancer in a ten-year period from 1944, but no increase at all in larynx cancer deaths. The lung, of course, is more exposed to air pollutants than the larynx.

South Africa's Dr. Dean notes that Durban, which suffers from a serious air-pollution problem not entirely dissimilar from that of Los Angeles, has twice as many cancer victims as Johannesburg or Capetown, cities with much less air pollution.

Medical authorities in recent years have also observed a notable increase in lung cancer among animals in zoos.

More than a score of studies in Britain and elsewhere have established the role of air pollution in chronic bronchitis. The ailment has taken more lives in Britain in some recent years than lung cancer and tuberculosis combined, and is one of the leading causes of death in that country.

In the decade when California's automotive population grew the fastest – from 1950 to 1960 – mortality rate from emphysema, a chronic lung disease that many physicians contend is aggravated by foul air, quadrupled. The most notable increases, twice as many, in fact, were experienced by urban as compared with rural regions.

Dr. W. C. Hueper, chief of the Environmental Cancer Section of the National Institutes of Health in Bethseda, Maryland, describes modern man as "living in a sea of carcinogens." The cancer-causing agents, says he, include such ingredients of combustion exhaust as benzpyrene, arsenic, benzol, tar, asphalt, carbon black, creosote oil, paraffin oil, and a variety of metal particles.

According to some authorities, air pollution is already so bad in some cities, notably Birmingham, Alabama, that the mere process of breathing may cause the intake of as great a quantity of cancer-causing substances as the smoking of two packs a cigarettes a day. Medical authorities have measured the intake by inhalation of as much as 200 milligrams yearly of benzpyrene, which results from the incomplete combustion of fossil fuels, such as coal and oil. They figure this is a third more benzpyrene than one would take into his system if he smoked forty cigarettes a day throughout the year.

Hearing the observation stated at an international conference on air pollution, the National Broadcasting Company commentator Martin Agronsky was moved to comment: "I am really very grateful," said he, "that I am able to bring word from this meeting to my family, my friends, and my neighbors, the very happy news that they have been worrying about their smoking producing lung cancer but they can now stop worrying, just relax, and keep breathing, and get lung cancer without any effort at all."

A good many air-pollution experts believe some urban areas may be setting themselves up for air-pollution disasters in the not too distant future. At least three such disasters have occurred in modern times. In 1930, a heavy pall of industrial pollutants blanketed the Meuse Valley in Belgium for several days, leaving 63 dead in its wake. In 1948, aerial wastes snuffed out the lives of at least 18 persons in Donora, Pennsylvania, and brought illness to thousands of others, whose life spans were believed to have been shortened as a result.

In 1952, a fog steeped in smoke and soot that could actually be tasted squatted for a full week on London, England. Before it lifted, 4,000 deaths were attributed to its content. The mortality rate on certain days was higher than in any peacetime 24 hours in a century with two exceptions: during the influenza epidemic of 1918-1919 and during the cholera epidemic of 1854. The smoke content of London's air during the incident was as much as 9 times the normal amount.

The London week brought 10 times as many deaths from bronchitis, 7 times as many from influenza, nearly 5 times as many from pulmonary tuberculosis, and nearly 3 times as many from heart and circulatory failures as in a normal winter week. Some 90 percent of the victims were over 45 years of age, and a good many of the other 10 percent under 5 – two groups especially susceptible to respiratory problems.

Emanuel Landau, chief of the Biometry Section of the Public Health Service's Division of Air Pollution, suggested to an audience in San Francisco late in 1960 that air pollution may be responsible for slowing down the advance against infant-mortality rates in many parts of the United States in recent years.

In 1958, the Commissioner of Health for Philadelphia, Dr. James P. Dixon, stated that unless man's "somewhat submerged" instincts for self-preservation were aroused on behalf of saving the air necessary for life, "gas masks may be as common in a hundred years as shoes are today."

Sound farfetched? Perhaps, but postmen in Manchester, England, have already run tests on a transparent plastic face mask containing ammonia crystals to combat contaminated air. In London, St. Bartholomew's Hospital issued ammonia masks to volunteer members of its medical staff not long ago to gauge the effectiveness of the masks in reducing the incidence of respiratory and other diseases.

Surgeons in Los Angeles have been known to postpone operations during smoggy periods after observing that patients did not do so well during these periods as they did when the air was cleaner. One physician in that city's Samaritan Hospital makes it a standing practice to shift patients with known lung diseases to special "clean air" rooms during periods of high air pollution. Some medical authorities believe it won't be long before physicians prescribe protective masks for aged persons suffering from respiratory ailments in periods when air pollution is particularly bad.

In Osaka, Japan, a public vending machine dispenses 20-second whiffs of clean oxygen for the yen equivalent of just under three cents.

Air-conditioner manufacturers for some time now have been selling their appliances on their air-purifying as well as their cooling virtues, and several manufacturers have even placed air purifiers on the market. A portable model air purifier made by the General Electric Company, for instance, was advertised in Los Angeles department stores early in 1962 for $59.95. The units were said to be capable of delivering 44 cubic feet of "clean air every minute." Some pollution authorities, however, are skeptical of their value as purifiers of the air.

A survey of physicians by two professional medical groups in Los Angeles in 1961 indicated 77 percent believed smog to be detrimental to health. Nearly one-third of the 350 physicians responding said they themselves had considered moving because of the dangers of smog. They further stated they had advised some 10,000 of their patients to move from the area, though only about one-fourth had heeded the advice.

Los Angeles' smog chief, S. Smith Griswold, believes air pollution can be lessened substantially by 1970 in the

Southern California metropolis by the use of emission control devices on automobiles. But he warns that the volume of aerial wastes will probably rise again after 1970 as the increase in the automotive population combines with increased industrial activity to more than offset the reduction in smog output from each individual vehicle.

Some progress, in fact, has already been made against air pollution by automobile manufacturers without any notable relief for the average citizen. Automobiles of 1959 and 1960 vintages have been found to produce 600 parts of hydrocarbons per million parts of air, or less than half as much as 1953 and 1954 cars, according to Mr. Griswold. But, he notes, pollution levels are believed to be as high or higher than they have ever been because there are far more cars on the road – and a greater number of industrial plants.

Air, not water, insists Mr. Griswold, is the most critical factor limiting Southern California's growth. "Water apparently will be available in adequate supply and quality," he has declared, "but the supply of air is fixed, and we can do nothing to increase it."

There's no question about this. No measure that may conceivably be taken now or in the immediate future is likely to prevent the atmosphere of this planet from becoming even more unhealthy for humans in the future. United States industrial output in the decade to 1970 alone is expected almost to double. The nation's human population in the same period is expected to increase at least 25 percent; the number of automobiles in use is expected to rise twice as fast.

Because population and industry are concentrated in metropolitan areas and because these areas still cover only a small portion of the nation's total surface area – including mountains and waterways – the concentration of air pollution is considerable. About half of it is believed to be issuing from a land area no greater than 1.5 percent of the total surface of the continental United States. A special issue of the magazine *Power*, which noted this fact, went on to warn rural dwellers against complacency: "While it is true that cities will always be subjected to greater air pollution potential than suburban areas, suburban potential will increase as time goes by."

A top official of the Public Health Service told a meeting of the American Academy of Occupational Medicine in February, 1960, that "unless our knowledge of how to deal with air pollution increases even faster than the present-day forces which are constantly multiplying its sources and intensity, we are going to bequeath to our children a sorry legacy indeed: an ocean of air unfit to breathe."

Humans have been fighting polluted air for centuries, and chances are they will still be fighting it centuries from now, if contamination of one sort or another hasn't cleansed them from the globe by then. King Edward I, son of Henry III, passed the first Smoke Abatement Law back in 1273, shortly after Britons began burning bituminous coal. The problem grew so bad by 1306 that the Parliament formed a special committee to rid the nation of the nuisance. A proclamation forbidding the use of coal in furnaces was issued shortly thereafter, and within the year a violator was executed for failing to heed its dictates. But the prohibition against burning bituminous coal didn't stick.

Five centuries later, air pollution was an even bigger headache in Britain. In 1881, another commission, this time with broader representation from the community, was set up to find a solution to the problem. That same year, on the other side of the Atlantic, the city of Chicago adopted the first ordinance giving a municipality authority to control smoke emission by industry and others. In 1894, commissions to study the problems of air pollution were created in France and Germany as well.

In 1905, Dr. Harold Antoine Des Voeux, a noted British physician who coined the word "smog" to designate the combination of smoke and fog that was becoming increasingly common in Britain's industrial centers, called for an alliance of householders, factory owners, and government officials to study the causes of air pollution and develop means for its control. He got nowhere and, in fact, was regarded as something of a crank for his dire warnings on the subject.

Today, from Milan to Mexico City and from Paris to Pretoria, civic bodies are becoming increasingly concerned over what their residents are breathing. And well they might: the normal adult inhales some 15,000 quarts of air daily, about 10 times as much by weight as what he eats and drinks in the same period.

The focus on the control of air pollution is particularly sharp, of course, in the Los Angeles area, largely because of its climate and its vast automotive population. Vehicle registrations in Los Angeles County totaled more than 3 million in 1960 – nearly 5 times the figure for the entire state of Florida.

These traveling combustion chambers, like any other combustion devices, spew forth a certain amount of unburned gases – ingredients for the airy stew. Sunshine serves as the cooking element in the photochemical process. The container, for all intents and purposes, are weak winds which prevent the ingredients from being lost out the sides. And the lid is provided by a phenomenon known as "temperature inversion."

Temperature inversion is produced when a layer of warm air sits atop a layer of cooler air, thus inhibiting the normal processes of vertical ventilation from the rising of warm air.

Los Angeles gets a steady diet of inverted temperature conditions – about three-fourths of the year, in fact, from winds that blow eastward from a predominantly stationary high pressure area about 1,000 miles out to sea and a little to the north. The lower level of that moving air mass is cooled by the sea. Since the cooler air is already low, there is no vertical ventilation from normally rising warm air. Only if the cool air is high enough, 1,500 feet or more, is there enough vertical movement within the cooler surface layer itself to provide the necessary vertical ventilation.

INVERSION PUTS THE LID ON LOS ANGELES' AIRY BREW

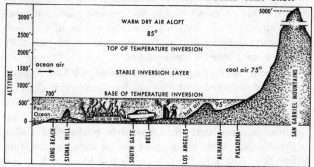

Temperature inversion is not peculiar to Los Angeles. It happens up and down the West Coast from San Francisco to San Diego and even farther south. In fact, practically all coastal areas, except in turbulent polar latitudes, experience it where high pressure areas customarily lie in the direction of their prevailing winds – to the west in northern latitudes and to the east in southern ones.

Thus, if the surface winds are weak, as they frequently are in Los Angeles, if the "lid" of temperature inversion is on (that is, 1,500 feet or lower), the sun isn't hidden behind the clouds, the ingredients are poured into the bowl, and the stew known as "smog" in Los Angeles and by other names elsewhere, isn't long in the serving.

The fact that Los Angeles is ringed in by mountains had long been considered as an aggravator of its smog, turning the basin into a bowl in still another sense, but it may actually help reduce smog: some meteorologists believe mountain slopes act as escalators, heating cool air and sending it gradually upward. Whatever the case may be, Los Angeles would probably have smog with or without its mountains.

Since inversions are common throughout the globe, weak winds not unknown, and sunlight reasonably frequent, only one ingredient is needed to produce the troublesome kind of pollution that plagues Los Angeles: enough unburned gases in the air, especially hydrocarbons and oxides of nitrogen. And these are being provided in more and more places by the growing horde of automobiles.

The poor ventilating characteristics of the Los Angeles basin were observed centuries ago by the Spanish explorer Juan Rodríguez Cabrillo, when, in October, 1542, he dropped anchor in what is now known as San Pedro Bay. Cabrillo recorded that while mountain peaks were visible in the distance, their bases could not be seen. Smoke from Indian fires rose into the calm air a few hundred feet and then spread across the valley, known to local Indians as the "Valley of Smokes." Los Angeles is presently getting between 30 and 50 days yearly of bad smog, most of it in the hotter months of July, August, September, and October.

Air pollution in Los Angeles, of course, is not the same beast that it is, say, in London. Nor is air pollution in New York the same stew brewed in the air over San Francisco. For one thing, pollutants themselves differ: automotive exhausts may dominate in one city and smoke from burning trash or coal fires in another. The air itself may differ: Los Angeles' air is generally dry, while London's is often wet. Climate, topography, and other factors also exert an influence. The principal targets of air-pollution campaigns thus may vary in different areas.

Too often in the past, problems of air pollution have been regarded as the peculiar product of an unlikely conspiracy of circumstances or the bad habits of a highly unique area. Yet, air pollution has proved time and time again that it may squat almost anywhere for uncomfortably long periods of time. Moreover, the air pollution for so long held peculiar to Los Angeles is proving that it can get around with an automobile as well as any motorist, perhaps better.

A recent study of meteorological and other records revealed that a nine-day siege of air pollution in New York in November, 1953, which is now believed to have taken at least 170 lives, was caused largely by the same phenomenon of "temperature inversion" so often considered peculiar to Los Angeles. In New York's case, the inversion was caused by a combination of weak winds, which might have provided horizontal circulation, and an unusual combination of high- and low-pressure belts.

If Los Angeles' air-pollution experience is a portent of things to come in the air of cities elsewhere, the strategy of combating the problem may similarly be of growing interest – as, indeed, it has been.

The county first took action against air pollution in 1948 by banning burning in open dumps. The city of Whittier nearly seceded from the county because it did not like the idea of incurring added expenses for the disposal of its rubbish by other methods, such as incineration. In all, there were some 54 open-burning rubbish dumps in the county, most of them municipally operated. They were considered a principal contributor of air pollutants at the time.

The banning of open burning, however, proved to be only a preliminary step in the city's arduous war against its ethereal foe. Nine years later, homeowners were prohibited from burning refuse in their backyard incinerators. The edict forced the scrapping of an estimated $48 million worth of the concrete-and-iron backyard furnaces. Detroit, Pittsburgh, Philadelphia, and other cities have since followed Los Angeles' action in banning open burning on dumps and in backyards.

Los Angeles' move against homeowners was followed up within two years by regulations prohibiting the use of smoky fuel oil in the summer months by commercial and industrial establishments and apartment houses. Fuel oil containing over 0.5 percent sulfur was thus banned from burning between the period from April 15th to November 15th throughout the basin. Since fuel oil generally contains more sulfur than that, the regulation, in effect, forced a switch to cleaner but costlier natural and artificial gas during these months along with the installation of equipment necessary to effect the changeover.

The Southern California Edison Company, for one, figured the rule tacked 6 percent, or $3 million, on to its annual fuel bill.

Petroleum refiners came next. In 1960 they were told they would be given a specific period of time – later extended to 1963 – to reduce from approximately 18 percent to about 12.5 percent the olefin content of their gasolines, so that autos burning their products would send fewer objectionable gases into the atmosphere. Automakers in the same year were warned by the state that as soon as a specially constituted board certified two or more devices as effective in reducing exhaust gas emissions, they would have to install one of those devices on all new vehicles sold thereafter.

A year later, buyers of used cars were to be compelled to do the same. By the end of the third year, all motorists were to be required to install an approved unit on their vehicles at a cost that was expected to exceed $50 per vehicle.

Approved devices were to eliminate at least 80 percent of the hydrocarbons and at least 60 percent of the carbon monoxide emitted into the air. Nothing was said about nitrogen oxide and other pollutants, which were believed to be less troublesome and anyway threatened to be more difficult to deal with.

Beware of the Air

Increased number of vehicles, experts agree, will eventually offset the effects of control devices. The devices have to become more and more efficient if they are to prevent the rising number of vehicles from increasing the total volume of pollutants. Ultimately, the solution might lie only in the development of new engines whose waste gases, if any, at least will be less dangerous to the species that must live among them.

It doesn't take much in the way of foreign particles and gases to pollute air. There are about 30,000 tons of air over a square mile at the height of a single-story building. As little as 0.03 tons of pollution in that area – or just one part per million – is enough to make the air unpleasant to breathe. It is not uncommon for a ton of coal to be burned per minute over one square mile of urban dwellings or industry in areas using that fuel in homes or factories. On the average, that volume of coal will produce 0.05 tons of sulfur dioxide and other gases and particles, not counting carbon dioxide.

In automobiles, the waste product emitted in greatest volume is carbon monoxide: autos spew 5 to 6 times the volume of carbon monoxide as they do hydrocarbons and oxides of nitrogen, the chemical compounds that make the most trouble in the air. While carbon monoxide is not particularly troublesome at the moment, experts fear its sheer volume may one day create pollution problems.

Automobiles are the principal producers of air pollution in many cities. Los Angeles' Air Pollution Control District figures the 1,630-square mile Los Angeles basin, which includes more than half of Orange County as well as all of Los Angeles County, received 80 percent of its air pollution from that source in 1961. Its seventy smog-patrol cars wrote some 2,500 notices and citations for excessive exhaust smoke from automobiles in that year; fines for such violations range up to $50.

Los Angeles air-pollution authorities maintain they have

reduced – temporarily, at least – both the severity of their smog and the number of days in which smog is bad, but they admit they have not succeeded in arresting its geographical spread nor in keeping down the number of days of moderate smog. The vast San Fernando Valley, a rich agricultural smog-free area until recent years, for instance, is now almost as severely plagued with the malady as Los Angeles itself.

Los Angeles' "smog alerts," sounded when the dreaded ozone content exceeds 50 parts per 100,000,000 parts of air to exhort the public against unnecessary travel or combustion, declined from as many as 15 days a year prior to 1956 to no more than 7 days in any 12-month period thereafter to the time of this writing. Nevertheless, the Los Angeles County Air Pollution Control District reported 96 days "with some degree of smog" in 1960, for example, compared with an average of 88 such days a year over the 7 years through 1960; 31 of the 1960 days were classified as days of heavy eye irritation. Quantities of nitrogen oxide, in the meantime, were observed to be reaching new peaks, rising to a record 3.93 parts per million on January 3, 1961, compared with the previous maximum of 2.00 ppm on January 5, 1960.

Air pollution is growing more widespread on a global scale as well. In Durban, South Africa, the City Council not long ago asked the Standard-Vacuum Refining Company temporarily to close its multimillion dollar refinery after local residents complained of loss of sleep, nausea, and vomiting from fumes that were said to be issuing from the plant; the company averted the shutdown only by installing a battery of costly control devices. In Japan, the city of Kobe, which has come to be known as the "smoky city," is the scene of increasing clamor for action to clean the air. A thickening mixture of chronic fog and industrial smoke has become a matter of concern among residents of the peaceful Po Valley in Italy. And even Paris in the springtime is not as pleasant as it used to be: the French Association for the Prevention of Atmospheric Pollution reports chimneypot emissions, combined with a growing volume of automobile traffic, are blotting out upper portions of such famous landmarks as the Eiffel Tower and the Montmartre Cathedral.

The Communists are wrestling with the problem, too. A visitor to the Hungarian capital of Budapest reports smog is increasingly obscuring the hills of Buda from the plains of Pest.

Indeed, even the idyllic archipelagoes of the warm Pacific may not be spared the airy blight. Air samples analyzed in Hawaii reveal the presence of increasing quantities of contaminants which may have had their origins many miles distant, perhaps in the continental United States.

In the United States an increasing number of communities that did not believe themselves susceptible to problems of air pollution have been given cause to change their mind. In 1956 only 194 communities in the United States were collecting pollution data; two years later twice as many did so. Now more than two dozen states and over a hundred municipalities have laws for punishing air contaminators.

The city of Dayton, Ohio, in one recent year issued as many as 437 violation notices while collecting some 3,000 complaints against alleged air-pollution culprits. Phoenix, Arizona, in recent years has developed the same type of eye-irritating smog that previously caused its citizens to pity Angelenos. In Tucson, city authorities recently prohibited auto wreckers from burning their old cars in open lots lest the act contribute further to a fouling of the air in that once desert-clean city; the vehicles piled up for many weeks before the wreckers were convinced the city meant business and turned to other, more costly, methods of skeletonizing the vehicles.

The Minnesota Department of Health in 1961 reported 38 of its counties had "air contamination in sufficient concentration to cause discomfort or inconvenience." Sacramento, which once had one of the clearest atmospheres in the entire state of California, reported that in the fall of 1958 air pollution crossed the threshold of human discomfort 20 times.

In Denver, where the mixture of smoke and haze is known as "smaze," the municipality recently banned incinerator burning during certain hours of the day. In New York City, under a measure signed into law in November, 1961, the open burning of all materials was to be banned outright beginning January 1, 1964.

Though California was getting most of the publicity in its search for pollution-arresters for automobiles, some 18 other states were studying automotive smog-control legislation of their own in 1962. In Pittsburgh a citizens' committee early in 1960 suggested an ordinance be adopted to compel motorists whose cars were idle for any prolonged period of time to shut their engines off. Senator Abraham Ribicoff in mid-1961, while he was Secretary of Health, Education, and Welfare, warned United States automakers that if they didn't equip their cars with certain control apparatus – known as blow-by devices – by 1964, he would seek federal legislation forcing them to do so. They chose to provide the devices.

Ivan A. Nestingen, Under Secretary of Health, Education, and Welfare, told a gathering of engineers in the nation's capital in 1961 that some 90 percent of the American population "live in localities which have air pollution problems." He further stated: "It is estimated that all 232 communities with populations over 50,000 have air pollution problems and about 40 percent of the communities of 2,500 to 50,000 population." In all, he stated, some 6,500 United States communities had air-pollution problems of varying degrees for which action programs "should be initiated or strengthened as soon as practicable."

Only 106 of the 6,500 communities with air-pollution

problems in the United States at the end of 1961 had full-time staffs devoted to gauging and attempting to control the menace, according to Dr. Richard A. Prindle, Deputy Chief of the Public Health Service's Air Pollution Division. And only 28 of these staffs, said he, had as many as 5 full-time employees. Though estimates have placed the cost of air pollution in absenteeism, cleaning bills, and other losses as high as $65 a year for every man, woman, and child in America, the average expenditure on its control, said Dr. Prindle, amounted to only 10 cents a head in 1961 – and half of this sum was spent in California.

Political boundaries make the control of air pollution especially difficult. St. Louis, which claims to have largely solved its once notorious smoke problem, complains it is helpless when the wind blows in from East St. Louis, in Illinois, where its ordinances do not apply. More than a score of communities are involved in air-pollution problems in the San Francisco Bay area. Los Angeles, which has more than 70 independent cities, long since decided to leave its air-pollution control tasks to the county, so it is relatively free of jurisdictional hassles, at least on this subject.

The expense of keeping gaseous garbage from turning the air above into one huge atmospheric cesspool has been brought home to the general public in a variety of ways. Air pollution hikes laundry bills, damages and discolors fabric, necessitates repainting and repairs to damaged surfaces, and causes other personal expenses as well, to say nothing of higher taxes from municipal pollution-combating efforts. And the sum is rising sharply. The United States Public Health Service placed the national total as high as $7.5 billion in 1960 – at least twice and perhaps as much as four times the 1950 figure. California's 6 million motorists face the prospect of spending $35 million to $70 million to equip their autos with pollution-control devices in the years ahead; and other states, such as New York and

Illinois, indicate they won't be far behind in requiring their motorists to take similar precautions.

Industry has been spending considerable sums for many years in the war against pollution. According to the trade magazine *Steel,* about 10 percent of the capital investment of the foundry industry goes for equipment and processes to keep waste materials out of the air. Chemical companies, petroleum producers, electric-power utilities, and others also spend vast sums of money to combat air pollution.

So stringent have Los Angeles County's rules against refinery-caused air pollution become, that Air Pollution Control District Chief S. Smith Griswold was moved in 1956 to predict, "They'll never build another oil refinery here." "They" still hadn't done so by 1962, despite the area's rapid growth.

When the aerial refuse from a new 150-foot-high stack on one side of San Francisco Bay wafted across wheatfields on the other side, complaints forced a raising of the stack to 600 feet; it cost $500,000 to add the extra 450 feet that finally abated the nuisance. A Chicago Sanitation Department official notes he has had to more than double the height of incinerator chimneys since the 1930's because of the growing menace of air pollution, raising them to 255-foot heights by 1962 compared with just 120 feet in the 1930's.

A number of suits have been brought against alleged contaminators of the public's airy domain. In Santa Cruz, California, residents sued a cement company for $1 million in damages to their property which they said resulted from excessive quantities of dust kicked up by the cement company in its operations. At Clarkston, Washington, a pulp and paper mill was sued by a private individual for $2,000 worth of damages to his property, $750 of it for alleged paint discoloration caused by air contaminants. A Joint United States-Canadian Commission in 1930 awarded $350,000 in damages to farmers in Washington's Columbia

River Valley for damage done their trees and crops by a copper smelter in British Columbia about 40 to 60 miles from their fields.

The American Municipal Association, representing some 13,000 of the biggest municipalities in the United States, figures air pollution causes over $200 million worth of depreciation to property values yearly as people and industry choose to move elsewhere.

Dr. Arnold Beckman, an adviser on air-pollution problems in Los Angeles and president of Beckman Instruments, Inc., says the smog was a "contributing cause" to his company's decision to move from South Pasadena to outlying Fullerton in 1954. The Pasadena area, scene of the famous New Year's Rose Parade, is one of the more pollution-plagued regions of Los Angeles County.

What about the costs that cannot be counted in dollars and cents or even in human life? The costs of physical and psychological discomfort from eye irritation, raspy throats, reduced visibility, lost sunlight, and the general pall of gloom that goes with a smudgy aerial environment? Vernon G. MacKenzie, Chief of the Public Health Service's Air Pollution Division, contends: "There is probably no single phenomenon which affects man in more different ways than air pollution."

A civic leader in Pittsburgh, which, like St. Louis, has done much since World War II to solve its smoke problems by regulation and urban renewal, bemoans the loss of valuable residents who chose to move elsewhere rather than cope with the city's air and other problems. Dr. Edward R. Weidlein, retired president and board chairman of the Mellon Institute, referring to the period before Pittsburgh made great strides against its smoke nuisance, notes: "We just couldn't get talented young people to take jobs in the city. One look at our grimy building and sooty air and they and their wives simply decided Pittsburgh wasn't for them."

A few cities such as Cincinnati and Toronto keep a

"soiling index" to warn housewives of the risks they're taking by hanging up their wash at any given time. At 9:38 A.M. on April 17, 1958, for example, the index stood at 7.8 in Toronto – meaning the atmosphere was nearly 8 times as dirty as on a clear, breezy day.

Air pollution exacts a toll against vegetation as well as against humans and their properties. Skeptics of air pollution's destructive power need only travel to the corner of southeastern Tennessee to bear witness to its ravages. There, near Ducktown in Polk County, they will find a circular area almost ten miles in diameter devoid of vegetation – the result of an event that took place over one hundred years ago! A smelting plant, using the heat-roasting method for purification of its ore, blanketed the countryside with enough sulfur over the years to kill off all trees and plants in the region. During the Depression years of the early 1930's, a detachment from the Civilian Conservation Corps was sent into the area in an effort to get vegetation growing again and stop the rains from further eroding the naked earth. Except for a limited amount of success along the fringes of the area, the attempt was a dismal failure. The plant, with modern smoke-abating devices, continues to operate. Workers who live in its environs must use imported soils to grow lawns and flowers there to this day.

Wheat, oats, rye, spinach, sugar beet, endive, avocado, romaine, and a variety of fruits, including peaches, apricots, oranges, and lemons, and many flowers, particularly gladioli and orchids, have all proved susceptible to damage from air pollution. At Bartow, Florida, a citrus grower some years ago sued the operator of a nearby phosphate plant for $20,000 worth of damages to his crop; phosphate was all right in the ground, where it feeds roots, he reasoned, but not on the skin of his citrus where it produces diseases. California in 1960 awarded farmers in 25 counties some $8 million for damage to crops due to smog –

including stunted growth, malnutrition, and the fomenting of diseases.

Some plants are so sensitive to the aerial environment, in fact, that they are being used in the war against smog. Kaiser Steel keeps two greenhouses near its plant in Fontana, California, one with filtered air and the other with air from the atmosphere itself, to warn mill managers to cut down on their chimney emissions; the plants, fortunately, react faster to the pollutants than the public does.

Different plants are susceptible to different pollutants. Ozone, for example, is spotted with special ease around spinach, oats, sugar beet, endive, and alfalfa. The degree of smog will also cause different reactions among plants: smog of low concentration, for example, tends simply to close the stomata, or openings, of plants, while higher concentrations may cause sap to ooze or leaves to become discolored as cells are killed off.

Factory smoke has been blackening tree trunks in the English countryside for so many years that more than 70 of England's 700 species of moth which depend for survival on their protective coloration have changed their natural colorings for darker hues – a pattern which is being carried through to their progeny. The magazine *Scientific American* in its issue of March, 1959, called the occurrence "the most striking evolutionary change ever witnessed by man."

Animals, along with plants and humans, are susceptible to bad air. A factory was held responsible in the state of Washington not long ago for causing the death of all but 100 of a herd of 2,000 cattle through air pollution.

Air pollution has been known to cause cutouts in electrical service. These occur particularly in humid weather when electrical "flashovers" result from the settlement of a film of pollutants on the surface of high-voltage insulators found on transmission wires.

Iron in smoky Sheffield was found to rust three times as

fast as iron in countrylike Farnborough, in Hants, England. Practically all metal objects corrode more rapidly in towns than in the rural areas.

Combined with rain, pollutants become soluble, working their damage on all kinds of building materials, even stone. A British authority in 1930 estimated that air pollution was then causing the equivalent of many millions of dollars' worth of damage to structures in that country yearly.

A Soviet air-pollution scientist at an international air-pollution conference in Los Angeles in 1961 reporting findings that air pollution is capable of shortening tempers and souring dispositions. He claimed experiments conducted in Moscow showed certain common air pollutants have a measurable effect on human brain-wave activity at subliminal levels – levels below which the pollutant can no longer be detected by human senses. The Soviet scientist Professor V. A. Ryazanov said Moscow was being placed on a 100 percent natural-gas-burning basis by 1965 largely because of the threats of air pollution from other fuels. Natural gas produces only 10 pounds of pollutants, compared with 70 pounds from fuel oil of the same heat content and a considerably greater amount from coal.

Over the course of time, a number of villains have occupied the position of Public Air Pollutant Number One. For centuries the enemy was bituminous coal. The air is being relieved of soft coal's sulfurous fumes today, but it is dirtier than ever with petroleum's airy wastes. And radioactivity even from peaceful pursuits may cause worse headaches in the future.

"When one dragon is disposed of there will inevitably be another," said the *Los Angeles Times* in a recent editorial. Air-pollution authorities from New York, Los Angeles, and Washington, D.C., recently issued a joint statement, apparently to keep citizen's hopes from rising too high: "The history of technology," they stated, "suggests very strongly that patterns of emission from all sources will change in the future. The precise direction in which these changes will occur cannot be predicted but that they will occur is certain."

A case in point, perhaps: oxides of nitrogen. When preliminary rules were laid down by California authorities for auto exhaust-control devices, this air-pollution ingredient was not mentioned because medical and other data were insufficient to identify it as a cause for deep concern. Since that time, however, its place has been established as a highly dangerous if elusive element in automotive smog.

Air-pollution problems may become more troublesome in the future even if the volume of contaminants doesn't increase. As human beings age, they are less able to withstand the onslaught of bad air. With the number of oldsters increasing rapidly, the problem of polluted air is bound to loom larger in the years ahead, compelling more and more individuals to seek homes where pollution is at a minimum.

Says St. Louis' Mayor Tucker: "The study and treatment of air pollution has become a permanent part of city government and will probably stay that way." The statement is particularly notable coming from Mayor Tucker – a man who achieved the reputation which sent him to City Hall by cleaning up that city's notorious smoke problem as chief of its Division of Smoke Regulation. The fact that that agency, however, is still in business under a different name illustrates the mayor's contention. As the Air Pollution Division largely concerned with St. Louis' new air-pollution problem, automotive exhausts, the agency had twenty people on its full-time staff in 1961.

CHAPTER FOUR

Water: Filthier and Farther

"EVERY time you take a glass of water from a faucet in St. Louis," says Richard Amberg, publisher of that city's morning *Globe-Democrat*, "you are drinking from every flush toilet from here to Minnesota."

The rival afternoon paper, the *Post-Dispatch*, commented not long ago on a Public Health Service report concerning pollution of the Mississippi in this manner: "The world's cleanest people, using only the purest oils and spices in exorcising grime witches, are drinking the garbage dump trickles of whatever town lies up the line. We bathe with scented fats and drink a factory's slime."

St. Louis is not unique among the nation's cities. A good many municipalities these days are drinking water that contains the inadequately treated discharge of communities upriver from them. And a good many more, from the looks of things, will be doing so in the future as water use increases along the nation's streams.

The prospect is not a pretty one. It was painted in vivid strokes some years back by Congressman Brent Spence, Kentucky Democrat: "I was born in sight of the Ohio River and I lived most of my life in a home that overlooked the river. I have seen it turn from a beautiful river in which I swam as a boy to a polluted sewer." The open sewer got so bad that eight states finally banded together in 1948 to form the Ohio River Valley Sanitation Commission to clean up the stream. By mid-1962, over 1,000 cities representing all but 13 percent of the area's population had poured over $1 million into sanitation facilities, and the job still was not complete. The multi-state body hired a helicopter to film the dumping of oily wastes into the river by factories along its banks for showing to the general public, in the hope of pressuring industry into cleaning up its liquid waste before discarding it.

The tide, apparently, is finally being turned against the forces of pollution on the Ohio, but it is rising on a good many other waterways. The father of our country is fortunate he's not crossing the Potomac today. A joint House and Senate committee on the capital's urban problems recently found the river so foul as to have become entirely uninhabitable to a wide variety of marine life that once thrived there.

Tulsa no longer draws water from the Arkansas River, it is so fouled with briny discharge. Chicago, which has spent over $400 million on sewage-treatment facilities to remove some 90 percent of the solids from its sewage, still disturbs communities as far as fifty miles downstream with its discard. And in Utah, contamination of the Great Salt Lake has become a matter of increasing concern to recreation-minded municipalities on that vast inland sea.

Authorities estimate well over 50 million pounds of solid wastes are pouring into the nation's waterways daily. Municipal sewer systems were already dumping twice as much waste into streams in 1961 as the maximum that was considered allowable as recently as 1955. A fourth of all the wastes cities are sending into streams is raw sewage. Another third is sewage that has had only the most cursory treatment. According to Dr. Abel Wolman, former chairman of the National Water Resources Board and more recently a top official of the National Research Council in Washington, D.C., practically every major waterway in the United States is now polluted in one degree or another.

President John F. Kennedy told Congress: "Pollution of our country's rivers and streams has – as a result of our rapid population and industrial growth and change – reached alarming proportions."

Water authorities figure that unless pollution is more effectively arrested at the source, the chemical methods that most cities use for treating water, when they treat it at all, will be incapable of producing palatable water by 1980 in many metropolitan areas.

The United States Senate Select Committee on National Water Resources has predicted the nation's daily discharge of used water will nearly double between 1954 and 1980 – from 17 billion to 29 billion gallons. By the year 2000, it forecasts, that volume will rise another 50 percent. The late Senator Robert S. Kerr, the Oklahoma Democrat who headed that committee, told the National Watershed Congress in Tucson in 1961: "Well before the end of the century most Americans will be drinking, cooking with, bathing in and otherwise using secondhand or thirdhand water."

The problem, for the most part, is not a lack of water. The United States as a nation has been well endowed in this respect. Besides its vast lakes, rivers, and groundwater resources, its average replenishment from precipitation is a deluging 4.3 billion gallons daily – an average of 30 inches a year across the nation's entire surface. Nearly three-quarters of this precipitation, mostly rain and snow, is lost through evaporation, runoff to the sea, and seepage. Only about half of the approximately 1.2 billion gallons that remain is considered economically recoverable. Still, this quantity of new fresh water was double the nation's 1960 usage. Furthermore, only a small portion of the water that's used disappears from circulation altogether. Only about 10 percent of it, in fact, is lost through evaporation, manufacturing, and other processes. Most of the rest is used and then discarded.

Hence, even though the nation's water usage is expected to double between 1960 and 1980 to approximately 600 billion gallons a day – about equal to the volume considered economically recoverable from precipitation – there is little concern, except in the more arid regions of the country, over actual water shortages. The worry, rather, is over a shortage of clean water. More and more water that's needed for home, factory, and other uses will have to come from sources that have already served one, and in some cases, several purposes.

In reusing the fresh water available to them, municipalities face a dual problem: not only is the volume of pollutants rising but the pollutants themselves are growing increasingly complex and troublesome. Until relatively recently, man's watery wastes posed no special problems to the processes of nature: they were largely organic and therefore easily decomposed by bacteria. Technological progress, however, is releasing a swelling variety of substances extremely impervious to nature's ways. And more are being developed all the time. It is estimated that well over four hundred new chemical substances are created yearly in the nation's research laboratories. Many of them participate in industrial processes and end up in the discard.

Furthermore, a vast increase in factory waste is in prospect. Industrial activity is expected to treble between 1950 and 1980, and the use of water for manufacturing purposes to rise even faster – perhaps to six times the 1950 level. The headaches of tomorrow are thus likely to be many times greater than those of today. And not all of these have been particularly easy to handle.

Consider one liquid miracle wrought in the recent past: the household detergent. It came into common use shortly after the end of World War II and now does about three times the wash volume in this country that natural soaps do. Detergents are customarily made from petroleum derivates, which means they are practically impervious to breakdown by bacteria. They have been known to retain their chemical identity even in water that has been treated several times. And, to the great dismay of treatment-plant operators, their sudsing ability is similarly unimpaired. Whether their sudsing ability helps them wash better is highly questionable, but market surveys consistently show housewives think they do, so manufacturers make them sudsy.

The indestructible suds whip up all kinds of trouble at the sewage plant. Porter W. Homer, City Manager of Tucson, Arizona, recalls seeing "suds froth as high as 10 to 15 feet in our primary treatment beds. When the wind came along," says he, "it would take a big foamy gob full of partially treated sewage and spread it over the neighborhood, on lawns and backyards and even on some of the clean laundry hanging on the line that perhaps helped produce it in the first place."

Sewage plant operators are attempting to keep the foam down with overhead sprinklers. The installation runs as high as $200,000 per plant, and even then the suds are not destroyed. They may bubble up all over again on the journey downstream, perhaps to other users of the water.

Some twelve thousand residents of the town of Chanute, Kansas, were somewhat taken aback not very long ago when they found water issuing from their taps foaming like beer. A severe drought had turned the town's usual water source, the Neosho River, to a trickle. To make up for the loss, the city decided to recirculate its sewage plant effluent through its treatment plant and dilute it with fresh water stored behind a dam. Five months of the circular expediency resulted in the accumulation of enough detergent to put a head on water flowing under pressure from city faucets.

Canadian physicist C. E. Hollborn recently reported detergents were turning Lake Winnipeg into a "giant bucket of suds." In the United States, a Senate report in 1959 stated that "most surface waters" and "many ground waters" were showing traces of detergents in them. Britain,

West Germany, and other countries where the use of washing machines has increased considerably in recent years, have also had to grapple with the problem. Bargemen on the Neckar River in Germany complain that banks of suds three feet high are menacing navigation.

In Britain, where greater population densities cause fresh water to be more carefully husbanded, a standing committee of the Minister of Housing and Local Government reports regularly to the public on what the chemical industry is doing to come up with less vexatious detergents. Several promising new "soft" varieties have been developed as a result and at least one city, Luton, has banned the sale of any other type of detergent to householders in its environs. In the United States, however, chemical companies say they are hard at work on the problem but have yet to come up with a cleanser with destructible suds that housewives will buy at prices that would make their manufacture worthwhile.

Several states, including Wisconsin, have considered outlawing the use of synthetic detergents altogether. The process is not likely to prove easy, especially on a national scale: some 40 million American housewives are estimated to be using detergents at the present time and they apparently are quite pleased with them. A building management firm in New York recently reported no success whatsoever in its offer to supply upper-story dwellers with a low-sudsing detergent free, so the suds would not back up in the tubs and sinks of tenants in lower apartments as they had been doing. High-sudsing detergents will enlarge themselves as much as 17,000 times in a 15-story fall.

The San Diego City Council recently appealed to housewives in that city to wash their clothes on Sundays or in the middle of the week instead of on the Fridays, Saturdays, and Mondays generally popular for the chore so the volume of suds would not grow so high. The city had just been warned against the nuisance by pollution control authorities.

The broader use of chemicals in agriculture, particularly insecticides and weed killers, also poses a threat to water supplies. Since the advent of DDT in 1944, more than a hundred synthetic insecticides in thousands of different formulations have appeared on the market. The effects of many of these substances have yet to be determined. Very few of the chemicals are removed by treatment plants.

Agricultural chemicals are used in tremendous volume. More than 30 million acres of United States cropland are presently being sprayed with some kind of chemical at least once yearly. In addition, forests, highway rights-of-way, and other large noncrop areas are also being chemically dusted against weeds, fire, and other hazards. The nation's production of synthetic organic pesticides alone is said to exceed 500 million pounds a year. Another million pounds of inorganic chemicals, arsenics included, are also produced annually. All told, American farmers are presently spending over $250 million a year on agricultural chemicals, exclusive of fertilizers.

Radioactive wastes threaten to vastly compound the water-pollution problem in the future. By the year 2000, atomic reactors are expected to be producing 750,000 megawatts of heat against 10,000 megawatts in 1964. Other nuclear industrial activities will likewise increase.

Mother earth is taking some of the radioactive discard at present. Such wastes occupied some 1,125,000 cubic feet of the Atomic Energy Commission's main burial ground at the end of 1960, compared with 316,000 cubic feet in 1955. Some of it is going to sea. Some 21,000 concrete-lined barrels containing radioactive wastes had been dumped in the Pacific and another 23,000 in the Atlantic by 1962. The United States in 1962 spent close to $6 million to prevent the nation's radioactive discard from contaminating water and other valuable resources, but the future task is likely to be costlier and more difficult still.

"The waste problem may prove the most difficult hurdle in the advancement toward broadscale peaceful use of atomic energy," a Select Senate Committee stated recently. Radioactive contamination from atomic subs and other nuclear naval craft is already stirring apprehension for the multimillion dollar shellfish industry at Hampton Roads, Virginia. Concern over the 38,000-acre shellfish resource has resulted in a rising clamor for limitations on use of the port by nuclear vessels.

More and more cities are monitoring their municipal water for radioactivity. The Department of Health, Education, and Welfare in 1958 found approximately 30,000 persons in southwestern Colorado and northwestern New Mexico using Animas River water that ranged 40 percent to 160 percent above maximum permissible levels of radioactive content.

Water men claim the removal of radioactive wastes, once identified, poses no insurmountable technical or economic problems. But they are not having the same good fortune cleaning certain other pollutants out of their fluids. A recent Public Health Service analysis showed water treated after a single use still contained more than twice as many foreign particles as is generally found in unused water. Some cities, however, are already reusing water as much as six to eight times.

Pollution of surface water is serious enough, but when contaminants find their way into groundwater supplies, which meet almost a fifth of the nation's needs, the problem may be infinitely worse. A Senate Committee on National Water Resources put it this way: "When streams become polluted, the situation can usually be remedied by treatment or by removing the source of pollution. In any case, the polluted waters move rapidly downstream and pass out of the picture in a relatively short time. Underground waters, on the other hand, are out of reach and move perhaps only a few feet a day. Years or decades may pass before pollution is detected, but once it has occurred, recovery may require an equal number of years." The affected water, the committee warns, "may never again regain its original quality."

Crowding too many septic tanks or cesspools in an area is one way to contaminate groundwater. And altogether too many suburban housing subdivisions have been doing exactly that. Where they should have provided sewage systems or forgone development until such systems were practical, some subdividers have packed up to eight times as many septic tanks in a given area as soil conditions were deemed to allow. Water contaminated by septic-tank seepage has been drawn from wells in such places as Peoria, Illinois; Dania, Florida; Lac de Flambeau, Wisconsin, and elsewhere.

Sewer lines, however, are costly to lay in communities where residents are widely scattered and connections to other systems are remote. Thus, they may not be constructed until the consequences come home to roost in danger or disaster. The Minnesota Health Department recently tested wells in a suburban subdivision with septic tanks just outside Minneapolis-St. Paul. Some 24 percent of the wells it tested produced water too contaminated for use in baby formulas. In the nearby town of Bloomington, 80 percent of the wells "showed traces of contamination from sewage."

On New York's Long Island, Suffolk County Executive H. Lee Dennison calls the threat of contamination to groundwater in that area "the most desperately urgent problem in the history of the county's development." Glasses of water from the area's wells have been known to overflow with suds before they were half full. Residents call their well water the "detergent cocktail," but they don't think it's very funny.

As late as 1955, approximately one-third of all new

homes being built in the United States had no sewage facilities other than septic tanks, according to the magazine *House & Home*. It calls this "too high" a share of the nation's new housing to be using septic tanks. If a septic tank "went wrong on a farm," the magazine states, "there was so much land it didn't make much difference." In crowded housing subdivisions, however, it warns, such an event can be disastrous. The Federal Housing Administration, in an effort to nudge negligent communities into constructing sewer systems, is beginning to refuse loan guarantees on new homes until such construction is authorized.

Pollution's stature as a wholesale killer of marine life, threat to human health, and robber of scarce recreational facilities is everywhere in evidence.

A United States Public Health Service survey for the year to June 1, 1960, turned up nearly 300 incidents of water pollution that killed a total of over 6,000,000 fish. In the Pacific Northwest, oysters taken from Lake Washington in 1957 were found to contain only one-tenth as much meat as they did before urban waste polluted the lake; the Washington Pollution Control Commission reported the meat yield from a bushel of oysters had declined to 0.1 gallon in that year compared with the 1.0 gallon or more harvested in the years before 1949.

Pollutants tend to downgrade marine life. Streams which jumped with trout and bass now sport only less-demanding carp if they have any marine life in them at all. Marshes of the Hackensack River in New Jersey which once hosted as many as 250,000 wild ducks are now almost barren of the webfooted creatures because of water pollution, according to a recent report by the New Jersey Audubon Society. Pollutants have also been known to cause quail to lay infertile eggs or produce chicks incapable of survival.

Pollution is sealing off vast recreational areas at a time when they have never been needed more. New York City has spent many millions of dollars creating long stretches of clean beaches, yet its waters are sometimes so badly polluted that much of its shoreline must be barred to swimmers. So much sewage has been pouring into Puget Sound and Lake Washington – an estimated 14,000 gallons per second, enough to create eight good-sized lakes yearly – that officials of nearby municipalities have taken to pouring vast quantities of chlorine into the lake near the shoreline to make it safe for swimming. Even idyllic Lake Tahoe, tucked away in the Sierra Nevada Mountains between California and Nevada, is suffering pollution of "serious proportions" because of a growing population of vacationers and residents, according to a recent report by a joint Nevada-California commission.

True, the consequences of water pollution were once vastly more tragic in terms of human life than they are today. Housewives in England up to a little over a century ago still emptied their chamber pots from their windows with little more concern for the folks below than a hardy "Gardy-loo!" The cholera epidemics in London and Paris in the early and middle 1800's have all been traced to watery wastes, and typhoid carried in polluted waters to this day remains a vicious killer of humans in many parts of Asia and other less-developed regions of the world.

While water pollution is not the menace to human life in most parts of the globe that it once was, thanks to advances in water-treatment technique, new threats to human health are beginning to appear. Scientists at the Robert A. Taft Engineering Center in Cincinnati, for example, recently reported an explosive outbreak of poliomyelitis in Edmonton, Canada, was "reasonably correlated" with sewage pollution in that area. Polluted water was a prime suspect in a spate of polio cases reported in Nebraska. Senator Kerr in his book *Land, Wood and Water* (Fleetwood, 1960) cited a report from Camden, New Jersey, which showed "an amazing statistical connection" between paralytic polio cases in the area and open sewers; all but one of the cases reported over a period of eight years came from areas with open sewers.

Polluted water of late has also brought an upsurge in another, less frequently fatal but highly debilitating disease known as infectious hepatitis. The federal government's Communicable Disease Center in Atlanta traced thirty-two cases of the disease in 1961 to oysters taken at the highly polluted mouth of the Pascagoula River in Mississippi. The state dispatched two patrol boats to stop all oyster gathering in the area until the pollution problem was cleared up.

Some forty cases of hepatitis in the northeastern United States in 1961 were traced to the eating of raw clams taken from highly polluted Raritan Bay between New York and New Jersey. Another seventeen cases were traced to clams collected off Greenwich Point, Connecticut. Cooking shellfish generally kills hepatitis germs, but steaming them may not be enough: two of the Connecticut victims were found to have eaten steamed oysters.

Hepatitis, which is caused by a virus, can also be brought on directly by drinking polluted water. Contaminated well water reportedly caused hepatitis recently among 52 schoolchildren in West Virginia. Chlorination doesn't always prevent the disease, either: polluted drinking water treated with chlorine was suspected of causing several cases of hepatitis in one eastern community in 1961.

Hepatitis, like water pollution, is riding a sharp upward curve. The United States Public Health Service estimated the total number of reported hepatitis cases in 1961 at a record 60,000 – 50 percent over the 1960 figure and three times the 1959 total. Unreported and undiagnosed cases are probably ten times the reported totals, medical authorities estimate. The Public Health Service has begun describing hepatitis as "a major infectious disease." It says the disease, which can cause confinement for three months or longer and recurs with the slightest strain or overindulgence in food and drink, is generally spread by contact but that the "most explosive epidemics" appear to be waterborne.

The damage bad water does to human health is not always immediately obvious. The Baker Water and Sanitation District just outside Denver recently investigated complaints of dirty water in its territory. As it did so, it turned up the fact that the area had twice as much intestinal illness as a nearby water district where there were no pollution complaints.

Considerably less than half of the nation's municipalities and only about a fifth of its factories are bothering to treat their sewage before dumping it into streams, according to authorities. Representative John Blatnik, Minnesota Democrat, reciting the record to the United States Conference of Mayors in 1960, declared that only 6,700 of the 11,600 municipal sewage systems then in operation, and only 2,600 of 10,400 known factory waste outlets, had any treatment facilities whatsoever for their outflow.

Many treatment plants now being operated have long since been considered obsolete. The Public Health Service in 1959 estimated about one-third of the municipal treatment plants then in operation were in desperate need of modernization. Sewer lines may be in similarly poor shape: a recent survey of New York City revealed that not one of its five boroughs met sewer maintenance and repair standards set by the Water Pollution Control Federation, a Washington-based organization of sanitation specialists and municipal officials.

Water pollution can become a legal hazard to the municipality that fails to do something about it. A resident in North Carolina not long ago won a $9,000 suit against his city when he produced traces of toilet paper from his well water. Foul odors and debris left on banks when river waters receded have moved property owners to haul more than one municipality into court in recent years. Dairy farmers have successfully sued cities for polluting streams by proving their cattle died after partaking from them.

Water: Filthier and Farther

Larger populations and increased industrialization, of course, reduce opportunities for getting rid of watery wastes. Coastal communities which used to send their sewage out to sea in outfalls along the shore or in elongated pipes along the ocean bottom are having this avenue closed to them by growing numbers of beachgoers along the shore.

Chicago, which has been using a tributary of Lake Michigan to flush its sewage down the Mississippi River by means of a connecting canal, is now in federal court fighting efforts to prevent it from using the lake for flushing its sewage down the great river. Opponents of the practice claim it deprives power plants as far away as Niagara Falls of needed water to turn turbines faster, forces ships to load more lightly on the lakes, and causes other economic loss. They want Chicago to return its treated discard to the lake.

The Public Health Service figures the need for additional sewage treatment plants around the country tops by more than 50 percent the 7,500 in operation in 1962. It estimates that over 4,000 new sewage treatment plants are needed and that 1,700 of those in operation in 1962 needed modernizing. It says industry needs 6,000 more facilities, and if fully effective pollution control is to be achieved, the United States will have to spend twice as much per year on pollution control during the decade to 1972 as the $300 million it was spending for that purpose in 1961.

Smaller communities are at a special disadvantage in meeting the need. Treatment plants designed to serve a community of 1,000 persons cost about three and a half times as much per capita as one designed to serve 100,000 persons. The Water Pollution Control Act amended by Congress in 1961 recognized this handicap by earmarking at least 50 percent of federal-aid funds for sewage treatment to communities under 125,000 in population, but a good many medium-sized communities still fail to ante up the cost.

Sick Cities

The federal government, which previously had authority to clamp down on polluters of interstate waterways, was empowered by law in 1961 to bear down on offenders within states as well once the governor summoned its assistance. Governor Albert D. Rosellini, of Washington, a Democrat, became the first to request such help when he called for Uncle Sam's assistance early in 1962 to force seven big pulp and paper mills to cease dumping an estimated seven million pounds of waste solids daily into Puget Sound. The industry had balked at spending another $35 million atop the $30 million it figured it had already spent to clean up its discharge.

Neither cities nor manufacturers should need the federal government to compel them to do something about their liquid waste. The sad fact is that they often do. "Two hundred years ago," says an official of a manufacturer of sanitary equipment in Stamford, Connecticut, "it was universal in American and European cities for each householder to empty his chamber pot into the gutter in front of his house. Theoretically, we don't do that anymore. Actually, many of us are, in effect, using a bigger chamber pot and a bigger gutter. We don't dump our garbage on our neighbor's lawn," he argues, "and we ought to cease sending our raw sewage into his water supply."

How are cities going to cope with their pollution problems? It's a safe bet a good part of the job will not be done at all. The federal grants-in-aid program that began in 1956 and builds up to $100 million a year from June 1, 1964, is obviously not going to turn the tide. One likely consequence: pollution will have to become an even greater peril than it is today to evoke additional expenditures from municipalities for the purpose. Another: industry will be hit by stricter regulations and fees on its own watery waste.

Some types of industrial wastes may be refused altogether. Professor Don E. Bloodgood, of Purdue University's Department of Sanitary Engineering, recently urged

124

city officials to outlaw the discharge into public sewers of such highly troublesome commodities as gasoline and other explosive solvents, which pose special dangers; feathers from poultry houses, which have a tendency to clog filter nozzles; hair from tanneries, which mats up in plant digesters; and lime sludge from water-softening and acetylene-generating plants, which is simply too hard to treat.

A recent study by the International City Managers Association showed that three times as many cities were levying special charges on industrial wastes in 1960 as did so in 1950; the I.C.M.A. survey listed 300 cities over 5,000 population levying these charges in the beginning of 1960 compared with 100 in 1950. About 10 percent of those levying charges in 1960 stiffened their rates if the type of discard was especially difficult to treat.

Homeowners and other domestic water users likely are also going to have to share directly in the burden of higher pollution costs.

One convenient method for the municipality to obtain such funds is to hike water rates. About 75 percent of the nation's population gets its water from publicly-owned systems, so the diversion of such funds for sewage purposes does not pose any insurmountable difficulties. Water rates, of course, were originally designed to pay for supply facilities, but more and more communities are using the device to meet climbing pollution costs as well. Water remains a bargain nevertheless: the American Water Works Association, which represents the public water supply industry, figures the 50 to 60 gallons consumed daily by the average residential user for such purposes as drinking, bathing, laundering, watering the lawn and washing the family car, cost him less than four cents. It figured the total water bill works out to about $13.50 a year per person, on the average.

In addition to higher water rates, residential users can look forward to tacking a new item on to the family budget or increasing one that might already be there: the so-called "sewage charge." The charge is generally based on water usage and is rendered with the water bill, so, for all intents and purposes as far as the use is concerned, it might just as well be a higher water rate.

Over 60 percent of the nation's larger cities (over 10,000 population) were levying sewage charges by 1961. Only 20 percent did so in 1945. In addition, some 75 percent of those levying sewage charges imposed charges for connecting new homes to municipal sewer lines, ranging as a rule anywhere from $50 to $100. Though such fees are generally paid by the builder, they are reflected in higher home prices to the buyer.

Not all forces are working against cities in their fight against water pollution. Technology, in addition to presenting bigger problems, is also fashioning new ways for treating water. New chemicals, processes, and filters are helping to make the job of cleaning up dirty water both more effective and cheaper. One of the most promising approaches, the Zimmerman Process, involves the use of high pressures and temperatures to 560 degrees Fahrenheit. Another attempts to freeze water clear of its contaminants, which generally do not freeze quite as easily. A third removes waste particles through the use of electrically-charged membranes.

However, it all costs money, which many municipalities are reluctant to spend on so thankless a purpose.

CLEAN WATER

To meet soaring demands for clean water, cities are having to reach farther and farther. Winston-Salem, North Carolina, didn't have to go anywhere for its water before 1949: it simply fetched what it needed from Salem Creek, which runs through the town. In 1949, however, it decided it needed more than the eight to nine million gallons it was getting daily from that source, so it started a $4 million pipeline to haul another 30 million gallons down from the Yadkin River, 14 miles away. By 1962 even that added amount threatened to prove insufficient.

San Francisco got all the water it needed from lakes just 25 miles from the city back in the early 1930's; today its reservoirs are as far as 150 miles away. Amarillo, Texas, in 1961 faced the prospect of having to go 55 miles for water it had been getting from only 14 miles away until then.

Detroit is getting all the water it needs right now from the highly convenient Detroit River, but rising requirements, says City Controller Henry P. Dowling, "will shortly force us to dip into Lake Huron, 60 miles from the city." New York City is spending over $30 million for a 10-foot concrete tunnel running through five miles of bedrock as much as 900 feet below sea level to meet an anticipated population boom on Staten Island following completion of the $330 million Verrazano-Narrows Bridge from Brooklyn.

Denver, on the dry eastern slope of the Rocky Mountains, realized a decade-old dream in 1962 when it finished six years of boring through 23 miles of Continental Divide to get to the Blue River at the foot of the well-watered

PIERCING THE CONTINENTAL DIVIDE FOR WATER

Cross-section of Roberts Tunnel through the Rocky Mountains, Colorado western slope. Known as the Harold D. Roberts Tunnel, the $50 million project has nearly doubled Denver's flow of water, from 60 billion to 110 billion gallons a year – enough to meet anticipated needs for the rest of the century.

The most ambitious water undertaking of them all is California's multipurpose Feather River Project, which will enable the arid southern part of the state to draw water from melting snows and running rivers as far north as the Sierra Nevadas above Sacramento. The network of dams, tunnels, pumping stations, concrete channels, and other facilities are expected to cost close to $2 billion by the time the project is completed in the early 1970's. Los Angeles will then be drawing its water from as far as 550 miles away, more than 200 miles farther than it is now reaching. Even so, plans are afoot to start tapping water sources still more distant, at the northern end of the state almost at the Oregon border.

Cities are having to dig deeper as well as reach farther for their water. Municipalities in the Chicago area, for instance, which still get much of their water from underground sources, had only to dig their wells a century ago and let natural pressures bring water to the surface. Such artesian wells are now unknown in the area. Well water in these regions currently has to be pumped to the surface from depths as great as 2,000 feet and more.

In a recent series of articles in the Dallas morning *News,* staff writer Allen Quinn noted: "The underground water on which the suburbs [of Dallas] have depended is failing." The average depth of wells in the state of Mississippi is said to have sunk 400 feet in just ten years' time.

The lowering of water tables poses a special problem in coastal areas. Lowering of the fresh water "wall" permits seawater to enter, and thereby pollute vast quantities of fresh water. Industries on Long Island, New York, using over 100,000 gallons a day are now required to pump their

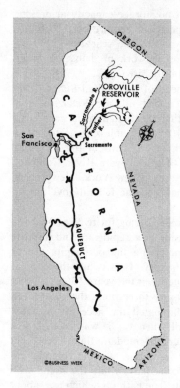

OVER 500 MILES
— *for a drink.*

discharge back into the ground so this water will act as a barrier against the sea.

Even in areas where there would seem to be plenty of water, swelling populations are making it altogether too risky to depend on the vagaries of nature for supplies. Storage facilities, dams, and reservoirs thus become vital in areas which never knew them before.

Washington, D.C., is a case in point. The capital's metropolitan-area population is expected to rise to 5 million by the year 2000 from 2 million in 1958. The region has no important dams and almost no storage capacity at present. By 1980, however, it is expected to require over 90 billion gallons of storage capacity and by the year 2000, 700 billion gallons. A $500 million network of dams and reservoirs has been proposed for the area.

Colonel T. H. Setliffe, head of the United States Corps of Engineers' Philadelphia District, told the Water Research Foundation not long ago that the Philadelphia area faced a water shortage "within 10 years" unless it started work on a $437 million network of 58 dams in the Delaware River Basin by the 1970's. The Delaware River Compact, a recent creation of four states (New York, New Jersey, Delaware, and Pennsylvania) and the federal government, has been shaped to tackle the task.

The nation's water needs are soaring for two reasons: the population, of course, is rising at a rapid rate and improving living standards are increasing the per capita use of water at home and in the factory. Thus, while the population is expected to double between the years 1960 to 2000, water needs are likely to rise to three times the 1960 level.

The tap itself, which eliminated the necessity to fetch water from an outside well whenever it was needed, was the first great water spender of modern times. A recent survey showed the average farmhouse without running water uses 10 gallons per person daily, while the home with running water uses about 60. The bathtub, which uses about 20 to 25 gallons with each filling, once seemed so extravagant in its use of water that the city of Boston, which was providing municipal water service even then, banned its use altogether in 1845. But the edict, fortunately, didn't stick. Some modern appliances, however, make the bathtub look like a water miser. The automatic dishwasher uses almost as much water as a bathtub every time it cleans a load of dishes. The automatic washing machine may consume even more. But the air conditioner is the greatest water user of all. A 1,000-ton unit, common in restaurants and other commercial establishments, may use as much as two million gallons of water a day, enough to meet the normal needs of nearly 40,000 people. Because they are such prodigious water users, large air-conditioning units are being hit increasingly by municipal regulations requiring the installation of recirculating apparatus. The water-conservation gear also helps reduce another curse of the air conditioner: it keeps water demands for air-conditioning purposes from all coming at the same time in a sort of "rush-hour" of the water main.

Urban sprawl adds to water demands. The more homes there are, each with its own lawn, garden, and two-car garage, the more water is needed to keep the vegetation alive and family buggies clean. The spread of home ownership also enhances the propensity to pool ownership. The aquatic amenity has helped lift water usage to three times the national average in certain sections of Los Angeles.

But the fastest rising of all water demands are those of industry. Industry's water use rose tenfold from 1900 to some 160 billion gallons a day by 1962. It is expected to soar to 400 billion gallons by 1980.

The amount of water needed in industry for cooling and other purposes is staggering. The manufacture of a ton of paper, for example, takes 25,000 gallons of water; a ton of finished steel, 65,000 gallons; and a ton of rayon fiber, 200,000 gallons. A pulp mill capable of turning out 300 tons of paper a day requires 15 million gallons of water for its operation.

Water shortages, of course, are not unknown even in this well-watered nation. Over a thousand United States cities and towns have already been forced to curtail water service at one time or another in recent years, and their number, say experts, is certain to climb. Such shortages, however, are more often due to inadequate distribution facilities, such as pipes and pumps, than to inadequate supplies. Boston and Milwaukee, two cities that lie close to water sources, for example, have both had to restrict their lawn-watering, car-washing and other "nonessential" water-using activities in recent years because their pumping capacities were not up to carrying the load.

In the future, however, supplies as well as distribution facilities will be under greater pressure in certain areas of the country. According to the 1960 annual report of Resources for the Future, a nonprofit organization that oversees usage of the nation's natural resources, five of the country's 22 geographical regions will be short of water by 1980 and nine by the year 2000, because of increased demands. Others, it warns, may have to restrict certain uses in some periods of peak demand. The necessity to conserve water through reuse and other means will thus take on added urgency in these areas.

The problem will become even more acute beyond the year 2000, if population continues to rise. By that time, water-storage areas will become difficult to come by. "With the growth in population and an ever-increasing premium upon land," says the Resources report, "reservoir storage areas will not be found easily, especially in the more developed regions of the country."

New York City in 1949 and 1950 received a mild taste of what may be in store for water-short metropolitan areas in the years ahead. Water wardens were assigned to report wastage to the police so appropriate fines could be levied. Leaky faucets bore penalties ranging from $2 to $5 apiece. One real-estate firm was fined $100 for an unusually bad runoff it failed to remedy. Restaurants were asked to cease serving water except on request, dentists to turn off their chairside taps except when they were being used, and barbers to stop issuing hot towels unless specifically asked. The washing of airplanes, taxis, delivery trucks, and other commercial vehicles, as well as that of passenger autos, was prohibited. So was the use of water for such purposes as flooding ice-skating rinks and indoor swimming pools.

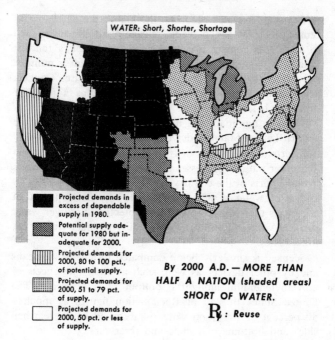

WATER: Short, Shorter, Shortage

Projected demands in excess of dependable supply in 1980.

Potential supply adequate for 1980 but inadequate for 2000.

Projected demands for 2000, 80 to 100 pct., of potential supply.

Projected demands for 2000, 51 to 79 pct. of supply.

Projected demands for 2000, 50 pct. or less of supply.

By 2000 A.D. — MORE THAN HALF A NATION (shaded areas) SHORT OF WATER.

R̶ : Reuse

The scarcer water gets, the hotter the rivalry tends to become over what remains. There is nothing new in such conflicts, of course. The word "rival" itself has the same Latin origins as the word "river"; it referred to parties that shared the same water source and were therefore frequently in conflict. Today, the rivalries are bigger and more numerous than ever. Fortunately, those that take place within the United States are confined to the courts. California and Arizona have been vying in this manner for years over the Colorado River, which rises in the Rocky Mountains north of Denver and flows through the arid southwest into the Gulf of California, south of the Mexican border some 1,450 miles away.

133

The scarcer water becomes, the higher the degree of its reuse. In Las Vegas, Nevada, sewage plant effluent is used to keep golf courses green at some of the city's fanciest hotels. Even sludge, which remains after effluent is pumped out of the treatment plant, is put to good use. Cooked, dried, and otherwise processed, it is sold as a fertilizer under such lofty names as "Green Goddess." The city of Milwaukee has marketed its "filter cake" for years in the eastern United States under the brand name "Milorganite."

Efforts to cut the loss of fresh water through evaporation and other natural processes are being increased. Reservoirs in some parts of the country are losing as much as 40 to 50 inches of water a year to Ole Sol. The development of chemicals that will spread a thin protective film over water surfaces without harming water quality is under way to cut these losses.

Seepage is similarly being combated by chemical means and by other devices as well, such as spreading sheets of polyethylene film along the bottom of a reservoir. The United States Bureau of Reclamation figures as much a 50 percent of irrigation water is absorbed by the earthen sides and bottoms of canals and reservoirs.

Artificial "rainmaking," strongly ballyhooed just after World War II as a possible solution to the water ills of parched areas, however, is one panacea which seems destined for stillbirth. The legal problems have proved insurmountable, principally the threat of suit from those who may claim their rain was intercepted.

The oceans, of course, are almost a limitless source of water. They account for about three-quarters of the earth's surface and reach depths as great as 6.5 miles (off the Philippine coast). The ability to convert seawater into fresh water at low cost could solve man's water-supply problems once and for all, though he would still be faced with great distribution needs. Cheap conversion techniques, however, are not yet at hand. Though the federal govern-

Water: Filthier and Farther

ment put the first of five seawater conversion plants into operation in 1961 to test various methods aimed at producing fresh water for as little as 50 cents for 1,000 gallons, even that cost is approximately ten times what it costs to clean up soiled fresh water.

CHAPTER FIVE

No Place for Fun

IN Bellflower, California, just outside Los Angeles, it is not uncommon for as many as 1,000 people to show up on a Sunday afternoon for picnic tables capable of accommodating only 300 persons. The city, with a population of 50,000 in 1960, has only one 12-acre park, and no prospect of adding others because of dense residential and commercial development. Families who persist in picnicking, have one of two choices: deposit Junior at an unclaimed table around seven o'clock in the morning to stake their claims or drive ten to fifteen miles to Long Beach to take their uncertain chances there.

In heavily populated eastern-seaboard states, local radio stations periodically announce waiting times at local golf courses. A recent Tri-State New York Metropolitan Region report noted that wielders of the iron were lining up "before daylight" at various courses and waiting hours for an opportunity to play. Public greens were the most congested, it reported.

Campers toting trailers to state and national parks many miles from crowded cities are being greeted increasingly these days by signs that might have come straight off a downtown parking lot. They read: "Sorry, full camp." Those willing to keep the vigil for a vacancy are required in some places to make twice-daily appearances at the camp entrance to ensure their place on the waiting list. And even then, they may be limited on the length of their stay once they get inside. California state parks, for example, generally ask campers to leave in ten days. Those seeking cabins may have to reserve them as far as six months in advance, or do without.

The frustrations of the would-be picnicker, the anxious golfer, and the hapless camper are typical of many shaping up around the nation which threaten to make the pursuit of outdoor pleasure more trying in the years ahead. That much all recreational experts are agreed upon.

Marion Clawson, in a report published by Resources of the Future, Inc., a nonprofit corporation aided by the Ford Foundation, declares, "We are approaching a grade-A crisis, unprecedented in both size and character."

How come? Is there not plenty of open space still available in this great land?

Yes, there is plenty of open space. Very little of it, however, is readily available to the growing megalopolises that need it most. Sizable park plots within the city are growing exceedingly scarce, while open land outside it becomes less and less accessible.

The point is well documented in a report submitted to President Kennedy early in 1962 by the Outdoor Recreation Resources Review Commission headed by Laurance S. Rockefeller, brother of New York Governor Nelson Rockefeller and Chairman of the philanthropic Rockefeller Brothers Fund. The slick-papered volume notes that no less than one-third of the nation's land is in federal ownership at the present time. Two-thirds of Uncle Sam's real estate, however, is located in Alaska, whose population at the time of the 1960 census was barely a fourth that of Rhode Island.

The commission finds that one-eighth of the total land area of the country consists of public areas designated for outdoor recreation. But it finds only 4 percent of that acreage in the northeastern part of the United States, where one-quarter of the population lives. Nearly 90 percent of federal recreation land is located in western states which contain but 15 percent of the population. Even in the

South and North Central regions, where the balance is not quite so out of line, 12 percent of the federal government's recreational acreage serves 30 percent of the population.

Very little of the land that has been set aside for public recreation is close enough to urban centers for easy weekend driving. Parks owned by local and state governments, those generally most accessible to the urban public, account for only 4 percent of total lands set aside for recreational purposes in the United States.

By the year 2000, with a population almost double that of 1960's enjoying shorter workweeks and longer vacations, and with more money to spend getting places, the demand for outdoor recreational opportunities is expected to treble. Swimmers, campers, hikers, and players of outdoor games will nearly quadruple in that period, the commission predicts. There will be more than three times as many boaters, almost three times as many picnickers and nearly three times as many hikers as there are today. Fishermen, cyclists, and horseback riders will be at least twice as numerous as they were in 1960.

And the most popular outdoor recreational pastime of them all – woe to the nation – driving for pleasure is expected to soar from 872 million "participations" in 1960-1961 to over 2.2 billion in the year 2000. It already accounted for slightly more than one-fifth of all the time Americans put into recreation in 1960 and twenty times more than they devoted to camping.

Pleasure driving may be no form of activity at all, except for the family automobile, but it is an indicator of the numbers who will be taking to the road for open vistas in the future. In addition to more highways, the pastime requires resting places and rest rooms, facilities for refreshment, and other opportunities for relaxation.

Americans in the year 2000, it's estimated, may be logging an average of 10,000 miles of travel yearly, double the 5,000 they put on in 1960 and nearly 20 times the

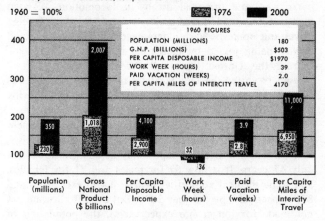

ESTIMATED CHANGES IN POPULATION, INCOME, LEISURE, AND TRAVEL
For the years 1976 and 2000, compared to 1960

1960 = 100%   ▒ 1976   ■ 2000

1960 FIGURES	
POPULATION (MILLIONS)	180
G.N.P. (BILLIONS)	$503
PER CAPITA DISPOSABLE INCOME	$1970
WORK WEEK (HOURS)	39
PAID VACATION (WEEKS)	2.0
PER CAPITA MILES OF INTERCITY TRAVEL	4170

Population (millions): 230 / 350
Gross National Product ($ billions): 1,018 / 2,007
Per Capita Disposable Income: 2,900 / 4,100
Work Week (hours): 36 / 32
Paid Vacation (weeks): 2.8 / 3.9
Per Capita Miles of Intercity Travel: 6,950 / 11,000

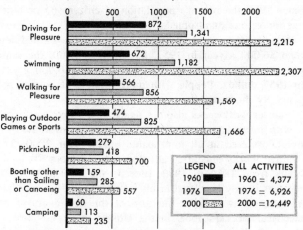

NUMBER OF OCCASIONS OF PARTICIPATION IN OUTDOOR SUMMER RECREATION   1960 compared with 1976 and 2000 (by millions)

Driving for Pleasure: 872 / 1,341 / 2,215
Swimming: 672 / 1,182 / 2,307
Walking for Pleasure: 566 / 856 / 1,569
Playing Outdoor Games or Sports: 474 / 825 / 1,666
Picknicking: 279 / 418 / 700
Boating other than Sailing or Canoeing: 159 / 285 / 557
Camping: 60 / 113 / 235

LEGEND	ALL ACTIVITIES
1960 ■	1960 = 4,377
1976 ▨	1976 = 6,926
2000 ▒	2000 = 12,449

Projections of The Outdoor Recreation Resources Review Commission,
Laurance S. Rockefeller, Chairman—submitted to President Kennedy, Jan, 1962.

500 miles they journeyed, on the average, back in 1910 when the steam locomotive, the electric streetcar, and the horse were the principal means of locomotion. A good many of these additional miles will be added in foreign travel, but domestic vacationers generally keep pace – and they're being joined by increasing numbers of foreigners touring the United States all the time. Some 600,000 foreigners visited the United States in 1960; national parks and historic shrines are usually high on foreigners' touring lists just as they are on American itineraries.

Longer life expectancies and more generous retirement plans are adding to the ranks of year-round recreationists, as well. The average life expectancy at birth in 1900 was only 47 years. It is now 67 for males and 71 for females, and some medical authorities believe it will exceed 80 and 85, respectively, by the year 2000. But even if allowance is not made for longer life expectancies, the population of retired persons is expected to be 50 percent greater in 2000 than the 15 million who were retired at the end of 1960. Since 1900 the nation's population of citizens 65 or older has more than quadrupled.

Nearly 60 percent of the nation's families earned less than $6,000 a year in 1957. By the year 2,000, the same proportion is expected to be earning over $10,000 a year in 1957 dollars. People with more money, of course, are generally more mobile.

Shorter workweeks also are likely. A 28-hour workweek – with three-day weekends and seven-hour workdays – is not considered at all improbable by the year 2000. The average workweek, after all, was reduced from 70 to 40 hours from 1850 to 1950. Indeed, one British authority believes it may be illegal in his country to work more than 16 hours a week after the turn of the new century. An electrical workers' local in the United States has already won a 25-hour workweek.

While demand for recreational space is soaring, its availability is rapidly diminishing. In the New York metropolitan area as much raw land was covered with homes, factories, roadways, and other urban structures in the 30 years to 1960 as was turned to urban purposes in the previous 300 years, according to the Regional Plan Association. The R.P.A. forecasts another doubling in the region's urbanized land area by 1985 to 4,000 square miles. At this rate, the R.P.A. figures, the New York metropolitan area will run out of raw land altogether by the year 2010 even if no provision is made for additional recreational acreage.

Senator Harrison A. Williams, Jr., New Jersey Democrat, told the United States Conference of Mayors in 1961: "In the last ten years, we have put more than half as much new and unspoiled land to urban use as we did in all the previous years since this country was founded. We have," he added, "been pushing the urban fringe out from the central city at an unprecedented rate. And as we have laid out seas of subdivisions, we have pushed nature's horizon farther and farther away from more and more people."

His concern? Lest the youngsters of today and tomorrow be deprived of the opportunity "to get out in the open air, climb trees, and get the self-confidence that comes with being on your own in a bit of open land." Too many subdivisions, the senator lamented, have failed to provide "a single area where the kids can play a game of football, or basketball or baseball."

George Hjelte, retired General Manager of the Department of Recreation and Parks for the City of Los Angeles, says he knows of only one instance where a subdivider in that city reserved land for a baseball diamond. One community of over 50,000 persons within the city, says he, has only one area big and flat enough for a game of baseball. A nearby city of 83,000 people, has only one diamond, while a third, with 170,000, has but three. "And this," says he, "is the country of the wide open spaces."

Recreational areas have themselves fallen victim to the

inexorable urban bulldozer. Washington, D.C., for example, has lost some 600 park acres to highways, school sites, and other urban "improvements" in recent years. One-fifth of San Diego's Balboa Park has fallen victim to the construction of schools, hospitals, and highways. In Flint, Michigan, a fire station, a parking lot, and an armory have all claimed pieces of local public greenery of late. The biggest thief, by far, is the automobile and its need for highways.

In Los Angeles, a new stretch of freeway severed three holes from two different 18-hole municipal golf courses in 1962; the highway also roofed over a lake in Hollenbeck Park, on the east side of town, placing boaters in the rumbling shade where once they enjoyed sunny California sky. In Bergen County, New Jersey, road planners not long ago sliced the 1,100-acre Overpeck Marine Park into six disconnected sections in the process of grabbing 200 acres for a projected state highway.

If highways and other urban structures continue to eat up park space at the present rate, warns Fred Smith, Director of the Council of Conservationists, "we will wake up one day to find we no longer have traditional parks. We will have a new kind of urbanized area, not for living in, like a city, but for standing in line in, for playing in with such competition, vengeance, purpose and breathless determination that there will be no point in going there at all."

Highways should avoid parks, or go under them if they cannot avoid them, but the cheaper solution of slicing through them is proving too irresistible for public bodies – and it doesn't arouse nearly the public clamor that relocating people does. The fact that this open space may be worth considerably more to the community in terms of recreational opportunity than its dollar cost would suggest is rarely evidenced by an apathetic general public.

Harvard City Planning Professor Charles W. Eliot reports federal highway engineers were once instructed to "head for the nearest parkland – you can get it free." Boston's Fenway Park, he notes, was described by one road-builder as "just some trees and bushes with a dirty stream running through it." Professor Eliot thinks highway and other public authorities who commandeer recreational acreage for their own purposes should be compelled to donate "equally adequate and accessible" acreage for parks elsewhere in the community even if it means having to buy and raze existing structures to do so. Very few highway departments make such provision at present; one authority claims most park departments are lucky if they end up with funds to buy more than half the land taken from them.

Park authorities are not about to insist, except in certain instances, that highways detour around recreational lands. But they do believe the loss of strategic recreation land can be avoided if parks, roadways, and other facilities were planned in advance. Where they are not planned in advance, the result almost invariably is greater cost and sometimes unnecessary sacrifices of recreational facilities.

Cities occasionally are desperate enough for property tax revenues to permit conversion of park lands or prospective park lands to apartment, office, or other high-value developments. The move is often shortsighted, even from the purely fiscal point of view. With more and more of the working population seeking out pleasant places to live more leisurely lives, employers increasingly favor office and factory sites which afford good recreational opportunities and pleasanter living environments. In addition, parks may ward off blight that could be costly to the community in crime as well as in renewal need.

The skeptic may ask what, specifically, is the usefulness of park space in contrast, say, to a road that will speed the movement of goods and people? What is the value of a lily-speckled pond against a factory that pours forth widgets to ease the housewife's burden and provide employment for her spouse? What, precisely, justifies the expenditure of public funds for recreational indulgence? Poets and philosophers for years have sung the praises of open land, but what, exactly, is its practical purpose?

The late Bernard De Voto, writing in *Harper's Magazine* in defense of an unspoiled half-acre of nature threatened by a roadway, confessed his own tastes were "metropolitan," and admitted he had "no urge to be active in the wilds." Yet, he stated: "I agree with the outdoorsmen: life would be intolerable if I could not visit woods and mountains at short intervals. I have," he stated, "got to have the sight of clean water and the sound of running water. I have got to get to places where the sky-shine of cities does not dim the stars, where you can smell land and foliage, grasses and marshes, forest duffs and aromatic plants and hot underbrush turning cool.

"Most of all," he added, "I have to learn what quiet is. Nothing in this," he insisted, "is sentimental or poetic. It is necessity – and it is necessity to a hundred million other Americans." In nature's habitat, Mr. De Voto concluded, one could "learn a little, reflect a little and refresh the spirit."

"The physical well-being of the community," says Alfred B. LaGasse, Jr., Executive Secretary of the American Institute of Park Executives, "requires space for exercise of the body, especially when it comes to children and young adults. The community also needs playgrounds, golf courses, and tennis courts, but it also needs preserves for education in the processes of nature. And it needs all kinds of water areas – from swimming pools in parks to open areas for boating – for the teaching of water safety. It also needs areas for social get-togethers, picnics and family gatherings. And it needs to preserve its historic aspects so it can pass its heritage on to its children."

Says Mr. LaGasse: "Children who enter into any activity

– whether it's the Boy Scouts, church or anything that is capable of consuming their interest, are better for it – and a park as much as any other place points up the truth of that."

Burt L. Anderson, Executive Secretary of the California Recreation Society, puts the argument this way: "A child," says he, "has to play. If there's no place for him to play in the parks, he'll play in the streets – and if there's nothing to play with, he'll experiment. He'll swipe an apple, perhaps. Maybe he'll smoke; if he smokes, he might later try dope."

Mr. Anderson adds: "There is no assurance a child is going to be good if he can go to a park. He needs direction there, too. It used to be that a lad could seek his own harmless activity, fishing or hiking in the hills. But the Huck Finn of today rarely has such places to go; the Huck Finn of today is the prospective delinquent of tomorrow. And it's all the more tragic when you realize these same energies can be turned to the cultivation of interests beneficial to both the child and the society in which he lives."

Dr. Howard A. Rusk, a world-renowned authority on human rehabilitation, maintains: "Recreation is more than just having fun. It is fundamental to physical and mental well-being." In his proposed master plan for Paramount, California, veteran Los Angeles city planner Gordon Whitnall states: "The words 'recreation' and 're-creation' differ only phonetically. They are actually synonymous. Recreation is not luxury. It is an essential to life."

Recreational authorities admit there's nothing sacred about a park. They are the first to concede a park can be poorly placed, so it serves the function of a park hardly at all. They recognize it can also be misused, so it becomes a haven for misanthropes. These are not arguments against parks, they contend, but, rather, for their better placement and more intelligent administration. Parks, they insist, cannot just be provided – they must also be supervised, and in some areas they must be supervised more than in others. Such supervision, they contend, should not be of a negative character, but directed toward the stimulation of healthy interests and activities.

"The average juvenile delinquent," says L. R. Preyer, Judge Pro Tem of the Municipal County Court in Greensboro, North Carolina, "is a person whose sense of adventure has been frustrated by his surroundings and he finds his outlet for it in the cops and robbers game of crime. We no longer have any western frontier where adventurous youth can pioneer," he notes, "but we do have the substitute available, in the form of recreational activities and sports. If juveniles' activities can be channeled along these lines, the problem of juvenile delinquency would be largely solved. It is far more important than enacting laws or setting up special courts to deal with juvenile delinquency."

Parks may also be capable of making a contribution in the campaign to keep youth from dropping out of high school, a bane of educators and employers alike. Children who derive enjoyment from normal high school years, which means at play as well as in the classroom, are more likely to see their education through to graduation, maintains George Nesbitt, Director of Consulting Services for the National Recreation Association, a nonprofit service organization for professionals in the field.

Recreational facilities for the aged also have a practical as well as a philosophical bent. Older people who participate in recreational programs have been found to visit physicians' offices and clinics about half as often, contribute about 50 percent as many general hospital occupants, and have one-eighth as many psychiatric breakdowns as persons in their age bracket who do not participate in such activities. Part of this may be due to the fact that healthier people are the ones who tend to participate in recreational activities to begin with, but the proportion would indicate the cause-and-effect relationship goes both ways.

Recreational fibers are woven into the fabric of a nation. The love of one's country is steeped in the pleasant memories of vales and meadows where one has spent reflective moments. There is some question as to whether concrete cities devoid of natural beauty can long fire national loyalties to high heat. A nation addicted to television and other passive pursuits of pleasure, whose working activities are more and more oriented to offices and machines with progressively less opportunities for fresh air and exercise, can do worse than fritter away financial resources on intelligently planned recreational facilities.

Where is the need greatest? At the moment, it is in the city and county parks that cater to daytime uses. These, of course, were the recreational needs that developed first – and have been neglected the longest. Until relatively recent times, in fact, city folks in need of brief respite had almost nowhere else to go for it except to the public cemetery, Greenwood Cemetery in New York drew as many as 60,000 visitors yearly in the early nineteenth century.

The acquisition of land for Central Park in New York City in 1853 seemed to many at the time to be highly unnecessary and an extravagant way to spend the city treasure. Manhattan was then largely countryside north of Twenty-third Street, and the acquisition of 700 acres north of what was much later to become Fifty-ninth Street was roundly criticized as indulgent. The park, which takes in 840 acres at present, has been regarded more recently as an outstanding example of civic foresight.

Today the provision of park facilities in urban centers is considered a necessity by most city planners and civic leaders. The National Recreation Association's general rule of thumb calls for at least one acre of close-in park land for every 100 inhabitants. The national average presently works out closer to a half-acre for every 100 inhabitants.

For every acre provided in city parks, another, by generally accepted standards, should be provided in county or metropolitan regional parks. Few cities or metropolitan areas come anywhere near these targets – yet they are not unduly high in the view of most recreational authorities. Los Angeles, for instance, sets its objectives at one acre of park for every 70 persons, though it, too, falls far short of that objective. No standards have been set for state or federal parks.

To eliminate irksome waiting periods at public golf courses, recreation specialists figure one hole should be provided for every 3,000 population, which works out to one eighteen-hole course per 54,000 population. California, for one, estimates it will need three times as many golf courses in 1980 as it had in 1960 to meet these standards. And many other municipalities are nowhere near so well endowed with golf courses as the Golden State. At the same time, the threatened conversion of golf courses into residential and other development has never been greater: with property values soaring and taxes based on the "highest and most valuable potential" use, more and more private courses are trading their green for the green from developer's pockets.

In all, the nation's inventory of city and county parks was estimated at approximately 750,000 acres in 1959. Its need at the time was calculated at close to 1,500,000 acres.

Facilities for day outings, such as state parks and federal reservoir areas, are somewhat more difficult to gauge because of vast regional differences. Western states, for the most part, are reasonably well endowed with such expanses. In the more densely populated East, such facilities are not nearly so plentiful. Yet demand for the all-day acres is expected to increase more rapidly than demand for local parks and playgrounds – about four times as fast, in fact. The current inventory of 9 million acres in state parks and federal reservoir sites will have to rise to at least 35 million acres and perhaps as high as 70 million by the end of the century if uncomfortable overcrowding is to be avoided, according to recreational authorities.

Unlike city and county park sites, these more distant resources are not yet too costly to come by. Land capable of conversion to all-day park sites is still available in some areas for as little as $300 to $500 an acre. Recreationists fear the tab may be far higher in the years ahead if, indeed, the properties are available at all.

The urban crowd is likely to converge most heavily, however, on the broader, remoter preserves of the national parks and forests. These areas have been insulated from human inundation up to now largely by limited incomes and vacation periods. With substantially higher incomes and month-long vacations in prospect, such facilities are bound to become the objective of an increasing proportion of a growing population. About 40 times as many Americans may be visiting national parks and forests in the year 2000 as did so in 1960, recreational authorities believe. In contrast, the 40 million acres in recreational land in 1960 is considered expandable by approximately five times. Any increase beyond 230 million acres is likely to be exceedingly costly, say recreation officials.

Moreover, improved facilities tend to bring even more visitors to recreational lands, thereby resulting in even greater crowding.

Might projections of recreational demand be exaggerated? Experience would indicate otherwise. In the decade to 1960 alone, visits to national parks nearly trebled. In the period from 1920 to 1956 the number of visitors to the Grand Canyon increased fifteen-fold. Those to Yellowstone in the same period rose 18 times – and to Glacier National Park in Montana, 33 times.

It is perhaps physically possible, through additional clearings and roadways, to accommodate 40 times as many people in federal park and forest lands. But, says Mr. Clawson,

"Long before that unlikely goal could be reached, the special attractions that draw people to the parks and forests would be gone. The one-time grandeur and quiet, the sense of being close to nature, would retreat in the face of paved roads and parking areas, trodden vegetation and human bustle."

The State of California, which recently peered into the year 1980 to estimate its recreational needs, concluded it would probably have to limit campers to one-night stays in more congested areas by that time, that waterfowl and pheasant would be in much shorter supply for hunters, that skiers would find parking space difficult to come by, and that fishermen would have to content themselves with fly-casting from rocky coastal shores instead of streams and rivers.

The most dismal picture of all, in California as elsewhere, is painted for the beachgoer. California has lots of coast – 1,200 miles of it, in fact – but three-quarters of it is privately owned. Much of the public shore, moreover, lies in sparsely settled areas. In built-up regions, much of the beachfront is privately owned – and getting exceedingly expensive to come by. A typical stretch of Corona Del Mar beachfront in Los Angeles County that sold for $900 in 1934 commands over $50,000 today.

To help their beaches from becoming too crowded, communities in Connecticut are already raising barriers against nonresidents. Bridgeport, for one, slaps a 60-cent daily parking charge on nonresident autos with Connecticut plates and an even stiffer $1.50 on those from other states; its own residents park free. Nearby Westport charges nonresidents $4 for access to its beaches on a Saturday or Sunday, about twice as much as residents pay. In Greenwich, nonresident bathers are barred outright except as guests of residents.

Boaters as well as bathers will have an increasingly difficult time of it in the future. Writing in *Sports Illustrated* in April, 1960, Henry Romney noted: "Boating is gaining so rapidly as a sport that if the present trend continues, by 1980 every Californian will own five boats: 30 million Californians . . . and 150 million boats." The breakneck dash to boat ownership, of course, will taper off long before that point is reached. But its rise will be considerable nevertheless: 1.1 million Californians, it's predicted, will own boats in 1980 compared with 300,000 in 1961. Says one authority: "By 1980, we may be using dry lake beds, flooded only sufficiently to keep the dust down."

Already New York and Connecticut suffered more deaths in boating accidents on a recent July 4th weekend than they did on the highway. In all, there were some eight million boats on the nation's waterways by the end of 1961 – about one to every eight passenger cars.

Parking has become a problem along the shore as well as on dry land. Detroit recently installed 25-cent-an-hour parking meters along its public marina frontage to force boaters to haul their vessels out of the water or take off; policemen ticket violators.

The motorcar has given rise to some recreational pastimes of its own which also are increasingly difficult to accommodate. Los Angeles, particularly, is being pressured for paved strips where hot rodders can test their vehicles without menacing ordinary motorists through their unlawful speeding. Though the issue has not yet been resolved as to whether the provision of such facilities is a public responsibility or not, one area has been considered for the purpose: the usually dry concrete bed of the Los Angeles River. It is perhaps a sign of the times that even this ribbon of urban real estate has assumed several functions in recent years, among them, as training grounds for drivers of official cars and as a testing area for smog-control devices on automobiles.

As uncrowded recreational space disappears, the pressure on private owners – farmers, lumbering firms, and others – to open up their property for public purposes will mount. Many private owners already invite hunters and campers to use their lands for recreational purposes. To get still more to do so, public bodies are pondering such incentives as direct subsidy payments, tax remissions, "recreational" leases, and the provision of habitat improvements free of charge to the landowner.

As they seek to extend their recreation acreage by buying appropriate property, park authorities are running into more and more opposition. Back in 1954, the National Park Service, following a survey of 3,700 miles of United States coastline, designated a 30-mile stretch along Massachusetts' Cape Cod shore as a "top priority" project for inclusion in the national seashore program. The area was said to have been within a day's drive of some one-third of America's population and a particularly easy trek for the residents of two major metropolitan areas: New York and Boston. It was also held to be a region without a single national park and severely short of public beach.

Residents, quite understandably, didn't relish the prospect of an estimated 40 million or more visitors a year basking on their beaches, clogging their streets, and littering their lawns. They fought the effort for some seven years. It wasn't until August, 1961, that the Cape Cod National Seashore Program was finally signed into federal law and land acquisition got under way, making it the first such endeavor in the United States.

A second, the 53,000-acre Point Reyes National Seashore just north of San Francisco, was authorized in 1962. Earlier, subdividers had attempted to frustrate proponents of the park plan by creating and selling off some 125 homesites, more than a dozen of which were subsequently built up with luxury homes. The homes may be allowed to stand since there is some private property in many national parks but if they have to be torn down, it's likely to be at Uncle

Sam's expense since he is required to make fair compensation.

Cities as well as individuals can frustrate recreational efforts pressed by higher levels of government. Los Angeles County had the experience recently when it sought to create a new 35-mile public beachfront. Three of the several shoreside communities whose approval was needed for the project demurred. Exclusive Palos Verdes Estates didn't want the traffic, Hermosa Beach the police problem, and El Segundo the loss of acreage that might be leased to industry for sorely needed public revenue.

In addition to the problems imposed by scarcer space and growing crowds, recreation authorities have also to cope with demands for additional comforts and amenities. Not the least of these is parking space. But there are others as well. Campers, for instance, have come to expect not only hot and cold running water and city-type toilets in camping grounds, but even electrical outlets for electric frying pans and blankets. The phenomenon of the comfort-seeking camper isn't confined to the United States, either: campers in Italy are reportedly renting tents with clean linen and floor mats in them and getting their meals served by waiters in canvas-covered commissaries.

Despite the fact that they're faced with the prospect of more patrons than they can handle, park administrators are anxious to make their facilities more pleasant and useful. The new Children's Zoo which opened in New York's Central Park in 1961 on a $500,000 donation from former Governor and Mrs. Herbert H. Lehman, for example, sports mock-up whales children can walk through, a Noah's Ark they can board, a turreted castle they can explore, and a Hansel and Gretel gingerbread house – all for a ten-cent admission charge designed to cover the costs of upkeep.

An estimated hundred such "fairylands" have been created in public city and county parks in the United States in recent years, and many more are likely to be provided in the future. Some of the installations come equipped with tape recorders for the periodic telling of fairy tales or for otherwise enhancing the effect. The storybook touch is held to make parks both more entertaining and more educational, but it also adds significantly to construction costs and maintenance. "The kids lose interest when the paint fades," notes one park authority. Only a few such fairylands are sufficiently well endowed from private sources to relieve the municipality of these added costs.

Parkgoers are also being protected increasingly these days against the vagaries of nature itself. Concrete canopies at $6 a square foot protect picnickers from summer rains. A new insect spray used in Los Angeles in 1961 was said to have almost exterminated the bee population in that city's vast, 5,300-acre Griffith Park. Grizzly bears wander around Yellowstone National Park with tiny transmitters hung around their necks on plastic collars to broadcast their whereabouts to special monitoring stations; actually, the monitors are at least as interested in protecting the bears as in protecting visitors, since the bears, unlike the visitors, are growing exceedingly scarce, and park authorities want to know why.

Nature is even being tricked into serving man's recreational wants more and more. To permit visitors to observe nocturnal life during convenient daytime hours, the Bronx Zoo recently constructed a lightproof "world of darkness" in which the creatures are fooled into thinking day is night through the use of infrared lights only humans can see. At night, bright lights burn which are visible to the animals, causing the confused creatures to take their 40 winks when ordinary self-respecting humans do. Another recent addition to the zoo enables visitors to overcome natural physical handicaps by running ramps up to treetop levels so humans can view bird and other high life otherwise hidden from them.

Zoo authorities are trying to make their facilities more

realistic as well as more versatile. Fences and iron bars that mar the objective are rapidly being scrapped. In a five-year program that won't be completed until 1966, the Bronx Zoo, for instance, is putting close to $4 million into the construction of moats, glass paneling, walls, and raised vantage points to give visitors the illusion of being at one with the creatures of nature. The zoos have proved safe enough so far: San Diego's Balboa Park has been operating its zoo in this fashion for over twenty years and has yet to report its first fatality among men or beasts.

The development of more ambitious recreational facilities is likely to stir a good deal of debate in the future. One controversy raging at the moment centers around the proposed construction of an 18-story hotel that would run up and down the mile-long slope of the south rim of the Grand Canyon, with each room given to a spectacular view. No one believes the Canyon is yet in danger of becoming a sort of depressed Manhattan with canyon-scrapers blanketing its sides, but opponents don't like the idea of the "great loneliness," as Theodore Roosevelt put it, being violated. Whether the hotel ever gets built or not, that "great loneliness" is hardly likely to be preserved much longer in the Grand Canyon than it is anywhere else.

The demand for recreational comfort has its favorable as well as its unfavorable fiscal aspects. It needn't constitute an economic burden alone but may afford revenue opportunities too. No less in the operation of hotels than in the letting of food and drink concesisons, these needs can be served at a profit to the public body that holds the land. Such earnings could be used to offset deficits in other park activities or for the acquisition of additional land. Automatic laundries and even hairdressing shops, which can be sensibly located, have already demonstrated a certain degree of popularity in the few parks where they've been provided so far.

Altogether too small a portion of the recreation dollar

is being garnered by public park authorities at present. Total revenues of the National Park Service in 1961, for example, accounted for less than 1 percent of the $20 billion Americans spent in the pursuit of outdoor pleasure, counting outlays on transportation, boats, and related expenses.

Recreation officials are stepping up their search for revenue opportunities, and the hunt is bound to grow keener. Charges of one kind or another are likely to be imposed or increased, not just to keep existing park facilities from becoming still more overcrowded, but to permit park authorities to keep abreast of climbing road and other maintenance costs. Entry to vacation campsites, which now run $2 to $3 a head at national park sites, for example, would be increased to as much as $25 or more per visit if some authorities had their way.

New York's Central Park slaps a fee on commercial photographers simply for using the facility in their background shots. The professional shutterbugs pay a flat $10 where ten or fewer models are used, plus $5 for each animal and $5 for equipment. By issuing the permits only for specific locations, park authorities are able to guard against the bootlegging of backgrounds through periodic checks on occupied lensmen.

More and more cities are imposing charges for amenities not generally considered among basic recreational services. San Diego in the fall of 1961, for example, began imposing special fees for a number of programs its city and county parks had been providing free for years. A charge of $3.50, for instance, was slapped on 16 weeks of half-hour weekly lessons in ballet, tap, ballroom, and square dancing. Nine months of instruction in "competitive swimming," provided two hours a day five days a week, was tagged with a $20 charge.

California in 1961 installed two toll gates for admission of tourist autos to forest areas. The gates swing open on insertion of half a dollar into a slot. In four other wilderness sites, parking meters have been installed with $1 charges (two 50-cent coins) for overnight use and 50 cents for daytime picnicking. United States Forest Service employees check motorists periodically to be sure they have the proper tickets.

There's some difference of opinion among park men on the issue of recreational fees. Opposition comes largely from those who believe that recreation, like education, should be available to all youth on an equal basis – a view which still allows for special charges on adults, particularly where the use of special facilities or equipment is involved. Others point out that the principle of charges for certain costlier forms of recreation, such as swimming pools, has long since been established and that so-called higher levels of recreational service have to pay their costs or risk depriving the community of other services it might have been able to provide for greater numbers of users with that money.

There has been relatively little effort so far to make the imposition of fees easier on those less able to afford it. Some park authorities argue that it is in the very nature of the fee itself to place the service on a more discriminating user basis. "There are hundreds of recreational activities available free all over town," says one such proponent.

Nevertheless, there are means for rendering such services available to underprivileged children. One, particularly important, is through the interest of service clubs and other charitable organizations. The system works in San Diego. A city-county camp started just after World War II, for instance, was created to give all sixth-graders an opportunity to live in a natural setting and study nature for a week at a total cost of $14 to cover lodging, transportation, and other expenses. Underprivileged youngsters are generally subsidized by the area's philanthropic organizations.

There's no reason why cities themselves can't show

greater ingenuity in making recreational ends meet. Municipal forests, for instance, may offer excellent opportunities in some areas for raising revenues and providing recreation acreage at one and the same time. Three-quarters of the woodlands of Switzerland, for example, are of this type. According to the United States Forest Service, there are well over two thousand such forests in the nation at the present time, many of them planted by women's clubs, Boy Scout organizations, and other civic groups with trees donated by state and federal agencies as well as by private donors. The town of Troy, in Maine, has used the proceeds of lumber sales from its municipal forest to finance the rebuilding of its schools. Such forests also serve to protect city watersheds, conserve wildlife, and otherwise preserve the pastoral scene that might have been marred by urban growth.

Funds for recreational facilities will be sorely needed in the years ahead. Authorities figure public bodies between 1960 and the year 2000 will have to spend a staggering $50 billion just for land acquisitions and improvements needed to accommodate the growing numbers of recreation seekers. The total expenditure in 1961 for all purposes – maintenance and acquisition – was estimated by the Rockefeller Commission at approximately $1 billion. If that same annual expenditure went for nothing but land acquisition it would still fall short by 20 percent of the Rockefeller Commission's projected acquisition and improvement needs.

No matter how dedicated one may be to the principle of "open space," however, there is a danger in the unrestrained accumulation of undeveloped land. Open space may be set aside for supposed future recreational use when the real purpose of such action is simply to make local government more economical by forcing up population densities. Low population density is the enemy of municipal economy: sewage lines, police and fire service, and other provisions of local government are far cheaper to provide in compact than in sparsely settled communities. Where the cry of "open space" is used principally as a device for achieving greater economy in local government over and beyond what is justifiably reserved for anticipated needs, the community is deprived of open space in another and equally vital form: as part of one's residence, with the opportunities for privacy and convenience it affords. The opportunity to enjoy such private space must be preserved as long as the communal need and real-estate economics will allow. Wanton destruction of that opportunity for the sake of municipal efficiency is as much a violation of the spirit of recreation as is the wanton development of open space required for communal use – and may be in far greater need of protection in the years to come.

CHAPTER SIX

Help, Police!

T H E R E was a time in the past, not too long ago, when the average citizen could expect to go through life suffering no more serious act of unlawfulness than a picked pocket or, perhaps, a stolen purse. Though radio communications, the automobile, and other scientific and technological advances have tended to favor the law more than the lawbreaker, this is no longer true. Anyone living to age 60 or beyond these days can expect, according to statistical averages, to fall victim at least once in his life to some serious crime ranging from the theft of property valued at over $50 to aggravated assault, rape, or even murder. And, as the years pass, unless the trend is suddenly reversed, the law of the jungle will continue to stage its comeback in this space-age civilization.

The surge in crime in recent years has, in fact, assumed such proportions as to make public complacency itself almost criminal negligence.

According to the Uniform Crime Reports issued by the Federal Bureau of Investigation, the number of serious crimes committed in the United States in 1960 was at a record high – up 98 percent from 1950 to nearly 1.9 million at a time when the nation's population, according to the United States Bureau of the Census, was rising just 12 percent, from 151 million to 179 million. The increase in crime from the previous year alone amounted to 14 percent! According to the FBI report, someone was being murdered in the United States every 58 minutes throughout 1960, raped every 38 minutes, robbed every 6 minutes, and

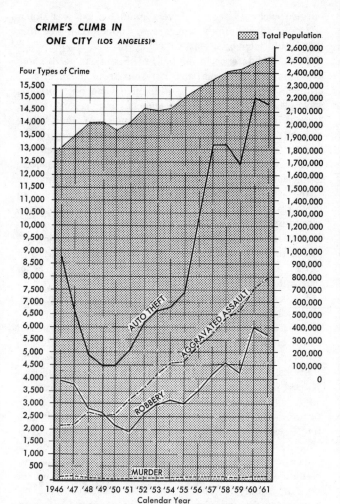

CRIME'S CLIMB IN ONE CITY (LOS ANGELES)*

Four Types of Crime

Total Population

*One of few major U.S. cities in which figures are reliable and comparable over this period.

burgled every 39 seconds; every minute a car was stolen and every fourth minute someone was undergoing a beating that would later be described as "aggravated assault."

Public indifference in the light of these facts needs some explaining. In part, perhaps, it results from the nature of crime itself; its victims are individuals and not, directly, society as a whole, so that the tendency is to regard the act as someone else's uncommon misfortune. Another lulling element may be found in the public-relations policy of police departments, which are understandably more interested in conveying an image of police efficiency than in depicting the alarming growth of lawlessness. A third factor may lie in the community's own adaptation to rising crime rates in the form of insurance coverage designed to cushion property losses arising from illegal acts.

A fourth factor may likewise be at work in causing the public to accommodate itself to a high and rising rate of crime: a certain resignation to its inevitability, the belief that little can be done about it anyway.

FBI crime statistics are not reassuring in this respect. They almost suggest that it is safer, these days, to be a criminal in fear of the law than a law-abiding citizen in fear of the criminal – certainly, at least, when it comes to certain types of crimes. According to the FBI's 1960 crime statistics, over 60 percent of all reported robberies and over 70 percent of reported burglaries resulted in no arrests at all – and only one-third of those that did resulted in convictions. The proportion who go unpunished is even higher for lesser crimes. Indeed, even these statistics do not portray the situation fully since they are compiled from official police records, which, for one reason or another, may not contain all the crimes reported to those agencies and do not, of course, include the many crimes which are not reported to the police at all. The federal agency until recent years did not accept the crime statistics of the New York City Police Department at all because it believed the department's figures so understated. Chicago's new police chief, when he took over in 1960, declined to make comparisons of the city's crime statistics with earlier periods because he was not satisfied with their accuracy, even though the Chicago figures had been used by the FBI.

Though the federal and state governments in the last half-century have taken on a number of policing functions, responsibility for keeping the peace falls primarily on local police departments. And, as crime mounts, population increases, valuables accumulate, and more cars take to more roads, that responsibility assumes the form of an immense financial burden as well – one which very few municipalities manage to carry adequately. That burden becomes heavier still when it is compounded by the rising wave of juvenile delinquency, stemming from a breakdown in family relationships and increased ethnic mobility that puts low-income groups into areas unaccustomed to assimilating them in such numbers.

Even automation, as desirable as it may be from other points of view, has contributed to police problems. Among other things, it has opened new opportunities for the criminal and the pervert. The self-service elevator and the automatic subway train, for example, lend rapists, muggers, and other lawbreakers a free hand for their molestations in the late hours of the night, particularly. Even the coin-operated phone box makes things easier for the thief; a foggy night in Los Angeles has been known to veil the raiding of several miles of such installations along a single thoroughfare. Ultimately, the combating of crime connected with automation may have to be fought with the same means: automated surveillance in the form of television cameras mounted at such strategic places as the ledges of high buildings over deserted streets, inside commuter trains, and even in the lobbies of public housing or other buildings fraught with crime.

Municipalities are not spending anywhere near as much

on law enforcement as they should be spending, but these expenditures are greater than all outlays of local government except education, the construction and maintenance of streets and highways, and, by a 4 percent whisker, treatment and conveyance of sewage. The nearly $1.3 billion spent on city police departments in 1960 was 33 percent above the 1956 figure. Yet it represented only a small percentage of what crime and its prevention were costing the nation. According to FBI Director J. Edgar Hoover, the cost to the United States of crime and its prevention, counting such items as prison maintenance, police budgets, and the volume of stolen property itself, may have approached $22 billion in 1961. No one knows exactly what the figure is, of course, but Mr. Hoover's educated guess at least suggests the magnitude of crime's measurable costs. In terms of human suffering and anguish, crime's toll cannot begin to be tallied.

Police capabilities for coping with this toughening assignment leave much to be desired. The likelihood, therefore, is that crime will continue to outpace both law enforcement expenditures and population growth in the years ahead. With few exceptions, police management is not keeping pace either with the increase in police personnel or with the greater complexities of law enforcement in urban areas any more than the law enforcement bodies themselves are keeping pace with lawlessness. Inadequate procedures for self-policing, outmoded recruitment practices which create artificial manpower shortages and prejudice the hiring of more capable personnel, the lack or complete absence of satisfactory training methods, the poor allocation of manpower and facilities, meager or nonexistent research efforts, and a general failure to summon or heed outside professional advice are just a few of the maladies presently endemic at police headquarters generally around the nation.

Not all police departments, needless to say, are guilty of all of these management crimes. St. Louis and Chicago are notable examples of cities which have made great strides in recent years in reshaping their departments, while Los Angeles has long been known for its use of modern techniques and manning procedures. But the progressive, well-trained, efficient department, authorities agree, is exceptional. "We're still in the horse-and-buggy days when it comes to the policing that is supposed to make life and property safe," declares a leading police consultant.

There is no dearth of evidence to back up that conclusion, either. Take training. Quinn Tamm, Director of the Field Service Division of the International Association of Chiefs of Police in Washington, D.C., notes: "A large number of communities in the United States, particularly smaller ones, have no training requirements for their police and there wasn't a single state, before 1960, that required any. By 1961 one did so: New York." Recently, two municipalities in New Jersey were held responsible by the courts for injuries to children sustained from guns which went off in the hands of policemen later deemed to have been inadequately trained in the use of firearms.

Police pay has improved considerably in recent years, but many authorities contend it still is not adequate to attract enough men of intelligence and integrity in most cities. Los Angeles, one of the better-paying cities, was starting its policemen at $6,540 a year early in 1962 compared with $3,828 a decade earlier. New York, whose wage scales are also considerably above the national average, paid its top-ranking patrolmen (those with at least three years' experience) $7,276 a year in 1962; its ceiling was only $4,150 in 1952.

A good number of cities, however, still pay their police substandard salaries. Despite two raises granted in rapid succession, a police chief with 30 years' experience who headed up a force of some 154 men in the capital city of one of the larger eastern states received less than $6,000 in 1961. The starting wage for patrolmen in the biggest cities of the nation averaged out to less than $100 a week in the beginning of 1961.

The executive officer of the police department in Burlington, Vermont, which was hit by scandals of police thefts early in 1962, was himself receiving $5,400 a year at the time – $1,200 less than a privately-employed plant security patrolman with no responsibility other than that of checking signal boxes.

The reluctance of municipalities to hike police pay stems more from a desire to keep the cost of government down than from a lack of recognition of the need for raises. Personnel costs account for approximately 80 percent to 95 percent of police department budgets, with the biggest cities showing the highest percentages. Police budgets, furthermore, have risen sharply in recent years as police work-weeks have been reduced, in some instances from as much as 76 hours in 1945 to 40 hours at present.

"The reduction in the work week was largely responsible for the doubling of police budgets across the nation in the fifteen years following World War II," notes Donal E. J. MacNamara, Dean of the New York Institute of Criminology and a consultant in the field of police administration. More holidays, longer vacations, and other fringe benefits, such as better disability coverage and improved uniform allowances, have also hiked police personnel costs without fattening dollar sums on individual paychecks.

Taxpayers had best brace themselves for still higher personnel expenditures. Chicago's Police Superintendent and former head of the School of Criminology at the University of California in Berkeley, Orlando W. Wilson, argues: "Quality is influenced by price. If we're going to raise police standards, we're going to have to raise police salaries as well."

Chief Wilson, who came to Chicago to overhaul a scandal-ridden department in 1960, says he'd "like" to have his recruits with at least two years of college but he does not think that is "nearly as vital as character and intelligence." It is going to take money, he argues, to snare such prospects from jobs in government or private industry.

To supplement their income, policemen often hold down second jobs. A good many authorities are highly critical of that practice. Chief of Police Robert V. Murray of Washington, D.C., believes the two-job policeman comes to work tired and tends to avoid making arrests the day before his day off so he won't have to appear in court when he is supposed to be on another job. Chief Murray is also disturbed by the possible conflict between enforcement of the law and loyalty to an outside employer. And he is afraid of losing desirable men: "The better men who take part-time jobs often do well enough to develop these jobs into full-time positions and then they quit the force altogether," says he.

A good many police departments prohibit "moonlighting," as the practice is called, but few enforce the ban lest they lose too much of their force. A top official of the Policeman's Benevolent Association in New York City recently estimated 60 percent to 70 percent of that city's policemen were holding down other jobs despite the fact the department is among those prohibiting the practice. Former Police Commissioner Stephen P. Kennedy aroused considerable wrath among the rank and file when he tried to enforce the ban. His successor, Michael J. Murphy, did not press the issue.

Police dishonesty has often been blamed, in part at least, on moral erosion from substandard pay scales. It has been said low pay makes police officers susceptible to offers of free meals, cigarettes, and other small favors from local merchants and that such practices tend to be followed by more generous gifts later. Then, when they are not forthcoming, there is the dropped hint and, finally, the outright request for gratuities. Whatever truth there may be in this contention, when the "shakedown" is standard procedure throughout a department, as it was revealed in 1961 to have been for years in Denver, it is more reflective of a serious neglect of discipline within the department than of the level of police pay.

"The police service reminds me of George Bernard Shaw's comment on marriage," says the youthful Planning Director of Chicago's Police Department, Richard E. McDonnell. "The reason it's popular, he said, is that it combines a maximum amount of temptation with a maximum amount of opportunity. The absence of internal controls over police conduct makes for the same condition."

The tendency of police management to ignore or show too much leniency toward erring members of the force has been documented repeatedly in various departments around the country, albeit seldom for public eyes. Failure to institute procedures which might more readily bring police malpractices to light have likewise been noted. Many of the more than forty policemen implicated in Denver's 1961 police scandal were found to have been cracking safes for at least a decade; police authorities contend the most rudimentary controls would long before have indicated something was awry with so many members of the force involved.

One reason disciplinary procedures are not more common in police departments is that police supervisors want a maximum of discretionary authority to deal with situations in their departments as they see fit. And they do not want their decisions in this realm questioned, which fixed procedures would make easier. The desire is understandable, but the facility with which it is realized is a luxury in laxity communities can ill afford.

Among the most important innovations Chief Wilson made in the Chicago force when he began to reorganize the department in 1960 was the institution of an Internal Investigation Division consisting of some 90 plainclothesmen. Since the entire department had 10,800 men at the time, that meant assigning the equivalent of nearly 1 percent of the force to police the police. Among other things, the division was to be responsible for recording and investigating every complaint filed against a policeman. It was also to do some investigating on its own. For example, its personnel were instructed to deliberately exceed speed limits on various streets and thoroughfares and then attempt to get out of the ticket by flashing a five-dollar bill, long considered the going rate for a ticket "fix" in Chicago. More than one police officer has been trapped in this manner and dismissed from the force.

The detection of police dishonesty is self-defeating if prosecution is not swift and certain. Chicago resorted to wholesale dismissals of suspect policemen as a result of Chief Wilson's cleanup efforts, but leniency rather than severity has been the rule in many departments in the past. The late Bruce Smith, one of the nation's foremost police experts, in a little-publicized and exceedingly illuminating study of the New York Police Department completed in 1952, cites the case of a police officer who got drunk off duty and used his weapon to take a man's life. He drew a five-day sentence for the act.

Another officer, brought to trial 40 times for various offenses in the course of 20 years, and found guilty 36 times, received penalties totaling less than 33 days' pay, according to Mr. Smith. In all, of eight police officers who were tried and found guilty on at least 20 different accounts, only two were finally dismissed from the force, he notes. "Very few charges," he stated, "are brought against sergeants and almost none against lieutenants or officers of higher rank, unless and until criminal proceedings are initiated against them by other public agencies. Such puny efforts toward discipline," he declared, stood in "unhealthy contrast" to the sentences that would have been imposed by a criminal court on members of the general public had they committed the identical acts.

Just as police authorities have sought to protect their men in the past, regardless of wrongdoing, so have they frequently been guilty of understating the occurrence of crime for the purpose of preserving "community confidence" in their performance. In his book *The Trouble with Cops,* published in 1955, the late Albert Deutsch noted the effect of an overhaul in New York City's crime-reporting which had been too lax for the FBI to include in its Uniform Crime Reports. "When the record system was improved," said he, "the number of known burglaries reported was multiplied 13 times and the number of robberies fivefold as compared with the last previous period for which figures were available."

St. Louis, a model among record keepers, submits its crime statistics to regular audit by the Governmental Research Institute, a nonprofit business-supported organization which strives for better local government. The agency, inspired for many years by a hard-working dedicated public servant, the scholarly Dr. Victor D. Brannon, has helped institute many modern management techniques in its police force as well as in other local government bodies.

Police officials in many cities have long complained of their inability to hire qualified personnel needed to bring their forces up to authorized strength. However, one retired police consultant, Edwin O. Griffenhagen, of Lake Geneva, Wisconsin, who headed his own firm for forty-five years prior to his retirement in 1959, is "not so sure it is as difficult to get good men as police officials frequently make out."

Many cities, authorities agree, needlessly hamstring themselves by barring the hiring of nonresidents or otherwise limiting the geographical scope of their recruitment. The Police Department of New York City, until late 1961 when it stepped up its recruitment efforts in nearby Connecticut and announced it would also seek men farther afield, was among those most frequently bemoaning its hiring difficulties. The practice has only one purpose: to dispense political patronage within a given voting area. Departments that adhere to it and then blame personnel shortages on the community's niggardliness in paying its police apparently don't trust truth too far.

Reports the District of Columbia's Chief Murray: "We had always been short of our authorized strength until November, 1960, when we sent four teams of two men each into 101 communities in the East and Midwest designated by the Labor Department as high-unemployment areas. Shortly thereafter we had not only filled every one of the 180 vacancies we had at the time, but we developed a backlog of men waiting for jobs." The International Association of Chiefs of Police, for its part, has been a vigorous critic of residence requirements in the recruitment of police personnel. Many communities and departments persist in applying them nevertheless.

The recruitment of detectives comes in for special criticism. Too much emphasis, it is said, is often placed on physical attributes and too little on tested aptitude for analysis and problem-solving. "We might clear more of our crimes with convictions if we were more selective about mental abilities among our detectives," maintains one consultant.

Police department officials can stretch police manpower by employing more civilians to handle clerical and other tasks which don't require the capabilities of a patrolman for their performance. The Los Angeles Police Department figures that in the decade from 1951 to 1961 it freed over 400 police personnel for enforcement duties – and saved the city up to $500,000 a year in the process – by taking them off typewriters, switchboards, filing, stenographic work, and even photography and fingerprinting, and giving those chores largely to clerk-typists. The clerk-typists were paid $246 less per month, and, of course, their qualifications weren't nearly so difficult to come by. According to the city's law-trained Police Chief, William H. Parker, 23 percent of the department's 6,100-person mid-1961 payroll was made up of civilians, compared with only 13 percent of the 4,757 persons the department employed on December 31, 1950.

In Oakland, California, Police Chief Edward M. Toothman recently replaced police personnel with civilians in 30 jail positions and in 18 of the 20 posts in the department's radio room. Civilian personnel already accounted for nearly 25 percent of the department's total employment by 1962. Colonel H. Sam Priest, President of the St. Louis Board of Police Commissioners, reports that even his Research and Planning Division is 100 percent civilian-manned and has been ever since it was established in 1957; the department's training director is also a civilian.

In contrast, only 227 of the 2,973 persons working for the Boston Police Department on the same date, or 7 percent of its total employment, were civilians. New York City's percentage at the time was even lower: approximately 1,250, or 5 percent of its total payroll. Jacob S. Katz, Deputy Police Commissioner in Charge of Administration, notes the proportion of civilians to total department personnel in the city's force has been almost unchanged for "20 years or longer." A visitor to the department in 1961 could have found police personnel performing a wide variety of clerical tasks, including the issuance of licenses for the operation of dance halls, secondhand stores, taxicabs, and other enterprises whose activities are supervised by the department. Deputy Katz blames the scarcity of civilian employees on poor civilian pay for police department positions and undesirable working hours and conditions.

New York Police Commissioner Michael J. Murphy says he "tried to get the Civil Service Commission to provide a differential for civilians working in the department at night, but I haven't gotten anywhere so far." The department at the time had authorization for 24,590 sworn personnel, however, nearly 25 percent more than the 20,000 it had seven years earlier.

A number of departments are easing their manpower problems at low cost and helping to meet future personnel needs as well through the use of police cadets. The system provides for the hiring of young men between the ages of 17 and 21, too young to qualify as police officers. For the most part, they are assigned to clerical and other nonenforcement tasks. The theory is that police aspirants too young for service may thus become better acquainted with it, and it with them, for mutual benefit on future application to the force. The program has a further advantage to the department: its cost is exceedingly modest. The city of Buffalo, New York, launched its cadet program in mid-1961 with a going wage of $2,400 a year; it aimed to have 40 in the corps within four years. Detroit at the time boasted a police cadet corps of 55. A new program in Fresno, California, had cadets experimentally replacing "meter maids" in tabbing overparked cars; the cadets were expected to prove less susceptible to illness, bad weather, and the abuse of motorists than the female meter corps had been.

Some police authorities argue women could be employed to a far greater extent in police work, particularly in certain aspects of detective work, in laboratory and identification assignments, as desk and communications officers, in traffic control and in other roles where personal safety is not in jeopardy.

Another device for stretching manpower, whether the department is utilizing the cadet system or not, consists in the cultivation of an auxiliary or volunteer force. Such forces are being created increasingly by broadening the role of civil defense units. Comprised essentially of males, though conceivably women could be used as well, the auxiliary is expected to purchase its own uniforms and gen-

173

erally is not paid. Candidates are customarily screened first for character. Denver, which turned to the idea in mid-1959 when it had about as much trouble recruiting cadets as recruiting policemen, boasts an auxiliary of approximately 150 members previously organized as a civil defense unit; the group meets monthly for training purposes. It supplements the regular police force in disasters and parades, directs traffic from ball games and other special events, and helps out on such community chores as the posting of Christmas lights. An official of the Denver department finds some of the city's volunteer police "better trained and more enthusiastic than some of our regular officers." They are also taking some of the load off the department from increased traffic, which forced the assignment of 120 men to that function in 1962, twice as many as in 1950.

The International City Managers Association, in a report published not long ago, notes the "widespread organization and use of civilian auxiliary police since World War II." Many of these units, it adds, remain principally "civil defense" in character.

Facilities, as well as manpower, are not being used anywhere near as efficiently as they should be. Bruce Smith, who has followed in his father's footsteps as a police consultant from a base in Norfolk, Virginia, maintains: "Most police station locations in our older cities were laid out before the day of the automobile and the telephone, when they had to be within walking distance for public and patrolman alike. But advances in transportation and communications since that time, which cause the public to phone rather than personally visit stations when they need help and which also permit the dispersal of patrolmen by bus or squad car, make many stations obsolete and unnecessary."

The elder Mr. Smith in 1953 suggested New York City did not need more than 75 stations – but it was still operating five more than that nearly a decade later. In mid-1961, the so-called Blyth-Zellerbach Committee reported that San Francisco could be effectively protected with just four stations; it had nine at the time. In Boston, one of the most heavily-policed cities in the nation in relation to population, City Councilman Gabriel F. Piemonte not long ago pointed to four police stations from the window of his office, all within a five-minute walk from one point. The four, he insisted, could be consolidated into one to cut custodial services, heat and light bills, and eventually the salaries of three of their four captains simply by failing to fill their positions when they retired. The need for lieutenants, sergeants, and clerks to man these stations would similarly be reduced. The elder Smith called for the closing of seven Boston police stations, but not a single one had been shut down thirteen years later.

Police chiefs generally agree on the desirability of operating fewer stations, but they often argue as Washington, D.C., Chief Murray does: "We tried consolidating some stations a few years back, and the people who were losing their station howled from the rooftops. We had to give them back their stations again." To save money on the real estate investment, and communications equipment as well, a small number of cities are housing some police stations with fire companies, a joint tenancy not altogether unknown in the past.

As cities grow together, the principle of local control, which was devised to prevent the concentration of police power in too few hands, tends also to foster conflict, confusion, duplication, and waste. A woman who stopped overnight at a motel in El Portal, near Miami, recalls she had to phone three different police departments to report a suspected prowler outside her door before she got through to the right department; fortunately, she was either mistaken or he moved on, since there was ample time for anyone nearby to fulfill any suspected intentions and move on before the police arrived. In Shelby County, Tennessee, sheriff's cars were having to drive 13 miles to get outside the city of Memphis to begin their patrol but, says Memphis Mayor Henry Loeb, "they would be even less centrally-located if they were headquartered in the county itself." An estate owner summoning police aid in an eastern metropolitan area one day found two squad cars pulling into his driveway; one, it turned out, was a county car with jurisdiction over that particular address and the other was a city car which normally patrolled the area and therefore knew it better. In Los Angeles, not long ago, a speeding motorist managed to accumulate police cars from seven different municipalities before he was finally caught.

A recent study by the Northwestern University Law School found 90 law-enforcement agencies in Chicago's 954-square-mile Cook County. Writing in the *Journal of Criminal Law, Criminology and Political Science,* Gordon Linkon noted these separate agencies "operate for the most part without coordination and many times without knowledge of what other forces in the County are doing or attempting to do. The combined strength of law enforcement in Cook County is so weakened by the discoordinated structure that the process of law enforcement is seriously impeded."

According to the *Municipal Yearbook,* published by the International City Managers Association in Chicago, there were over 40,000 autonomous police jurisdictions operating in the United States in the beginning of 1961. "The political design of law enforcement in this country," says Los Angeles' Chief Parker, "is a tragedy in view of our modern mode of living. We are trying to maintain village-type autonomous law enforcement in areas which have long since outgrown it." Retired consultant Earle W. Garrett, one of the nation's leading police authorities, observes that local municipalities "cling to the police service they know they can control, even though such service is far less efficient than one that would result from a coordination of police departments."

After investigating the highly fragmented metropolitan regions of Cook County, Illinois, in which Chicago is located, Bergen County, New Jersey, and Los Angeles County, the United States Senate Crime Committee, otherwise known as the Kefauver Committee, declared in 1951 it found "no centralized direction of control and no centralized responsibility for seeing that a uniform law-enforcement policy is applied over the entire geographic area of a county. The situation," it went on to state, "lends itself to buck-passing and evasion of responsibility which can only inure to the advantage of gangsters and racketeers. It makes it possible for hoodlums to find those cities and towns where law enforcement is low and to concentrate their operations there."

Widespread agreements calling for mutual aid between police departments, authorities say, are pitiful countermeasures against vice and syndicated crime which know no municipal boundaries. They can also present legal problems for police departments which are parties to such agreements. In Santa Monica, California, a policeman who was shot answering a call for help on the Los Angeles side of a street forfeited his workmen's compensation because he was not legally a ward of the City of Santa Monica when he answered the call outside Santa Monica. The situation has since been remedied by an exchange of benefits between the two cities, but a good many other areas in the country have no such reciprocal arrangements.

Feuding or jealous departments which hide evidence from one another or don't call for assistance until it is too late, needless duplication of records and other facilities, and a thinning of resources which might otherwise be used for better service are just a few of the consequences of fragmented police authority.

Few police experts believe the solution lies in the creation of a single police force for the entire nation. Such an organization would probably be too big even for efficiency, not to say anything of the dangers it might pose to the nation through its concentration of power. A good many police authorities, however, argue the police function would be better served through the consolidation of several departments in a given metropolitan area or at least through the combination of certain of their functions, criminal identification and recordkeeping, for instance.

The lack of communication between departments becomes rather surprising at times. For instance, the Police Department of Oakland, California, in 1956 came up with a system for getting a patrolman's routine reports into the station without his having to come to the station to type them himself or even dictate them by phone, which often leads to errors. The periodic report is one of the big consumers of patrolmen's time in many cities even today. One police authority has estimated patrolmen spend up to 20 percent of their time on reports when they have to type them in the station. The Oakland Police Department simply had its men write their reports on the street in longhand and leave them in the police callbox where a patrol car or wagon picked them up on its regular rounds. "We tried everything," Chief Toothman recalls, "even having the reports phoned in to a tape for transcription by a stenographer later, but nothing has been as cheap or as foolproof as this system." Yet, he admitted, the system had never been written up or otherwise reported to the profession, and, so far as he knew, no one outside the Bay Area had much knowledge of it. A police chief of one of the biggest cities in the area whose own men were still coming into the station to type out their reports five years after the Oakland innovation began, confessed recently to having "heard" about the Oakland system but not being "too familiar" with how it was working out.

Because manpower accounts for so large a portion of

the police budget and because its more effective use is crucial in the combat of crime, new techniques and devices for increasing its effectiveness are vital. Some of the new techniques appear to offer some promise. In mid-1961, for example, the St. Louis Police Department launched its Special Deployment Squads. Two, each consisting of twelve men and women dressed in civilian clothes, roamed high-crime areas night and day as decoys for muggings, purse snatching, holdups, and other crimes. Concealed miniature two-way radios kept them in touch with "cover" cars positioned ahead and behind them. In their first month of operation, the two squads apprehended more than half-a-dozen persons. The squads proved so effective, Police Chief Curtis Brostron decided to place two more just like them on the city's streets only two months after the first two began operating.

St. Louis has also established a special "Mobile Reserve" to saturate heavy crime areas with speedily dispatched forces. The unit in 1961 consisted of 65 men and some 30 cars. It is generally on duty from 7:00 P.M. to 3:00 A.M., though the shift varies as the situation warrants.

San Francisco's "Operation S," created in 1958, goes into action when the crime load becomes too great for its special 12-man night Crime Prevention Squad to handle. In 1961 some 72 officers and 36 squad cars were assigned to the unit. When they're not needed, the men and cars of "Operation S" serve on routine patrol.

Radio communications and recordkeeping leave much to be desired in a great many police departments around the land. Boston claims the distinction of having placed into operation the first police radio system in the United States as far back as 1932. It was still operating the same system in 1962. Recently, when it made a pitch to the city for $250,000 for a new radio network, the department produced a technical report which showed the new unit would pay for itself in five years in gasoline savings alone, since patrol cars would no longer have to race their motors to maintain transmitting power.

New York City's Police Department was unable as late as 1962 to broadcast simultaneously to all patrol cars. It had to relay these calls from one borough to the next. Its radio network was also burdened with some 300,000 ambulance calls yearly. Because of the network's limited capacity, emergency calls may not be taken for several minutes during periods of particularly heavy traffic.

Identification procedures likewise are often cumbersome and slow. St. Louis recently completed the installation of electrically powered card-filing machines which helped reduce its clerical force substantially while also reducing to a matter of minutes identification procedures which previously took half an hour or more. The new automated record room, however, is highly unusual among police departments. Most continue to hobble along with facilities and procedures outdated decades ago.

The weakness of management science in police administration would seem to be further demonstrated by the accumulation of controversy, rather than thoroughly researched evidence, in a surprising number of techniques that are no longer new. Nowhere does that controversy rage more heatedly than around the polygraph, or the lie detector, as it is more commonly known. Essentially, the lie detector is only an instrument for measuring such physiological phenomena as respiration and blood pressure. Its use in crime detection is based on the theory that most people are afraid of getting caught in a lie and show that fear by altering their normal patterns of respiration and blood pressure. The device, however, is not infallible. Some persons just aren't that afraid of being caught or of the instrument's ability to betray them. Others, though innocent, behave as if they are telling a lie when they really aren't. For these reasons, the lie detector is not admissible as evidence in most courts.

But its value as an investigative tool has been proved over and over again. A Los Angeles police official relates how the instrument was used to find a murder weapon: a series of Yes and No questions was put to the suspect until the place where the weapon was hidden was narrowed down sufficiently to permit a search. A gun was subsequently found within feet of the location where the polygraph indicated it might be.

The Police Department of Evanston, Illinois, recently hired the services of a polygraph specialist to screen police candidates who had passed all other qualifying exams. Through use of the device one aspirant who admitted to no crime record was discovered to have committed eight burglaries. Another, who went similarly undetected through interviews and written procedures, was found to have participated in five armed robberies. Still another, who qualified on all other accounts and who might otherwise have been appointed to the force, was identified as a sexual pervert.

Impressed with Evanston's results, the St. Louis Police Department in 1961 hired the same polygraph specialists to screen 50 of its applicants. At $150 a day for an examiner capable of handling 8 applicants in his 8 working hours, the department considered it a bargain: an investment of $16 to $18 per applicant, it figured, might be saving many times that cost in terms of training, equipment, and the betrayal of public trust which might otherwise ensue if due precautions weren't taken. St. Louis, along with other cities, is also submitting applicants to psychiatric examination to reduce chances of hiring sadistic persons or persons otherwise unsuited to the responsibility who may not have betrayed that fact on a crime report. Psychologists have long noted the tendency of police work to attract a certain percentage of maladjusted individuals, but it is still the exceptional force that tries to weed them out with every means at its command.

Indeed, some police forces turn their back even on the polygraph, for this or any other purpose. The New York Police Department is among those who ban its use. New York Police Chief Murphy explains the policy by stating simply that "they're not admissible as evidence in court, so we don't use them." A number of critics contend the use of the polygraph is sometimes prohibited by departments who fear it may be turned against their own police to discredit testimony or for other purposes.

Another practice still debated among police authorities which is not exactly new is the use of dogs in police work. Baltimore, for example, has used German shepherds for searching dark warehouses, controlling unruly gangs, and for other purposes, since 1956. Police Commissioner James H. Hepbron had read of their use in London and dispatched representatives of the department to study the value of dogs in police work firsthand. Within four years, Baltimore had a K-9 corps of 39 dogs. A number of other cities, including Pittsburgh, Houston, St. Louis, and Minneapolis, followed suit with K-9 corps of their own. The dogs are useful, the contention goes, as a deterrent to such crimes as burglaries and robberies and for flushing suspects out of hideaways. They are not trained, however, to kill. The first sign of viciousness generally brings a canine elimination from the force.

Some police authorities, however, remain skeptical of the value of dogs in police work. One consultant argues that "their main use is to produce newspaper stories for publicity-minded chiefs," though he concedes they may have such limited application as routing perverts from parks. "In crime patrols," says he, "they're more of a nuisance than a help."

What about the two-man patrol car: is it really necessary or can the community get more mileage out of its patrol dollar by splitting its men up and giving them a car apiece? This debate, too, has been raging for years without any thoroughgoing effort to investigate scientifically its pros and cons, its dangers and possible means for lessening them. Practices, possibly as a result, vary sharply. Except for a single squad car which is manned by two men only during hours of darkness, the city of Oakland, for example, has been using one-man cars exclusively with no apparent ill effects. New York City, on the other hand, was not operating a single one-man patrol car anywhere in the city in 1961. A top executive contended this was because "driving in New York City occupies all of the driver's attention and one-man patrol cars are anyway unsafe in criminal situations."

Proponents of the one-man car are critical of flat bans against it, arguing that foot patrolmen generally walk their beats alone without even the benefit of a radio, which a man in a squad car has. As for the contention that the driver's time is fully occupied with driving in a city like New York, critics argue that there are sections of the city, residential areas in Queens, for instance, which are no more difficult to drive in nor any more dangerous from the standpoint of crime than the suburbs of many another municipality which does use one-man cars. They further justify the use of one-man cars on the grounds that the mere presence of a police car is reassuring to the public and serves as a deterrent to crime.

The issue of the marked versus the unmarked patrol car is similar unresolved, and likewise a subject of highly divergent practice. The use of unmarked patrol cars, that is, cars which look like any other on the road, is common in such states as Colorado and Connecticut. The theory, of course, is that the unmarked car is more likely to catch violators and discourage others from speeding. Police authorities in other locales, Los Angeles for one, argue the presence of the law should be made as conspicuous as possible as a means of deterring violations of the law which, they argue, is after all their principal function. The

183

same philosophy gives rise to the removal of motorcycle cops from behind billboards and their making themselves conspicuous even to the extent of moving along with traffic, if at a slightly slower pace.

While police experts go on debating such basic issues as the unmarked car, the one- and two-man patrol, the use of dogs, and the pitfalls of the polygraph, they generally agree on one point: that more research is needed on these and other aspects of police administration and that very little research of this nature is being conducted at present simply because no one department is large or rich enough to finance it, and even if one was, the application of its findings to other cities might be questioned. They agree on the need for – but don't yet foresee – the creation of a national agency which might carry on these functions independent of individual departments.

Whether police departments generally would follow the findings of such an agency or continue to go on their own ways as they see fit is another question. Few departments even now bother to call in outside help for advice or scrutiny. One organization particularly well qualified to provide it, as it often does, is the International Association of Chiefs of Police, with headquarters in Washington and a field staff roaming the nation. The organization, however, will make only those investigations requested of it by a department's chief of police. If he does not care for its advice on a particular subject, for one reason or another, it makes little difference who exhorts it to do so, the I.A.C.P. will not investigate. Boston officials found that out recently when they attempted to get the I.A.C.P. to make a study of the city's police department at a time when former Boston Police Commissioner Leo J. Sullivan was being asked for his resignation by Governor John A. Volpe following a television show which depicted as many as ten Boston policemen entering and leaving a bookmaking establishment.

Police departments which will go out and hire outside consultants of their own accord are rare. Again, St. Louis stands out in this respect. That city's Board of Police Commissioners in 1957 authorized the independent Governmental Research Institute to do whatever consulting work it considered necessary, including the hiring of other outside authorities at the Department's expense; G.R.I. hired the services in 1957 and 1958 of Orlando Wilson while he was still at the University of California, and subsequently of Sanford Shoults, who had gone from a high-ranking post with the Detroit Police Department to the faculty of the School of Police Administration at Michigan State University and then to the University of Arizona to develop courses in police administration.

Mr. MacNamara, of New York's Institute of Criminology, however, figures: "There are over 40,000 police jurisdictions in the country, but I doubt if more than 20 of them a year hire consultants to look into the way their departments are run and to make recommendations."

Not too many, it might be added, want the looking glass lifted before them. Until they do, however, the growing burdens of mounting crime and spreading urbanization will continue to catch them off balance.

A WORD ON JUVENILE DELINQUENCY

ONE factor which is likely to aggravate policing problems in the years ahead is the persisting rise in juvenile delinquency. The number of youngsters in the critical 14- to 17-year-old age group will swell nearly 50 percent in the decade to 1971. Because the jobless rate is about three times as high among unskilled youth as it is among adults, unemployment could strike hard at those failing to pursue their education into higher institutions of learning. Climbing divorce rates and the deterioration of family relationships that previously nourished respect and compassion for others are also likely to contribute to the rise in youthful lawbreaking in the future.

A great many efforts – federal, state, and local – are being directed against the surge in juvenile crime, and some may yet be successful. But they probably will not be found in the bargain basement. Keenly aware of that probability, the Congress in 1961 passed an act authorizing the expenditure of $10 million yearly for a period of at least three years to stimulate local efforts in combating juvenile delinquency. The first project to gain its support, $1.9 million to be provided over a three-year period, was a massive effort aimed at reforming the entire Lower East Side of New York City at a total cost to local, state, federal, and private agencies over the period of some $12.6 million. The area's 107,000 population at the time had an average family income of $69 a week; only 15 percent of its adults had ever finished high school. The program, which got under way in the summer of 1962, was fashioned by an organization known as Mobilization for Youth, Inc. It was designed, in the words of then Attorney General Robert F. Kennedy, to give the area's youth "a stake in conformity."

The project, a sort of Golden Gate of social engineering, ran the gamut from organizing the play of seven-year-olds to providing jobs for 16- to 21-year-olds in an Urban Service Corps, repairing tenements, beautifying the neighborhood, and otherwise dressing up the cityscape and enhancing municipal services. An "adventure corps" on paramilitary lines was to be provided for boys 9 to 13. In addition to a host of special facilities, including three "cool and jazzy" coffee shops featuring art and folk music, 300 "homework-helpers" were to tutor failing pupils, teachers' home visits were to be stepped up, educational and cultural efforts were to be aimed at adults as well as their offspring, and welfare programs tailored to troubled families, addicted youth, and other social diseases were also to be provided.

The task nevertheless was awesome: delinquency rates among those 7 to 20 years of age had risen from 28.7 per 1,000 in 1951 to 62.8 in 1960.

In the past, combatants of juvenile delinquency have produced almost as much confusion as they have practical results, and sometimes more. So many organizations have become involved in the battle and so much has been written on the subject, that two new libraries were created recently to specialize in this field alone: one, by the National Institute of Mental Health, and the other by the National Research and Information Center on Crime and Delinquency. In Los Angeles County, over 90 autonomous community groups are estimated to be working on the problem.

Some of the techniques for combating juvenile delinquency appear to be working in some areas, at least for the time being. Plainclothes patrolmen in Jersey City who get their leads from school authorities have proved effective in getting problem youngsters in for medical and psychological treatment before they end up in court. Clubs organized by businessmen and other public-minded citizens in such cities as St. Louis and Columbus have succeeded in directing the interest of youths toward athletics and the arts and away from diversions that lead to violence and destruction. Supervised recreation in parks and community centers has also helped direct youthful energies into healthier channels. Work programs and efforts to keep youngsters from dropping out of high school also apparently are achieving results.

Despite these efforts, expenditures, and occasional accomplishments, however, the wave of juvenile delinquency is on a sharp upgrade. According to the Children's Bureau in Washington, 1960 was the twelfth consecutive year in which juvenile crime rose to a new peak – up 6 percent from 1959. According to California Probation Officer Karl Holton, the number of San Quentin inmates under 25 years of age rose 40 percent in the 15 years to 1962; the California Youth Authority, he notes further, had 5,000 boys and girls in its correctional schools compared to 1,200 in 1941. Former Attorney General Kennedy repeatedly warned that the problem of juvenile delinquency would be "unbeatable" if it were not licked before the 1960's were out. He figures that by 1970, some 7 million high school dropouts will be entering the labor market – 2 million of them without ever having finished the eighth grade.

The rise in juvenile delinquency is not only making vast sections of the nation's larger cities unsafe, it is rapidly spilling over into the suburbs as well. A Senate Judiciary Subcommittee late in 1961 reported juvenile crime was rising considerably faster in suburban and rural areas than in central cities. The Family Service Association of Nassau County, one of metropolitan New York's richer counties, was getting a hundred calls a month in 1961 from parents seeking help in controlling delinquent youngsters.

Juvenile delinquents rarely grow up to become good husbands, wives, and parents, though they marry and have children like everyone else. With their own flock of problem children to add to those society is already producing, the problem is one that could multiply many times over.

As with so many of its other urban ills, the nation could do worse than to look to foreign lands for a clue to the solution of its problems, in this area as in others. In this respect, Switzerland, particularly, bears study. That mountain land under the social microscope reveals not only close family ties but also a severity that prohibits youngsters under 16 from entering motion picture houses and those under 18 from obtaining drivers' licenses. The nation has succeeded in producing generation after generation of youngsters dedicated to hard work, the vigorous pursuit of sports, and a healthy respect for their elders and the law.

The nation, it should be noted, also has one of the lowest divorce rates in the world, has traditionally placed its teachers in high financial and communal regard, encourages thrift through small allowances, and fosters discipline through a brief period of military service required annually of all youths from ages 21 to 33.

Whether these phenomena are responsible for the remarkably high state of social health among Switzerland's youth, of course, has yet to be proved. It would be surprising, however, if delinquency rates rise in that country in the future while these stanchions still stand.

It is hardly likely that similar measures could be widely adopted in this country, but there is no reason why the vein cannot be mined for some useful ore.

CHAPTER SEVEN

Fire!

THERE'S a town in New Jersey with a population of approximately 20,000 and another in the state of Washington with 12,000 which have twice as many fire trucks as men to man them. One has ten trucks with five men on each shift and the other eight trucks with four men.

The New Jersey and Washington towns are extremes, to be sure. But they are becoming increasingly typical in one respect: more and more paid fire departments around the country are finding themselves unable to keep their companies up to strength. On the one hand, sharp and continuing reductions in the fireman's workweek are yanking manhours out of the firehouse. On the other, increases in pay are leaving fire departments with scant means to go out and hire the additional men needed to maintain round-the-clock strength, much less expand it to meet the added requirements of urban growth.

Notes Warren Y. Kimball, Fire Service Department Manager of the National Fire Protection Association, a Boston-based nonprofit organization: "In the vast majority of cities, the undermanning of fire companies is so critical as to seriously cripple the ability of the fire department to promptly combat anything more than the smallest fires." John A. Neale, retired Chief Engineer of the National Board of Fire Underwriters, contends: "With the exception of a handful of our largest cities, not one city or town fire department in the U.S. is adequately manned, and it's getting worse as the workweek gets shorter."

So widespread has the practice become of sending out

fire equipment with one driver or a driver and just one companion aboard that the vehicles have come to be known among professional fire fighters as "our $25,000 taxis." Fire burdens and fire hazards, in the meantime, have been vaulting with the spread of new homes and other structures across the landscape and with the rise in property values generally. Despite the wholesale replacement of tinderbox frame construction by fireproof steel and glass edifices, many new dangers are presenting themselves in the form of bottled gas used in more and more rural homes and recreation places, the broader use of an expanding variety of electrical appliances, the more widespread installation of certain types of fibrous board, soundproofing, and plastics which, while they may not be inflammable in themselves, are speedy spreaders of flame.

It is true that some particularly troublesome problems, pumps at gasoline stations, for instance, are nowhere near the fire hazard they once were. But there are also new problems to face: windowless buildings, even those made of steel, may turn into blazing furnaces, building up temperatures well above the 200 degrees (Fahrenheit) firemen can normally stand even with protective gear. Buildings with windows, on the other hand, permit heat to escape through the broken glass.

The nation's losses from building fires rose 70 percent in the decade to 1960, according to the National Board of Fire Underwriters. Counting automobile, aircraft, ship, forest, and other nonstructural fires, the nation in 1960 suffered the direct loss of more than $1.5 billion worth of property by fire. Another billion over and above what burned, went for insurance coverage on what, fortunately, didn't burn; it's estimated that approximately 85 percent of what burns is covered by the more than $2.5 billion that is paid out annually in fire-insurance premiums. Still another $1.65 billion is spent yearly on fire departments and other suppression activities. Including an estimated

$700 million in added building costs to comply with fire codes, the annual cost of fire and the threat of fire to the nation is estimated at close to $5 billion a year.

There are also the indirect costs of fire – wages lost from injuries, lost production and idleness during the period of reconstruction, or permanently lost jobs when reconstruction is not feasible. One fire that blazed in the town of Ayer, Massachusetts (1960 population: 15,000), in June, 1961, destroyed both of the town's two biggest industries, throwing 20 percent of its breadwinners out of work for several weeks.

Incalculable, of course, is the cost in human lives. Some 11,700 persons perished in fire in 1961, about 6,100 of them in residential dwellings. Half the victims were children, one-third of whom had been left home alone. All told, single and two-family homes accounted for 542,000 of 880,000 building fires reported in the United States in 1959; fewer than 38,000 of those units were apartments.

Fire officials complain it is often easier to get communities to buy a new piece of apparatus, which they can see, than it is to get them to hire the men needed to man the apparatus they already have. It is also much cheaper: figuring the average life of a fire truck at a minimum of 15 years, even a $30,000 vehicle works out to only $2,000 per annum, about a third or less than what a rookie fireman must be paid a year. Even then, it takes approximately four firemen to fill one round-the-clock duty position every day of the year.

How does the average citizen know when his department is seriously undermanned? An N.F.P.A. pamphlet suggests he has only to count the men on a fire truck the next time it answers a call. If there are only two men and a driver, as often happens in small and medium-sized cities, the equipment, says the N.F.P.A., cannot possibly be operated anywhere near as effectively as it was designed to operate. The National Board of Fire Underwriters, on the basis of

half a century of fire experience, maintains that at least
five men are needed on a pumper, including the driver,
who is as much a fireman as the rest of the crew, and at
least six men on a ladder truck. Some fire chiefs believe
they can get by with one man less on each vehicle in districts of moderate hazard, but even by these standards a
great many fire departments around the country are sorely
undermanned. And their number, according to the N.B.
F.U., is rising constantly as two- and three-man fire crews
become increasingly common. The truck with just two men
leaves only one for entering a burning building, because
one must operate the apparatus. The board calls the one-
man entry, for either fire-fighting or life-saving purposes,
"entirely unsafe."

The manpower shortage in the nation's firehouses is not
due to inability to find men willing to do the job. Three
years after it had given its last exams in 1958, Chicago
still had 2,000 qualified applicants on its waiting list,
according to William E. Quinn, Administrative Assistant
to the Commissioner. Many other cities also have long
waiting lists for firemen's jobs but lack the budgets to
hire them.

It's not the pay that attracts firemen so much as the
work schedule and the opportunity it affords for holding
down a second job. Most big cities in 1961 were paying
new recruits only a little over $5,000 a year, but giving
them 20 full days off for every 32 they worked, generally
on 24-hour shifts which permit sleeping from approximately 10:00 P.M. to 7:00 A.M.

Most cities make no effort whatsoever to prevent their
firemen from holding a second job. Some permit it under
certain conditions. Only about 10 percent prohibit the
practice altogether, according to a recent survey by the
International City Managers Association. Where restrictions exist, they are customarily directed against strenuous,
hazardous, or undignified labor and against soliciting, par-

Sick Cities

ticularly fire insurance. And even departments that ban the practice altogether, such as New York's, often find it more practical to turn their heads the other way, as so often happens in the police service. Others with restrictions enforce them with varying vigor.

THE FIREMAN'S TIME

FIREMAN'S CALENDAR
ON A 63-HOUR WORK WEEK
32-DAY CYCLE

On Duty: 24 hours,
shifts changing at 8 A.M.
20 full days (and nights) off
in 32-day period

Sun	Mon	Tue	Wed	Thur	Fri	Sat		No. Days Per Week On	Off
1	2	3	4	5	6	7		3⅓	3⅔
8	9	10	11	12	13	14		2⅓	4⅔
15	16	17	18	19	20	21		2⅓	4⅔
22	23	24	25	26	27	28		3⅓	3⅔
29	30	31	1					0	4
							Total	12	20

One city manager who attempted to enforce his city's ban against "moonlighting" by both police and firemen recently reported his experience anonymously to the I.C. M.A. "Approximately a year ago," said he, "I endeavored to enforce the rules of the police and fire department which prohibited outside employment in order to provide more jobs in this industrial city which was rather hard hit by the recession. The fire fighters immediately brought action in court to enjoin me from enforcing the rules. After prolonged discussions, the City Council decided against any stringent regulations of this sort, and as a result, the portion of the Municipal Code governing employees was amended. The amendment, in effect, allows every employee to hold two jobs as long as it is not incompatible with his municipal employment."

Some cities require firemen holding second jobs to sign waivers freeing the municipality of its responsibility for providing workmen's compensation, sick leave, and other benefits that might be necessitated by outside employment.

194

Many municipalities continue to provide such benefits, however.

The proportion of firemen holding second jobs has been estimated as high as 70 percent in some cities. Fire Chief C. D. Williams of Las Vegas, Nevada, early in 1962 figured his men were averaging about 20 hours a week of outside employment. He estimated their average outside earnings at about $50 a week.

The average fire department workweek in 1960 totaled 63 hours, with the smallest cities averaging 68 and the larger ones 56. Since most cities operate their fire departments on a 24-hour shift, a 63-hour week gives firemen 20 full days off in every 32. And the pressure is on in some cities to lower the workweek further. Before World War II, the fireman's typical workweek was 70 to 72 hours. Today, 48- and even 40-hour weeks are not uncommon among fire departments in large cities, and few work longer than 56 hours a week.

New York City firemen went to a 40-hour workweek January 1, 1963, but it is run on a five-day, eight-hour basis. Firemen in some cities have been pressing for a 40- or even a 48-hour week to be performed in a single session, thus giving them five days off for every two they are on. Such workweeks, however, are still unknown.

Shortened workweeks, of course, play havoc with fire-department manning requirements. A 33 percent reduction in the workweek, from 84 to 56 hours for instance, boosts personnel needs 50 percent after allowing for days off and vacations, notes William B. Marx, Staff Assistant for the International Association of Fire Chiefs, headquartered in New York. It takes 2.92 men to fill one fire position on a round-the-clock basis in a department on a 64-hour workweek, but 4.44 men on a 42-hour basis, the I.A.F.C. notes.

Demands for shorter hours, moreover, have been coupled with pressure for better pay. Though their average workweek was reduced a third or more in the fifteen years following World War II, firemen's pay in the same period doubled. From 1947 to 1957 alone, it rose from a big-city average of $2,389 a year to $4,350 a year, according to the I.C.M.A. And it has risen considerably since. Los Angeles, for instance, gave its firemen an 11 percent pay hike in mid-1961, raising rookies to $6,900 a year.

Because they are better organized than they ever have been, firemen may be even more effective in pushing their demands in the future. The majority of paid fire departments, in fact, have been unionized since the end of World War II. Some 80 percent of Chicago's 4,500-man force were counted as members of the AFL-CIO International Association of Fire Fighters by 1962. In Los Angeles, where the local police and firemen's protective association has represented firemen for over 35 years and still claims 95 percent of the department's membership, the number of men who have also inked allegiance to the AFL-CIO rose from approximately 300 in 1956 to over 3,000 in 1961. The AFL-CIO in 1962 claimed to represent some 100,000 men, or 96 percent of the men paid to fight fires in the United States; it had 1,400 locals around the country at the time, more than twice as many as it had in 1942.

Public law, reaffirmed in most cases by union constitutions, prohibits firemen from striking. But the fact that they are better organized and can bring their influence to bear on legislative bodies is significant nevertheless. Says one Southern California city manager: "There's almost nothing they want that they don't get from their state legislatures – if not on the first try, then on the second or the third."

Big cities, of course, are highly dependent on professional fire fighters. Small ones rely heavily on volunteers. This is the principal reason why fire protection costs roughly twice as much per person in big cities than in small ones.

The community's protection against fire is not to be found entirely in the adequacy of its fire force. Sufficient water at the right pressure in the right place at the right time may be even more important. One of the worst fires in American annals started in a house across the street from a fire station in Shreveport, Louisiana, on September 4, 1925. Because the city's water system was out of service at the time, owing to a break in the main, 196 homes were consumed before the fire spent itself. In contrast, a few adept home-owners manning nothing but garden hoses were able to prevent their roofs from igniting in the midst of the holocaust that swept palatial Bel Air, California, for three days in November, 1961, destroying some 500 homes.

No one is about to contend a good water system makes professional fire fighters unnecessary. It is significant, however, that in evaluating the level of fire protection in a given city for purposes of insurance classification, the National Board of Fire Underwriters places greater weight on water systems than on fire departments. An inadequate water supply may bring the municipality up to 1,700 deficiency points, or 34 percent of the 5,000 possible, but the worst conceivable fire department will penalize it only 1,500 points, or 30 percent of the possible maximum. The next biggest items are structural conditions (700), the effectiveness of its fire-alarm system (550), its fire-prevention measures (300), and its building laws (200). The deficiency points are then used to rate cities, from Class 1 (0 to 500 deficiency points) to Class 10 (4,501 and over).

Because the board's classification is so important in the calculation of fire-insurance rates, it frequently shows good financial sense as well as sound precautionary judgment for cities to spend a little extra to improve their ratings one way or another. The town of Kettering, Ohio, recently put $146,000 into additional fire hydrants and other improvements in its water system, more fire-fighting apparatus, and a new fire station to house its fire services. In doing so, it raised its fire grade sufficiently to save property owners an estimated $46,000 in insurance premiums annually, enough to pay for the investment, with interest, in less than three years' time.

Alarm systems are also vital to cities seeking to protect themselves against ravage by flame. Unfortunately, however, there can be false signals as well as valid ones. False alarms have been the bane of fire departments since the invention of telegraphy enabled cities to put emergency call boxes on the street with the pull-down handles so tempting to youngsters. False alarms endanger firemen and others by putting fire trucks on the road and by temporarily robbing the community of a certain amount of fire protection. More firemen lose their lives in traffic accidents on their way to fires, in fact, than are killed fighting fires, according to the I.A.F.C.

False alarms also add to expenditures. The city of Boston figures the 4,285 false alarms its fire department answered in 1960 set the city back over $400,000.

Though the national average for maliciously-sounded false alarms runs around 13 percent of all fire calls turned in, some communities are plagued by a much higher proportion. As a result, scores of municipalities in recent years, figuring that most of their fire calls were coming in these days by telephone anyway, have yanked out their old alarm boxes or, in the case of new developments, not bothered to install them in the first place. Some of these communities, young and old alike, have turned toward the installation of a relatively new type of emergency alarm system consisting of a telephone inside a red metal call box, much like those used by policemen on street corners. The telephone is linked directly to a switchboard in the city's fire dispatch center, so its location is known as soon as the phone is lifted from its cradle in the same manner that the location of the telegraph box is known as soon as the handle is pulled. The phone, however, has several obvious advantages over the telegraph type of alarm: the opportunity for imparting additional information may enable the fire dispatcher more accurately to gauge equipment needs; in the case of an automobile fire, he might send a single truck instead of an entire company. And, of course, the telephone-type alarm permits the reporting of other emergencies besides fires, such as broken water mains or the need for ambulance or police service.

More than fifty cities around the country are currently estimated to be using emergency telephone alarm systems. Exactly how effective the telephone system is in reducing the number of false alarms, however, is difficult to determine. The jingles often outnumber the false alarms that used to be turned in over the old system, possibly because children are too familiar with telephones to be awed by them, where they might hesitate to pull a lever. Like the old-fashioned alarm boxes, the telephones are located about four feet off the ground – not a difficult height for a child on a tricycle.

San Pedro, Los Angeles' port, replaced its old-fashioned alarm boxes with more than 300 telephone units back in 1957. In the ensuing five years, according to a fire department official, it recorded some 12,000 voiceless signals – "not a single one of them," says he, "a valid fire report." San Pedro figures it is getting about three to four times as many "voiceless signals" as the false alarms it got with the old equipment, but it isn't yanking the phone apparatus out yet. The city notes that almost every one of the voice reports that do come in are valid and that most of them are informative enough to permit the department to dispatch fewer vehicles than it ordinarily would on a "blind" alarm. The system is also being used about as often for reporting nonfire as for reporting fire emergencies, thereby, theoretically at least, increasing its usefulness to the community.

Some fire departments manage to solve the problem of the voiceless signal by ignoring them altogether. They do not even bother to log them, though this is against N.B.F.U. rules.

Some fire authorities argue that alarm systems of all kinds have been rendered unnecessary, at least in residential areas, by the ordinary telephone. A 300-day survey in Miami revealed 88 percent of its fire calls were phoned in from ordinary telephones in homes or public places. "Except in business and commercial districts where an ordinary phone is unavailable at night and on weekends," says one fire chief, "the alarm box – even the telephone type – is an obsolete and, in fact, a very costly device." Few fire authorities, however, are willing to do away with the firebox altogether, even in residential districts.

The task of the city in improving or even protecting its level of fire protection is being made infinitely more difficult by suburbanization. Vast new areas suddenly need fire protection. Thicker traffic must be negotiated over longer distances. And a growing number of independent municipalities have to fend for themselves, on fire protection as on other vital services. All this at a time when many central cities are themselves falling into a state of disrepair and city planners are laying out suburban patterns that, while they may serve other needs, seldom make fire fighting any easier. Cul-de-sacs, for instance, those bulbously-rounded dead ends designed to keep through traffic out of residential streets, are adding as much as a mile to fire department runs in some Los Angeles areas, according to Captain Virgil C. DeLapp of the L.A.F.D. The city in 1960 had only one fireman for every 34 city blocks; more compact cities, such as New York and Chicago, had one for every 16 and 11 blocks, respectively.

The instrument that has carved the urban scene across the rural landscape, the automobile, has contributed to the fire problem in a direct manner as well. It is making fire as commonplace on the roadways of some communities as it is among residences. It is also aggravating the need for public ambulance services, often the responsibility of fire departments. The city of Los Angeles, for instance, assumed that function in the San Fernando Valley in 1957 when it decided it did not like the renewal bids it was getting from private ambulance firms. Those departments which have been providing municipal ambulance service for a good many years are having to increase their rescue activities. With 18,000 more ambulance cases to handle yearly, the Chicago Fire Department in 1962 was operating 23 ambulances compared with 17 in 1957. Fire department ambulance service is generally provided free of charge, though it is customarily limited to hardship or emergency cases.

Like police departments around the country, fire departments are also burdened these days with an increase in juvenile delinquency. Approximately 50 percent of the fires chargeable to arsonists in the United States in 1959 were probably set by juveniles, according to a study of the Arson Committee of the I.A.F.C. Pranksters and demented adults used to be the principal pyromaniacs before World War II, according to fire authorities.

Technological as well as sociological factors are tending to boost fire-protection costs. It is true, of course, that every new device which helps prevent a fire or reduces the costliness of one that has started also lightens the fire department burden. More often than not, however, the savings tend to accrue in the form of lower insurance premiums and reduced fire losses rather than in perceptible savings in the fire department budget. Indeed, the budget may have to be increased because of the availability and demand for better and more effective equipment.

One of the more noteworthy advances in fire-fighting equipment is the so-called "snorkel" or "aerial platform" pioneered by the Chicago Fire Department. The cranelike structure, mounted on a special vehicle, can thrust as many as five men 80 feet or more in any direction in a matter of seconds with a nozzle braced, ready for training on fires several stories above the ground, if necessary. The apparatus is useful also for conducting reconnaissance, such as peering over roofs to see where a blaze may be coming from, and for life-saving purposes where it is not feasible to raise a ladder.

Ordinary fire trucks have themselves become more versatile. Turbine engines, the same type used in jetliners, are enabling big ladder trucks to negotiate steep hills with ease and speed in such cities as San Francisco and Seattle. They are priced well above the usual ladder truck, however.

Fire departments must keep abreast of strides in communications as well as in transportation. Two- and three-way radio enables fire trucks to make rounds of the community on prevention missions and still be available for emergency service. In 1959 the Los Angeles Fire Department put a vehicle into service known as a "command post," complete with radio transmitters and receivers, detailed maps on plotting tables, and other equipment for directing strategy and coordinating efforts in major disasters.

Fire departments are turning to television, too, as a means of making their efforts more effective. Chicago in 1961 began experimenting with the use of an infrared camera capable of being thrust through a window at the end of a snorkel or other device to peer through smoke so the exact location of a flame might be determined and a nozzle directed at it. The department has also used closed-circuit television to direct strategy at the scene of large fires, warn firemen of collapsing structures, and for other purposes. Television is also being used by fire departments for training personnel by bringing lectures, demonstrations, and films to firemen on duty in the station.

Some fire authorities believe the day may not be too far off when special radio-controlled drones will be mounted on strategic rooftops throughout the city for dispatching over a fire area as soon as the alarm is sounded. The dummy missiles, as they see it, would hover over the fire scene telecasting the view to vehicles still making their way on the ground. The picture, picked up on the screen of a small receiver on the fire truck, would ease the mapping of strategy and the understanding of instructions, and thereby save precious minutes. Missiles capable of spreading fire-retarding chemicals, such as borates, have already been designed for use in fighting forest fires.

Technology, in fact, is lifting the fireman in many ways from the customary medium – the surface of the earth and sea – and giving him new fire-fighting and salvage opportunities in the air and even under water. The Los Angeles Fire Department laid out $54,000 in 1961 for the purchase of its fire helicopter – painted in bright fireman's red – to reconnoiter remote fire areas, direct strategy, and for special purposes such as helping to lay hose over vast distances or dropping water or other fire retardants on otherwise inaccessible blazes. A number of major cities have trained firemen as frogmen to fight wharf and other marine fires, conduct undersea salvage, and perform rescue operations.

Technology presents new tasks as well as new opportunities for fire fighters. The jetliner, with its horrendous potentiality for spreading disaster in mishap, is a noteworthy example. The automobile, of course, is another.

Technology's effects, fortunately, are not all on the burdensome side. One of the biggest of all recent fire-fighting advances, in fact, consists simply in the use of spray or "fog" nozzles whose effectiveness in speedily snuffing out fire was amply demonstrated by World War II shipboard experience. Besides being more efficient in the use of water to lower temperatures over a wider area, the fog nozzle reduces the manpower required to manipulate hose. A big hose 2.5 inches in diameter generally entails the use of four men for its control where a stream nozzle is used; three is usually enough if it is a fog nozzle. Because it uses less water to do the job and is responsble for less flooding, the fog nozzle also helps reduce losses due to water damage. It is more hazardous under certain circumstances, owing to the danger of superheated steam in confined areas. Nevertheless, the fog nozzle is now in common use among fire departments throughout the country, generally as a combination unit which can be switched from fog to straight stream, as conditions require.

To increase the effectiveness of the fog nozzle still further, a number of fire departments are experimenting with large portable blowers mounted on a vehicle to direct the spray over still greater distances. The additional weight of the blowers and their limited use, however, may make it impractical for ordinary fire trucks to carry blowers in their present form.

Communications advances coupled with speedier vehicles are making it possible for fire departments to eliminate many stations erected at only five- or six-block intervals in an era when fire wagons were drawn by horses and alarms were borne by foot. Fire administrators, however, haven't proved much more successful with this opportunity than have their colleagues at the police station – for much the same reasons. For one thing, there is a natural reluctance in the department itself to trim the size of its organization. For another, there is frequently considerable opposition to the closing of a facility from those in the immediate neighborhood. The economies from such consolidations, however, can be considerable. Los Angeles figures it saved $125,000 a year in salaries alone when it used one new fire station in 1961 to replace two old ones.

"Altogether too many stations are operating only seven or eight blocks from other stations," contends one fire authority. The N.B.F.U. figures a single fire station should be capable of covering a radius of up to three-quarters of a mile in high-value commercial districts, 1.5 miles in ordinary residential areas, and three miles in areas where buildings are scattered.

Fire!

Some big-city fire departments are attempting to stretch their resources by laying greater stress on volunteer help. There's nothing new in the idea, of course. The first fire department in the American colonies, set up in Philadelphia in 1735 largely on the instigation of Benjamin Franklin, was a volunteer force. It was not, in fact, until the late 1800's that any American municipality started employing full-time paid firemen. Even today, volunteer firemen outnumber their paid counterparts by approximately 1.5 million to 1 million. Paid firemen are almost unheard of in communities of less than 15,000 population. Some 90 percent of the nation's 20,000-odd fire departments in 1960 were volunteer departments.

At least one small community, Castlewood, Colorado (1962 population: approximately 600), has a daytime volunteer force consisting entirely of women. The petticoat brigade has responded to as many as six or seven calls in a single week, including grass fires and traffic accidents, within its 24-square-mile area just south of Denver.

Chicago has turned several of its civil-defense auxiliaries into volunteer fire brigades in recent years. It also uses members of two fire-fighter clubs, known as the "511 Club" and "The Fire Fans Association," to augment its strength at extra-alarm blazes. Members of the clubs responded to a total of 163 calls in 1960.

Few fire experts, however, expect any real solution to the fire manpower problem to come from volunteer help. Sprawling urbanization, increased traffic congestion, the rise of suburban industry, and the greater variety and complexity of modern fires all conspire against the effectiveness of occasional part-time assistance in the fighting of fires. The strongest hope for combating growing fire problems, authorities agree, lies in getting property owners and others to make their contributions against fire by preventing or frustrating it in the first place through the broader use of fire-retardant and fire-resistant materials and through the wider use of overhead sprinklers and automatic alarms.

A sign of things to come on the residential fire scene was quite possibly posted in the town of Quincy, Massachusetts (population 50,000), early in 1958 following a series of bad fires, when an ordinance was enacted requiring all homes built after July 1st of that year to contain automatic detection and alarm equipment. The ordinance, which added about $100 to home-construction costs, requires provision of standby batteries for automatic use should customary power sources fail. Besides protecting the home itself and its occupants, of course, the unit also promotes the safety of neighboring persons and property. Similar ordinances have been debated in other Massachusetts communities since, but the price is more than many, apparently, care to bear.

The installation of automatic sprinklers, fire alarms, or other devices in residential units could lighten fire losses considerably and thereby reduce both insurance rates and fire-fighting budgets. Their installation would not have to be compelled by law. Tax concessions, or penalties, might well be used to spur their adoption. Tax concessions for this purpose could conceivably pay for themselves over the long run. The universal adoption of automatic sprinkler systems in Boston's new $50 million-plus Prudential Center is credited by city officials as making unnecessary the provision of a fire station which might otherwise have been required on the site.

The United States has traditionally employed about three times as many firemen in its big cities as European nations, yet its fire losses customarily run anywhere from three to six times as high. The difference in fire-fighting records between American and European cities is explained in part, of course, by differences in the use of building materials. European structures, at least until relatively recently, were commonly built of stone. In the United States, wood has long been the predominant building material. Wood shingle roofs, a particular fire hazard, have been much more commonly used on American than on European dwellings, though the English and other Europeans employed a more dangerous roofing material still for some centuries previously: thatching.

The fire menace imposed by wood shingle roofing came in for special attention following the blaze that did $24 million worth of damage in the fashionable Bel Air section of Los Angeles late in 1961. Popped by the heat and carried by raging winds, some blazing shingles traveled half a mile away, over the eight-lane San Diego Freeway, starting fires and destroying scores of additional homes in the expensive Brentwood section of the city farther to the west. Instances have been recorded in previous conflagrations of burning shingles starting fires as far as three miles away and, in one case, of landing on the deck of a ship eight miles at sea. Because of the dangers they present, wood shingles also tie up fire fighters protecting roofs when they are urgently needed to combat the fire itself. Over 600 communities in the United States have banned the use of wood shingle roofing.

Some fire experts believe basic fire prevention philosophy, at least as much as differences in building materials, explains the better fire records of European countries. France and Germany, for instance, fix the responsibility for a fire on the party experiencing the fire. Unless he can prove it was not due to his own carelessness or neglect, he is held responsible for any damage done to the property of others and even for a certain portion of the municipality's costs in fighting the fire on his own premises. The insurance premiums of the Frenchmen and the Germans customarily reflect these liabilities, and generally rise when the individual's fire record is a poor one. In certain German cities and elsewhere, the insurance operation is owned by the municipality, with a portion of insurance profits going toward fire-department costs.

The principle of pinning the blame on the victim doesn't set too well with Americans but the idea of placing added emphasis on prevention is gaining wider currency. "Practically no fire department in the country was doing any real fire prevention work when I entered this field in the 1920's," N.F.P.A. General Manager Percy Bugbee recalls. "Now," says he, "most of them do so." Departments in bigger cities, in fact, have rather sizable staffs to do nothing but fire-prevention work – along educational, inspectional, and other lines. The city of Los Angeles in 1962 had some 130 men engaged exclusively in fire-prevention activities; in addition, its entire on-duty force was assigned to such work for approximately five hours a day three days a week – Mondays, Tuesdays, and Wednesdays.

Fire departments are carrying their prevention activities increasingly to the home, sending their vehicles into the community with trained personnel to carry out inspections and instruct homeowners against hazards. Though such activities are for their own benefit, residents sometimes resent the intrusion – or, unconsciously perhaps, the reminder of unpleasant realities they would sooner not face. To overcome such resistance, fire departments have taken to promoting their product – prevention – in much the same manner that those selling commercial wares and services do.

Many departments, including that of Covina, California, distribute leaflets to remind homeowners that they are after all paying for prevention services as taxpayers and that they should ask for them. Nearby Anaheim occasionally purchases television time for the same purpose, in the hope of sharpening the community's fire-consciousness as well as its appreciation of the department generally. The city of Del Mar, just north of San Diego, achieves its prevention objectives at almost no cost at all to the community by using a volunteer Women's Fire Brigade to make its house-to-house calls; the women receive professional instruction in lecture sessions at the firehouse.

Prevention efforts are not aimed solely at oily rags in overloaded closets. Attention is directed against the most common causes of fire and lost life. They run the gamut from smoking and the handling of matches as the Number One cause of fires (over 141,000 of the nation's 890,200 total in 1960), to faulty wiring (76,500 fires in 1960 at fixed installations and another 53,400 from power-using appliances), overheated or defective heating and cooking equipment (known to have caused over 137,000 of 1960's fires), and the incautious use of inflammable liquids (nearly 59,000 fires). Other hazards that loom large on fire preventers' targets, according to N.F.P.A. figures, include neglected rubbish (almost 54,000 fires) and children playing with matches (implicated in 38,600 of 1960's blazes – a bigger menace than lightning, which caused 25,500 fires in the same year).

Though most municipalities have mutual aid agreements to assist one another in an emergency that threatens to get out of hand, many are reluctant to send their men and equipment to the aid of nearby communities with no fire departments of their own even when those communities are willing to pay for the service. Some 40 percent of 1,000 cities responding to a recent survey by the City Managers' Association reported they did not permit their fire departments to answer calls for assistance outside their city limits unless the fire constituted a danger to the municipality itself. One reason for this reluctance is to be found in the law: fire departments can be held responsible for undue damage from water or other causes involved in fighting the fire itself, and may risk losing workmen's compensation for firemen killed or injured outside their jurisdiction. Also, of course, there is a certain reluctance to see the city left unprotected while a call is answered many miles outside.

Sick Cities

Of the 60 percent reporting they did answer calls outside their bailiwicks, half stated they provided such service without charge. The other half computed their charges in a wide variety of ways – among them, by flat hourly rates (some Wisconsin towns charged as much as $300 an hour), by fixed annual charges (Lafayette, Indiana, collects $25,000 per township served), and by more elaborate fee schedules based on the type of equipment used, the mileage run up, the number of fire fighters involved, and other factors. One of the most detailed of all fee schedules of its kind is that of Sanford, Maine, whose levies include a penny for every foot of hose laid; a recent listing of its rates included also a flat charge of $35 for each 500-gallon pumper used, $25 for each truck, $1.50 an hour for every fire officer, $1 an hour for each fireman, and an override of 75 cents a mile on total distance involved.

Besides returning a certain amount of revenue to the city, the fee system has another advantage: it tends to discourage unnecessary calls from communities which otherwise are not bearing their share of the cost of the fire service. One Florida municipality which was getting 55 to 60 calls a year from outside its borders, or 25 to 30 percent of all the calls it made during the course of a year, was summoned on only three calls in the twelve-month period following the institution of charges.

Some municipalities are seeking the solution to their fire-fighting needs through the hiring of private companies in business to make a profit. One such concern is the Rural Fire Protection Company of Scottsdale, Arizona, whose services are sold to individual property owners under a yearly subscription arrangement – generally $12 a year for homeowners and $15 for business firms – and to municipalities under contracts providing fixed monthly fees. Going into 1962, the company had some five stations and 20 pieces of apparatus in operation to serve half a dozen Arizona communities ranging in size from tiny Paradise

Valley, with a population of 1,500 and little Youngstown, with 2,500, to Scottsdale itself (15,000). It also held contracts with the cities of Phoenix and Glendale to serve areas newly annexed by those cities pending the provision of permanent city fire service.

The device is not altogether new. Insurance companies in Europe for many years, and in Colonial America for a shorter period of time, maintained their own fire departments for the purpose of minimizing their clients' losses. The metal seals they imbedded in the front of buildings purchasing their protection so they would know which ones to attempt to save can still be seen on ancient structures, particularly in Europe. It is hardly likely the newer version of the old profit-seeking fire-protection company will come into such broad use, however, unless present-day political philosophies undergo drastic change.

MERGING FIRE AND POLICE

ANOTHER remedy to the fire problems of the small municipality which is being tried on a somewhat broader scale calls for the combination of police and fire functions into a single "public safety" service. The roots of this idea are dug even more deeply into the ancient past. Emperor Augustus created such a force in A.D. 29. Known as the vigiles, they were traditionally pictured with a short sword in one hand and a fire bucket in the other.

More than two dozen municipalities in the United States and Canada were operating combined police-fire departments in 1962. One of them, Shawinigan Falls in Quebec, has had a public-safety rather than separate police and fire departments since it was incorporated in 1901. Others operating such departments range in size from little Sewickley Heights, Pennsylvania, with a population of less than 1,000, to Dearborn, Michigan, and Winston-Salem, North Carolina, both with populations of more than 100,000. The plan has also been considered by larger cities, such as San Diego (population: 600,000) and Seattle (575,000) but rejected, often because of fierce campaigns waged against it by fire-fighting groups. The fireman's way of life, to be sure, is changed most under the scheme which, in effect, makes every public-safety officer a policeman until he is summoned to a fire. At that time, public-safety officers cruising the streets in squad cars in a certain vicinity are radioed to rendezvous at the fire scene, using the helmet and other fire gear they carry with them as a matter of course in the squad car, usually on the floor behind the front seat. The fire trucks are usually taken out solely by drivers. Safety officers who arrive before the fire trucks are expected to engage themselves in lifesaving tasks or the clearance of traffic while others not summoned to the fire maintain police protection in the community.

Champions of the public-safety service contend it saves money through the more efficient use of police-fire manpower. A survey published by the city of San Diego in mid-1961 indicated firemen in that city spent only 1.3 percent of their workweek responding to alarms but 36 percent of their time eating and sleeping. It is also argued that combined police-fire operations permit more selective recruitment by stretching the city's dollar so it can pay better salaries for fewer men, that it places personnel more quickly at the fire since they are already out in the community, and that it generally provides a higher level of both police and fire service by making more men available for either function as they are needed. City Manager Perry Scott of Sunnyvale, California, which has operated a unified public-safety service since 1957, figured the system saved Sunnyvale over $300,000 in 1961 – the equivalent of 30 cents on its tax rate, which was then running $1.37 per $100 assessed valuation. Though most of the savings came from the department's ability to keep its total police-fire manpower down to 110 persons – at least 40 fewer than it would have required to provide comparable protection with separate departments – economies were also realized in not having to duplicate buildings, communications centers, record departments, and other facilities.

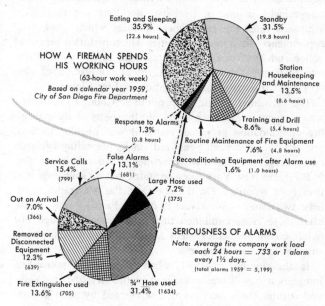

HOW A FIREMAN SPENDS
HIS WORKING HOURS
(63-hour work week)
*Based on calendar year 1959,
City of San Diego Fire Department*

Eating and Sleeping
35.9%
(22.6 hours)

Standby
31.5%
(19.8 hours)

Station
Housekeeping
and Maintenance
13.5%
(8.6 hours)

Training and Drill
8.6% (5.4 hours)

Routine Maintenance of Fire Equipment
7.6% (4.8 hours)

Reconditioning Equipment after Alarm use
1.6% (1.0 hours)

Response to Alarms
1.3%
(0.8 hours)

Service Calls
15.4%
(799)

False Alarms
13.1%
(681)

Out on Arrival
7.0%
(366)

Removed or
Disconnected
Equipment
12.3%
(639)

Fire Extinguisher used
13.6% (705)

Large Hose used
7.2%
(375)

¾" Hose used
31.4% (1634)

SERIOUSNESS OF ALARMS
*Note: Average fire company work load
each 24 hours = .733 or 1 alarm
every 1⅓ days.*
(total alarms 1959 = 5,199)

Based on study by City of San Diego of its own department
during period September 9, 1959 through October 7, 1959.

As for the speed of response to fires, Sunnyvale recently published the results of a study conducted during a six-month period to December 31, 1959, which showed the first two patrol cars arrived at the scene of a fire on the average of 2.6 minutes after the alarm was sounded against an average of 3.3 minutes for the fire trucks. The difference, proponents argue, can be crucial in the saving of lives, which they argue is the fireman's first duty.

Critics of the combined operation toss many arguments at it – including some blatant falsehoods which, at times, have been highly effective in defeating further consideration of the measure. The *California Fireman*, a monthly publication of the California Firemen's Association, stated categorically in one of its issues not long ago that "fire insurance rates are far higher in cities which integrated departments" than in communities which maintain separate police and fire forces. And a statement to the same effect was read into the record at a recent convention of the AFL-CIO International Association of Fire Fighters.

The Missouri Public Expenditures Council, however, which made an extensive study of all aspects of the police-fire consolidation proposal, stated it was unable "to find one city that had been penalized" in its fire rating because of a merger of the two departments. An official of the N.B.F.U. in New York likewise states that no such case has ever been recorded. On the contrary, the fire grades of at least two cities – Sunnyvale and Oak Park – were raised after these cities combined their departments, though officials credit the achievement as much to improved water supplies as to anything else.

In the summer of 1961, when the issue of police-fire integration was being considered in the city of San Diego and further study was deemed warranted by such groups as the local Chamber of Commerce and the San Diego Tax-payers' Association, William H. Gibbs, president of the San Diego Fire Fighters Association, Local 145 of the AFL-CIO union, made a statement which received wide publicity and was generally credited with a role in shelving further consideration of the proposal.

Mr. Gibbs said: "I have a quote from Mr. Edwin Flood, president of the San Diego Insurance Association, and he says, 'You can quote me – if the Police and Fire Departments are integrated (in the functional, not the racial sense), San Diego will go to a four classification (a poorer fire rating than it had at the time) and raise the fire rates 8 percent.' " Later, when he was confronted with the statement, Mr. Flood contended he was misquoted. What he actually said, he explained, was "that *if* integration caused San Diego's fire rating to go from grade 3 to grade 4, the rates then would be 8 per cent higher. I didn't say integration would cause the change in rating," he stated. The record was never corrected, however, before the plan was shelved.

The criticism is often made that a combined police-fire force does not produce as effective a fire-fighting team as personnel assigned permanently to work together on a single piece of apparatus. That team capability, the argument goes, may be less vital in a predominantly residential community with little industry or dense development, but it can mean the difference between success and disaster in fires where high densities and values are involved. And those, they contend, are the fires that cause the most damage; 10 to 15 percent of all structural fires, they note, customarily account for 90 percent of the annual fire loss.

There is no doubt that a certain amount of teamwork is lost by assigning a fire squad police duties. Exactly what part of that loss can be overcome by better planning and training is difficult to determine. Proponents of the system claim they can overcome a good deal. They also turn the same statistics to their own use: 85 to 90 percent of all fires, they note, are too minor to require even the laying of hose, much less a high degree of fire-fighting strategy and teamwork.

Another argument levied against the combined department says, in effect, that one man cannot do two jobs without one job or the other suffering by the attempt. Often cited in this connection is an incident that occurred in Canada some years ago in which thieves set several diversionary fires around town and then proceeded successfully to rob a local credit union of some $120,000. Champions of the plan, however, argue thieves would not have any better stealing opportunity in a city with a properly manned public-safety department than they would have in a city with separate departments and that anyway it is the rare thief who is prepared to add arson to his list of crimes.

Fire-fighter groups have carried their opposition to police-fire consolidation into state legislatures in an effort to outlaw the practice where persuasion has not been entirely effective on other levels. They nearly succeeded in getting Illinois to outlaw the combined operation in 1959, thereby forcing half a dozen communities in the state to revert to separate departments, but were thwarted by a gubernatorial veto. The fire fighters have been more successful in Massachusetts, however, where they managed to get state legislation the same year to prohibit combined departments in cities of more than 40,000 population; there were no integrated departments in the state at the time.

The most crucial test of public safety's effectiveness, perhaps, lies in the experience of communities which have had it in full operation for some time. A pamphlet published in 1959 by the AFL-CIO fire fighters to help members combat the plan under the title "Fight Back!" makes this statement on its first page: "Almost without exception, those communities that have given the plan a trial have returned to separate fire and police departments. The experience of seven California cities," it states, "is typical. The cities of Buena Park, Chico, Fremont, Hawthorne, Monterey Park, Sanger, and San Marino tried combining the two departments and reverted to separate fire and police departments. . . . It may have taken a disaster to prove the unworkability of the scheme. In most cases, however, it was community dissatisfaction with lowered fire and police service that brought the return to separate departments."

In October, 1961, the Cleveland Bureau of Governmental Research, Inc., now the Governmental Research Institute, published a 77-page survey entitled "Police-Fire

Integration in the United States and Canada." The study revealed that only 15 of 88 cities which ever got as far as combining even a portion of their police and fire personnel into a single public-safety service at the working level subsequently abandoned the system. Of the seven California cities mentioned in the IAFF pamphlet, three – Chico, San Marino, and Fremont – never carried consolidation beyond the stage of appointing a single public-safety director to head both forces. And in at least two of the other communities, according to public officials there, unification was abandoned principally because of dissatisfaction among department personnel rather than because it failed to work after it was given fair trial.

In the search for solutions to the fire problem, and perhaps to the police problem as well, serious, honest consideration of the advantages and disadvantages of the public-safety plan would appear highly warranted, certainly by smaller, fast-growing communities predominantly residential in nature. For communities facing the transition from purely volunteer fire forces to paid departments or the prospect of having drastically to trim the workweek of a small fire force, such a study would appear especially pertinent. In large cities, where specialization may be both vital and more economical, the alternative to bigger firefighting budgets quite possibly lies in only one direction: more effective prevention through better building codes and practices on the part of property owners.

Says Boris Laiming, a consultant and writer on fire problems for over forty years: "Municipalities, and perhaps state governments as well, must write laws to make buildings more self-protective through the greater use of fireresistive construction, compartmentation, automatic sprinklers and other precautionary provisions. Public laws," says he, "should also create inducement for safer building by imposing a special tax burden on structures which contain features inviting the spread of fire."

Sick Cities

Mr. Laiming, a retired geologist who acted as an adviser to the United States in its incendiary raids on German and Japanese cities during World War II, also believes American cities could go a long way toward reducing their fire burdens by letting some of the European philosophy rub off on them, by fixing responsibility for fires on the people who have them unless they can prove the negligence was someone else's. He doubts, however, the American public is willing to go quite that far in its pursuit of safety from fire.

CHAPTER EIGHT

School Bells – and Burdens

EDUCATOR. Baby-sitter. Counselor. Trainer. Instructor of the handicapped. Companion. Motivator. In a phrase, ersatz parent.

This, more and more, is becoming the role of the school in the nation's central city. But ersatz parents are costly. High-income families who might otherwise help carry the burden of providing them have fled to suburban communities, often paying their taxes instead to less needy, better-heeled school districts. In their place have come greater numbers of low-income, minority groups with larger broods.

The problems that sprawl showers on urban education thus tend to fall more heavily on the central city that is left behind in sprawl's outward dash than upon newly created suburbs. True, new communities need schools and the staffs to man them; older metropolitan areas, on the other hand, have both schools and, at least to start off with, the staffs to man them. But the means to build new schools and provide them with the finest of staffs are not lacking in the relatively affluent suburb. For the most part, in fact, those funds have been summoned with relative ease despite the outcries and the attention they have brought.

Moreover, the suburban child typically is the benefactor of an educational resource far more vital to education than those money can buy: concerned parents capable of providing the strongest motivation and all the trappings to go with it, from private study space and well-chosen books to provocative conversation at the dinner table, an occasional evening at the theater, or a Sunday afternoon in the museum.

If sprawl has any serious implications at all for education in the suburbs, it likely will not be found in the two phenomena that have commanded the most attention in the past: the shortage of classrooms and of teachers. There is considerable evidence, in fact, that, despite the lamentations, these shortages are being overcome and, quite possibly, could speedily be eliminated if teachers and classrooms were used as efficiently as they might be. Indeed, suburbia is more likely to find the most vexatious of its educational headaches, in the longer run, in a complacent affluence than in overcrowded classrooms. The influence of television and teenage automobile ownership and, still more ominous, of more homogeneous student bodies resulting from the increasing separation of racial and economic groups, are problems suburbia has yet to reckon with.

But the most serious of all schooling challenges to the community are not likely to be found in the suburbs at all. They lie, rather, in the deteriorating areas of the central city with its highly limited means and growing needs. Here, a catalog of welfare functions is thrust upon school systems to meet the needs of underprivileged youngsters who must be fed before they can be taught and assured before they can be interested, of teenagers who lack the diligence or wherewithal to acquire the learning so vital for secure employment in an increasingly automated economy, and of adults who do not themselves understand the uses of education, much less desire its assiduous acquisition by their youngsters.

Bigger burdens and smaller budgets also handicap central city school systems by placing them at a disadvantage in the competition for quality teachers. Many suburban school systems, because of their safer, pleasanter, and more satisfying environments, no longer find themselves desperate for teaching help, but can pick and choose among teacher candidates; shortages of good instructional help, on the other hand, grow increasingly acute in the central city, where substitute teachers can refuse assignments to fourth-grade classes when they cannot get more easily controlled second-graders, or a third-floor walkup when they cannot get one on the ground floor.

Time and technology, too, work against the central city school system by aging and obsoleting its plant. Where land lies vacant and relatively cheap in outlying suburban areas, it comes costly and generally built upon in the central city. Central city land purchases not only entail higher acquisition prices but, frequently, expensive razing costs as well. Seldom are new schools, in fact, built in the inner metropolis unless there is the most dire need for additional facilities or an urban renewal project is under way. Central cities, which have yet to make a significant dent in their overall renewal needs, have hardly begun to tackle the job of accommodating their schools to the opportunities afforded by new technology and educational techniques.

Along with their own particular handicaps, school systems in the central city, as well as those in the suburbs, are being weighted more heavily with new responsibilities. Beyond their original objectives of instilling five "R's" – reading, 'riting, 'rithmetic, the ability to reason, and a sense of responsibility – the nation's public schools are expected today to combat all manner of handicap, mental as well as physical, social as well as economic. In addition, they are being called upon to raise educational levels to meet the challenges of scientific achievements in the race for space and nuclear supremacy, to cope with the complex demands of world leadership, properly channel the use of lengthening leisure, and otherwise equip an amorphous electorate for a better understanding of complex political, economic, and sociological change.

The raising of educators' sights necessitates special attention to the needs of the slow learner, the special capabilities

221

of the gifted and, indeed, the custom-tailoring of education to the entire student body as a collection of individuals with varying capabilities in different subjects at different ages. New subjects must be taught and old ones taught better. Abilities and achievement must be more precisely determined and guidance more painstakingly provided, moreover, if broadening alternatives are to be intelligently selected.

These diverse assignments are being dumped on educators when tax burdens, in city and suburb alike, are taut with the needs of the national defense, the burdens of past wars, efforts to bolster the economy, and of unprecedented endeavors to meet the entire gamut of urban urgencies from the relentless rise in crime to the spread of blight. They come at a time, too, when pressure for higher teacher pay, by far the biggest item in the school budget, is mounting, and when the increase in population, along with the desire for longer schooling, are kiting enrollments to consistently greater heights. The nation's public school enrollment climbed 44 percent in the decade to 1960, from just over 25 million to more than 36 million, and is expected to rise another 55 percent by 1980, to over 56 million. By 1962, one-fourth of the nation was already enrolled in learning institutions, from kindergarten to graduate levels.

Increased mobility, the result of higher incomes and of jet and auto travel, further magnifies the need for educational facilities by unpredictably shifting populations from region to region and from city to suburb.

TEACHER SHORTAGES, CLASSROOM SHORTAGES, AND DOUBLE SESSIONS

ANY effort to assess the cities' progress, or lack of it, in overcoming teacher and classroom shortages must be placed in the context of constantly rising standards of classroom intimacy. For, despite the frequently cited shortages

SCHOOL BURDENS — Past and Prospective

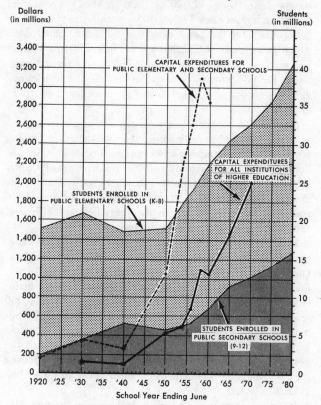

of teachers and classrooms, that intimacy has been growing steadily greater. According to the United States Office of Education, the ratio of pupils to teachers has been trimmed from 36 to 1 in 1900, to 29 to 1 in 1930, to 26.8 to 1 in 1948, and to 24.5 to 1 in 1962.

Benjamin C. Willis, General Superintendent of the Chicago public schools, figures that every time the ratio is lowered by just one pupil in the city's elementary class-rooms alone (some 12,000 of them in 1962), his current operating budget rises $3,250,000 – without any allowance being made for the construction of additional classrooms, which average about $32,000 apiece. It would cost another $13 million, he figures, to provide classrooms for the additional 12,000 students. Chicago, nevertheless, had trimmed its pupil-teacher ratio from 36 to 1 in the beginning of 1959 to 32 to 1 by 1962.

Statistics on median class sizes are not regularly kept on a national basis, but indications are that these are coming down along with pupil-teacher ratios. Studies by the National Education Association, the teachers' professional organization with headquarters in Washington, D.C., show median class sizes have decreased from over 35 in 1946 and even higher than that in the years before the Second World War, to approximate 30 today.

It is interesting to note, as author-lecturer Roger Freeman does in his volume *School Needs in the Decade Ahead* (published by the Institute of Social Research in 1958), that if the pupil-teacher ratio of 1929 (29 to 1) were maintained today, "We would have a surplus of almost 200,000 teachers." Educators are clamoring for still greater intimacy in class sizes on the theory that the learning process benefits thereby, though research has yet to establish the point. Indeed, some studies indicate that just the opposite may be true: that children often learn better in large than in small classes.

It is true, of course, that many teachers are holding their positions today solely on the strength of temporary or emergency credentials because they lack the necessary college credits to qualify on a permanent basis. Many of these teachers have proved fully as capable as their certificated colleagues; but even if the figures are taken at face value, they show an element of unmistakable progress. The 90,000 teachers on temporary credentials in the 1961-1962 school year, a figure which has been both considerably higher (97,000 in 1959-1960) and considerably lower (75,000 in 1954-1955) in recent years, represented just over 6 percent of the total teacher force that year but was more than 8 percent of it a decade earlier. The relative decline in emergency credentials is all the more remarkable for coming, as it does, not alone in a period of lower pupil-teacher ratios and much higher enrollments but also when teacher qualifications themselves have been continually on the upgrade.

Back in 1921, only four states required anything more than a high school education of their public school teachers. By 1962, over 60 percent were demanding college degrees. And qualifications are still being increased. Elementary-school teachers seeking certification in New York State after September 1, 1966, for instance, will have to have had five instead of four years of college training.

The prospective climb in enrollments, of course, means still heavier demands for teachers in the years ahead. The N.E.A. not long ago estimated the need to meet replacement requirements and enrollment growth at roughly 150,000 a year. The nation's colleges, however, are turning out just over 130,000 yearly, and a fourth of these are not going into teaching. Teacher colleges, in other words, cannot be expected to provide more than 100,000 of the projected annual teacher need under present circumstances.

The outlook would appear ominous indeed were it not the fact that many graduates of teacher colleges who do not immediately go into teaching do so eventually, while many others who quit the profession return. An N.E.A. study published in 1957 showed roughly half the teachers who were teaching in April, 1956, but not the year before, did not come directly from teacher colleges. Some 29 percent of them had been homemakers; 15 percent were in nonteaching jobs; 3 percent were in military service; and 4 percent were in "other occupations."

Higher teaching salaries and the growing appeal of the

profession generally, due both to a slower rate of economic growth and to changes in the profession itself, could cause more youngsters to choose this means of livelihood in the future.

Teacher groups and the federal government itself, in fact, have tended to underestimate the number of teachers who would be in the profession on a future date. Roger Freeman notes that in each of the two years immediately prior to publication of *School Needs in the Decade Ahead,* the Office of Education underestimated by more than 5 percent the teacher corps that later was found to have been practicing during those periods, the forecasts having been made in the fall for the school years then getting under way.

But there is also the basic question of whether the existing teacher force is being used anywhere near as efficiently as it might be. Many teacher manhours are currently being wasted on such routine chores as roll-taking, monitoring the lunchroom, supervising playgrounds, and a wide variety of other tasks nonprofessionals can perform, often more effectively. Only a meager beginning has been made in the use of nonprofessionals to replace teachers in such activities. Also, the broader use of devices such as television, teaching machines, films, and sound tapes might likewise stretch teacher talent if their use were not so largely relegated to supplementary teaching roles. Ironically, the use of such devices to free teachers for other tasks is often vigorously opposed by teacher groups who, on the one hand, publicly proclaim the seriousness of teacher shortages and, on the other, act as if the real menace were the threat of a teacher surplus.

Charges on the inadequacy of teaching pay similarly warrant closer examination. Average teaching salaries in the decade to the 1960-1961 school year rose from $3,126 to $5,389 per annum, or better than 72 percent; personal income in the same period increased less than 60 percent.

The question of whether pay rates have increased more rapidly in other professions and occupations is capable of eliciting almost any result, depending on what years are chosen for the comparison. Teaching salaries suffered less during the depression, for example, than did those of most other occupations. Since the end of World War II, teachers have fared better in obtaining pay increases than most government workers, manufacturing employees, and some professions, though they have not done nearly so well as doctors.

President Kennedy's former Education Commissioner, Sterling M. McMurrin, once stated that he personally would not be satisfied until teachers were paid well enough to make the calling "competitive" with any other in the minds of the "top 10 percent" of the student body. He said this did not mean teachers would have to be paid as well as doctors, say, or lawyers. Those professions, after all, have the attendant costs and early deprivations of self-employment as well as other disadvantages. On the basis of total attractiveness, however, he argued, teaching pay must match those of other professions if the nation is ever to get the quality of education he and many educators deem necessary.

Educators for years now have complained that otherwise dedicated teachers, particularly men with families, were unable to remain in the profession as their financial needs grew with maturity and better opportunities beckoned elsewhere, often in wholly unrelated lines of endeavor. If the argument is valid, as it seems to be, it would suggest opportunities for advancement in teaching may be more urgently needed than higher starting salaries if the profession is ever to become more than a way-stop for women between a sheet of sheepskin and the altar. Even a crude system of merit pay, it would appear, might prove preferable to the present preoccupation with seniority in which no differentiation is made among veteran teachers.

The lower rung of the teacher salary ladder may already be better pegged with respect to other callings than is generally recognized. Comparisons, of course, must take into account, though they often conveniently do not, the fact that teachers generally work a 36- or 37-week year, after allowing for summer vacations and week-long Christmas and Easter holidays, compared with the 48 or 49 weeks put in by most other trades and occupations. The teacher's school day itself rarely exceeds six or seven hours, though teachers reluctant to do their paperwork during classroom hours (for fear of "robbing" their wards of valuable instruction time) often invest additional hours of their own after class, marking papers and otherwise keeping abreast of day-to-day routine. The broader use of nonprofessional aides could considerably lighten that after-hours load, however.

The percentage of college graduates who prepare for teaching actually has been increasing in recent years. It rose from less than 27 percent in 1950 to over 30 percent by 1957, according to the N.E.A. The percentage of male teachers to the total teaching force has likewise improved from 14 percent in 1920 to 22 percent in 1940 and 29 percent in 1960. Provided teaching salaries continue to be raised to more competitive levels, particularly when it comes to opportunities for advancement, there is every reason to expect teaching to attract a still larger proportion of college students into the profession.

What about the "classroom shortage"? That signal, too, appears to be considerably more shrill than the facts would seem to warrant. Office of Education figures established the shortage in the fall of 1954 at some 370,000 classrooms. By the fall of 1961, the agency reported, the shortage had been reduced to 127,000 units. The rate of construction in 1961 was running at 70,000 units yearly – 10,000 above estimated average annual needs to 1970 after allowing for obsolescence and increased enrollments. This construction over estimated annual needs could eliminate the shortfall entirely by the early 1970's.

Here, again, however, the question may be asked: Is the nation really short of classrooms, or are existing facilities, like teachers, grossly underused?

The chief evil of the classroom "shortage" as it is deemed to exist today revolves around the concept of the "split" or "half-day" session. The shortage of 127,000 classrooms in the 1961-1962 school year was said to be committing some 500,000 youngsters to "split" sessions, which means they attended school either in the morning or in the afternoon but not both times, as most youngsters do.

Taking the concept of the double session first at its face value, it should be noted that progress is being made toward its elimination as additional classrooms are built over and above new annual needs. In 1956-1957, for example, some 870,000 students were said to have been on double session. Thus the reduction in only five years' time amounted to over 42 percent. Those on double session represented only 3 percent of total public school enrollment in 1961-1962, but few would argue that even this proportion should not be a cause of valid concern if it meant thousands of youngsters were being short-changed in their education. The question is: Are they?

The Los Angeles Unified School District is fairly typical of big city school systems operating double sessions. It is also fairly typical of urban areas where the pressure on classroom facilities has been consistently high: the district must build the equivalent of one average-sized elementary school of 15 classrooms every week of the school year to keep abreast of its enrollment growth, a requirement it often has difficulty in meeting. To the extent that it has not been able to provide new facilities fast enough, Los Angeles has had anywhere from 10,000 to 50,000 students on double session in recent years. These students, however, are actually attending classes only 20 minutes less than those on normal full-time schedules. And even this 20-minute "loss" may be insignificant: teachers generally find they must spend at least that much time after the noontime meal recess settling their students so they can resume serious work.

Indeed, some authorities think the double session should be extended, not eliminated. They argue that by working the school plant longer, first with one set of students and teachers and then with another, and possibly by extending the usual 180-day school year to make up for any time which may be deemed to have been lost in the process, the usefulness of existing facilities could be increased notably, and education dollars that would otherwise go into brick, mortar, and real estate would be liberated for the hiring of additional teachers, improving teacher pay, or used for other worthy educational purposes. The idea, however, is highly unpopular among parents who look to the school for "baby-sitting" as well as educational services, and among teachers who fear being stuck with a longer day when positions cannot be filled on one shift or the other.

Over 80 percent of the schools in Soviet cities, nevertheless, are reportedly operating on at least two (and sometimes three) sessions a day, with schedules that may run from eight o'clock in the morning until eight in the evening. Nearly half the students in West Germany attend school on the double-session principle. The practice may not be a desirable one, but it is not the most serious threat to urban America's education.

SPRAWL'S SUBTLE THREAT: THE SEPARATOR

By nurturing into being communities which are more homogeneous socially, economically, and racially than cities historically were before them, sprawl is exerting a "settling out" effect on urban development which substitutes a "separator" action for the "melting pot" role cities once served. "Mixed" schools thus become less and less common, and, unless many of the greatest educators of the past are wrong, living laboratories in democracy cease to be.

Indeed, the modern urban school is more likely to serve as a pressure cooker for differences, resentments, rivalries, and intolerance than as an instrument capable of the greatest achievement of education, the sowing of respect for others, regardless of creed or color. The penalties for this failure may be exacted from society in many ways: through the aggravation of police problems, the erosion of national loyalties, the diminution of stimuli that are otherwise found in the questioning of prevailing patterns of life and thought, and in the waste of human resources that results from too narrow an appreciation of individual worth.

The measure of such penalties cannot be easily taken, but the extent of the "separator" process is not difficult to delineate. City cores increasingly are becoming repositories of low-income minority groups, while families more capable of coping with their economic environment move as far away from the central city as their incomes will take them and commuting will allow. A recent survey of 704 public schools in New York City showed 455 were dominated at least 90 percent by a single ethnic group, either Negro, Puerto Rican, or white. Negroes and Puerto Ricans accounted for 35 percent of the city's public school enrollment in 1962; by 1970 they will account for 45 percent.

Newark's proportion of nonwhites rose from 17 percent in 1950 to 34 percent in 1960, Washington, D.C.'s, from 35 percent to nearly 55 percent, New York's from just under 10 percent in 1950 to nearly 15 percent in 1960, Chicago's from 14 percent to nearly 24 percent and Los Angeles' from nearly 11 percent to nearly 17 percent. Population in the outlying regions of the 12 largest metropolitan areas, on the other hand, has remained almost unchanged since 1930 at the high rate of from 93 percent to 99 percent white. University of Wisconsin researchers Leo F. Schnore and Harry Sharp, reporting on a study of racial changes in metropolitan areas from 1950 to 1960, cited evidence of outlying portions of some of the nation's larger metropolitan areas, in fact, becoming "whiter" still with the passage of time, as real-estate prices, building codes, and scarcer transit writes "finis" to more and more of that ancient institution known as "shantytown." The Negro suburb, they noted, is rare.

The way income patterns likewise follow geographic lines was pointed up not long ago by a study of the area of metropolitan Detroit. It showed that those living within a six-mile radius of the central business district were considerably worse off in 1959 than were those living in that area in 1951; their monetary incomes increased 3 percent in a period when the cost of living rose 12 percent. Those living between the six-mile radius to the city limits, however, were 5 percent better off after allowing for the increase in living costs. Those living beyond the city limits, however, were 37 percent better off in terms of real income than those who lived in that region were in 1951.

The phenomenon of the poor settling at the metropolitan core and the wealthier as far outside as their means will take them is well illustrated by the diagram of Metropolitan Washington (page 233).

Percolation of the classes is causing serious fiscal hardship in many central city school systems where the suburbs are actually separate cities. Suburban cities, of course, usually have more money to spend on education than the central city does. Too, the suburban education dollar is not likely to be unduly weighted with the burden of having to educate neglected, impoverished youngsters. That poor families are often prolific ones as well is a point that hardly needs to be labored. The city of St. Louis watched its population decline from 857,000 in 1950 to over 750,000 in

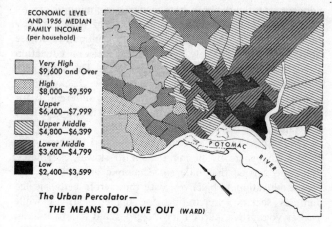

ECONOMIC LEVEL
AND 1956 MEDIAN
FAMILY INCOME
(per household)

Very High
$9,600 and Over

High
$8,000—$9,599

Upper
$6,400—$7,999

Upper Middle
$4,800—$6,399

Lower Middle
$3,600—$4,799

Low
$2,400—$3,599

POTOMAC RIVER

The Urban Percolator —
THE MEANS TO MOVE OUT (WARD)

1960, but its school enrollment rose from nearly 85,000 to nearly 96,000.

The development of more homogeneous schools may hold other unfortunate implications for education besides financial ones. Where different groups of youngsters are raised and educated apart, education itself is bound to lose some of its potency. Not only is group consciousness likely to be carried more sharply over into adult life, but the schools themselves suffer the loss of the controversy that stems from diversity and nourishes the desire to find answers for oneself to some of life's most crucial questions.

Conformity, mediocrity, and indifference – these are only too often likely to be the attitudinal hallmarks of the average, comfortably homogeneous suburban school. They are all the more unfortunate for coming at a time when original thought and individual conviction were never more urgently needed to balance the molded patterns of look-alike living, herded striving, and institutionalized moneymaking.

Teaching techniques and the readiness of communities to experiment with new learning methods similarly suffer from such conformity. "It's not easy to introduce any new concept in a tightly knit, homogeneous community of any kind," says one pioneering educator, "and it is infinitely more difficult to do so in a suburban community whose adult population is likely to have fixed ideas on education based on their own schooling experiences. The same people, mixed up in a community of diverse backgrounds, will likely be more willing to try something different, if for no other reason than because this may be the line of least resistance," he maintains.

The "mixed school" is sometimes berated for penalizing bright youngsters by hitching them to slower classmates. It is also argued that different economic groups have different educational objectives, with those from better-heeled families seeking preparation for higher learning while poorer youngsters, particularly Negroes and Puerto Ricans, must think in terms of obtaining and holding down a job. The argument, however, is directed more against the mixing of abilities than the mixing of ethnic and economic groups as such. Mixed schools or classes differentiated only by varying standards or areas of specialization, such as science or music, should benefit students of all abilities, below average as well as above.

For those who fear the envy that might arise among youngsters toward those more fortunate than they, several considerations may be borne in mind: first, that envy is perhaps inevitable among youngsters even in the most homogeneous of groups. Second, such envy may not be undesirable if, as often happens, it causes students to strive harder. Finally, a certain amount of envy can be avoided, for example, by prescribing modes of dress, at least among students in elementary schools.

At the high school level, the problem of divergent means may be more complex. School administrators, particularly in western cities but increasingly in eastern ones as well, are witnessing the rise of the automobile as an important symbol of status in suburban high school society. The inability to purchase and maintain an automobile may undermine grades and, perhaps more often than is generally realized, underlie the decision of many students to leave school for full-time employment.

A recent insurance company survey of 20,000 high school students in 29 states showed 50 percent of those holding part-time jobs did so *solely* to earn money for car upkeep. The survey also showed that the more a youngster worked, the lower his grades were likely to be. And it found twice as many failing students among those using their cars four or more nights a week as among those using it less often. Even if one allows for the likelihood of the less studious tending to go out more often, the automobile's skill as a thief of time and interest can hardly be doubted.

Not the least of the troublesome problems that tend to settle in the central city is that of the "dropout," the youngster who never does finish high school. The problem is becoming increasingly urgent with every advance in automation that reduces job opportunities for the unskilled as elevator operators, gandy dancers on the railroad, and other rapidly disappearing hard-backed, softheaded tasks. It becomes more serious, too, as the need to understand and to vote intelligently on complex issues grows.

Taking the population as a whole, the proportion of dropouts has actually been declining over the years. Fewer than a third of the nation's seventeen-year-olds fail to receive high school diplomas today compared with the two-thirds who failed to do so in 1930 and the 98 percent who went into the adult world without high school diplomas when Massachusetts passed the nation's first compulsory education law in 1852. However, the fact that dropouts are much more distinctly the exception now, and because job requirements have become so much more demanding, the dropout is a much more serious social problem than he has ever been before. Dropouts are also more of a problem because, while they are not increasing as a proportion of the entire student body, they are increasing in terms of sheer numbers. If present trends continue, the number of sixteen- and seventeen-year-olds leaving high school without diplomas will rise to approximately one million by 1970. In 1962, they totaled 600,000.

EDUCATION AND SOMETHING MORE

ANY effort to raise the educational level of low-income minority groups must inevitably come to grips with a wide range of difficulties. As Robert L. Baker, Director of Secondary Education for the St. Louis Public School District, puts it: "These children don't get discussion of world affairs at the dinner table. They're just told to shut up. Some of them come to class so hungry in the morning, they can't absorb anything unless they're fed first." In some instances, the school system is doing exactly that. But its undertakings also extend well beyond the breakfast platter. One extra-curricular program, for instance, attempts to raise aspirations of "culturally deprived" youth by taking them to concerts, getting them part-time jobs that will sharpen their appreciation of the value of education, and otherwise attempting to fire ambitions.

Many uplifting programs are aimed at parents as well as at their progeny. Raymond L. Hilliard, Director of Welfare for Cook County, Illinois, explains why. "Ignorance," says he, "is infectious. Children in relief families often follow in the footsteps of parents who have no skills, no education and no prospect of employment. Many parents can't even read their children's report cards."

"Teachers have known for a long time," says Richard I. Miller, Associate Director of the N.E.A., "that the family relationship determines, to a significant extent, attitudes and learned abilities the child brings to school with him." Not alone divorce, which already afflicts an average of one in four American marriages, but other shortcomings in the family relationship as well may have an effect on the learning motivation and the ability to concentrate at home and in the classroom.

Illiterates receiving public assistance in Cook County recently were being required to attend late-afternoon or evening sessions in the public schools to learn reading, writing, arithmetic, and other basic subjects under the threat of being dropped from the county's relief rolls. Some 50,000 individuals were said to have attended such courses throughout the county in 1962.

General Sessions judges in New York City recently began sentencing delinquents to night school to learn English, American history, and other subjects which, it was hoped, might turn them into more responsible citizens. A survey conducted not long ago by the New York City court system revealed that as many as 75 percent of delinquents have difficulty reading.

To assimilate older Puerto Rican children newly arrived in the United States with no previous schooling, New York City some years ago instituted "vestibule classes." They were not, as the name might have suggested, classes held in the corridor, but were intended, rather, as "corridors to learning." They were designed to provide older children with individualized instruction in the English language and in the ways of their new environment. The city also attempts to bring the youngsters' Spanish-speaking parents into the schoolhouse after hours to sharpen appreciation of the importance of their youngsters' education.

So teachers themselves will better understand the background of their Puerto Rican students, the city in recent years has also been sending a certain number of qualified teachers for summer learning sessions in the Caribbean land.

In 1962, with the help of a Ford Foundation grant, New York City launched a program aimed at preparing three- and four-year-olds from slum areas for some of the special problems that may face them when they enter kindergarten.

Attempts to salvage the nation's human resources are being extended to individuals handicapped by nature as well. Massachusetts schools in 1962, as a result of an act of the state legislature, began bringing into their classrooms "emotionally disturbed" youngsters previously confined to homes or institutions. The law required at least four hours of instruction weekly, with visits by teachers where the youngsters could not be brought into the public school. William Ohrenberger, Deputy Superintendent of Boston's public schools, figured at the time he would need about ten teachers for every fifty such children to be served, though he had no idea how many would ultimately be included in the program. A similar educational effort for the physically handicapped had been broadened to provide four instead of two hours of weekly instruction in 1959.

In 1960 the state of New Jersey launched an attempt aimed at educating children who had suffered brain injuries before or during birth. By 1962 it had ten such classes, consisting of from six to eight children each.

The provision of extra-educational services, of course, is nothing new to school systems. Nor is their mounting costliness. School lunch programs, among the oldest of the schools' welfare services, ran the nation's public school systems well over $300 million in the 1961-1962 school year against less than $180 million only a decade earlier. Medical and dental services, likewise more lavishly offered, set 40 major cities around the country back an average of $500,000 each annually, according to a survey the St. Louis public school system conducted in 1958; variations in expenditures were found to range from $0.19 to $14.00 per pupil annually.

So commonplace has the provision of free bus service become that the Elementary School Principals Association of New York City, where some 20,000 youngsters are transported daily, was moved recently to request the installation of phones in school buses at an estimated cost of $85,000 a year for use in emergency road breakdowns and for allaying parental fears when youngsters are unduly late.

In addition to becoming more of a sociological problem, education, of course, is also becoming more of an educational problem. Ever since Sputnik took to the heavens on October 4, 1957, the emphasis on science studies, particularly, has grown, spurred in part by federal aid under the National Defense Education Act. Freshmen entering Los Angeles high schools after September, 1961, for instance, were required to complete 170 semester hours of science study for graduation – 20 more than previously. The stronger accent on science, at the same time, has sharpened awareness of shortcomings in related subjects, such as mathematics, and even of some less related ones, such as economics and physical fitness. Stiffer academic requirements are causing school systems to refuse promotion to many more students than previously.

At the same time, youngsters are also being permitted to carry heavier loads. The Chicago city school system has done away altogether with restrictions that permitted only the top 10 percent of junior and senior high school classes to take a fifth major. Anyone who wants to can do so now, in any grade, provided he is deemed capable of carrying the extra load. Edwin A. Lederer, Associate Superintendent in Charge of Operation Services for the city's Board of Education, notes that the increase in permissive studies eliminates altogether the study period in which no teacher is required. He figures the option, which is widely chosen by students, is swelling high school instruction costs by approximately 20 percent.

The soaring popularity of publicly-supported junior colleges is also adding substantially to the cost of tax-supported education. Nearly 700 of the freshman-sophomore institutions were operating in the United States by early 1962. They contained some 25 percent of all the nation's college freshmen. By 1970 they may account for as much as 50 percent of all college freshmen. Some 4 million youngsters were enrolled in the nation's colleges in 1960; the total is expected to rise to 6 million in 1980.

Some efforts are being made to reduce the costliness of higher education to the public. A two-year community college begun recently in Norwalk, Connecticut, operates in the late-afternoon and early-evening hours at a local high school whose classrooms, library, and other facilities would otherwise be lying idle during this time. Florida not long ago made it possible for students to finance their higher education through loans by passing a law making minors legally liable for sums borrowed for that purpose.

NEW TECHNIQUES AND SOME HELPERS

THERE may be a good many other opportunities for reducing the costliness of education – or at least of making such education considerably more effective without substantially increasing budgets at the same time. Some of the most exciting of these opportunities are to be found in sharp departures from prevailing teaching techniques. Prominent among these are the systems known as "team teaching" and the "nongraded school."

"Teach teaching" is designed to do away with the concept of fixed class sizes and single-teacher instruction, and substitute instead "learning groups" whose size may vary from one student (for individualized instruction) to more than a hundred students (where a mass presentation, such as an introductory lecture, is involved). Groups of approximately 15 to 20 students are arranged in seminars for discussion purposes. Any member of the "teaching team" – the master teacher, an assistant teacher, or a nonprofessional aide – may take over any one of the three types of instruction, depending on the nature of the exercise. An aide, for example, might supervise drill or an examination.

An assistant teacher may deliver an "intermediate" lecture, and a master teacher the introductory one.

"The principle of team teaching," says Dr. Ovid Parody, Chief of Secondary School Instruction at the United States Office of Education, "is the same as that of not using an engineer to change a radio tube."

The system, which has many variations and is employed both at the elementary and at the high school level alike, has come into increasing use since the early 1950's in such states as Florida (at the Englewood Elementary School in Englewood, for instance), California (the Sierra Vista Middle School in Covina), Connecticut (the Dundee Elementary School in Greenwich), and Arizona (Flowing Wells Elementary School No. 3 in Tucson), Michigan (Lessinger Elementary School and East Elementary School, both in Madison Heights), and in Colorado (the Marie Creighton Junior High School in Jefferson County just outside Denver). Several schools have been especially designed for the concept, with several auditorium-style rooms for the general sessions, clusters of smaller classrooms for the seminar-style discussion groups, and cubbyhole spaces for individual study and instruction.

Dr. Robert Henry Johnson, former Superintendent of the Palo Alto City Schools in California and of the Jefferson County Schools in Colorado and one of the nation's leading authorities on team teaching, contends the system provides better instruction for the school dollar by making more efficient use of teaching talent. Also, he notes, it affords more of the opportunities for the advancement that educators believe is so sorely needed in the profession. In Palo Alto, for example, master teachers earn $1,000 more per year than the $8,000 annual salaries usually paid to top-bracket teachers in conventional systems. Clerical aides pull down less than $4,000 a year.

"A master teacher is chosen solely for his ability to organize and put subject matter across, not by seniority or any other mechanical method," notes James D. Laurits, Principal of Cubberley High School, one of Palo Alto's team-teaching institutions.

Team teaching has its drawbacks, of course. For one thing, it is still too new and too much in a state of flux to be winning wide acceptance as yet even among school administrators. For another, it involves logistical problems in scheduling students and teaching assignments. In addition, there is also the human angle: particularly the jealousies aroused among teachers when one of their number with lesser training and experience is selected as a "master" teacher and others are bypassed. Some teachers do not like the idea of losing "control" over students by having to share them with others.

The other revolution in teaching technique which is stirring up a good bit of interest among educators these days is the "nongraded" school. There is really nothing new about the basic concept except its high degree of refinement. The one-room schoolhouse, with its students of varying ages studying different lessons in the same classroom at their own learning pace, was a nongraded school. The real newcomer on the educational scene, in fact, was the graded school. Though prominently used in Germany much earlier, the graded school first came into being in the United States when the Quincy Grammar School opened its doors in Boston in 1848.

The nongraded school does away with grade levels as such, or at least so highly fragments them with its various "achievement levels" within the same "class" that they become groupings rather than grades. More common in elementary than in high schools, it has the child moving up from kindergarten to "first-grade reading," for instance, assigned to one of three achievement levels within that broad grouping, depending on the progress and capability he demonstrated in kindergarten. The teacher's attention is usually directed toward only one of the three groupings at any given time, the other two being expected to carry on with their own activity in the meantime.

A number of "appraisal points" during the course of the school year afford an opportunity for reshuffling students, so those who fall too far behind in the lowest achievement level or advance too far ahead in the highest level can be shifted to a middle achievement level in the "class" above or below. Students also may move from one level to another within the same "class" at any time, depending on their progress in the given subject. That progress is recorded from time to time on a "progress report" which can be used to place a child in his or her appropriate grade in the event of transfer to a graded school. The progress report also takes the place of grades in a given subject. The student thus neither "fails" nor is "promoted," though this, in effect, is what happens as his learning pace is appraised.

Grade levels, such as the first grade or "2B" are eliminated, and instead some general designation is used, for instance, "P" (meaning "primary" where the general level is equivalent to one of the first three grades in elementary schools), with the teacher's name after it.

One of the most widely acclaimed features of the nongraded system, in fact, is its elimination of competition between students and, in general, the relief from tension associated with promotion and subject grading. The student, rather, is in competition with himself, attempting to accelerate his learning pace in a given subject. The system permits the bright child to finish elementary school two or more years ahead of what might otherwise be his normal time, and has generally been well received by teachers, parents, and youngsters alike.

A survey of some 804 of the nation's 85,000 elementary schools published by the N.E.A. in 1962 indicated approximately 12 percent of the nation's elementary schools were then using the nongraded system at least in part. Five years earlier, only 6 percent did so. By 1966, if the survey proves valid, 26 percent will be at least partially on a nongraded program. The plan remains a rarity among high schools, however, because of administrative difficulties relating to larger student bodies and the greater variety of subjects offered.

The nongraded school has been used in combination with team teaching, with various achievement levels within a "class," for example, participating in general auditorium presentations and individual achievement levels engaging in seminar discussions. John I. Goodlad, an author of three books on the nongraded school and a Professor of Education and Director of the University Elementary School at the University of California at Los Angeles, sees such developments as television instruction and the teaching machine enabling still broader use of the nongraded system by permitting a greater degree of individualized instruction. Says Dr. Goodlad: "The system breaks the lock-step of graded structure."

School systems presently using the nongraded plan include Milwaukee, which began it in 1942 and has had it in effect longer than any other city, Philadelphia, St. Louis, Los Angeles, Chicago, and more than forty smaller cities and towns, including Melbourne, Florida, where one of the few high schools using the plan is located.

It does not take a revolution in teaching methods, however, for teachers to be used more efficiently. The Thomas Jefferson Elementary School in Bay City, Michigan, proved that in 1953 when it hired eight housewives with no training at all as teachers to help out with such routine classroom chores as monitoring lunchrooms, policing playgrounds, putting on children's leggings, filling out attendance sheets, collecting class funds, and handling much of the other paperwork normally required of a teacher. The city's then Superintendent of Schools, Charles B. Park, figured as much as 26 percent of a teacher's regular school time was being wasted in such nonteaching chores. Mr.

School Bells – and Burdens

Park's strategy for reducing this waste – hiring aides to help teachers just as nursing aides help nurses and dental assistants, dentists – proved so successful that it has since become famous as the "Bay City Plan." Among its unexpected by-products are more teachers, the result of aides becoming sufficiently interested through their introduction to the profession to obtain education degrees themselves. Arthur D. Morse notes in *Schools of Tomorrow—TODAY!*, published by Doubleday & Company in 1960, that some 42 Michigan school systems were using the plan six years later.

Teaching aides with somewhat greater training are being used as well for more specialized functions. The "Rutgers Plan" was devised by English teachers on Ford Foundation fellowships at Rutgers University in the summer of 1959 to make use of adults with a background in English to correct test papers, supervise spelling exercises, and examine homework. Chores performed in the classroom were paid for at the rate of $2 to $3 an hour; those at home, somewhat less.

The Chicago school system in 1961 experimented with the hiring of five "lay theme readers" to permit students more practice in composition without imposing more of a load upon the teacher. English teachers were thereby able to assign each student four papers a month instead of two; two continued to be read by the teacher while the other two were read by a lay reader. The program was sufficiently successful, according to Evelyn F. Carlson, Assistant Superintendent in Charge of Curriculum Development for the city's school system at the time, that the school system decided to hire twice as many lay theme readers the following fall for assignment at nine different high schools. Three of the first five persons hired for the purpose were women with bachelor degrees in English. Their rate of pay, $1.50 per hour, gave the school system almost twice as many theme-reading hours as it got from teachers, and spared that hard-to-recruit personnel for other teaching tasks.

Efforts to conserve teacher talent sometimes meet with considerable resistance. School systems in West Virginia which tried to trim expenses on their driver-training programs by having drivers of school buses conduct driving lessons in their off hours were speedily braked by a state association of driver education teachers. Currently provided by over three-fourths of the nation's high schools, driver training has become the costliest of all high school programs; an unusually high degree of individual instruction and the need for special equipment both inside and outside the classroom accounts for much of the $15 million to $20 million budgeted annually for this purpose by the nation's schools. A study by the Los Angeles City School Districts in 1961 placed the cost per pupil hour of driving instruction approximately nine times as high as the average high school course. There is some question whether the course of instruction should be provided at all, much less free of charge, but the school system that levies a fee for such instruction is rare.

Though the first course in driver education was first offered as far back as 1903 (by the YMCA), "only one or two schools," according to the Automotive Safety Foundation, were offering it in the mid-1930's. Some states, such as California, attempt to meet costs of driver instruction through an override on traffic fines; others, such as Michigan, attach an extra charge on drivers' licenses for the purpose. Much of the cost, nevertheless, continues to fall on school budgets.

School systems are looking increasingly to interested parents for assistance in the teaching task. A University of North Carolina psychologist who studied the childhood patterns of twenty famous people of outstanding ability, including Goethe, Voltaire, Pitt, and Coleridge, noted that all of them enjoyed a high degree of attention from parents. The Denver public school system in 1960 sought to make the reservoir of such interest more effective by undertaking the production of a television series designed to show parents how they can teach their preschool youngsters to read. "Parents with this kind of help frequently make very good teachers of the preschool child," says Denver public schools' Superintendent Kenneth E. Oberholtzer.

So other school systems might make use of the Denver series, the programs have been recorded on videotape with the help of a $65,000 Carnegie Foundation grant. Reception of the series was favorable enough in Denver to encourage the planning of a second series to assist parents in teaching their offspring a foreign language and in the process, of course, learning it themselves. Enthusiastic, Dr. Oberholtzer thinks the principle can be applied to advantage in almost any subject.

The student himself, of course, can take a load off the school system, particularly with the aid of such equipment as tape recordings, teaching machines, and TV. Though such devices tend to increase school budgets, many educators believe they can improve the effectiveness of the learning process without placing an additional strain on teaching staffs. Such professional presentations can produce more effective learning for the educational dollar while freeing teachers for more individualized attention.

James D. Finn, former Professor of Education at the University of Southern California and head of the Technological Development Project of the N.E.A., predicts: "The biggest change ahead for education in the coming years will be the emergence of a 'logistics of instruction' in which a wide variety of machines, materials, films, tapes and other apparatus will be used along with special teaching staffs to attain, by psychological and other means, a given educational objective. But," he warns, "such techniques are not likely to lower school budgets."

American educators are using television for a gamut of educational purposes, ranging from brief programs to stimulate interest in art in elementary grades to complete courses leading to a junior college diploma. One of the most ambitious of all video undertakings to date in education got under way in the fall of 1961. Known as the Midwest Program on Airborne Television Instruction (MPATI), the project makes use of two converted cargo aircraft which take turns flying figure eights 23,000 feet over Lafayette, Indiana. The planes beam taped language, history, English, mathematics, and other courses to over a million elementary and high school students in six Midwestern states – Illinois, Indiana, Michigan, Ohio, Kentucky, Wisconsin, and a small section of southern Canada. The general public, as well as students, can tune in. Many of the 7,000 school districts expected to participate in the program (with a total enrollment of over 5 million) are too small to afford the quality of education coming to them, literally, from out of the blue. The project's initial cost, $10 million, is being borne by the Ford Foundation, but local school districts are expected to assume the expense once that sum runs out.

Television teachers for mass audiences are selected not so much for their teaching experience or even their academic backgrounds as for their ability to get a subject across. As such, they may be finer actors than teachers in the sense that they may not themselves have thoroughly absorbed the subject they are presenting. The material, however, is generally prepared by professionals.

Dr. Lawrence G. Derthick, Assistant Executive Secretary for Educational Services at N.E.A. and former U.S. Commissioner of Education, says even if television and other new devices heap costs on school systems, as he suspects they will, the outlay should help bring a higher standard of learning long overdue. "We never did spend enough on education," says he. "Somewhere between 2 percent and 5 percent of the educational budget has traditionally gone into educational materials, including paper, books for libraries and, in many districts, school bands. We just never did give teachers and students enough of the tools they needed. Often, even their maps were outdated. Television should provide greater flexibility in our school systems, but it won't reduce budgets. The difference, however, is the difference between flying across country in a jet and riding across it on a horse. One is costlier in immediate outlay and the other is costlier in intangibles, such as time."

New devices, somehow, seldom do reduce education costs, perhaps because educators do not often give them a chance to do so. Some authorities, however, believe substantial savings can be achieved in schooling costs through the intelligent use of such apparatus as television. Alexander J. Stoddard, former chairman of the N.E.A. Educational Policies Commission and once a school superintendent in such cities as Los Angeles, Denver, and Philadelphia, has estimated television intelligently used could eliminate at least two positions in the average school – about 200 in a city of 500,000, or 50,000 throughout the country. Prospective saving: half a billion dollars a year.

The role of teaching machines in education is even more controversial at the moment, largely because of their variety and the art's speedily changing state. Some 83 types were being marketed or developed by some 65 different companies in the beginning of 1962; they ranged in price from a simple desk-top affair operated by buttons for $4.95 to complex systems for an entire classroom complete with tape and slides for $150,000. One teaching machine currently under development involves the use of a computer with master controls at the teacher's desk; it would cost about $2 million.

The tendency of schooling to grow more costly as it grows more complex is well illustrated by Los Angeles' experience with the so-called "language laboratory." "Before the 1950's," notes Virgil Volla, Associate Superintendent of Los Angeles City Schools, "we had no language laboratories in the public schools. Today, our foreign language rooms come equipped with tape recorders, earphones, playback equipment, individual sound booths for each student and control equipment for the teacher. The student gets a chance to hear the language correctly spoken and to record and correct his attempts at imitating it. It's an enormous help for turning out linguists, but it is also costly." Mr. Volla figures the average language lab contains about $14,000 worth of equipment. Nevertheless, he notes, practically every high school built in Los Angeles today is equipped with at least one such facility.

"A classroom used to be nothing but a blackboard, a few benches, a coal stove and a water bucket for the kids to take a drink," notes Dr. Shirley Cooper, Associate Executive Secretary of the American Society of School Administrators in Washington, D.C. "Now we have a vast array of laboratory equipment, projectors and recording devices, automobile and other workshops, banks of typewriters and bookkeeping machines and even air conditioning in some instances." He adds: "The cheapest course you can teach is one in philosophy, where you can get by with nothing but a book and kids. But spread your offerings to vocational subjects, languages, sciences and the like and there's no escaping it: you're adding to education costs."

TRICKS IN NEW FACILITIES

ONE of the few areas in which educators see any hope at all for achieving economies in school budgets lies in innovations in the school plant. Los Angeles, for instance, currently devotes as much as a fifth of all its new construction to collapsible structures capable of being moved from site to site as population shifts dictate. A specially designed two-room schoolhouse with knock-down walls suitable for toting by a single truck went into use in 1961. It reduced by nearly 50 percent the average $1,600 moving cost previously incurred on structures of that size.

School Bells – and Burdens

In Colorado, the Jefferson County School system is buying houses strategically located in new subdivisions for use as "cottage schools." Served largely by traveling teachers who provide an hour or two of specialized instruction before they move on to the next "cottage," the units accommodate children through the third grade. When the facilities are no longer needed, they are placed on the market for sale as homes. The average "cottage" cost the county $15,000 in 1961 – about half the usual $30,000 cost of a conventional classroom in a conventional school building; proceeds from the sale of the home, of course, further reduce the outlay.

A public housing project approved by the New York City Board of Estimate in March, 1961, for construction on the site of the old Polo Grounds baseball stadium provides for a 40-room schoolhouse on the lower floors of one of four buildings. The facility is convertible to residential use when and if it is no longer needed as a school. A public housing development built in France in recent years incorporates a schoolhouse on its roof so children still can get some sun and sky.

The City and Country School, a well-known progressive school in New York City, private but nonprofit, planned to begin construction in 1963 on a $1.8 million structure that would not only provide it with educational facilities but would bring it some income at the same time. The trick is being turned with a neat four-in-one complex of structures consisting of a parking garage on two subterranean levels, a medical center on the two levels above it, and a twelve-story residential tower. The school, a three-level affair complete with eleven classrooms, library, lunchroom, gymnasium, a print shop, and special facilities for art, music, and science instruction, sits on a plaza atop the medical center while providing a terrace on its own roof for residents of the tower. Fully rented, the complex is expected to return the school approximately $55,000 after

taxes and depreciation. Valuable land which otherwise
constitutes a costly item in the budget of the urban school
is thereby turned to advantage.

Economies and other objectives are being achieved in
some instances by combining schools with other public
facilities, such as parks and libraries, on a single site. The
combinations present problems some authorities say they
have never been able to lick, but others somehow manage
to do so. Parks, for example, raise the necessity of policing
against perverts. The city of Grand Rapids, Michigan,
however, began combining its park and school sites back in
1951, and by 1961 had sixteen combination school-park
facilities, with three others under construction. It was also
planning to provide similar recreational space for every
one of its schools still in need of them even if that meant
buying nearby structures and razing them to the ground if
the land could not be obtained in any other way. The secret
of its success is to be found in one word: supervision. A
recreation leader, whose salary is paid half by the school
and half by the park system, is in attendance at the park
from ten o'clock in the morning until eight o'clock in the
evening, all year round. His presence affords insurance not
only against perverts but wards off vandalism to the school
as well, which is particularly bad during the summer
months when the schools are customarily closed down for
vacations and left unattended. New York City figures that
vandalism, 80 percent of it in broken windows smashed
mostly in July and August, runs it in excess of a million
dollars a year.

Library authorities, particularly, object to marrying their
facilities to schools on the grounds that such libraries are
generally avoided by adults and by children from other
schools. Indianapolis and Kansas City, however, have both
turned the trick and managed to conserve reading and
reference materials, as well as library help, in the process.
The combination has also been turned to advantage by

using library personnel to teach classes in the rudiments of library use, thereby freeing schoolteachers for other tasks. By turning the library away from the school and by other techniques of good design, such facilities, while close to the schools that use them most, are nevertheless set sufficiently apart that adults and children from other schools continue to think of and use them as separate libraries.

Efforts are under way to make fuller use of the school plant itself, for instance, by lengthening the school day and even the school year. Summer schools, generally six-week sessions with teachers paid extra for their time, are being used increasingly as a means of speeding up student progress, rather than solely for the remedial work that once characterized it. Various school systems from time to time have experimented with the so-called "four-quarter plan" which has all children attending school for consecutive quarters of 12 weeks each, with 13-week vacation staggered throughout the school year. Another plan, generally proposed in connection with wider use of the split session, would have students attend school for as many as 225 days a year instead of the customary 180. Though the year-round school meets considerable resistance today from both parents and teachers who do not wish to disturb traditional vacation patterns, it was common a century ago; New York City, for instance, operated its schools on a 49-week basis, Chicago on a 48-week basis, and Buffalo for the full 12 months back in 1840.

Some energetic, imaginative school administrators have succeeded in making their structures useful even on Saturdays – with the help of volunteers recruited from the ranks of their more talented or accomplished citizenry. A famous art collector in Roxbury, Connecticut, recently held eleven-year-olds spellbound with tales of art history. A writer in Orangeburg, New York, fascinated fifth- to twelfth-graders with the finer points of composition.

To achieve economy in construction, school designers

are specifying painted concrete block instead of plaster walls, lowering ceilings to eight feet from the customary twelve, and, where land costs permit, going in more for sprawling buildings capable of using low-maintenance concrete-shell roofs. Standardized factory-built "modules," which can be fitted together in varying combinations or refitted as requirements change, are similarly stretching school construction dollars. The implementation of these and other economies helped to contain the rise in school-building costs during the 1937-1957 period to 150 percent, while the cost of other construction was climbing 210 percent.

School districts have been immeasurably more successful in squeezing tax dollars from the general public than have other local governments, but they have nevertheless found it necessary to badger the federal government and state governments for bigger and bigger helpings of educational aid. Some 60 percent of state aid to local governments, in fact, goes for school purposes. The fact that most school districts are highly dependent for their revenue on a single well-worked levy, the property tax, makes it more and more difficult for them to substantially increase their own tax take. And even if they were successful in doing so, they could not hope to eliminate the wide divergence in educational means that exists between school districts within a given state, let alone between states.

One of the purposes of state aid, of course, is to narrow the gap in educational opportunities between school districts within the state. One of the purposes of federal aid, likewise, is to reduce that discrepancy between states. Whether such aid, state or federal, must inevitably lead to tighter controls over local education by these authorities is at least debatable; federal assistance to land-grant colleges, it is generally agreed, has not resulted in such control after more than a century of operation. Also worth considering is whether the establishment of minimum standards of education at the federal level is not preferable to the blatant neglect of any standards at all by some states.

The late Senator Robert A. Taft, an early supporter of federal aid to education, notwithstanding his conservative views, defended the principle thus: "The youth of our country," said he, "are not only citizens of the states in which they reside but also citizens of the entire nation."

Extraordinary divergencies in educational opportunities, nevertheless, continue to prevail among school districts both between and within states. In the 1959-1960 school year, for example, New York and California were spending $698 and $589, respectively, per pupil on their public education, based on average daily attendance, compared with $255 and $298 by South Carolina and Mississippi, respectively. A University of California survey in 1958 turned up one school district in the Golden State with $12 million in assessed valuations behind every one of its elementary classrooms – and another with only $48,000; the same study showed one county in Ohio with $4,700 in assessed property behind each pupil compared with $238,000 in another county.

State aid to education, of course, has been soaring sharply. It presently accounts for close to 40 percent of all school revenues, up from less than 20 percent in the 1929-1930 school year. Federal aid, in contrast, accounts for less than 4 percent of total school revenues.

In terms of what the dollar was worth in the 1955-1956 school year, the United States in 1899-1900 was spending $40.25 per pupil ($20.21 in actual dollars at the time) on public education. Half a century later, in 1949-1950, it was spending $212.18 on the same price-adjusted basis. Slightly more than a decade later, the sum in the same fixed dollars exceeded $300. The processes of urbanization and the workings of a new social and educational philosophy more than likely will rocket these costs to still greater heights in the years ahead.

CHAPTER NINE

Libraries and a Couple of Nuisances: Noise and Birds

IN Soviet Russia, delinquent borrowers of books from public libraries are reported to their job supervisors or labor union officials for discussion of their "lack of discipline." The procedure may be too arbitrary for a democracy, but American library officials with some knowledge of the technique say it appears to be effective in the Soviet Union.

In the United States, public library authorities with similar problems have to rely on fines. Enough books remain unreturned, however, to rank the burden high among those that library administrators have to bear. So much so, in fact, that public library systems in most of the nation's major metropolises employ one or more full-time collectors to do nothing but trace overdue books.

The New York Public Library has eight full-time literary retrievers on its payroll, three of whom make their rounds fully armed. Borrowers of books more than ten weeks overdue which have set the library back more than $10 after allowing for its 40 percent discount are subject to a personal visit. Known as the Special Investigators Department, the unit also employs six full-time clerks to send out reminders and otherwise ride herd with the necessary paperwork. New York's investigators never have had to use their guns, but they have hauled in as many as 1,500 books from a single residence: the apartment of a mentally disturbed girl in Greenwich Village who said she was interested in books but "didn't realize" what she was doing.

Libraries and a Couple of Nuisances

Libraries rarely fine delinquent borrowers more than the cost of the books. And courts tend to be lenient even in the most extreme cases because the offense rarely seems overly onerous to them. But more drastic action has occasionally been applied in an effort to contain the abuse. Early in 1961, for example, officials of the Public Library of East Orange, New Jersey, turned their worst cases over to the local police department, which proceeded to raid the homes of more than a dozen errant borrowers in the wee hours of the morning. Five who could not raise the necessary $100 bail spent the night in jail. Several were slapped with $25 fines. The raid aroused so much local opposition, however, that it is not likely to be tried soon again in East Orange or anywhere else in the United States, for that matter.

The Boston Public Library has traditionally made use of state police to call on persons with an excessive number of long-overdue books. The system has been reasonably successful, but police agencies generally argue they are already too overburdened with crime, traffic, juvenile misbehavior, and other such social sorrows to take on library abuses as well.

No one knows precisely how many library books go unreturned throughout the nation each year. Dr. Edward G. Freehafer, Director of the New York Public Library, figures that his system, with its more than 90 branches, loses some 25,000 or more volumes annually through nonreturns. Harold L. Hamill, Chief Librarian of the City of Los Angeles, estimates that city's 50-branch system has to write off about 12,000 books a year as irretrievable.

Though the unreturned book accounts for only about one in every thousand circulated, the loss along with the cost of retrieving others that were reluctant to return, reduce by approximately 10 percent the book-buying ability of public libraries. Los Angeles, for instance, estimated its book-buying volume at 235,000 copies during the year in which it lost 12,000 – and spent the equivalent sum they cost in recovering others. The problem of an unreturned book – and its kindred woe, the stolen book – is only one of the many types of headaches that beset librarians these days, and by no means the most vexatious of them.

Larger, better-educated populations are imposing greater demand for library services at the same time that information-hungry industry and enrollment-swollen college libraries are luring away competent library personnel. Television, apparently, is also stimulating the public's reading appetite through book discussions and the treatment of serious subjects. Heightened foreign travel is similarly channeling mass curiosity more deeply into the realm of the printed word. And, of course, the body of knowledge is itself increasing.

A more motorized, sprawling clientele, in the meantime, is settling many library users beyond the taxing jurisdiction of the local government supporting central library services. New facilities, nevertheless, must be constructed in the suburbs, and even then children and others with limited mobility must be served increasingly with bookmobiles capable of only the scantiest of literary selections. Parking spaces must be added to both new and existing premises. The city of Los Angeles was providing no such facilities at its libraries before 1957. It now allocates 20 to 30 spaces at every new branch it builds.

Soaring school enrollments are inundating public libraries with more calls on books and librarian time. With education budgets already overloaded, many public schools are passing the reading and reference buck to the public library. It is not just a matter of more pupils, either: increased emphasis on individualized instruction and self-study broadens the need both for more varied reading matter and for special guidance.

Increased leisure time, longer life spans, and a greater number of oldsters similarly sharpen the accent on reading. Business and professional needs for knowledge have never been greater. A survey of some 6,000 people who used the Newark, New Jersey, public library in one recent two-week period, revealed as many seeking "information relative to business, trade or professional needs" as were there for "general informational purposes" or for "recreational reading."

The greater demand for books is reflected in circulating rates. According to the Office of Education, persons served by public library systems borrowed an average of 4.2 books in 1960 compared with 3.4 in 1950. The books they are borrowing are also costlier than they used to be. Eleanor Ferguson, Executive Secretary of the American Library Association's Public Library Division in Chicago, figures the circulation of science books, for example, increased approximately 75 percent in the decade from 1950 to 1960, while the circulation of fiction rose but 45 percent. The average science book, she notes, costs libraries about 50 percent more than fiction does and is also more quickly outdated.

The nonresident user is a special problem to hard-pressed central city libraries, and a growing one. Recent surveys by the Newark Public Library in New Jersey and the Providence Public Library in Rhode Island indicate nonresidents may now be accounting for as much on-premise library use of big-city systems as residents. The Newark survey, conducted over a thirteen-day period in December, 1960, sampled some 5,000 library users in its main library and business branch; 50.8 percent were found to be nonresidents. They hailed from 189 different cities in New Jersey and from 38 other cities in 14 states other than New Jersey. The Providence sample, taken during a fourteen-day period in October, 1960, revealed 43 percent were nonresidents; Providence taxpayers are estimated to be subsidizing nonresident users of their library system to the tune of about $160,000 a year.

To the extent that nonresident users pay state and federal taxes which in turn go to aid library systems, they are, of course, helping support such institutions. However, only twenty-one states were providing state aid to local library systems in 1959, and federal aid, under the Library Services Act of 1956, is limited to communities under 10,000 population. Though special charges are generally levied on non-residents who want a library card so they can borrow books, those who forgo that privilege can use the facility nevertheless for reference, relaxation, or library service free of charge.

Plagued at the same time by the loss of professional personnel to burgeoning, better-paying business and college libraries, a number of public libraries have been compelled to curtail service on occasion. In the San Fernando Valley of Southern California, three new library branches that opened in 1961 were unable to keep their doors open on Saturday, and in one instance during weekday evenings as well, because they did not have the staffs to man them. In Minnesota, the opening of a new library was delayed 13 months because of the lack of personnel.

Some 15 percent of authorized public library positions were estimated to be unfilled in 1961, and the percentage is expected to double by 1965. Openings in public libraries presently outnumber library-school graduates seeking careers in their profession by approximately 20 to 1, according to the American Library Association.

Recent studies show only 28 percent of library-school graduates are going to work in public libraries compared with 72 percent who are taking positions in school, industrial, and commercial libraries. In Southern California, a librarian with a master's degree recently commanded $541 a month in private as against $464 in public service. Willard Woods, Executive Secretary of the Special Libraries Association, figures there are now some 10,000 corporation and other special-purpose libraries in the United States compared with only 1,600 in 1947. Opportunities in attractive academic atmospheres are also on the rise with the increase in enrollments.

Despite the lag in pay behind private industry, public library spending rose nearly 50 percent in the decade from 1950 through 1960. According to the United States Office of Education, libraries serving cities of more than 100,000 population ran up operating costs of $148 million in 1960 against just over $100 million in 1950. Personnel costs, which nearly doubled during the period, now account for approximately 70 percent of the average public library budget. With some 18 percent of that budget going for the maintenance of books and buildings, only 12 percent remains for the acquisition of additional volumes and other loanable materials. Yet the demand for books, as already noted, has never been greater.

Despite the pressures of climbing demand and increasing costs, library administrators are continually attempting to enhance the value of their facilities and services. They want the public to know what they have acquired and to make use of their acquisitions – not only books and periodicals but, increasingly, of recordings, films, and prints as well. In the long run, they are undoubtedly forcing library budgets still higher by such activities. To the extent that they increase library traffic, however, they hope to put the library dollar to better use, and thereby lower the cost of library service on a per-user basis.

The Municipal Library of Pomona, California, advertises regularly in that city's local newspaper, the daily *Progress Bulletin*. Its ad budget is relatively small – approximately $500 a year – but the ads win a goodly share of public interest by calling attention to reading matter that is newsy or of seasonal interest.

Pomona City Librarian Raymond M. Holt insists the ads more than pay for themselves by making Pomona's library more useful to more people and thereby perhaps also making future bond issues more acceptable when expansion becomes necessary. City ordinances which prohibit libraries from buying advertising space or from engaging in promotional activities handicap library authorities in extending public awareness of these services, and therefore limit the usefulness of the library itself. Libraries without such formal authority, however, need not be paralyzed in their pursuit of public attention. A number of libraries succeed in assigning personnel to public relations duties without ever identifying them as such while others manage to perform the function in various ways. Pomona's Mr. Holt, for instance, serves up a stimulating column on literary subjects for his local newspaper once a week. The paper is more than pleased to have the contribution, which costs it nothing, interests readers, and, at the same time, performs a public service.

The public library system of the County of St. Louis began locating branches close to shopping centers in 1956 on the theory that increased traffic would more than make up for the higher rental or the price of property. By 1962 it had three such facilities in operation. "Shopping centers provide us with the foot traffic we've been losing almost everywhere else," an official of the system reports.

Library authorities are also reaching out for patrons via radio and television and less dramatically through the use of the telephone, the mails, and even displays at public events. The library system of the city of Miami in 1962 was taking to the air for 15 minutes every Sunday at 8:30 A.M. with a radio show called "Let's Look It Up." On Tuesday nights during the school year it puts on a half-hour television show staged by a college professor on an educational TV channel at a cost of only $900 a year. Glib library administrators have managed to talk their way into free space at conventions, exhibitions, and other public gatherings; home shows, for example, are used for the display of books on gardening with due attention to the public library making them available.

Libraries and a Couple of Nuisances

In Clifton, Tennessee, public librarians conduct discussion groups in private homes, with library materials being provided as they are needed.

A number of public library systems make it standard practice to phone or drop a postcard to an individual who has expressed a special interest in a given field whenever a new book arrives or an article is published on that subject. Some systems levy a small charge for the service, generally just enough to cover the cost of the postcard or phone call, but many perform it gratis. The public library of Charlotte, North Carolina, uses the procedure to keep local officials abreast of developments on municipal issues.

Almost all large public library systems compile bulletins listing newly arrived materials. The bulletins are generally free. But some tailor their lists to special purposes and derive a fee in the process. The Toronto Public Library, for instance, sells a monthly index of thirty Canadian business and technical publications on a subscription basis.

As a corps, public library administrators are highly conservative individuals who often lack the imagination, energy, or courage to promote and extend their usefulness beyond traditional lines even where the question of charges is not at issue. One of the most effective devices for strengthening the ability of public libraries to cope with their problems, judging from the almost universal experience of those relatively few public library systems which have made use of it, is the organization of civic-minded citizens into groups generally known as "Friends of the Library." Such organizations have proven their value repeatedly in helping to campaign on behalf of a bond issue, providing volunteer help for a variety of clerical and non-clerical tasks to ease the burden on professional staffs, encourage the contributions of books and financial beneficence, and for many other purposes as well. Friends of the Seattle Public Library, for example, read and criticize manuscripts produced by a class in creative writing for persons over sixty years of age.

The New York Public Library had so much success with its special Committee on the Dance Collection in receiving advice on what volumes to carry, in staging special benefits to raise money for purchasing them, and in scrounging what it could from private collections, that it was already busy in 1962 planning the organization of such committees to serve many different departments in a like manner. In Greenwich, Connecticut, some one hundred volunteers donate a minimum of three hours a week to the public library – and lose the "privilege" when they miss two weeks' service in a row; they buy their own uniforms and are awarded hash marks on their sleeves, army-style, according to their length of service.

One reason "Friends" groups are not more widely cultivated by library administrators is to be found in the fear, as the chief librarian of one major eastern system put it recently, "that Friends tend to meddle." It is true, of course, that almost any interested and devoted group of Friends will, from time to time, make suggestions – sometimes, perhaps, rather uncomfortable ones. The capable administrator, of course, will welcome aid from any quarter and manage to run his own show nevertheless; the incapable one has good reason to fear more intimate knowledge of his operation by the community. Such "Friends," after all, are more likely to be Friends of the Library than Friends of the Administrator unless the two allegiances do, in fact, prove compatible.

There is no doubt about it: public libraries need all the help they can get if they are ever to rise above the role of mere custodians of the printed word and become what they should be – active participants in the community's continuing education. The opportunity of public libraries to serve adult citizens, whose formal education may long since have ended, is far too great to be lost through lack of vision or vigor. If what public library systems need for this purpose are enterprising administrators and capable managers rather than professional librarians hidebound to the concepts of another age, perhaps that is what they should be getting.

At the present time, this "affluent society" is spending only a pittance on its public libraries measured by almost any standard. Big-city library systems, those serving communities of more than 100,000 people, spent only $1.85 per capita on library service in 1960. That is low enough in itself, but it is vastly under what the American Library Association figures is necessary for the provision of minimum standards. The ALA puts that figure for larger cities at $3.50 a head. "We spend $5,000 on 12 years of formal schooling for each child," says one educator, "and we then spend less than $100 over his next 60 years to provide library service through which he can profit from that early investment." No one, of course, would contend that library expenditures have to come anywhere near those for public education, particularly in the age of the paperback, but the 500 to 1 proportion seems blatantly neglectful of library service, considering its potential role in the community.

A nation that prides itself on scientific achievement and universal education and aspires to greater cultural and intellectual heights can afford to spend considerably more for facilities that serve the deepest needs of young and old alike, business firms no less than private individuals. Gilbert Highet puts the case for public libraries in his volume, *Man's Unconquerable Mind,* in these terms: "The smallest local collection of books," says he, "may contain unique treasures or inspire a genius. Every library is an assertion of man's durable trust in intelligence as a protection against irrationalism, force, time and death. A town or church or school without an adequate collection of books is only half alive."

Public libraries are highly limited in their ability to fend for themselves financially. Their traditional fees and charges – on such items as cards for nonresident users, overdue books, and special rental collections – rarely meet more than 5 percent of their annual expenses. One reason for this fiscal anemia is to be found in the nature of the library service itself. Though some libraries have gone to a five-cent daily rate on overdue books, most stick to two- and three-cent charges for fear of discouraging return of their volumes altogether. Rental fees have been raised in some instances from three to five cents a day, but competition from paperbacks limits this increase, too. "Our rental customers generally were our more well-to-do patrons, and they would just as soon buy the book in paperback for 50 cents or a dollar as rent it for five cents a day," observes the chief librarian of a large eastern metropolis.

Des Moines is among the few cities which have boosted nonresident fees as high as $10 a year from the customary $1 to $5. Most library administrators, however, say high nonresident fees are more useful for discouraging nonresident borrowing than for raising revenues. Though some librarians wish to discourage nonresident use, most are dedicated to making the facility of the widest possible service to the metropolitan community as a whole.

As for levying fees on residents, library administrators are vigorously opposed to any such efforts. They argue that the practice would set the clocks back two centuries to the time when Benjamin Franklin first laid the groundwork for the institution of free public library service by launching the "subscription library." The subscription library opened vast institutional and other previously restricted collections to the use of anyone willing and able to pay a nominal fee to help defray library costs. It was considered an important advance in bringing literary treasures closer to the public, but the institution of free library service late in the nineteenth century is regarded with more reverence still.

Must devotion to the institution of free public library

service slam the door shut on all efforts to develop revenue sources within that function? Many library administrators claim it does, that once they start charging for some services the pressure will be on to neglect others. Yet the fact that public library systems do charge for certain privileges and services, and have done so for years, on rental collections, for instance, would seem to contradict that assertion. The provision of public library service free of charge to the general public need not preclude the generation of a "luxury" level of services capable both of enhancing the overall usefulness of the library and of defraying expenses of free services as well.

How, for instance, might the institution's purposes be compromised through a trial combination baby-sitting-storytelling session open to all comers at a nominal charge in the shopping-center branch of a public library? The service might be provided at little or no cost to the system itself if volunteer storytelling baby-sitters were used and might conceivably expose to the delights of the literary world youngsters who might otherwise be insulated from them at home.

Getting librarians to use volunteers for reading, or any other purpose for that matter, is often difficult. They argue volunteers don't always show up when they are supposed to. Yet, the problem can be overcome easily enough through a stand-by system consisting of other volunteers or paid staff, and some libraries have used it with excellent results. The argument is also made that "storytelling" is a "highly skilled art" which "only the professional librarian can perform." The contention, of course, is ridiculous. Almost any sizable community can produce highly talented readers, whose skills are wholly unrelated to training in professional library work. The volunteer reader, after all, need not select his reading material to perform his function; that exercise is, perhaps, more properly performed by the professional.

Just as some library administrators manage to make use of volunteer help, some also manage to supplement their income through the development of services they otherwise would not be providing. Early in 1962, for instance, the Library of Congress instituted a special reference service for businessmen, scientists, and others interested in being kept abreast of new developments in their field. The charge, $8 an hour, was intended solely to defray costs. By mid-1962, business was good enough to permit the library to maintain a two- to three-man staff specifically for the purpose, reports L. Quincy Mumford, Librarian of Congress. Previously, he notes, if a reference request were made which threatened to absorb too much of a librarian's time, a member of the staff was recommended for its performance on an after-hours basis at whatever rate he might negotiate for his own private purposes. That system continues to be followed in many public library systems throughout the nation today, though both library and staff would seem to benefit from a more formalized procedure under the library's own auspices.

Some public libraries, though fortunately not many of their patrons are aware of it, are prepared to invest all kinds of staff time on an individual research project at no charge whatsoever to the beneficiary. A few of these libraries even go to the trouble of putting the information in typewritten form, again without charge. Many users and prospective users of such services should be more than willing to pay for this type of service if that practice were instituted, but few public libraries attempt it. Indeed, the library's usefulness might be increased by such means. Many who would make use of such assistance are hesitant to do so lest they impose undue burdens on a public facility they have been told time and time again was overburdened and understaffed.

Library administrators are occasionally frustrated in their attempts to offer revenue-bearing services by inflexible municipal codes or city councils who, like a good many librarians themselves, continue to adhere to the concept that devotion to the principle of "free and universal library service" means that all library services imaginable must be rendered free to anyone who wishes to use them or not offered at all. The result is either to restrict the performance of extraordinary services altogether or to permit their pursuit only at the expense of the general public and, therefore, of purposes in still greater need.

The readiness to charge for special services could conceivably put public libraries in a better position to take speedier advantage of opportunities that may one day be presented by electronics and other advances in information retrieval. With the increasing pressure on personnel costs and less and less of the library budget left for the purchase of materials and equipment, the ability to make such investments pay off might considerably ease the task of convincing the taxpaying public of the wisdom of the outlay.

Most of the functions libraries might profitably perform, of course, are already being served by private enterprise – for the simple reason that they are profitable. And some which may seem to promise greater revenue may be self-defeating with respect to other library objectives. If fees for photocopying services, for example, were raised significantly above the 20 to 30 cents a page presently charged by most public library systems, more patrons might be tempted to tear pages out instead of going to the expense of having it copied. "Our photocopy service is principally one of self-defense," says one library administrator; "it's simply a means of reducing mutilation."

Nevertheless, there are services which public libraries would appear to be capable of performing profitably at no risk to themselves. The compilation of special bibliographies and abstracts updating material in fast-moving fields would appear to be worth more investigation than most systems have given it until now. Friends' groups, or the local business community, should be able to suggest other useful money-making services for the library to perform in a given community.

Greater efforts, of course, could be made to cut costs. Because personnel accounts for so large a portion of the overall budget, the most promising of these devices would seem to lie in the direction of stretching or conserving manpower through such techniques as the more widespread use of volunteer help. But there are other avenues to economy as well. By locating its new main library over a depressed six-lane city highway, for instance, the city of Hartford, Connecticut, saved over $100,000 recently in land acquisition costs even after allowing $80,000 for bridging the roadway, according to City Librarian Edwin G. Jackson.

The Hartford library and others around the country are saving money on parking space and providing patrons with better service at the same time by providing drive-up windows where patrons can pick up books they have telephoned for in advance. Mailbox-like bookdrops make the return of books easier from the curbside and are serviceable, of course, even when the library itself is closed.

However they might cut costs and raise revenues, it is hardly likely public library systems are going to be able to meet their growing problems and rise to their opportunities without heftier helpings of public funds. Says Eric Moon, Editor of the semi-monthly *Library Journal,* in New York: "It's inescapable. Library administrators are going to have to convince the general taxpaying public they need more money – and they are going to have to lean more heavily on state and federal aid as well."

Approximately 87 percent of public library revenues are derived from local taxes, 4 percent from gifts and endowments, nearly 3 percent from state grants and approximately 6 percent from other sources. The trend in state aid is highlighted by the recent experience of New York State. Albany multiplied its assistance to library systems in the Empire State more than tenfold between 1950 and 1960, from less than $200,000 to over $2 million. Federal aid to public libraries, which began with passage of the Library Services Act in 1956 and was subsequently extended to June 30, 1966, makes $7.5 million available annually but is available only to public library systems serving rural areas of less than 10,000 population.

It is doubtful whether there ever was a time when the importance of stimulating public interest in the potentials of the public library was greater than it is today. Technology affords the opportunity to make research and the pursuit of knowledge an unprecedented adventure with unprecedented rewards. New library designs and concepts – fireside lounges and the generous use of glass and light, for instance – similarly make it possible to transform libraries into highly inviting institutions. A society that spends millions inducing college youngsters to smoke, take another drink, and see the latest in sex and violence at the local movie house might well ponder the advisability of a little bit of extravagance at the local library.

A NOTE ON NOISE

To Dr. Vern O. Knudsen, Los Angeles physicist and former Chancellor of the University of California at Los Angeles, noise is "one of the waste products of the 20th Century – as unwanted and unnecessary as smog, polluted water or littered streets. It is," he contends, "one of the chief drawbacks to the enjoyment of modern urban living."

The late Bernard De Voto once maintained: "Our culture is more likely to perish from noise than from radioactive fallout."

There's no doubt about it: technology and urban growth have conspired to create a cacophony capable of jarring human nerves, sabotaging concentration, robbing the weary of needed rest, impairing human health and performance, and, in general, trespassing on man's most prized and private possession: his mental preserve.

A century or so ago, the highest noise level man customarily encountered in his daily life was conversational speech, about 60 decibels of sound measured from three feet away. Technology, however, has since raised that level sharply. In the past thirty years alone, the height of sound to which urban man has been exposed has increased from 120 decibels, produced by a pneumatic chipping hammer, to 150 decibels, created by a rocket engine. If that average increase of one decibel per year continues in the years ahead, the decibel dosage could begin seriously to jeopardize not only man's aural health but ultimately even reach a lethal level. Experiments have already shown that 160 decibels can kill small furry animals such as rats and mice, whose bodies convert sound into energy with resultant temperature increases greater than their furry bodies can dissipate.

Man is somewhat more durable, at least physically. Even so, exposure to 160 decibels of sound can make him deaf for life; it may also cause a piercing of the inner ear which, if accompanied by infection, can result in meningitis. Much lower dosages can also be damaging: exposure to 100 decibels for eight hours a day over a protracted period of time may induce permanent hearing loss, according to Dr. Henning E. von Gierke, an Air Force specialist. That sound level is only slightly higher than that of a subway train measured twenty feet away.

Persons living near busy jet airports are advised by authorities to take periodic hearing tests, because constant exposure to noise levels as low as 85 decibels can impair hearing if the noise is persistent enough.

High frequency sounds have been known to induce forms of epileptic behavior in laboratory animals. Whether there is any relationship between noise and epilepsy in human beings has yet to be established, but there is some suspicion noise may be a contributing or aggravating factor.

Loss of hearing, though it is caused by many other factors besides noise, is the nation's Number One physical impairment. A recent survey by a large pharmaceutical house found the disability accounted for nearly 25 percent of all noninstitutionalized physical impairments in the United States at the time. In all, it brought the total of persons suffering from hearing losses to approximately 6 million. By way of contrast, impairment in the use of arms, legs, and back accounted for 21 percent of all physical ailments between them. Nearly twice as many persons, it was found, suffered hearing handicaps as suffered visual handicaps.

Noise-induced hearing loss is not a new problem, but it is becoming "more important because of expansion of industry and development of high-speed machines," the drug company's researchers stated.

Truck drivers reportedly suffer hearing ailments more often in their left than in their right ears. The left ear, of course, is more exposed to traffic noise.

With more vehicles on the road than ever before and their numbers constantly rising, the so-called "freeway rumble" is assuming the same blighting role on property values once performed by elevated and surface railroad tracks. Decreased property values due to climbing noise levels near jet airports have influenced officials of the Federal Housing Authority to deny mortgage insurance on new homes in certain areas. Officials of the Urban Renewal Administration are also seeking to avoid the spread of urban blight under the noise umbrella by directing the course of redevelopment, wherever possible, away from jet flight paths.

"If it did nothing else but interfere with sleep," exclaims Dr. Knudsen, "noise would be a menace to good health. And this," says he, "it does on a gigantic scale." Though he lives in the relatively quiet Brentwood section of Los Angeles, Dr. Knudsen does not pass a single night without wearing a set of earplugs to bed. He figures the plugs have halved his nightly awakenings by snipping 30 decibels off his nocturnal intake of noise.

With the playthings of power proliferating in both the private and the public realm, in the garden with its power mowers as well as in the air with its helicopters and its jets, on the road as well as in the living room, and with population densities thickening, the evil threatens to mount.

Indeed, the city din may already be working permanent damage on urban ears. A New York ear surgeon, Dr. Samuel Rosen, surveyed more than 500 members of a primitive African tribe living in an isolated section of the Sudan near the Ethiopian border in the winter of 1960-1961. He found most male members of the tribe enjoyed as good hearing between the ages of seventy and eighty as did a random sample of twenty- to thirty-year-olds tested at a state fair in Wisconsin in 1954. Lower blood pressure, a meager protein diet, racial, hereditary, and other factors may have helped preserve the Mabaans' hearing. But the fact that they lived in an environment free of any noises louder than their own occasional singing, Dr. Rosen believes, is worthy of further investigation.

Though noisemakers of all kinds, roaring trucks and sports cars, clanging garbage cans and booming hi-fi sets, are getting more numerous, the most extreme offenders of the aural peace, of course, are the vehicles of the modern air age – the helicopters, jets, and, in certain areas, rocket engines as well. Such noise is often costly to its perpetrators as well as annoying to its victims. The average American jetliner has close to $100,000 invested in noise suppressors. The mere measurement of rocket-engine noise, carried out for reasons of human safety as well as to achieve technical improvements, is costing the nation an estimated $5 million to $20 million yearly. Winemakers in California's Napa Valley some years back complained that noise from a jet-engine testing facility was souring their grapes; the engine tester ultimately installed silencing apparatus to avoid suit.

The noises that are most common on the urban scene, however, are not aerospace noises at all – but those, paradoxically enough, that are the easiest and cheapest to eliminate. Engines in average-sized trucks are only two to three times more powerful than those in expensive automobiles; equipped with proper mufflers, such trucks need be no noiser than three or four Cadillacs whispering in unison.

Owners of noisy sports cars and motorcycles could likewise sublimate their egomania on the decibel scale at relatively modest cost. In some countries, like Switzerland and West Germany, they are compelled to do so. Owners of foreign sports cars in the United States, for the most part, are required to do nothing more to their vehicles than maintain the noise level of the original equipment despite the fact that in some instances such equipment would not otherwise have been deemed permissible.

What can cities do about noise, the seemingly inevitable by-product of busy urban life? Well, they can do more than sit on their hands and fret over their helplessness and lack of knowledge in the subject as so many of them are doing right now.

For instance, they can, and a few of them do, use zoning powers to keep residential developments from sprouting in the flight paths of noisy jetports. They can also compel builders to insulate their structures better against noise in the vicinity of airports by exercising existing provisions in their building codes or inserting them where they do not now exist. There is no excuse for not knowing where such measures are needed: the Federal Aviation Agency provides noise-level maps on request which are specifically designed for precautionary purposes.

Nor should cities be confining their assault on noise to airport areas. A leading acoustical authority contends the noise level in New York City, which draws some 300,000 police warnings and citations yearly, could be slashed by 80 percent by compelling trucks and buses to use effective mufflers, getting garbage collectors to install rubber pads on their rear shelves, and convincing homeowners to use plastic or other nonmetallic containers for their refuse.

Paris and Mexico City are among the cities which have demonstrated that civic silence is attainable even in this blaring era. Once among the din capitals of the world, they are now paragons of municipal quiet, thanks largely to the strict enforcement of ordinances against the blowing of automobile horns except in emergencies but also because of other measures. Paris, for example, is replacing noisy metal wheels on its subway trains with rubber-tired ones. Toronto's new subway system makes extensive use of glass fiber in the walls of its underground tunnels and beneath its station platforms as a noise-absorbent.

The Swiss government has been particularly successful in its enforcement of vehicle noise levels. Its police stop vehicles without warning and place them on test stands to measure their sound levels. The Swiss have achieved further compliance with the law by threatening to prohibit the use of noisy vehicles at night.

Under an antinoise law passed in Britain in 1960, a complaint signed by three persons is sufficient to obtain a summons against the offender. British common law holds freedom from noise essential to the full enjoyment of one's dwelling.

A number of stringent antinoise measures, including thrice-yearly muffler inspections, a ban against unnecessary horn honking, and the strict imposition of fines against howling pets, has earned Memphis, Tennessee, a reputation for relative serenity among U.S. cities. "If you hear a horn blowing in Memphis," says one authority who recently studied noise practices in various American cities, "you know one of two things: either a stranger is in town or there is about to be an accident. The police," says he, "are strict about enforcing the ban – and proud to do so."

Not many city officials, however, have the concern or the courage to enact, much less enforce, antinoise measures. Such regulation invariably costs the noisemakers money, however nominal the outlay may be, and thus arouses their wrath. The onus of punishment likewise stirs opposition. And the likelihood that enforcement of noise ordinances would add to the duties of already overburdened police departments similarly tends to reduce the crusade's appeal to city officials. The onus on the offender and the load on the police, however, can be lightened considerably when antinoise regulations are administered, as they are in some countries, by nonpolice personnel, such as building inspectors.

The late Fiorello La Guardia, early in his first administration as mayor of New York, sought to clad the city's horses with rubber instead of with iron shoes. He never got his way. Ultimately, technology removed the beast from the street. But it trotted worse demons of the decibel out to take its place.

A WORD ON BIRDS

ALONG with all their other problems, cities are having to wage war against growing flocks of urban birds. The winged creatures deface buildings, discomfort pedestrians, threaten health, and, lately, have even begun to menace jetliners by crashing through windshields and fouling air intakes. City officials have tried trapping, shocking, inebriating, hosing, blowing, poisoning, and shooting the feathery foe. They have attempted to scare them with tape recordings of other birds in pain, fool them with the faked sounds of such natural enemies as owls and snakes, and shoo them off with powerful searchlights and noisemakers. They have plowed up their breeding grounds and made their perches on buildings untenable by smearing ledges with sticky, foul-smelling, irritating, or just plain slippery substances.

But the majority of stratagems do not seem to work, while those which promise to do so are speedily vetoed by humane societies and the citizenry at large. So the feathery nuisances proliferate and spread across the map.

One of the most troublesome of urban birds is the varied species known as the starling. The robin-sized bird was unknown in the New World before 1890. And it might have remained unknown had it not been for a single mention of the species in Part 1 of Shakespeare's *Henry IV:* "I'll have a starling shall be taught to speak nothing but 'Mortimer.'" That single late sixteenth century sentence was enough to qualify forty pairs of starlings for free trips to the United States two centuries later at the expense of a wealthy New Yorker named Eugene Schieffelin, a lover of both birds and Shakespeare with the peculiar ambition of populating the United States with every bird mentioned in Shakespeare's plays. Many of the transplanted guests never survived. The starlings thrived.

From New York the birds spread to Connecticut, then into the Midwest and the South. More recently they have made their way to the Far West; Washington attracted them first with its apple orchards, but the California climate eventually got to them as well. Pest-control authorities figure at least 75 major cities around the United States are now starling breeding grounds.

Their hazard is becoming a serious one to air travelers of the human variety. On at least two occasions, the birds have been scooped in considerable numbers into the air intakes of jetliners. In one instance, the aircraft had not yet left the ground, so the pilot was able to taxi it back to the hangar for repairs. Another was less fortunate: it had an engine snuffed out and went crashing into Boston Harbor with a toll of 62 lives in October, 1960.

Because of the growing threat to air safety, the Federal

Aviation Agency early in 1961 transferred $100,000 of its funds to the United States Fish and Wildlife Service to help support efforts to rid the nation of the nuisance in a manner which would not stir the sensitivities of too many citizens.

That's the rub. Hamburg, Germany, has apparently succeeded in bringing its starlings under control by sprinkling white corn impregnated with strychnine on the pavements of its main square every morning at five o'clock; it picks up dead birds by the score before traffic gets rolling. In the United States and Britain humane societies have effectively thwarted such efforts to achieve any such "final solution" to the bird problem.

Extermination, of course, is easier to effect when it is not being carried out before many sensitive eyes. But that generally means the birds must be caught first. Traps, however, have so far proved both costly and generally ineffective.

Officials in Springfield, Illinois, thought they had the problem licked when they caught some 20,000 of the birds by luring them into a huge tent with powerful 1,000-watt lights mounted on the floor. The birds were subsequently gassed, but countless others swooped down upon the city a short time later.

Philadelphia, the City of Brotherly Love (and birdly affection), tried tranquilizing its birds not long ago. It soaked bits of grain in a liquid form of a sedating drug and sprinkled the grain in favorite roosting places. Other cities have been known to soak grain in gin for the same purpose. Verona, Italy, even tried mixing sleeping tablets in birdfood. But none of the chemical efforts succeeds in decimating much of the bird flock.

One product, marketed under the name Roost-No-More, is a sticky compound designed to make things uncomfortable underfoot and cause the creatures to go elsewhere. Its manufacturer, the National Bird Control Laboratories of Skokie, Illinois, more than doubled sales of the product in the five years to 1960, from $40,000 to some $100,000. And judging from the number of birds still hanging around, it can go on doing so for some time to come.

Albany, New York, and other municipalities have attempted to sting the feathery foe with electric wires stretched across roosting places. Sharp-toothed steel wire has also been tried to get the birds to move on. Metal slides set at sharp angles have been used to keep the birds from landing in the first place. Not long ago, the British Ministry of Works devised a slippery varnish that dries to an unbelievable slickness, causing the birds to skid all over the sprayed surface, Still, the birds always manage to find some place to go.

The city of Poughkeepsie, New York, periodically hoses birds from their roosting places with fire hoses. Newton, Massachusetts, once tried blowing them away – with a high-pressure tree sprayer manipulated by a city forester.

Practically everyone, at one time or another, has tried to scare birds away. Two biologists at Pennsylvania State University in 1953 recorded the screechings of a squeezed starling and then played the tape over a loudspeaker where other starlings were clustered. Others have tried luring the birds into traps by playing mating calls recorded on tape. Such devices have proved effective for only short periods of time.

Stuffed owls, fake snakes, and rubber mice have likewise caused bird hearts to palpitate for brief periods of time before the foes were recognized as impostors.

Noisemakers – from special shotguns with shells that explode in the air to low-flying airplanes with wailing sirens – have proved highly effective except that the annoyance is greater than humans themselves can bear. Supersonic sound waves, which birds can hear but man cannot, have failed to keep the birds away for long.

Blinking lights were once installed atop a building in Los

Angeles to keep the birds awake so they would go elsewhere for a good night's rest. Instead, the birds shielded themselves behind air intakes, chimneys, and other handy structures.

Recently, municipal authorities have sought to combat the nuisance with birth-control pills flavored to birdie tastes. The procedure, however, is exceedingly expensive. Some birds take more than their share, while others appear capable of shaking off effects in just a couple of months.

There is hope, of course, that some cheap, permanent means of sterilization may yet be found. In the meantime, the forces of biology work their awesome magic. One species of nuisance bird, pigeons, are capable of leaving as many as 100 or more progeny behind them in their ten-year lifespan.

At the same time that more humans seek to destroy nuisance birds, others attempt to protect them and even ease their plight. The Bird Guardians League of San Francisco spends an estimated $10,000 a year feeding pigeons in that city's parks. Recognizing the nuisance to city dwellers, the league's septuagenarian president, former silent movie star J. Edward Dahlen, launched a drive not long ago to raise $10,000 for an aviary south of the city where pigeons might live out their natural lives.

Now city authorities have only to convince the birds of the advantages of rural as compared with urban life. Or they might direct their persuasive powers at humans instead.

CHAPTER TEN

The City Dump

SPECTACLE Island, two miles offshore in Boston Bay, is aptly named. For 37 years, from 1922 to 1959, scows dumped 25 percent of Boston's refuse there. The garbage got so high – 35 to 45 feet across the island's 50 acres – it became uneconomical to pile it any higher. In 1959 the city put its first incinerator into operation – a plant capable of burning up to 900 tons of refuse daily, about 60 percent of all the rubbish Boston was then producing.

The other 40 percent of Boston's refuse was still being dumped on open land in mid-1961 when John Francis Flaherty, Chief of the Sanitary Division of the city's Public Works Department, declared: "We're running out of dump sites at a rapid rate. Before long, Boston will have to burn all its refuse in expensive incinerators and even then it will have to find someplace to bury the ash and noncombustibles like tin cans and glass."

Boston's disposal problem is becoming increasingly common among American cities. Indeed, a good many municipalities are in even worse shape because of their speedier growth. Dump sites become scarcer as they are built upon, and also less acceptable to folks who move nearby. And it's not just a matter of running out of space to dump trash. The refuse pile itself is getting more voluminous, partly because of expanding populations and partly because each individual is generating more waste on the average. According to the Department of Health, Education, and Welfare, the average American is presently producing close to 3½ pounds of refuse a day compared with approximately

2 pounds twenty years ago. About 1.5 pounds of this amount, it is estimated, come from within the home, including three-tenths of a pound of wet garbage, the rest comes from yard refuse, the result of a big boom in post-World War II home building. Persons in apartments, especially those equipped with sink-type garbage-disposal units, produce as little as 1.2 pounds of refuse daily, while others in highly affluent areas may average as much as four or five pounds a day.

"We can afford to buy more – so we have more to throw away," explains Harrison P. Eddy, senior partner of Metcalf & Eddy, a Boston engineering firm which has been designing incinerators since 1897. "Many more items," says he, "are wrapped in paper these days. Newspapers are thicker. Magazines are bought in greater quantity. Toys and gadgets break more easily. And, in general, the life of our goods is shorter than those our grandfathers used."

Paradoxically, higher living standards have actually reduced the production of garbage as such – the wet, deteriorating kind that results principally from food wastes. Trimmed prepackaged meats, shelled peas, and other convenience foods, along with the greater use of disposers that grind food scraps in the sink and flush them down the drain, have reduced the proportion of wet garbage in the total refuse pile from approximately 75 percent in 1940 to 20 percent in 1960. At the same time, however, the rise in homeownership has produced vast quantities of garden waste, while paper and other nonfood discard has also increased.

The federal government's Number One garbage man, Ralph J. Black, Senior Sanitary Engineer for Solid Wastes at the United States Public Health Service, figures the United States in 1961 produced about 110 million tons of residential and commercial refuse. In 1940, he figures, the residential and commercial total was less than 40 million tons. Industrial waste, of course, is also soaring, but its collection and disposal is not so much a municipal problem as it is the concern of industry itself.

Even cities which are losing population are being saddled with bigger collection and disposal headaches as a result of the speedier rise in per capita refuse generation. Washington, D.C., for example, suffered a decrease in its population from 802,000 in 1950 to 764,000 in 1960, but its discard in the same period rose from 2.7 million to 3.5 million cubic yards.

The cheaper way to dispose of refuse is simply to dump it in an open field and burn it. The procedure costs the municipality almost nothing, particularly if it owns the land. Supervision may be provided at big city dumps, but smaller municipalities generally do not provide even that. The Public Health Service reports about 40 percent of municipalities with over 5,000 population and 80 percent of those smaller are still using open dumps as their principal means of refuse disposal.

Urban sprawl, however, is making the unpleasant sight, the noxious smoke, and the menace to health of many open dumps less and less tolerable to nearby residents and public officials alike. The Public Health Service claims the practice has long since become "inadequate" for the disposal problems of urban areas as they exist today, and condemns it as promoting insect and rodent infestation and as a danger to neighboring communities.

Those who live near open dumps are only too familiar with the damage they can do. Rats and vermin flourish on their garbage. Swarms of flies nourished by them have been known to deface the walls of houses with their droppings. Crickets bred by them have consumed wallpaper off interior walls. Cockroaches that multiplied in a load of bad cotton constituted a scourge to the city of Bedford, Connecticut, for months.

Thrown suddenly into the proximity of open dumps while aspiring to a more genteel existence with rising incomes, hordes of suburban homeowners are speedily writing "finis" to the open dump. To meet their growing disposal needs, therefore, municipalities are having to turn to more expensive methods. The most satisfactory of them, for the cost, is a technique known as the "sanitary landfill." Basically, it is a fill-and-cover operation, with the refuse being spread over a given area by bulldozer or other means, and compacted by the weight of the vehicle in the process. When the compacted rubbish gets 4 or 5 feet deep, it is covered with a layer of soil approximately 6 to 12 inches thick, and the rubbish-spreading process continues until it is ready for "topping off" with a final layer of dirt approximately 2 feet thick, enough to discourage rats from digging into it and keep vermin away. The refuse is bedded down with a blanket of soil at least 6 inches thick every night to minimize health hazards, odors, and other nuisances, until it is ready for "topping."

Natural depressions such as canyons or marshes make ideal landfill sites. Where they do not exist, special areas may be excavated for the purpose, with the extra soil being hauled away or used for some other needy purpose. Where it is desirable to raise the level of the site above surrounding ground, to permit better drainage for agricultural land, for instance, the soil may not be moved at all. Often, the completed fill is turned into use as a park. Nowhere in the process is there a smoke nuisance.

Champaign, Illinois, pioneered the sanitary landfill method of refuse disposal as far back as 1904. But the technique did not really begin to get into the ground until after World War II when bulldozers came into common use and housing subdivisions raised the pressure on open dumps. According to the American Public Works Association, it is now being used at least in part by some 60 percent of the nation's larger municipalities (over 5,000 population) and more than 30 percent of its smaller ones.

Sanitary landfills, however, are not only costlier to operate than open dumps but they do not last as long either. The cost of operating an open dump is estimated at well under 25 cents per ton of refuse even when the land is privately owned and must be leased for the purpose with supervision provided. The cost of operating a landfill site runs anywhere from 75 cents to $1.25 a ton, depending on how much excavation or other preparation is necessary beforehand.

Because refuse is buried in a landfill site as is, without burning, it consumes space much more rapidly than an open dump, where the refuse is burned and soil blankets are not used. A 100-acre site operated as an open burning dump, for instance, will serve a population of 100,000 people for approximately a century, according to sanitation authorities, where a landfill site of the same size dug down to a typical depth of 25 feet will serve the same population only about 30 years.

Thus, whether they stick to the open dump or go to the sanitary landfill, cities are having to reach farther and farther out for land to dispose of their refuse. The cost of the longer haul is eased only somewhat by the use of transfer stations, where small collection trucks can drop their loads into larger ones which then proceed to the ultimate disposal site, sometimes 40 or 50 miles away, while the smaller vehicle resumes its residential rounds. The transfer operation begins to be economical when the one-way haul to the disposal site exceeds 10 miles.

As they go farther out for disposal sites, city sanitation planners are running increasingly into still another hard fact of sprawling urban life: city limits and the emotionally charged repugnance of one city toward the refuse of another. Yet, such accommodation of one municipality's refuse by another becomes even more necessary with urban growth for the simple reason that fast-growing communities are not equally endowed when it comes to that increasingly valuable urban resource known as potential dump sites.

286

The City Dump

Communities that are most heavily built up and, therefore, most in need of disposal sites are often the ones most lacking that resource.

Indeed, even approaches to dump sites are becoming increasingly difficult to come by.

The county of Los Angeles had its eye for years on a large canyon in the city of Glendale as a dump site. When, not so long ago, a proposal was made to put the topography known as Scholl Canyon to work for the purpose, the protest from homeowners along the canyon route was vigorous as they envisioned the danger to children, the noise, and other hazards which might ride the parade of rumbling garbage trucks on their way to the promised fill. The fact that Glendale's own refuse-disposal headaches were to be eased in the process, and two bits deposited into its coffers for every ton of refuse dumped for the provision of a future park and golf course atop the garbage heap, did little to allay the objections of roadside residents. The county finally won the use of the canyon as a disposal site only after it agreed to build its own road for the purpose over the back hills at a cost of $300,000. The road will keep the county's refuse trucks off Glendale's streets and Glendale will continue to receive 25 cents a ton toward the park fund.

As dump sites grow scarcer, the need for the sharing of dumping resources among municipalities, of course, becomes more urgent. The Pennsylvania Economy League for years has been attempting to mobilize the country's municipalities in an areawide disposal effort without success. Says Emery P. Sedlak, director of the League: "Pittsburgh's refuse disposal problem is bad enough, but the problem is far worse in the County, which has only three times Pittsburgh's population in 129 separate municipalities." The league's plan calls for the construction of two incinerators and the provision of nine landfill sites which would serve all of the county's municipalities.

Where scarce disposal sites are wholly or largely in private hands, the disappearance of dump sites may work special hardships on the community. This is especially true if collection activities are also conducted by private firms. Owners of scarce sites anxious to win rubbish-collection contracts themselves are not beyond making their disposal premises unavailable to other collectors. So strategic is his position, in fact, that the dump-site owner may himself be used for the exertion of pressure; not long ago an official of the Teamsters Union was found guilty of coercing a dump-site owner to deny dumping privileges to collectors using non-Teamster labor. The result of using dump-site monopolies to thin out the ranks of those bidding on city refuse-collection contracts is to raise collection as well as disposal costs to the community. The small community, however, often lacks the financial resources to buy the dump site, much less build an incinerator. Cooperation with other municipalities for a common solution to the disposal problem thus becomes essential, but the level of desperation must be comparable among would-be partners before it is likely to be realized.

Boston, which actually trimmed its refusal disposal costs from nearly $600,000 in 1949 to less than $400,000 by 1958 while holding its collection expense exactly at $2.2 million, credits the accomplishment to its acquisition of private dump sites. Sanitation Chief Flaherty claims the land is costing the city nothing since he figures the leveled properties will bring in at least as much as the city paid for them when it is ready to put them back on the market.

Communities with publicly owned dump sites have managed to achieve some notable economies on the collection end by turning collection activities over to private enterprise. Oak Park, Michigan, figures the switch from municipal to private collection enabled it to cut its costs per stop from 23.1 cents in 1961 to less than 20 cents in 1962. An ordinance passed by the city council in 1952 required the installation of sink-type garbage grinders in homes built thereafter; it is credited with helping to pave the way for private collection by reducing the health risk of refuse that might be delayed in pickup.

The growing scarcity of tolerable dump sites and the rising standard of dumping that discourages the use of open dumps even when they are not within the range of annoyance are just a few among several disposal avenues that have been closed to urbanites in recent years. The pig and even the ocean are no longer the receptacles they used to be.

For centuries, swine helped solve man's refuse disposal problem by eating up almost everything Homo sapiens discarded in the way of animal or vegetable matter. So common was the practice that pig farmers customarily bought additional small pigs in anticipation of the peak August-September garbage season. The creature was able to turn a ton of garbage into 50 pounds of pork simply by eating to his heart's content. The process was highly profitable for the farmer when, as was the case just before World War II, he could buy a ton of garbage for only $5.00 to $7.00 and get $20.00 worth of pork from it, or $0.10 a pound, at wholesale. Municipal officials also had good reason to rejoice as swine made fatter pigs of themselves on the community's discard: not only did it lighten and in some instances entirely eliminate their disposal problems but the income from the sale of garbage by the city helped offset collection costs as well.

A change in the nature of man's discard away from wet garbage toward such nonfood wastes as paper and tin cans, of course, made the pig less thorough a consumer of community waste. But the animal's usefulness in waste disposal suffered its most serious blow in 1952 when a disease peculiar to swine and often fatal to suckling pigs, vesicular exanthema, was discovered in California, Wyoming, and Nebraska and in more than a dozen other states. The discovery resulted in the slaughter of over 100,000 hogs valued at over $3 million. Worse still from the standpoint of future sanitation needs, it caused almost every state in the Union to ban the feeding of raw garbage to hogs altogether. The federal government similarly prohibited the practice among hogs or hog products involved in interstate commerce.

The need for cooking garbage before serving it to pigs promptly punctured its price. Garbage that was worth $5.00 a ton suddenly plummeted to 50 cents a ton. Many municipalities preferred to quit salvaging the stuff altogether, figuring it was worth 50 cents a ton to spare residents the trouble of separating their wet garbage from other refuse. The farmer, for his part, found commercial feeds a cheaper source of pork than garbage which had to be cooked.

Oceans, lakes, and rivers once served as important depositories for the refuse of many cities. But these opportunities are also being speedily sealed by increased urbanization. Soaring quantities of garbage simply cannot be accommodated by lakes and rivers whose waters are being used over and over again by increasing numbers of people. Even municipalities which dumped their garbage into the sea are finding they can no longer do so because their shorelines are now packed with bathers and other recreation seekers. New York, which in the 1930's used to dump a good deal of its refuse offshore, was forced by a Supreme Court action brought by New Jersey to discontinue the practice. No major city in the United States today dumps its refuse into the sea.

City sanitation planners must worry increasingly about water pollution even in dry-land disposal. Delaware County, Pennsylvania, decided to build three incinerators when potential landfill areas were found to lie in the watersheds of nearby reservoirs. Landfill sites elsewhere have been vetoed when it was feared the groundwater level might rise above the refuse base and thus become contaminated.

The City Dump

Before World War II, when dump sites were relatively close in and open burning was permitted, many people in small towns and the outskirts of big cities hauled their trash out to the dump site themselves. Indeed, it was something of a social occasion for some people: they would take coffee and even sandwiches with them out to the dump site on a Saturday or Sunday afternoon and swap stories as well as discards. These practices are also going by the wayside not only because dump sites are harder to find but also because traffic congestion conspires to discourage it.

Though a few municipalities have managed in recent years to achieve economies by turning the collection function over to private contractors, the trend in collection has been overwhelmingly away from private operation. Soaring costs and the public's reluctance to pay private collectors enough to offset these costs – the same pincers which have squeezed so many private companies out of the transit business – have resulted in the almost complete "municipalization" of garbage collection in the United States. Some 75 percent of American municipalities were providing garbage collection service in 1955, according to a survey by the American Public Works Association; only 25 percent, it discovered, relied on private contractors.

Municipalities, however, are no less immune to soaring costs than are private contractors. Climbing wages and other inflationary forces have conspired to send refuse collection and disposal expenses upward. The Public Health Service figures municipal expenditures on refuse collection and disposal quadrupled in the period from 1940 to 1960, from $300 million to approximately $1.2 billion. The continued exhaustion of close-in disposal sites will undoubtedly help push these outlays still higher in the years ahead, as will the persistent push by labor for better wages.

As their refuse burdens mount, municipalities will be trying harder and harder to get residents themselves to lend a bigger hand in the collection chore – by using household garbage grinders, for instance, easier-to-handle garbage receptables, or simply by placing their garbage cans at the curb instead of making sanitation crews fetch them from alleys and yards and return them there.

Several techniques, in fact, are already being used to lighten the collection chore. One of the most unusual was first tried by Denver in July, 1961. It was born from the belief that some folks will go out of their way to help the garbage man if they can conveniently get rid of their refuse a bit sooner. Denver didn't suddenly create a lot of free dumps at strategic locations around the city, but it did the next best thing: it assigned nine big garbage trucks to the parking lots of five well-located shopping centers and one drive-in bank each Saturday during the summer months with instructions to accept all grass clippings delivered between the hours of 10:00 A.M. and 6:00 P.M. Garden refuse, particularly grass cuttings which rot quickly, produce flies, smell, and are bulky, is especially noxious to homeowners.

It didn't take long for the idea to catch on. Lines of vehicles at corners where the trucks were stationed frequently contained more than twenty vehicles. Hosting merchants, unconcerned over the congestion, promptly began directing their advertising toward the Saturday crowds.

"It was the most popular thing we ever did," exclaimed William Shoemaker, manager of the city's Public Works Department, shortly after the operation began. The experiment proved so successful from the standpoint of the city's refuse economics, Mr. Shoemaker planned to continue it indefinitely throughout each grass-growing season, which runs from about the first of June to mid-September in Denver. One important economy comes from having the trucks remain stationary as one load after another is brought to them in rapid succession. When they are full, they take off for the nearest dump 10 to 15 miles away as empty vehicles take their places. Another economy results from the necessity for only one man per truck, since he and the motorist can easily dump containers of grass clippings into the truck's low-slung orifice at the rear of the vehicle. The driver gets paid overtime for working Saturday, but Mr. Shoemaker figures the system nevertheless produces an average of 3.5 truckloads of refuse per vehicle at a total cost to the city of just $40.00 for the day. He figures a vehicle on its normal rounds gets about two loads at a cost to the city of about $75.00 a day. Furthermore, the grass-clippings service speeds the garbage trucks on their normal rounds by reducing the bulk to be picked up at each home.

Another effort to ease the collection burden revolves around the disposable container. One version, tested by the West Virginia Pulp & Paper Company, and styled after systems used in Britain and Sweden, was tried in a 500-home section of Montclair, New Jersey, late in 1961. The bag is suspended from a metal lid which is attached to the side of the house and is protected by wire mesh against prying cats and dogs. It is made to hold the juiciest of garbage. The elimination of the old-fashioned garbage can not only reduces noise and weight but also saves the collector the time it takes to put the container back, at least at the curb. Cost is the big deterrent to the wider use of paper containers at the moment. Besides the $8.00 outlay required for the metal holder, there is the price of the bags themselves, which run about 8 cents apiece.

One way for the municipality to cut collection costs without necessitating additional investments on the part of the public is to require property owners to escort their garbage cans to the curb instead of expecting round-trip service from the yard or alley. Boston figures it saved over $125,000 a year when it eliminated its roll-out service in the spring of 1961, requiring homeowners to leave their cans at the curb instead. The attempt, however, often raises a lot of squawks. The mayor of one large western city believes he was beaten on an annexation attempt by the specter of prospectives annexees having to roll their garbage cans out to the curb, since that was the only kind of collection service the city was providing.

Collection economies have been somewhat easier to effect in commercial than in residential service, because of the greater volumes involved. A combination of specially designed containers and trucks which can lift them merely with a pair of prongs, turn them over to dump their contents into the vehicle, and then let them down again, is permitting the operation of refuse vehicles in some commercial areas by just one man – a driver who never has to leave the vehicle. The same degree of automation, however, has yet to be accomplished among residences nor is it likely until some way is devised to get all homeowners to use the same type of container.

Sweden has solved that standardization problem and achieved a measure of automation by leasing garbage cans to homeowners for a fee that is included in their monthly refuse charge. The cans are designed to fit a hydraulic lift at the rear of the truck, which raises, dumps, and lowers the container again, though it must still be wheeled out to the lift and back to the curb again. The system, however, permits dumping by one man while the lease arrangement makes it possible to keep the cans in good condition since they are easily washed in a fully automated central plant.

Unlike cities in many European countries, including Sweden, American municipalities rarely charge for garbage collection service. But the practice of charging is spreading. Lloyd A. Dove, Assistant Director of the American Public Works Association in Chicago, figures about 350 cities in the United States were levying such fees by 1962 compared with "perhaps 100" in 1950. The charges generally run between $1 and $2 a month on a single-family home.

Some rubbish authorities see the ultimate solution to the refuse collection and disposal problem in the more widespread use of grinding devices, not only for wet garbage but for all kinds of other refuse as well. It is hardly likely that the necessary masticating apparatus can be economically provided in each individual household, however, as is now done with sink-type disposers that chew up easier-to-crush wet garbage. An interesting attempt at solving that problem, at least in densely settled areas, was placed into operation some years ago in a Paris suburb. The technique, known as the Gandillon or "Garchey" system, permits householders to dispose of their garbage, tin cans, old newspapers, and other rubbish simply by dropping their discard into a special sink-like container and pressing a lever. The "bottom" of the sink-like unit then opens up, the rubbish falls inside, and it closes again, when a vacuum sucks the material through a large air-tight pipe to a nearby central grinder where it is pulverized and flushed through the sewer.

Though the system is theoretically supposed to take only refuse that decomposes readily, householders have reportedly been indiscriminate in its use without adverse effects. Cost, however, will very likely limit its use for some time to come.

The idea of a central grinder served by more conventional delivery methods, namely trucks, which would take all kinds of refuse, grind it up, and discharge the powdery-like remnant through the sewer system, however, may not be quite so far off. At least two cities, Baltimore and St. Louis, are already operating such units, though they are of limited size. The cost of grinding is still higher than that of incineration, and the added burden it places on sewer systems would likely necessitate the modernization of many underground pipelines now used for fluid waste, but some sanitation authorities believe both handicaps may be overcome.

One who is convinced the day is not far off when the central grinding of refuse will be cheaper than incineration, particularly in areas where vast expenditures are necessary for smoke suppression, is Frank R. Bowerman, Assistant Chief of the Sanitation Districts of Los Angeles County. "Sewage people," says he, "are resisting the idea of the central grinder just as they once resisted the idea of sewers being used to carry wastes rather than storm water alone because they were afraid waste would rot out their systems." Mr. Bowerman believes cities will ultimately recognize sewer systems for what they are: "vast municipal conveyor belts which are presently very much under-used."

Household garbage grinders now in use provide only a partial answer to the collection and disposal problem. That is because food wastes account for only about 25 percent of today's total refuse volume, and the proportion is constantly shrinking as other types of refuse mount. Even then, the garbage grinder is not in universal use and, in fact, is leading something of a Jekyll and Hyde existence when it comes to local law. New York and a number of other cities, particularly in the East, prohibit its use outright. Others, such as Detroit, encourage its use, and a few, in southern California especially, have attempted to devise effective methods for requiring it. The explanation for this apparent conflict can be found in the esteem of local officials for their sewer "plant." Those who regard it as up to date, of more than adequate capacity, and blessed with sufficiently sharp grades to keep things moving, see no threat in the additional load of solid wastes contributed by garbage grinders; those who are worried about the condition of their sewer systems, its capacity and its grading, on the other hand, resist the added load.

A study of data compiled over a five-year period, from 1956 through 1960, in the city of Aurora, Colorado (48,000 population in 1960), indicated that garbage grinders increased the per capita contribution of solid wastes to sewer systems by approximately 30 percent. However, since solids represent only a very small portion of the total volume that moves through the sewer line, the addition to the underground system is relatively insignificant. Sanitation engineers contend sewer systems can be built to accommodate that prospective load at very little additional cost. The cost of accommodating the ground garbage at the treatment plan is somewhat greater, but it is still substantially less than the savings afforded over the years in the reduction of refuse loads that have to be picked up, transported, and disposed of. Many sanitation authorities regard it as folly, a serious lack of civic foresight, to neglect that provision when it can be made at relatively little added expense during the course of new treatment plant construction.

Household garbage grinders offer other benefits to the community besides reducing its refuse load. By eliminating much if not all of the health menace in standing refuse, they also permit less frequent collection. The ability of garbage to generate flies was documented recently by the Contra Costa County Mosquito District at Concord, California, in the San Francisco Bay region. It found ordinary garbage lying in a can was capable of producing up to 23,000 flies a week. Its study also showed that only 3 percent of fly larvae escape from the can during the first four days, which accents the importance of collecting refuse at lease twice a week where wet garbage is involved, or wrapping it carefully in paper when the collection period is less frequent.

The Minneapolis-St. Paul Sanitary District made a study in the mid-fifties which indicated garbage grinders added about $1.28 each per year to operating costs of its sewage treatment plant. That cost is easily recouped by municipalities through the imposition or increase in sewage charges while the added cost of the installation itself, in the piping and the treatment plan, can be recouped through a hookup charge levied on the basis of a permit required for installation of the garbage grinder.

Sick Cities

The General Electric Company, a manufacturer of garbage grinders, sought in 1950 to turn the town of Jasper, Indiana, which had a population of 5,000 at the time, into a model garbage community in the hope of convincing other municipalities of its advantages; by 1952, some 900 grinders served 75 percent of the town's population, and a good many municipal officials were impressed with the results. Shortly after the Jasper experiment got under way, some big subdividers in California created a community that was later to become the city of Lakewood, with every home grinder-equipped; the city, which had a population of nearly 70,000 in 1960, has yet to pick up its first load of wet garbage from a residence.

Los Angeles County, in which Lakewood is located, boasted grinder usage in approximately 40 percent of its single-family residences in 1962. The units were estimated to be sending approximately 640 tons of garbage daily through the county's sewer lines.

Garbage collection and disposal is strictly an urban problem, and methods for solving it have been sought for centuries. An interesting system used in the Middle Ages for disposing of refuse on the spot in certain European cities consisted of a wagon with ceramic sides in which refuse was continually burned as the cart went on its collection rounds. The technique proved too much of a fire hazard, however, to survive, to say nothing of its inefficiency in reducing wet garbage and its smoke nuisance. Today, cities are content merely to compact their refuse mechanically in trucks while toting it away and let their reduction efforts go at that. The pre-World War II garbage truck merely hauled refuse away in the same bulk in which it was received.

Sanitation authorities are inclined to look more toward the disposal than toward the collection end for drastic remedies to their refuse problems, partly because this is the more urgent need at the moment, with landfill sites disappearing, and partly because disposal appears to offer more dramatic possibilities for solution than does the tedious collection process.

One approach to the disposal problem that has yet to take hold in the United States but may do so one day is the European and Oriental practice of turning refuse through bacterial action into compost for sale as a soil conditioner to farmers and gardeners. American earth, however, is not quite so "tired" from long, intensive use as the soils of much of Europe and Asia, and other conditioners are relatively more plentiful in the United States than abroad, so that the market for such relatively expensive compost is still not as good in the United States as it is in many Old World places. Many sanitation officials, however, believe that as cities become more desperate to dispose of their waste, and farmers perhaps more desperate for soil conditioners, the process will prove economically feasible in a good many metropolitan areas, especially those close to agricultural lands.

Compost operations are beginning in Phoenix, Arizona, and, to a lesser extent, in other parts of the nation, including Los Angeles and Norman, Oklahoma. The nation's largest compost plant was placed into operation in Phoenix in mid-1962. The $750,000 unit is designed to handle up to 300 tons of refuse daily, about half of what the city generates. Because it wanted to encourage construction of the plant, the city has guaranteed to deliver that much refuse to the plant each day – and pay its operators $1.25 a ton for taking it, about what it costs the city to get rid of its refuse by the landfill method, according to Sanitation Superintendent William C. McSpadden.

Plans call for the construction of three such plants, one of which is in operation, and the second to be built when the proper plant site is obtained. The contract further provides for the city's right to purchase the plants after twenty years' operation for the price of the land only.

Arizona Biochemical Company, operators of the Phoenix

facility, is hopeful of selling its compost at $5.00 a ton, which would return it a handsome, though unstated profit. The process it uses is a Danish one and consists in reducing the rubbish to small pieces through the use of a hammer-mill, adding water to it, and then allowing the bacteria to work the mixture up to a temperature of approximately 150 degrees (Fahrenheit). The process, it is claimed, produces compost in just eight hours' time, considerably faster than most other methods. Between one and two weeks' additional time may be necessary to cure the compost poperly, however, before it is ready for use.

Smaller composting plants have been built also in Norman, Oklahoma, by Naturizer Inc. of that city and in San Fernando Valley, by an affiliate of the Lockheed Aircraft Corporation using the Naturizer process. So far, they have been unsuccessful in luring nearby cities away from landfill and incinerator operations, however.

Once upon a time, salvage was a very valuable phase of garbage-collection activity. Though they have diminished in value, salvage rights are still sold to private scavengers by some municipalities, even those operating sanitary landfills. The salvage operation, however, is not nearly so rewarding in a sanitary landfill as in a well-supervised big city dump for the simple reason that the salvaging operation must be conducted daily at the landfill site if opportunities are not to be lost beneath each night's cover. In recent years, the salvage of space afforded by the plucking of cans, rags, and paper from the junk heap has become just about as important to the municipality for extending the life of its landfill as the materials salvaged are to the scavenger.

More and more municipal incinerator plants are harnessing the heat that used to go up the flue and using it to produce steam needed by nearby facilities. Boston's Sanitation Department grosses close to $200,000 a year by piping the steam from one of its newer incinerators to a 200-bed city hospital not far away. Potentialities for the sale of steam are figuring increasingly in the location of modern incinerator plants.

The fact that a larger portion of today's refuse is paper in contrast to wet garbage causes incinerators to burn hotter than they used to. New York Sanitation Engineering Director Casimir A. Rogus figures the heat content of a pound of that city's refuse rose by more than 40 percent in the decade to 1960 alone, from 3,500 BTU's in 1950 to approximately 5,000 BTU's in 1960.

Incinerators in the District of Columbia are especially well endowed in this respect. The United States Government uses approximately 150 freight carloads of paper daily, and that usage is constantly climbing.

As sanitary landfills grow more and more remote, incineration becomes more economical, since the haul is thereby shortened. Though the figure varies city by city, Los Angeles calculates it is better off with incineration once the haul to the landfill site exceeds 50 miles, even where transfer operations are conducted. Los Angeles turned to the use of relatively remote landfill sites in recent years only after costly smoke-control edicts forced it to close down most of its incinerators. It figures it will exhaust its first important landfill site – about 20 miles from the heart of the city in the Palos Verdes hills – around 1970. It then plans to turn to canyons 40 to 45 miles from the heart of the city for the purpose. Once these are exhausted, officials figure they will have to go back to incineration, by building new plants, if necessary, to cope with the smoke woe.

Other big cities are in considerably worse shape when it comes to landfill sites. New York City, which generates enough refuse daily to fill a freight train seven miles long, expects to run out of all of its feasible landfill sites by approximately 1985, according to Mr. Rogus. The city is now in the process of building 11 incinerators at a cost of over $90 million to take care of its trash. The first was completed in 1959, with the last of the nine to go into operation in 1968. By then, New York will be burning practically all its refuse. It was burning approximately 55 percent of it in mid-1961.

Chicago, which constructed its first incinerator in 1930 and did not build another one again for 25 years after operating costs proved higher than anticipated, aims to be incinerating practically all its refuse by 1965. Though there have been a number of innovations in incinerator operations since 1930 which make incinerators more economical to operate – automatic stoking and filling, for instance – Chicago's move from landfill to incineration is being dictated by the disappearance of landfill sites. "We're down to our last one now," Deputy Sanitation Commissioner Theodore C. Eppig announced in mid-1961.

Incinerators do not eliminate the need for dump space, however, since there are still the ash and noncombustibles, such as tin cans and glass, to get rid of. Noncombustibles account for about 15 percent of the total refuse volume and ash for about 10 percent, which means that about a fourth of the original volume is still in need of accommodation after incineration. Though it is not nearly so obnoxious as before it was put to the flame, that residue must still be discarded. When New York City not long ago proposed to use it to fill in marshes along the Jamaica Bay shore of Long Island, it promptly stirred the dander of every duck hunter and nature lover for miles around. Chicago, which hoped to use exhausted rock quarries for the purpose, was faced with the costly task of hauling dirt from considerable distances for cover.

Washington, D.C., which went 100 percent into incinerator disposal with the completion of its fourth incinerator in October, 1961, is also worried over the shortage of sites remaining to take its ash and noncombustibles. Says William A. Xanten, Superintendent of the District's

Sanitation Division: "We're going to have to face up to a $3 million annual transportation bill one of these days to ship our ash and noncombustibles by rail to sites in Virginia and Maryland because we're not going to have any place to put them within the district before very long." In addition to the longer haul, the nation's capital will have to pay other municipalities for the privilege of allowing it to dump its refuse in their environs.

Small municipalities with dump and landfill sites no longer open to them are again at a special disadvantage when it comes to the construction of incinerators. To be economic, an incinerator must be capable of burning at least 40 to 50 tons of refuse daily. It takes a community of at least 25,000 people to generate that kind of refuse.

Theoretically, several small communities could get together and build a large incinerator for their joint use. Such cooperation, however, has not proved easy to achieve in the past. More frequently than not, cooperative efforts have been paralyzed by disputes over such issues as the distribution of financing burdens and incinerator sites (few want the plant in their own city limits, but putting it too far away is also undesirable because it hikes haulage costs).

Cities seeking to operate incinerators are running increasingly into the air-pollution problem. Los Angeles County in the late 1950's decided to shut down practically all its municipal incinerators, more than half a dozen of them, after its autonomous Air Pollution Control District put regulations into effect which would have necessitated the expenditure of at least $100,000 per stack. Some of those incinerators, one of them in swank Beverly Hills, had been constructed as recently as 1955, and payments on their construction bonds will continue to 1975. Chicago, Phoenix, and many other cities have been compelled to raise their incinerator stacks or equip them with special smoke arresters to combat air pollution.

The added expense makes even more costly a disposal

operation that is dear enough in itself. A 1,200-ton incinerator, for example, which is among those more commonly built, costs approximately $4.00 to $5.00 per ton of refuse to operate. That's more than three to six times the cost of disposing of refuse by sanitary landfill, and still does not allow for unusual expenses in disposing of the ash. The cost of incinerator operation is reduced only slightly when steam is sold.

The twin menaces of air pollution and disappearing dump sites have caused several companies to design and market special incinerators for burning automobiles. Like municipalities, auto wreckers have found space for their junkyards increasingly difficult to come by. And their smoky efforts in preparing vehicles for scrap by burning out their upholstery and paint has become one of the more conspicuous air-polluting activities in automotive America.

Ironically, the biggest single feeder of automobiles to the junkyards are the cities themselves – as inheritors of unwanted vehicles conveniently left on city streets, generally because they are no longer capable of motion. Chicago figures it picks some 14,000 such vehicles off its streets yearly. All, of course, end up in the junkyard. Rarely are they worth the price of hauling them there, but the city has to get rid of them somehow.

Cities fall heir to other oddments deposited or abandoned on their streets as well, besides the usual blizzard of fallen leaves and empty beer cans. Los Angeles County in one recent 12-month period collected 366,711 dead animals from its autoways – including 147,000 chickens, nearly 93,000 dogs, close to 86,000 cats, over 16,000 rabbits, 300 goats, some 36 horses, and, from its coastal communities, 56 seals.

CHAPTER ELEVEN

The Public Purse

DESPERATE for revenues to meet substantial pay increases won by its employees atop a decade of mounting municipal expenditures, the city of Baltimore in 1957 reached back into history for a dusty old levy that once set the stage for a tea party in Boston and ultimately brought the American Colonies their independence. There were differences in the two levies, to be sure, and in the opposition they aroused, but the tax in each instance was based on an attempt by government to cash in on advertising expenditures, an effort that has long been regarded as opening the door to press censorship. In the case of the American Colonies, the so-called Stamp Act required the payment of two shillings (28 cents at today's rate of exchange but a relatively princely sum at the time) on every advertisement that ran in a newspaper or elsewhere. Objections were so fierce, particularly on the part of printers (one, Samuel Adams, organized the Sons of Liberty in protest), that the British Parliament repealed the measure only a year later, in 1766, though it used that occasion to pass another law reasserting the binding nature of its enactments upon the colonists. Attempts to enforce the latter measure, particularly in questions of taxation, culminated in the American Revolution.

The tax, ironically, was revived ninety-seven years later to help the federal government fight the Civil War and thus preserve the Union. However, it proved almost as disappointing a money-raiser as it was unpopular, and was promptly repealed shortly after the war ended. In 1935,

Huey Long tried imposing an advertising tax in Louisiana, only to have the courts rule the levy unconstitutional. Between then and the time Baltimore picked it up, an advertising tax of one type or another had been considered by several cities and states and was recommended by a legislative committee for use once again by the federal government during the Korean War in 1951; it got no further. As finally enacted by the city of Baltimore, the measure placed a 4 percent levy on all advertising outlays on one end and a 2 percent levy at the other on gross receipts by newspapers, outdoor sign companies, television stations, and others selling advertising space or time. A year after it was enacted, the Baltimore tax was similarly ruled unconstitutional as a threat to freedom of the press.

Only a short time earlier, in 1955 to be exact, another financially hard-pressed city on the other side of the continent, Yakima, Washington, tried supplementing its public income by leasing out advertising space on the back of its parking meters under the glass that protects the timing indicator. With a charge of $1 a month per meter, it was collecting $500 a month from this source, almost enough to hire another policeman, when the state's attorney general ruled the practice illegal. He contended that public streets were dedicated for public purposes and that the sale of advertising space on public property did not conform to that objective. The state supreme court subsequently overruled his decision, but Yakima, possibly because the litigation had already been so costly and might have been renewed, never resumed the practice.

The experiences of Baltimore and Yakima in attempting to garner public revenues from the field of advertising do more than demonstrate the incompatibility of Madison Avenue and the tax collector. They indicate also the desperation of city halls throughout the land for additional revenue sources. That desperation has an excellent and ever-expanding foundation. The exodus to suburbia not only increases demands on the city for the provision of streets, schools, sewer and water systems, and other public amenities, but it also compounds needs in less desirable areas the affluent leave behind. The low-income families with large broods that so often take their place, many of them migrants from another part of the country or the world and therefore new to the community, magnify the load on police, education, and welfare authorities. Their neglect of property and the dangers they often introduce to recreational and other public areas spread the blight that causes remaining residents who can afford to do so to move elsewhere. Thus, at the very time its tax opportunities are shrinking, the central city's needs are rising the fastest.

The central city's financial problem is further aggravated if, as is so often the case with older cities, the city actually makes up only the core of the metropolitan area and is surrounded by many other independent municipalities. As a result of that jurisdictional confinement, the central city loses the property-tax revenues of many of its better-heeled families who, in fleeing to the suburbs, thus become residents of another municipality with its own tax authority and responsibilities. Yet these same suburbanites, continuing to earn their living in the city, require more roads for their coming and going, more downtown real estate for their parking, and the continued provision of many other city services, from police and fire protection for themselves and their business properties to libraries and other cultural amenities.

The proximity of other municipalities also makes it exceedingly difficult for the central city to apply the necessary fiscal remedies. If it raises property taxes too sharply, it will speed the flight to the suburbs that much faster, and perhaps chase other valuable development away as well as make its own industry and commerce less competitive with enterprises located in other towns and cities. If it imposes or raises existing sales taxes above those of nearby municipalities, it may drive customers and business out of the municipality. If it obtains authority to levy an income tax, and does so, it may similarly encourage employers to locate in the suburbs. No matter what it does, the central city must be aware of the competition from surrounding municipalities. Worse yet, its own geographic growth may be sealed by their proliferation around its borders; thus, the metropolitan area's population grows and the central city's needs increase while its opportunities for tapping new revenue sources sharply diminish.

The core city thus trapped in the vise of climbing expenditures and a shrinking tax base is further handicapped in its attempts to extricate itself by the dismal facts of its fiscal legacy: despite vigorous efforts in recent years to diversify income sources through the imposition of new taxes and service charges, local governments are still straitjacketed in a single source for close to 80 percent of their tax income: the property tax. Many tax authorities and municipal officials believe the property tax is highly overworked. The average in Los Angeles County in 1962 worked out to more than $60 per resident – $240 a year for the average family of four, more than twice the figure only a decade earlier. And it is a good deal higher in many other cities. Though it is deductible from federal income taxes, thus making the effective payment at least 20 percent lower in most cases, the tax is nevertheless held to have reached a level that is preventing many from realizing the great American dream of homeownership. A good number of authorities contend the tax is also an unfair one, inasmuch as it strikes harder and harder over the years on a given piece of property, thus working undue hardship on those whose incomes do not keep pace, such as retired people living off fixed annuities.

Those who despair of the property tax being able to carry growing city financial burdens argue further that rate ceilings imposed by state legislatures (as a percentage of the property's fair market value) also tend to limit the tax's usefulness.

Whether the property tax can be made to meet the rising needs of the city may well prove crucial to the future health of the city, unless new resources are suddenly thrown open to it. Though they are in the minority, there are some who believe the property tax can measure up to the challenge. They point out that its detractors half a century ago claimed it was being pushed to its limit, yet its productivity has risen even faster in peacetime than the income tax, largely because new construction and the tendency for property values to rise has hiked propertied wealth even faster than personal income except during wartime. They further contend that if politicians really wanted to do so, they could wrest the municipality free of state property tax rate limitations simply by raising assessments closer to the full market value of property. Very few municipalities assess their property anywhere near this level at present. The national average, in fact, works out to just over 30 percent of market, with assessment practice in some areas running as low as 7 percent of market. Since debt limitations are stated as a percentage of property valuation, municipalities, at the same time that they were raising assessments, would also be raising their debt ceilings.

Champions of the property tax argue also that the levy could become even more productive than it is if some liberal exemptions were reduced or eliminated and loopholes closed. The value of tax-exempt property is estimated at over $200 billion at present; the ability of industries to escape the local property tax of a larger metropolitan area by incorporating themselves as independent municipalities is one of the most blatant of many loopholes surrounding the levy that could be closed by appropriate action at the state level, property tax adherents assert. Dr. Harlan Cleveland, former dean of the Maxwell Graduate School of Citizenship and Public Affairs in Syracuse, New York,

WHERE IT COMES FROM AND WHERE IT GOES

CITY INCOME (in millions of dollars)
Total General Revenue: $11,647,000,000

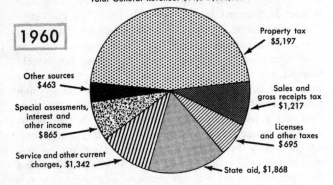

1960

Property tax $5,197

Other sources $463

Sales and gross receipts tax $1,217

Special assessments, interest and other income $865

Licenses and other taxes $695

Service and other current charges, $1,342

State aid, $1,868

CITY OUTGO (in millions of dollars)
Total Expenditure: $11,816,000,000
(Per Capita Expenditure shown in diagram = $101.84)

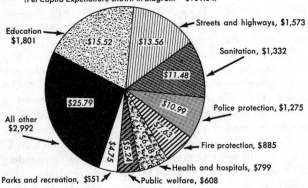

Education $1,801

$15.52

$13.56

Streets and highways, $1,573

Sanitation, $1,332

$11.48

$10.99

Police protection, $1,275

$25.79

Fire protection, $885

All other $2,992

$4.75

$5.24

Health and hospitals, $799

Parks and recreation, $551

Public welfare, $608

Source: Census Bureau, U.S. Department of Commerce

recently stated his conviction that "what brings Washington into the affairs of cities is usually the simple political fact that it is easier to get money from the federal government than to raise it from the cities' own citizens." The cities, he stated, were not so bankrupt in financial opportunity as they were "most of them, in imagination, organization, leadership and will."

Dr. Cleveland's contention is almost beyond argument. There is little doubt, too, but that the property tax will continue to prove increasingly productive in the future, if for no other reason than because municipalities will have to make them more productive. Assessments, no doubt, will be pushed gradually upward – as will tax rates. There is some doubt, however, as to whether the property tax yield, as a matter of practical politics, can be increased rapidly enough to keep up with soaring municipal needs. More than likely, local needs are going to have to be met from other sources as well.

Municipal officials, therefore, can be expected to go on badgering state and federal officials for increased aid. They will also be hunting harder for new revenue sources of their own. However, since almost every imaginable legal levy is already being worked over, and municipalities cannot lay their hands on levies used by states, whose creatures they after all are, they will also have to sharpen their persuasive powers toward getting the states to allow them to take over or participate more fully in those levies.

Municipal officials, until relatively recently, were thoroughly glum about their chances of persuading rural-dominated state legislatures to do anything more for big cities than they had to. They have become somewhat more hopeful, however, since the United States Supreme Court handed down its decision in March, 1962, based on a case in Tennessee, permitting federal courts to rule on complaints of voters for fair representation in state legislatures. Within three months of the decision, lawsuits were in preparation for redistricting in some 22 states.

The extent of disproportionate representation in state legislatures is notable. Los Angeles County, with 6,000,000 residents at the time of the Tennessee decision, was sending as many representatives to the state senate – just one – as another county in the northern part of the state which had but 40,000 inhabitants. In Connecticut, Barkhamstead, with less than 1,400 population, had as many representatives in the state legislature (two) as Hartford, the capital, with its more than 162,000 citizens. In Oklahoma, 23 percent of the people elected 75 percent of the state's lower house and 80 percent of its upper house. Vermont, which had not bothered to redraw its district lines since 1793, had given each town the right to send a single representative to the house; as a result, one with only 38 persons was sending as many representatives to the lower chamber as another with over 33,000. In Georgia, perhaps the most flagrant example of all, less than 6 percent of the people chose a majority of the state's senators in 1960.

For a number of years now, state governments have been kicking in with more aid to cities, just as the federal government has. State governments more than doubled their contribution to local governments in the decade to June 30, 1960, from just over $4 billion to just over $8 billion. In the same ten-year period, Uncle Sam hiked his help to local governments from just over $210 million to $450 million. In relation to the monies local governments have had to squeeze from other sources, however, these increases have hardly kept abreast. Federal aid accounted for only 1.5 percent of total local government general revenues in 1950 and only 1.8 percent in 1960; state aid actually declined, from 30 percent of the total local pie in 1950 to 28.5 percent in 1960. Local officials blame state legislatures for adding to municipal burdens, for example, by sharply reducing policemen's and firemen's workweeks while jacking up their pay.

To the extent local governments fail to do all the jobs thrust upon them, they will seek to pass as many burdensome and unrewarding functions as possible on to higher levels of government – the care and feeding of alcoholics, for instance, to county authorities, programs for the aging to the state, and those for the "underprivileged" to the federal government. Such transfers, however, may be more beneficial to taxpayers in the long run, since many such welfare-type functions can be carried out with greater administrative efficiency, at least, at a higher level of government. A good many of the tasks that cannot be passed on will simply be eliminated – or provided only for a fee where they once came free.

This is not to say the air-conditioned civic auditoriums won't be built, that municipal zoos won't come fancier, or even that subsidized public baths, like those in Boston, or child-care stations, such as those provided for working mothers in New York, will cease to be. For cities, buffeted as they are by political pressures, are no more rational in their spending than the people in them. The same inclinations that place more television sets than bathtubs in American homes are bound to reflect themselves in the public sphere even if public decisions are subject to broader exposure and, theoretically at least, to longer and more open scrutiny.

Municipalities, of course, differ in their degree of destitution. A few, where the average income is unusually high or industry flourishes without the burden of a needy residential population, are fully capable of meeting their public needs and will go on doing so.

Most municipalities, however, are not in this enviable position, and the ranks of the destitute are forever broadening as needs rise faster than the public's willingness to pay for them. If the nation suffers a severe or protracted economic setback and property values plummet, many of them may be worse off still. Even in relatively prosperous times urban needs are woefully neglected. The nation's largest city affords as good an example as any. Writes Professor Rexford Guy Tugwell of the University of Chicago in *Great Cities of the World,* published in 1957: "It is no exaggeration by now to say that New York City exists in a state of chronic bankruptcy. . . . Shortcomings affect every one of the three-hundred-odd services the city pretends to perform for its citizens."

A recent study placed the need for schools, libraries, sewer, and other "capital" projects in the New York metropolitan region in the twenty-five-year period to 1985 at close to $42 billion. At least one authority, C. McKim Norton, Executive Vice President of the Regional Plan Association, a nonprofit research group promoting closer governmental cooperation in the New York area, believes this is about twice as much as the area's local governments can possibly raise for these purposes under existing tax structures in that period.

In Philadelphia, Finance Director Richard J. McConnell recently estimated that city's investment requirements from 1960 to 1980 at close to $3.5 billion. "At the rate we're going now," said he, "it would take 37 years to come up with what we're going to have to spend in a little more than half that period."

Wendall R. Bailey, Finance Director for the city of Miami, predicts more than half the residents of that Florida metropolis still will be dependent on cesspools and septic tanks for their sewage in 1970 and possibly beyond, because Miami "just doesn't have the revenue to pay for a sewer system."

"Present-day city budgets," declares Joseph F. Clark, Executive Director of the Municipal Finance Officers Association in Chicago, "are going to seem absolutely delightful against those a few years hence. Only a catastrophic war or depression can stop operating and capital expenditures of the cities from increasing substantially in the years ahead – and even then many needs will go unmet."

Local governments more than doubled their spending in the decade to June 30, 1960, alone. Their general outlays rose from less than $15 billion in the fiscal year to June 30, 1950, to over $34 billion in fiscal 1960 (ending June 30, 1960). They came nowhere near meeting their expenditures with their own resources in 1950 and they did still worse in 1960. The gap between their spending and the monies they were able to raise through their own devices, principally by taxes and special charges, amounted to nearly $7 billion in 1950. In 1960 the shortfall amounted to $15 billion. The difference between what they took in, $8 billion in 1950 and $18 billion in 1960, was made up principally by state and federal aid and added debt – lots of debt.

Local governments, in fact, have been piling up debt more than 40 times faster than the national government since the end of World War II despite huge federal outlays for defense and space projects. In the fourteen years from June 30, 1946, to June 30, 1960, the federal government increased its indebtedness from just over $269 billion to just over $286 billion, or 6 percent, while local governments hiked their indebtedness 275 percent, from less than $14 billion to $51 billion, according to the Tax Foundation in New York. In the year ending June 30, 1959, for the first time ever, city taxpayers shelled out more in interest on local debt than for fire protection: their interest payments on general local debt came to $963 million that year compared with the $914 million they were spending for salaries, apparatus, and other fire department needs. Two years later, interest payments on local debt were 10 percent greater than fire department spending.

The costliness of debt, even in these days of installment living and credit-card confusion, often goes unrecognized by taxpayers who must foot the bill. One bond issue New York is seeking to redeem is particularly noteworthy in this respect. It traces its origins back to 1869 when two villages subsequently consolidated into the city, Morrisania and West Farms in the Bronx, decided to lay two miles of wood plank road between them. The undertaking was a good deal more than they were able to afford. So they floated a $377,500 bond issue that wouldn't mature until the year 2147. The long maturity enabled them to get a 7 percent interest rate and annual payments of manageable proportions. The road has long since been paved over – but the bonds have many more years to go to serve out their 278-year maturity. By the time the issue is fully repaid, unless New York succeeds in buying it in sooner, interest charges will have run to $3,064,000 – more than seven times as much as the road itself, which is no longer in use, cost to build.

Such recklessness, admittedly a good deal more common in the past than it is today, long ago caused state legislatures to clamp a tight lid on municipal indebtedness by statutory limit. In some cases they made bond issues, even within those limits, subject to voter approval wherever the city's own "full faith and credit," rather than revenues from the facility, such as tolls on toll roads, was pledged to their redemption.

Fiscal desperation, however, is sharpening the skill of municipal officials in avoiding these limitations. In Pennsylvania, Indiana, and Kentucky, for instance, school districts dodge such restrictions on their so-called "general obligation" debt by a neat device known as the "public building authority." The authorities operate on the order of the New York Port Authority and other special bodies of a self-supporting nature. As such, they own the schoolhouses they build. The schoolhouses are then rented to the school districts, which get their money, of course, from taxes. The rents paid by the districts are used to redeem the authorities' bonds. Because the bonds are technically redeemed by rental income rather than through taxes as such, they are considered revenue rather than general obligation bonds, and therefore do not come under debt limitations and do not require voter approval for their issuance. Theoretically, the authorities' bonds are self-liquidating and place no obligation whatsoever on any tax-supported government body but only on the self-sustaining authority itself.

If the authority somehow fails to make ends meet, that is, match its schoolhouse rentals up with bond payments as they fall due, bondholders are out of luck. In point of fact, it is hardly likely the school district would allow an authority to fall into that position, but, because of the possibility, lenders generally demand and get anywhere from one-half to one percentage point more on the interest rate than on a "G.O." issue. To illustrate, school bonds sold by a school district and paid from tax revenues might draw an annual interest rate of 3 percent; in that case, revenue bonds issued by a special school-building authority would command an interest rate of 3.5 or even 4 percent. The financing cost thus increases more than 15 percent, the difference between an interest rate of 3 and 3.5 percent. An increase of one percent on a million dollar bond issue maturing in 30 years adds $160,000 to its cost.

In Georgia, a State Rural Roads Authority has been set up to "rent" its roads to needy municipalities in much the same manner. School-building authorities also flourish in the state, whose constitutional debt limit for municipalities amounts to just $1 million.

Such restrictions on local debt are not entirely unusual. Some 80 percent of all the states in the Union have some kind of debt restriction on their municipalities, several at the million-dollar mark or lower. Furthermore, constitutions in about half the states of the Union do not permit voters to hike the limit. The only way they can do so is through amendment of the state constitution, which usually means securing a two-thirds vote of the legislature or a two-thirds plurality in a referendum of the people. That stringency was originally designed to protect local taxpayers against reckless spending by local politicians, and no one is convinced that danger is altogether passed even now.

The severity of debt limitations notwithstanding, the use of special authorities for such end runs around fiscal law comes in for some criticism. It is generally regarded as a costly means of avoiding the necessity of putting the debt issue to a public vote. Some municipalities have used the technique even where they still had some general obligation debt authority left; obviously, they wished to save it for other purposes. The practice is criticized also as affording municipalities an opportunity to pile up more debt than perhaps they should, if they are to have enough flexibility in the use of their tax revenues to meet other obligations.

Though the use of "revenue" bonds for such purposes as financing schools and roads with monies that are anyway derived from taxes is roundly criticized, their employment for the financing of facilities that might be made to pay for themselves, such as airports charging higher landing fees, is widely acclaimed. It is argued that revenue bonds used in this manner place the burden where it belongs – on the user. And, of course, civic officials like it because there is no need to obtain voter approval for the debt. In fact, ardor for the revenue bond is rising so persistently, it is beginning to worry some fiscal authorities even in this form.

Wade S. Smith, Director of Municipal Research for Dun & Bradstreet in New York, estimates approximately 30 percent of local debt these days is of the revenue-bond type compared with less than 10 percent in the 1920's. Mr. Smith is concerned over the growing role of revenue-bond financing because he fears many of these issues may prove incapable of weathering any economic storm that cuts their income: "If we had had in 1930 the degree of earmarking and revenue-dedication that exists today," says he, "we'd have had a lot more bond defaults than we did have during the depression years."

Municipalities, of course, are not interested only in running up debt. They are anxious also to increase their tax income. Many of them are beginning to despair of their opportunities to accomplish this objective speedily enough with the property tax. And even those more hopeful toward the property tax are looking lots harder for ways of raising revenue with the least possible squawk from taxpayers – or, anyway, from voters.

CITY INCOME TAXES

ONE device that is coming in for increased study in this regard, partly because it is considered more equitable by some and partly because it strikes out at residents who live in suburban municipalities outside the boundaries of the central city (and therefore don't pay its property taxes), is the income tax. At the present time, municipal income taxes are widely used in only two states, Pennsylvania and Ohio, neither one of which imposes a state income tax of its own. The levy is almost certain to be more widely employed in the years ahead, however, even in states with their own income taxes.

The municipal income tax, like its state and federal counterparts, is a highly productive one. Philadelphia, which has had a city income levy in effect since January 1, 1940, longer than any other big city in the country, collected almost as much revenue from this source in fiscal 1960 with its flat 1.5 percent rate as it did from property taxes. Its income tax yielded $66.9 million compared with its property tax revenues of $78.2 million, both exclusive of prior-year collections. A hike in the income tax rate to 1.625 percent, effective on January 1, 1961, was designed to increase its productivity another 10 percent.

A few cities already get more from their income taxes than from their property levies. Columbus in fiscal 1960 derived 70 percent of its total tax revenues from its income tax. Toledo's take was 57 percent of its total tax income the same year.

By 1962, over 100 cities in five states – some 60 of them in Ohio and approximately 35 in Pennsylvania – were levying income taxes ranging from one-eighth of one percent (in Williamsport, Pennsylvania) to 1.625 percent in Philadelphia. In addition, an estimated 800 school districts, 240 boroughs, and 40 townships in the Keystone State were likewise deriving revenue from income levies. Nine of the country's fifty largest cities obtained revenue from this source in 1962, including Pittsburgh, St. Louis, Cincinnati, Louisville, Toledo, Dayton, Columbus, and, since July 1, 1962, Detroit as well. The imposition of a municipal income tax had also been considered by other major cities, such as Chicago, Los Angeles, Dallas, Boston, Baltimore, San Francisco, Denver, Minneapolis, Atlanta, Fort Worth, and Kansas City, Mo.

Cincinnati Tax Commissioner George C. Schiele told a House Judiciary Committee in December, 1961, he believed the problem of city income taxes would one day "outweigh" even that of state income taxes. Some 36 states were then levying income taxes with rates running as high as 10 percent in New York (on net incomes exceeding $15,000), 10.5 percent in Minnesota (on incomes over $20,000), and 11 percent in North Dakota (over $15,000).

In all, municipal income taxes in the 12 months ended June 30, 1960, produced $254 million, more than three times the $70 million collected a decade earlier.

The legality of the tax, however, varies from state to state and even among cities in the same state, depending on whether they are "charter" cities and are permitted to levy any tax not specifically prohibited them by the state, or "general law" cities which require such authority. Los

Angeles and San Francisco, for example, are both charter cities. Besides Pennsylvania and Ohio, states specifically permitting their municipalities to levy income taxes in 1962 included Missouri, Kentucky, and Alabama – though each of these limited their authorization to specific cities by licensing authority or other means. In Missouri, only St. Louis was authorized to levy an income tax; in Alabama, only Gadsden. But more than half a dozen were permitted to do so in Kentucky, with rates ranging up to the unusually high 1.5 percent in Lexington and 1.25 percent in both Louisville and Paducah. Two other states which specifically permitted their municipalities to levy income taxes still had no takers by that time: New York and Minnesota.

In New York State, city councils which have to pass the necessary ordinances invariably have been stymied by local opposition to the tax. In Minnesota, voters can call for a referendum before any city income tax can go into effect; in the two cities where they have done so, Duluth and Minneapolis, the proposal has been defeated. The fact that both New York and Minnesota exact fairly substantial state income taxes may explain the stalemate in those two states. The two states where the municipal income tax is most widely used, as noted earlier, have no state income taxes.

The municipal income tax is generally imposed not only upon residents but also upon those who live elsewhere and work in the city, on the theory that those who work in the city also use its services and facilities and might not have their jobs at all if the city ceased to attract industry and commerce. In some states, such as Pennsylvania, however, suburban cities can strike back by enacting their own income-tax measures, in which case state law gives priority to the city of residence. Needless to say, many of them have done so, figuring that if anyone is going to tax their residents, it might as well be the resident city. Philadelphia's wage earners, however, cannot be taken from its tax collector; the state has given the city special dispensation to enable its income tax to supersede any that neighboring municipalities may impose.

In Ohio, the municipal income tax is pretty much a free-for-all. Individuals who live in one municipality and work in another can theoretically be taxed by both, though the city of residence has the right to grant relief to its doubly-taxed citizens if it wishes to do so.

One factor that may reduce opposition to the municipal income tax in the future is its ability to relieve property owners of the growing burdens they are having to bear. Cities rapidly raising these rates have also to worry about speeding the flight to the suburbs through their high levies on property; Toledo credits a reduction in its property tax rate afforded by the imposition of an income levy with having brought many suburbanites back into the city. On the other hand, cities imposing income taxes risk driving prospective commercial and industrial employers elsewhere, both because the income tax usually hits employers harder than the property tax does and because it introduces greater uncertainty about future costs, since increases tend to be proportionately sharper on income taxes than on property taxes because the property tax has been around so long and is already so high. Philadelphia attempts to deal with this uncertainty, at least in some degree, by making its income tax rates binding for at least four years at a stretch.

CITY SALES TAXES

THE danger of driving business elsewhere and making existing enterprises less competitive with those in other cities, twin risks that sprawl magnifies many times over by creating many more cities, is inherent also in another prospectively lucrative local levy: the retail sales or gross receipts tax. State governments that wish to do so, however, not only can make it possible for municipalities to exact the levy but can make it both practical and easy for them to do so. California, for example, where use of the tax is universal, makes local administration of the tax easy by collecting it on behalf of the local governments while it is collecting its own sales tax; it makes imposition of the levy practical by having the tax enacted at the county level, so the rate is uniform throughout a given area. Municipalities are entitled to their share of what is collected under the county rate as soon as they pass the necessary ordinances, as they invariably do.

Despite the fact that the municipal sales tax first came into use back in 1934 in New York, it was widely used in fewer than half a dozen states 25 years later. One reason: few states are anxious to encourage its use by municipalities because they depend on the levy so heavily themselves. It has, in fact, been the states' biggest revenue producer since 1944, when its revenues first passed those from the motor fuels tax. Some 36 of the nation's 50 states were exacting the levy in 1962.

That the sales tax is a potentially lucrative tax for municipalities as well as states, however, cannot be doubted. Its limited municipal use did not prevent it from accounting for some 17 percent of local tax revenues in 1960, for example, up from 13 percent a decade earlier. In addition to California, the tax is widely employed on a local level also in Illinois, Utah, and Mississippi. Two school districts use it in Alaska. Other states which have authorized its use by local government include Alabama, Arizona, Colorado, Louisiana, New Mexico and, to a limited extent, Pennsylvania, New Jersey, Virginia and, of course, New York.

A few states share their sales-tax take with their cities, and some of these, notably Arizona, also permit their cities to impose additional sales taxes of their own. Some 15 percent of Arizona's sales-tax collection goes back to the municipalities, with distribution based on population.

The importance of achieving geographic uniformity in rates of local sales taxes has been demonstrated time and time again. Philadelphia was one of several municipalities forced to give up its sales-tax effort because of competition from other municipalities which did not exact sales taxes. Cities which have been able to tap large transient populations, such as Atlantic City and Niagara Falls, have been successful, however, in imposing the tax at least on the sale of luxury items, since they gain more on tourist purchases of these items than they lose from their own residents shopping for them elsewhere; in addition, luxury items are not customarily bought with the same price-consciousness as necessities are.

More revenue from the property tax, the broader imposition of local sales and income taxes, and the heightening of old and the institution of new charges for municipal services – from the removal of sewage to the boarding of lost pets, and from the right to park in parks to the removal of dead trees in front of private homes. These are some of the future fiscal developments urban dwellers can anticipate.

MORE SERVICE CHARGES

THERE is nothing new about the service charge. It has long been common in public hospitals, where those who can afford to pay for their care are expected to do so, and among municipal airports, where airlines are required to pay for landing rights. The variety of its application, however, is spreading. Newly imposed recreation fees and the spread of sewage charges, detailed in earlier chapters, afford just two illustrations of its increasing use. Only a few municipalities, however, have carried the service charge anywhere near as far as opportunities permit. Among those that have carried it further than most are the cities of Sunnyvale, near San Francisco, and Riverside, near Los Angeles. Sunnyvale derived as much as 26 percent and

Riverside 24 percent of their total revenues from this source in fiscal 1959.

According to the United States Census Bureau, which classifies such revenue as "current charges," this income source produced close to 10 percent of local governments' general revenues in fiscal 1960. In fiscal 1946 the proportion was 5 percent.

The potential is impressive. A study of service-charge opportunities in Los Angeles back in 1940 indicated the city could raise another $70 million a year from this source – 40 percent of its total budget at the time. Lyman Cozad, City Manager of Colton, California, proposed a list of nearly one hundred service charges for broader general use in the March, 1960, issue of the magazine *Western City*. They included special charges for such services as tree removal and planting, zoo admission, an override on city utilities sold to nonresidents, the use of parking meters in parks, rates for the provision of police at dances and other social affairs, nominal prices for copies of ordinances and other civic literature now distributed free on request, charges for sidewalk, curb, road, and other repairs, boarding rates for animals kept in pet pounds on return to their owners, and fees for the use of school and other auditoriums by homeowner and similar nonschool groups.

The service charge has an advantage over taxes in its ability to pin the cost of a service more closely to its individual user, thereby promoting more discriminating use of the service. Also, it stirs relatively little opposition among those who have to pay it since they know precisely what they are getting for the money. The tax has yet to be discovered, however, that does not raise dissension among at least some segment of those who must pay it. However, the service charge is relatively easy and simple to collect and can be adjusted to changing economic conditions more readily than ordinary taxes can; tax collections have a nasty way of contracting in periods of economic adversity when city welfare and other needs are greatest.

SAVING MONEY

As difficult as it may be, finding new ways to raise public revenues appears to be a lot easier to municipal officials than finding ways to cut public spending or improve the efficiency of government. Even the elimination of "temporary" or outdated public programs somehow proves exceedingly difficult for public bodies to accomplish. Take the institution of the public baths in Boston, first conceived back in 1861 as a means of "giving the people an opportunity for habitual and economical bathing." That opportunity has long since been provided, even in the city's lowest rental housing, yet Boston in 1960 was still operating 15 public baths, one of them built as recently as 1953. The city's bath budget in fiscal 1960 came to $600,000, including salaries for some 180 employees. The *Boston Herald* noted in a critical editorial not long ago that commercial health centers were offering baths for just $3.00 – $1.87 less than it was costing the city to provide them in some of its public places. The city's Municipal Research Bureau calls the institution "a costly anachronism." And patronage continues to plunge: daily average usage fell from 6,865 in 1930 to 1,204 by 1957 – but the institution, despite all criticism and Boston's own financial desperation, manages to survive.

New York City set up a system of child care stations during World War II where mothers could leave their youngsters free while they were out working. Attempts to eliminate the service after the war "aroused too much opposition," in the words of one Gotham official. Result: child care stations were still costing the city $400,000 annually 15 years after World War II ended.

In Los Angeles, until a new mayor put a halt to the

practice in 1961, practically every department in the city was issuing a fancy, four-color "annual report" of its own, in reality, highly uninformative "sales brochures" which, if they had any purpose at all, were to prevent the citizen from finding out what the department's problems were and how successful it actually was in coping with them. That of the Bureau of Street Maintenance, for example, was costing taxpayers as much as $3.83 a copy; another, published by the Bureau of Engineering, ran $3.34 a copy; and still another, by the Bureau of Sanitation, $2.17 a copy.

Somehow, efforts to clean the grit out of the machinery of local government seldom get pressed very vigorously for very long. Scandal is occasionally uncovered, but the necessary permanent safeguards are seldom instituted. And a wave of public ire quickly subsides into the ocean of public apathy, perhaps not so much because the public is dull and doesn't care as because it has no effective means of ferreting out the truth and making its indignation speedily felt. That vigilance is thwarted, too, by public officials who use public money to insulate the public from the facts, not alone with printed propaganda but often by their own inaccessibility to the press and other public media.

There's no question but that local governments could achieve significant economies if the pressure were on or if they did nothing else but examine their own practices against the economies of others. Three that came to light in various publications on a single spring day in 1961 are perhaps typical: New York's mayor proudly proclaiming savings of $315,000 a year by chucking 92 vehicles off the municipal fleet, Los Angeles' Director of Public Assessments revealing that Angeleno taxpayers would be spared $28,000 a year by having the county bill for streetlight maintenance sent out with property tax notices instead of having the city do it separately, and the city manager of Gainesville, Georgia, boasting in the magazine *Public Management* how, by giving public work crews raincoats to work in, it was no longer necessary to excuse them from their labors on rainy days!

Police departments that are not wasting uniformed manpower in the performance of nonpolice functions are rare. In few cities has the pooling of purchases by various government departments to realize bigger discounts in bulk buying been fully utilized. Central garages for the repair and maintenance of city vehicles from various departments would appear to be one of the most obvious dictates of public economy, yet many large cities continue to operate several such facilities.

Notwithstanding these shortcomings on the part of the city itself, there's no denying the buildup in spending pressures. The burdens of population growth and, thanks to the automobile, its ensuing sprawl, are inescapable. The forces of inflation also strike hard at municipal budgets, since 80 percent of local government expenditure is devoted to

NOT EASILY AUTOMATED — A Government of Men

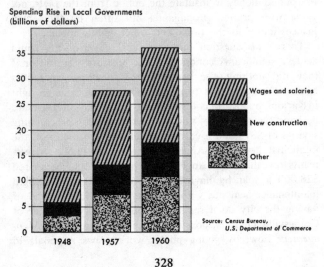

Spending Rise in Local Governments
(billions of dollars)

- Wages and salaries
- New construction
- Other

Source: Census Bureau,
U.S. Department of Commerce

1948 1957 1960

salaries. Local government employed 5.1 million persons at the end of 1961, up from less than 2.8 million in October, 1946. Including teachers, it presently employs about twice as many persons as the federal government, exclusive of Armed Forces personnel.

At the same time that they've been laboring under the pressure of rising population and climbing costs, cities have also been subjected to demands for fancier public services and facilities to keep abreast of improving living standards and the opportunities afforded by new technology. Educational TV stations, electronic traffic controls, turbine-powered fire trucks, and air-conditioned classrooms are just a few of the items that have been added to city shopping lists of late to raise the level of public services.

It's not just better apparatus, but "culture" as well that cities are more avidly seeking. A new art museum sets Birmingham back $80,000 a year in operating costs. Long Beach, California, recently poured $5 million into a new Commerce and Maritime Museum. A new artifacts museum for Milwaukee ran $7.5 million.

In addition to improving the "public plant" and keeping abreast of growing populations and rising wages, cities also have a stiffer fight on their hands against the ravages of time on aging structures. Greater sums must be spent, too, to combat human blight – the climb of crime and juvenile delinquency that originates in family disintegration and social ferment.

With these many challenges before them and the many obstacles in the way of expanding fiscal opportunities to meet them, cities will have to do a harder selling job not only in Washington and their state capitals but also for greater understanding and support at home, among the general public. Local officials may be at something of a disadvantage in that endeavor. Besides the impression of extravagance, waste, and dishonesty they have managed so well to convey, city administrators are also up against some natural disadvantages in attempting to sell the general public on the value of services that are not nearly so evident or as close to home as, for example, the education of children.

Charles T. Henry, City Manager of University City, Missouri, put it this way in the May, 1961, issue of *Public Management:* "School districts," said he, "enjoy tremendous public relations advantages inherent in their functions and organization in their competition with cities for property tax income. The effective work of PTA's supported by the natural desire of parents to look after the interest of their children above all else has resulted in positive action for schools. In contrast," he continued, "cities must buck wide assortments of ill will generated by the uncomfortable responsibilities of policing adults, telling them what they can't do, and levying fines and fees on them. These necessary city functions," said he, "do anything but facilitate acceptance of city tax increases."

Still, the wealth needed to solve metropolitan-area problems is nowhere if it is not in the metropolitan areas themselves.

CHAPTER TWELVE

Too Many Governments

"ONE of the most inspiring sights one could witness is the panorama of light and color of the spreading cities and populated county area of the Los Angeles basin when observed from a point on the partially surrounding mountain formation, especially from Mount Wilson on a smogless night. To the uninformed in local government matters, this is Los Angeles; to those who have been interested in metropolitan problems there is only a checkerboard of governmental areas in the third largest metropolitan area in the United States."

The words appear in a volume entitled *Metropolitan Los Angeles: Its Governments,* one of a series of studies on the area sponsored by the city's philanthropic Haynes Foundation. The volume was published in 1949. Today, the lights are spread even more broadly across the plains and amid the mountains which punctuate that vista.

The governments, too, are more numerous. Los Angeles County contained fewer than fifty cities in 1949. Today it has well over seventy, and more are being formed all the time. Counting school, water, mosquito-abatement, and hundreds of other districts and agencies which infest this once halcyon scene, there are presently over 600 different taxing bodies within the confines of the county.

Los Angeles' patchquilt of local governments is particularly interesting for the bizarre variety of its origins, but the pattern of administrative and fiscal frustration is repeated in practically every metropolitan area in the land. And it is getting considerably worse as sprawling growth

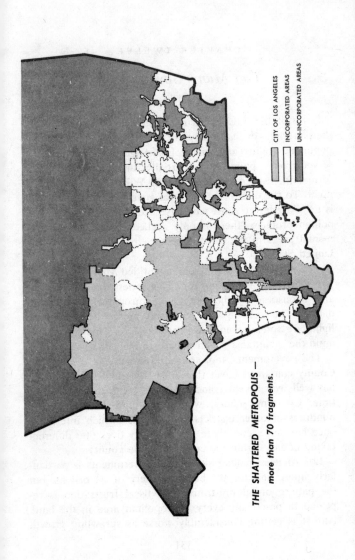

THE SHATTERED METROPOLIS —
more than 70 fragments.

CITY OF LOS ANGELES
INCORPORATED AREAS
UN-INCORPORATED AREAS

knits existing cities together, physically if not politically, and governments, if they do little else, proliferate. Dr. Luther Gulick, Chairman of the Institute of Public Administration and New York's first City Administrator, recently counted the number of local governments operating in various metropolitan areas around the United States. He found the Pittsburgh area had even more than Los Angeles and that Chicago's was higher still: over 950. New York's total was even higher: 1,100, some 550 of them cities, towns, and villages.

In the San Francisco Bay area, which has half the population of metropolitan Los Angeles, there were, at a recent date, 13 more cities and some 250 more governmental units than in Los Angeles. Bergen County, in New Jersey, has roughly half the land area of Los Angeles – but almost as many incorporated towns and cities. Bergen County had 70 at the time Los Angeles County had 73. Four of Bergen County's incorporated municipalities are less than a square mile; its largest is just over 25 square miles.

The mosaic of local authorities in a single metropolitan area should be of more than statistical interest to those who live among it or who one day might. It results in increasingly wasteful duplications of local services, conflict and confusion in their execution, inequities in taxation, and, in many instances, complete paralysis in the solution of more and more urgent areawide needs, from the provision of a single metropolitan transit system to effective policing, and from the control of air and water pollution to the execution of regional planning.

Probably no aspect of the modern metropolitan scene is more thoroughly criticized and lamented among students of local government and practical administrators than the multiplicity of local governmental units, many of them obsolete but almost all of them indestructible. As Dr. Gulick puts it: "Our system of local government in America was set up in the 1700's and 1800's to fit conditions existing

PATTERN FOR THE TWENTIETH CENTURY
— Eighteenth Century Patchquilt

then. And it was a marvelous and brilliant invention. But the conditions have changed. The living city is no longer within the old city limits. The problems we are asking local governments to wrestle with now sprawl all over the map.

"Take any problem, like water or traffic," says he; "not only does it reach beyond the lines of any one organized governmental body, but it falls in several independent and often competing jurisdictions. Thus, you have problems which cannot even be thought about except on a comprehensive and unitary basis, fractionated among a score of separate political action units."

Professor William A. Robson, of the London School of Economics and Political Science and past president of the International Political Science Association, in a volume entitled *Great Cities of the World*, declares: "It is obvious that a large municipality, surrounded by a multiplicity of small local authorities of various kinds, cannot hope to meet the social, political or administrative needs of a great metropolitan area. A medley of scattered and disintegrated local authorities cannot provide the unity required for a coherent scheme of development."

Catherine Bauer Wurster, author and lecturer on housing and city planning at the University of California in Berkeley, maintains that "after a century dominated by the growth of enormous cities and the resulting increase of urban functions and responsibilities, the city is weaker as an entity than it has ever been in its history. It controls neither its shape, its function, nor its density. It is smothered and paralyzed by its own offspring: the suburbs and satellite towns. The latter are themselves equally weak and helpless."

Consider, for a moment, the confusion produced by this welter of government. The city of La Mirada, which straddles the Los Angeles and Orange County lines, provided a poignant example not long ago. Residents of the city with "LAwrence" telephone exchanges generally were getting their fire service from the Los Angeles County Fire Department, but they weren't all doing so. New and nervous telephone operators occasionally became confused between which did and which did not. One day, a fire was reported in the two-year-old home of the John Broadbents. The operator mistakenly put the call through to the Orange County Fire Department. The department decided the call was outside its jurisdiction and passed it along to the police department of nearby Buena Park for action. The Buena Park Police desk made some quick checks and turned the call back to the Orange County Fire Department. Eventually, the call got to where it was supposed to go in the first place: the Los Angeles Fire Department. The LAFD had a station only two blocks from the Broadbent residence, but the house was wholly engulfed in flames by the time its engines arrived. A Los Angeles fire official testified later that the home could have been saved if the engines were dispatched correctly the moment the call was turned in.

Shortly after the incident, the Los Angeles Fire Station – Engine Company Number 29 – distributed cards among residents of the area suggesting that next time they have a fire to report they should dial FAirview 8-7366. It was subsequently pointed out that the number could not be dialed from LAwrence exchanges in La Mirada but would have to go through an operator first, which could easily set the train of confusion back into motion again. An official of the nearby Buena Park Fire Department noted at the time: "This is a bad situation, and everyone in the area is aware of it. We get reports every time La Mirada has a fire."

The effect of "balkanized" government on police service, where its debilitation is especially serious, has already been described.

For the most part, the price of governmental confusion is paid unknowingly by the average citizen. He suffers it in such forms as time lost in trying to find an address as the name of a street and even its numbers vary as it crosses imperceptibly from one jurisdiction to another, or through the receipt of a traffic ticket innocently incurred as the regulations of one city vary from another. In Orange County, California, motorists are subjected to five different speed limits on a single two-mile stretch of street. In nearby Los Angeles County, one major artery changes names three times as it moves through three different cities – Claremont, Pomona, and La Verne.

Conflict, as well as confusion, results from the profusion of local government. A former battalion chief of the Las Vegas Fire Department tells of orders he once received to take an engine to the city line and let it sit there while a fire blazed in a house just on the other side: "Our station was only two and a half blocks from the scene, and Clark

County's was a good deal further but the fire was in County jurisdiction. We arrived nine minutes before they did with orders to act only if the fire threatened city property. Some of the residents got angry and started throwing stones at the truck. It cost us more to repair the truck than it would have cost to fight the fire, but maybe they got the idea: if they wanted city services, they had to join the city."

"The Battle of Alameda Street," as it was known, raged for nine years before the city of Los Angeles finally succeeded in getting the industrial city of Vernon to help pay for a traffic light on an intersection of that heavily traveled street which divides the two cities. Los Angeles had been trying to get a traffic light installed there since 1939, but failed to get the city of Vernon to go along until a court order forced it to do so in 1948.

Conflicting codes and other municipal regulations penalize all manner of economic enterprise, which burdens business and makes for costlier products and services to consumers. An electrical contractor in the greater Miami area must obtain separate permits to work in different municipalities, permits that are not always easy to get. Gasoline distributors in the greater Los Angeles area are allowed to use aluminum delivery trucks in the cities of Torrance and Santa Fe Springs but not in most other areas of the county. Highway contractors in the greater New York region have been clocked through as many as 187 procedural steps before they were able to get their specifications approved by every governmental body involved so they could begin to award contracts.

As it thickens, the jurisdictional jungle produces further duplication of facilities and services – and other costly waste. "It wasn't so bad when the snow plow stopped at the city limits and there was nothing beyond, but it seems a needless waste for the vehicle to turn around and go back to the garage now when it is just as built up on one side of the city as on the other," exclaims Samuel Resnic, Mayor of Holyoke, Massachusetts. At least four municipalities in his area, Mr. Resnic maintains, could benefit by pooling their public works departments – Holyoke, Chicopee, South Hadley, and West Springfield – but years of talk have yet to produce results.

Tax inequities, as well as waste and confusion, flourish in the soil of fragmented government. "Eighty percent of the youngsters in Shelby County live in the city of Memphis, yet they get only 50 percent of the county's total educational tax money," declares Mayor Henry Loeb. "The other 50 percent goes to 20 percent of the county's schoolchildren. In fact, we have had to have a special city tax to make up deficiencies in the city school system."

Some communities, particularly those which are primarily industrial, set themselves up as incorporated municipalities largely for the purpose of ducking the tax burden they would otherwise have to help carry if they were part of a more residential city. The City of Industry in the eastern part of Los Angeles County is one of several such municipalities to be found around the country. Its origin is particularly interesting. Because California law required a minimum of 500 inhabitants before an area could qualify for incorporation as an independent municipality, Industry's aspiring city fathers who otherwise could not muster the necessary number had to include 173 inmates of a local mental institution, the El Encanto Sanitarium. A taxpayer inside the proposed city area who brought suit against the action was promptly bought out; the new property owner asked for withdrawal of the action and the incorporation went through.

Sigfrid Pearson, Executive Secretary of the Center for Urban Studies at the University of Wichita in Kansas, maintains that voters in communities capable of bringing pressure to bear at the county or state level against "tax haven" cities are either being hoodwinked into tolerating them or neglecting their opportunities for achieving fiscal justice. Says he: "Folks are scared off from mounting a campaign against this sort of thing when they're told that by compelling industry to bear a fair share of the community tax burden, they are going to chase it right out of the area and everyone will lose his job. On the whole, this is not true. And if that's the kind of industry that is being attracted to the area, the community shouldn't want it anyway."

The State of California has since amended its incorporation rules so no one can again include in its minimum of 500 inhabitants the inmates of a mental institution. Municipalities, however, continue to multiply in Los Angeles County as elsewhere. With only 16 percent of its land area still unincorporated by 1962, some authorities in the County of Los Angeles were predicting there would not be a square foot of unincorporated area remaining a decade hence. That phenomenon has long since come to pass in older, more heavily urbanized metropolises of the country, not alone in the East but in the Midwest as well, around such cities as St. Louis and Cleveland, for instance.

One of the most ominous of all the effects of splintered government is the paralysis it brings to the provision of necessary metropolitan areawide services. A special commission investigating government problems in the New York City area, recently found control of water pollution and the development of an adequate regional park system were suffering seriously from the failure of local governments in the area to take common action. It noted that vast sums had been spent by some municipalities on incinerators and sewage plants but that others were highly neglectful about where they dumped their refuse and raw sewage. Water conditions had become so bad in the region, it stated, that the city was faced with "having all its beaches closed by health authorities." It concluded: "Divided authority for planning and constructing sewers is a contributory cause preventing solution to the problem of pollution."

Highway planning is especially vulnerable to roadblocks thrown up by conflicting governments. The same New York study commission figured 33 years were consumed in the planning of the now-famous Sunrise Highway through wrangling among governmental units in the three counties involved, Brooklyn, Queens, and Nassau. The problem of obtaining coordinated action among local governments in the field of transportation is described as "the greatest one in the whole transportation difficulty" by Boyd T. Barnard, President of the Urban Land Institute, the Philadelphia-based nonprofit research group.

Splintered government also means splintered borrowing capacity, and splintered borrowing capacity rarely gets jobs done. Mary Tracy, who served two years in the city council of St. Petersburg Beach, a Florida town of less than 1,000 population, recalls how that municipality attempted to raise $700,000 in 1955 for an auditorium by floating bonds. "We wound up with only $300,000 and we had to pay dearly for that. We never did raise the rest of the money, so we just built a city hall with the funds and forgot the auditorium." Other small nearby communities, she notes, were suffering even worse financial setbacks at the time. The town of Pass-a-Grille had to withdraw a $450,000 bond issue for a seawall to save its beachfront after it failed to make enough progress in its sale. Pass-a-Grille, St. Petersburg Beach, and other municipalities in the area were similarly unable to summon the necessary credit for the construction of drainage systems sorely needed to prevent heavy rains from continuing to wash roads away and creating serious health hazards by causing septic tanks to overflow.

The most serious of all problems connected with the balkanization of local government, perhaps, is the inability of the central city to extend its taxing jurisdiction any further while its wealthier citizens and new industry are taking to the suburbs. "The heart of the metropolitan problem, not only in the central city but in a good many suburban cities as well," says Mayor Henry W. Maier of Milwaukee, "is the taxing problem." Not only are the core cities saddled with greater servicing needs at a time when their tax revenues are faltering, but suburban cities once able to support themselves "suddenly find they've a lot of kids to educate, so they start raising property taxes – and make it more difficult than ever to attract the industry they themselves vitally need to bolster their own revenues," maintains Mayor Maier.

A certain amount of conflict, waste, and confusion is probably inevitable in any system of decentralized government and, no doubt, in highly centralized systems as well. But there are ways to cope with and perhaps even reverse the trend toward shattered local government. The most effective method of all, perhaps, for cities which can still do so, is annexation of surrounding areas before they develop and incorporate themselves. That device, which has its political problems, is fully discussed in the following chapter. There are other methods, however – each with political debilities of their own.

METRO OR SUPERGOVERNMENT?

ONE which has received a good deal of attention of late and must inevitably come increasingly into the public eye is "metro." The term signifies "metropolitan area government," generally consisting of an upper tier of local government to exercise control over a variety of areawide problems, such as transit, sewage, recreation, and planning. As such, metro is similar to federal government on a national level, which handles such problems as defense and international trade and whose purpose would otherwise be

341

less effectively served were each state free to administer those functions as it saw fit.

The concept comes in for a good deal of criticism from those who view it altogether too simply as the great big bad bogey of "supergovernment." The label is too facile a substitute for the closer study that students of the subject, with rather striking unanimity, feel it warrants. Nor is it unique, as many of its critics make it out to be. Under attack most commonly in Florida's Metropolitan Dade County, where it has been struggling for survival since it came into being in 1957, it has been accepted in the United States over a much longer period of time in such forms as the Metropolitan District Commission, which operates in the Boston area, the city-parish government of Baton Rouge, Louisiana, which is a city-county government of the Miami-Dade County type and, above all, in New York City with its borough system.

New York City's "metro" government, in fact, came into being back in 1898, when the old city of New York was transformed into two boroughs – Manhattan and the Bronx – and three counties were also turned into boroughs, Kings County (which became the borough of Brooklyn), Richmond County (which became the borough of Richmond), and Queens County (which became the borough of Queens). Though the main functions of metropolitan-wide government were vested in the new municipality of Greater New York, certain local powers continued to reside in the county or "borough" governments. The city government has become more centralized over the course of time through various changes in the city charter, especially that of 1935.

The tendency toward centralization of local government is one of the most serious criticisms opponents level at "metro" government. Yet the governmental structure of New York City, possibly because it has experienced that centralization gradually, is rarely criticized on this account today. Indeed, it is perhaps more often criticized for not having kept abreast of the times: when Greater New York was created, its boundaries encompassed almost all of what was then the metropolitan area; those boundaries take in about 60 percent or less of that vastly expanded metropolitan area today.

The Metropolitan District Commission was established through an amendment to the Massachusetts constitution back in 1918. It came into being the following year to assume jurisdiction over three areawide functions which had been metropolitanized singly over the years as the Metropolitan Sewerage District, created in 1889 with jurisdiction then over the sewage of 33 towns and cities, the Metropolitan Parks District in 1893 with authority over 38 cities and towns, and the Metropolitan Water District in 1895, with responsibility over 22 municipalities. Today, the authority of the MDC extends over 43 cities and towns, including the city of Boston itself; their aggregate population totals more than 2 million persons and their area some 472 square miles, greater than that of Los Angeles County. The MDC also has its own traffic police, an outgrowth from its function of policing the area's parks. Though that police jurisdiction has been extended to include all streets "of a boulevard character" throughout the area, there is some sentiment toward turning it into a full-blown metropolitan police force to replace the more than 40 police forces presently operating in the area.

The city-parish government of Baton Rouge, Louisiana, came into being in 1949 with the powers of "home rule," which means it can exercise any taxing or other authority not specifically reserved for other levels of government or expressly prohibited to it. It is not a consolidated city-county government in which a single government replaces all those existing before it and thus abolishes cities as such which come within its jurisdiction. Rather, it is Dade County-style government, in a sense, since its individual cities continue to retain their separate identities and powers, just as the cities of Dade County do. Police and fire functions, for example, continue to reside in the cities of Baton Rouge and the parish's two smaller municipalities, those of Baker (population about 6,000) and Zachary (about 3,000). Parishes correspond to counties in most other states.

The city-parish government has jurisdiction over the construction and repair of streets and highways, but, more importantly, it can zone for the entire area and prohibit the incorporation of additional municipalities. Above all, it provides a means for applying property taxes collected from industrial and other outlying properties to needs of the metropolitan area as a whole, including those of the central city. That provision has been made somewhat more palatable to those outside the central city through a two-level property tax, with a lower rate applying outside the city; in 1962, for instance, the city property tax rate was $12 per $1,000 assessed valuation compared with $4 per $1,000 assessed valuation elsewhere in the parish, including Baker and Zachary. A one percent sales tax voted by the city-parish council, however, applies uniformly throughout the parish. The council, significantly, comprises seven members elected from the city of Baton Rouge and two from the rest of the parish, including the two smaller cities.

The city-parish government has the further advantage of being able to enact its own taxes rather than having to submit new tax measures to voters as weaker parishes, not enjoying the benefits of home rule, must do elsewhere; dissatisfied voters can express their sentiments when it comes to electing members of the city-parish council. After watching the Baton Rouge experiment for approximately a decade, voters of the Jefferson parish, with no core city and only two small municipalities, decided to ward off some metropolitan problems of their own by similarly extending the powers of their parish government to tax, zone, and prohibit future incorporations. The city of New Orleans, whose boundaries coincide with the parish of New Orleans, is in fact a single government, the city having extended its boundaries earlier through annexation.

Metros are becoming more common outside the United States, in such areas as those of London, Manchester, Paris, and, particularly, in Canada. Canada's first metro government came into being four years before that of Dade County, when the Metropolitan Toronto Corporation was formed by decree of the Ontario Legislature in 1953. Originally, it was to perform seven major functions for an area consisting of 13 independent municipalities, including Toronto: the provision of water supply, sewage disposal, arterial highways, parks, school financing, certain welfare services, and coordinated planning. In 1956 its functions were expanded to include policing, business licensing, and air-pollution control as well. The corporation has no power to tax directly, but gets its funds through assessments on each municipality based on the ratio their property assessments bear to the area's total. The corporation assesses all property in the region, which ensures uniformity.

Though Toronto officials naturally would have preferred to see the city gobble up its suburban municipalities as it first sought to do, the structure has been generally regarded as effective – so much so, in fact, that some of Canada's other large metropolitan areas have been following in its wake. Late in 1960, for example, fifteen suburbs threw their lot in with the city of Winnipeg to create the Corporation of Metropolitan Winnipeg. Metro Winnipeg began life by assuming powers formerly discharged by a confusing array of single-purpose districts and commissions over such functions as water, transit, sanitation, and planning.

Though Toronto carried the system furthest, the city of Montreal and fourteen suburbs created a metropolitan commission for purposes of financial control as far back as

1921. In 1939 the provincial legislature expanded the commission's jurisdiction to include the master planning of roads and highways, the provision of grants to hospitals, the regulation of traffic, the creation of parking facilities, responsibility for developing a system of mass transit and for coordinating opening and closing hours of commercial establishments. Further enlargement of the powers of Montreal's metro depend on common consent of municipalities concerned. However, they have not yet given their more venerable overseer as much authority as Toronto's metro has, for instance, over the provision of such basic municipal functions as police.

Dade County's metro was voted into being to tackle such problems as traffic control, sewage, zoning, and water for an area consisting of twenty-six municipalities, including Miami. Some of those municipalities, however, have fought metro tooth and nail, with the result that metro has yet to operate in the manner its founders originally envisioned. In some respects, it has become just another party in the governmental free-for-all. Nevertheless, it is showing some gradual, if painful, progress, particularly in the standardization of traffic laws and signs, the invigoration of its port authority, and in the assembly of a nucleus for areawide mass transit.

Nowhere are the difficulties of Dade County's metro better demonstrated than in its attempted reorganization of the courts. Under the provisions creating metro, traffic court administration was to become the exclusive domain of Dade County, though the cities were to be permitted to retain their courts for penal purposes if they chose to do so. By mid-1962, only three cities had handed metro their penal cases: Opa Locka, Hialeah, and Homestead. A number of other cities, particularly well-heeled Miami Beach, however, stoutly resisted metro's takeover even of the traffic courts. The city of Miami Beach, in fact, turned its traffic records over to metro only after the United States

Supreme Court handed down a ruling compelling it to do so. One reason for Miami Beach's reluctance: the last year it operated its own traffic courts it took in approximately $1 million in fines, nearly half the $2.5 million collected by traffic courts throughout the county.

Actually, metro is supposed to return the traffic fines it collects to the cities where they are collected, two-thirds of the sum within 30 days and the remainder, less the county's administrative costs, shortly thereafter. Cities like Miami Beach object to the system, nevertheless, on two accounts: first, because they feel the county's administrative take is an additional cost to them because their court systems are operating anyway to handle penal cases. And, second, they object because the county does not seem to be garnering as much revenue from its traffic-court operation as cities like Miami Beach were collecting. Judge Charles H. Snowden of the Metropolitan Court of Dade County pleads guilty to the latter charge with pride: "We are interested not only in punching a cash register. If suspension of a driver's license promises to be more effective than a fine, we prefer the suspension." Judge Snowden contends he would rather have a violator appear in court when an "accident-producing" violation is involved than have him mail in his fine, even if it is costlier to the court. Driver education, he contends, is more important than court revenue.

City officials of Miami Beach are generally well regarded, but there is no doubt that some municipal officials do not like to lose control over traffic courts for a very practical reason: when they do so, they also lose much of their ability to fix a ticket, a very valuable resource for any politician interested in perpetuating himself in office in the traditional manner. Indeed, the charter of the city of Hialeah permits the mayor to overrule a city judge if he chooses to do so, so he doesn't even have to bother fixing a ticket; the right became academic when the county took over operation of the traffic court, however.

The traffic-court tussle provides another insight into metro's difficulties: as of mid-1962, metro's cities still had some 37 judges on their payrolls, only three fewer than they had before metro came along. Metro itself had 13 judges. Thus, the metropolitan area actually had ten more judges three years after the metro traffic court came into being than it had before. Had the cities chosen to deliver up their penal courts as well, there would likely have been many fewer judges over metro than before metro came along – but they have yet to do so. In other words, metro afforded the means for economy if the cities chose to use it, but it imposed still another unit of government to discharge the functions where they chose not to do so.

As metro's chief, County Manager Irving G. McNayr, says: "Metro is only a compromise. Our intent in the 1950's was to consolidate the city of Miami with Dade County into a single government but we were defeated by something like 1,000 votes."

Time would seem to be in metro Dade County's favor if it can continue to survive persistent calls to do battle at the ballot box. The city of Miami, for instance, was already moving in mid-1962 to turn over its penal courts to metro. Such a move could give the metro court the momentum it needs to cause other reluctant municipalities to hand over their penal courts as well. Furthermore, metropolitan Dade County had already begun to move on port development by providing a larger tax base, and, therefore, bonding ability, than the city of Miami had by itself. And in 1962 metro began to create the area's first regional public transit operation by buying out four of the seven bus lines serving the region and initiating service in the territories of the other three. By breaking freeway-building roadblocks, standardizing traffic speeds, exercising exclusive jurisdiction over homicide and felony investigations, and by otherwise demonstrating its capabilities, metro is gradually making its chances for survival in south Florida slightly less precarious.

Is metro, then, the solution to the problem of fragmented government in areas in which annexation is no longer possible?

Students of local government, almost to a man, believe it is certainly a remedy worth serious study in many metropolitan areas. They recognize, however, that it is not very salable to voters. And its complexities, along with some preconceived notions and basic fears, make it difficult to merchandise.

The sicker the patient becomes, however, the more likely he is to reach for a "cure." Metropolitan Miami was in the throes of governmental problems when it reached for metro. And a good many other areas are already in at least as bad shape or worse. St. Louis is continually attempting to call the crowd of governments in its area to order by one means or another, and may yet succeed. The dictates of practical politics, however, make it necessary to seek other remedies for the metropolitan anarchy as well.

ALTERNATIVES

ONE of the more appealing of these remedies to theorists of government, except that it is even less salable to the electorate than metro, is the consolidation of municipalities into one another or into the county. The device proved highly successful in ultimately solving the problems of Passe-a-Grille and St. Petersburg Beach in Florida when, in 1957, they and two adjoining municipalities – Bella Vista Beach and Don-Ce-Sar – consolidated into the single city of St. Petersburg Beach so they could get on with their urgent urban tasks. Shortly after consolidation, the enlarged city, though it contained but 6,000 persons even then, succeeded in selling $2.1 million worth of bonds for a sewer system and $1.5 million for new roads.

Though consolidation efforts are under way almost continually in some part of the nation, they rarely succeed except where the area that would thus be absorbed is in desperate need of urban services such as water or sewers, and sees no other way of getting them, or in that rare instance where a single areawide vote will decide the issue rather than separate elections which have to be won in each separate jurisdiction. The metros of Baton Rouge and Dade County rode to victory on single areawide votes, while Canada's have been decreed mostly by provincial legislatures.

Consolidation efforts have been made in recent years in such metropolitan areas as Pittsburgh, Cleveland, Milwaukee, Detroit, and St. Louis, only to be beaten, usually in the outlying area. Of three consolidations that carried in 1961, Virginia Beach with Princess Anne County in Virginia, the town of Winchester with the city of Winsted in Connecticut, and the city of Port Tampa with the city of Tampa in Florida, not one matched partners where both were as large as 10,000 in population. Two relatively large consolidations failed altogether at the polls that year. Henrico County with Richmond, Virginia, and Durham with Durham County, North Carolina. In 1962, voters moved to create the nation's third largest city, in terms of area, by approving the consolidation of the city of South Norfolk (1960 population: 22,000) with the county of Norfolk (over 73,000); the new city, which was to come into being in January, 1963, was to have an area of 371 square miles – smaller at the time only than the area of Oklahoma City and the City of Los Angeles, though its population was to be considerably smaller than either. Virginia is hardly typical in its consolidation climate, however, since its courts have authority to order annexation even over objections on the part of the annexees. Thus, there is considerably more fear in outlying areas of big-city annexation ambitions. In the case of the Norfolk County-South Norfolk merger, the fear of further expansion by the area's dominant city, Norfolk, is considered to have eased the consolidation effort.

If metro conjures fears of supergovernment and a loss of control over local affairs, consolidation makes those prospects certainties. Municipalities that can manage to obtain necessary urban services without having to surrender their identity or their prerogatives naturally shy away from consolidation. As long as state laws require consolidation measures to pass individually in each political entity involved in the proposed consolidation, as practically every state law does, the smaller municipality can, in effect, exercise veto rights over any such attempt.

Consolidation, however, need not be effected on a total basis; it can be effected on a functional basis as well, and still leave municipal entities intact, much the way metro does. One commonly employed device for accomplishing this purpose is the special district or public authority. The special district is customarily tax-supported, where public authorities generally obtain their support from revenue bonds paid off by user fees on their services. Special districts for schools, water, sanitation, refuse disposal, and other such functions are common; public authorities are more likely to be found in transportation, operating toll roads, bridges, ports, and parking lots. Like the special district, however, the Public Authority is a single-purpose type of agency which, quite naturally, has its own objectives at heart to the exclusion of all others. A city official in Los Angeles County who serves on the boards of five special districts confesses: "There's absolutely no coordination between them. They fight each other to get the most money out of the County of Los Angeles."

Ben West, the vigorous Mayor of Nashville, Tennessee, described the limitations of the special district and the single-purpose authority in these terms not long ago: "They make it difficult to relate one function of government to another in terms of the community's resources. That's because every crow thinks he's the blackest." Critics of such governmental bodies refer to them as "the one-eyed agencies of government" for this reason. One describes them as "bodies legally entitled to make their spending decisions in an urban vacuum – a privilege they seldom forgo." Still another argues, "they destroy a sense of community."

In the city of Downey, almost in the center of Los Angeles County, homeowners pay one tax to the city of Downey, another to one of three different water districts, one of two school districts, a public-library district, a flood-control district, a sewer-maintenance district, a lighting-maintenance district, and a mosquito-abatement district (annual rate: $0.96 cents per $10,000 assessed valuation). A "Taxpayers' Guide," published by the auditor's office of the county of Los Angeles, lists 230 different governmental units levying taxes within the county of Los Angeles, many of them special districts of one kind or another.

Efforts to combine special districts or authorities into multipurpose units of government, a form of metro in the style of Boston's M.D.C., have not been particularly successful for the same reason that metro itself is not widely embraced: local municipalities fear such multipurpose districts will tend to accumulate other functions as well and ultimately turn themselves into a dominating metropolitan government. The Seattle Metropolitan Municipal Corporation, created by voters back in 1958 with legal powers over sanitation, water supply, public transportation, garbage disposal, parks, and planning continued to be confined as late as 1962 to the single function of sanitation.

One device for straightening out the spaghetti of local government, and getting rid of some costly, unwanted functions as well without midwifing a prospective governmental rival, is for one level of government to transfer those functions to another. In recent years county governments have taken over such services as civil defense from the city of Detroit, boiler and elevator inspection from the city of Nashville, and the jailing of alcoholics from the city of Los Angeles. County governments, often even more financially strapped than the cities themselves, generally resist such efforts, but the municipalities manage to bring political pressures to bear, through their respective state municipal leagues, for example. Such pressures are not generally difficult to amass, since the logic of government often calls for the function to be performed over a wider area anyway. Nor is the effort always stoutly resisted: weak county governments are sometimes only too happy for the opportunity to enhance their stature with additional tasks.

The strengthening of taxing and other authority at the county level in recent years by such states as California, Maryland, and New York places counties in a better position to assume these and other metropolitan-wide functions. The device may ultimately prove among the more attainable of solutions to the problem of metropolitan-wide local government, if for no other reason than because it lets metro in through the back door. Back-door metro, however, is likely to differ from front-door metro in one significant respect: it is bound to accumulate many more unrelated and largely undesirable services. If it is to serve as something more than a receptacle of unwanted governmental functions, metro must encompass services whose areawide performance is vital or more efficiently and effectively performed, though municipalities may wish to retain them for reasons of revenue, the dispensation of special privilege, or other reasons.

Another means of making greater use of county governments in the handling of metropolitan problems is the contract service system, or "Lakewood Plan." The system permits the county to "supermarket" local services to any municipality in its jurisdiction that wishes to buy anything from a third of a patrol car (8 hours of service) to an almost completely packaged city administration. It has come into especially broad use in Los Angeles County but is also used elsewhere, in St. Louis County, for instance. Los Angeles County has offered to contract out some of its services, in fact, since 1890; but the arrangement did not begin to flower until 1954, when a package of police, fire, and other services was worked out to help midwife the creation of the city of Lakewood, a new residential community just north of Long Beach. The Lakewood Plan of contract service permits almost any community that can scare up a mayor, a city council, and a corporate charter to have a complete city government ready to go merely by contracting with the county for essential services and levying the taxes to pay for them.

The county's services are priced as specifically as items in a supermarket; a round-the-clock patrol car, for instance, ran $93,903 a year in 1963. Some 27 of the county's cities were buying its police service that year; smaller municipalities have purchased as little as one-third of a patrol car – manned, mobile protection, in other words, for eight hours a day. Contract prices are intended to cover the cost of the service, including a certain amount for overhead. The determination, of course, is often exceedingly difficult to make. But the price usually represents something of a bargain to the purchaser, who might otherwise have had to make a considerable investment for limited use. One municipality in St. Louis County reports the tax-collection service it is buying from the county for just $40 a year cost it $750 a year from a private collection firm previously.

St. Louis County has used the contracting device to achieve ends of its own: it has managed to promote uniformity among municipalities in electrical and plumbing codes by requiring municipalities contracting for county inspection services to adopt the county code first. Attempts to achieve this same uniformity in construction codes, however, have caused municipalities only to perform that inspection service themselves.

The contract service system has proved so attractive since it was packaged in the "Lakewood Plan" that it is credited with encouraging the creation of more than a score of cities in Los Angeles County since 1954. County officials, including some who were instrumental in promoting the plan at one point themselves, are beginning to develop second thoughts about it as they have watched one profitable segment of the county after another peel itself off as a separate city to save tax dollars and sometimes for other purposes as well, leaving the county with the poorer, costlier areas to maintain itself. The plan and the whole contract service idea itself are also criticized for encouraging the very development that counties in rapidly urbanizing areas should be seeking to discourage: the further proliferation of government.

Frank P. Sherwood, Professor of Public Administration at the University of Southern California, is among those who believe the contract services system is self-defeating. "I'd prohibit the county from providing municipal services altogether," says he. "If a city can't provide its own services, it shouldn't be an independent municipality." He is opposed to incorporations of areas containing an assessed valuation of less than $5 million or a population vastly under 50,000. Well over a dozen of the cities that have incorporated themselves in Los Angeles County in recent years started off with populations less than a tenth that figure.

The best of all possible worlds, of course, would have municipalities voluntarily cooperating to eliminate conflict, needless duplication, and other wastefulness, to promote common objectives and make more equitable the sharing of public burdens. Areawide coercion and the governmental bodies needed to achieve it would thus be unnecessary, and local entities, however unsuited to conditions they might have become, could retain their identities with little or no loss to the metropolitan community as a whole. However, the need for closer cooperation between local governments, like exhortations against sin, is far easier to proclaim than to achieve. Most bodies of this kind prove more wistful than effective; their production of agreements in vital areas is exceedingly sparse. And many of those they manage often fail to be implemented, largely because of their voluntary nature. Such agreement must also be carried over from one administration to the next if time is not to chip it away.

Where such bodies are used as a smokescreen to keep the public from seeing how little is being done about their common woes and to content them with the promise that something shortly will be done, they are perhaps worse than useless.

One cooperative grouping of municipalities that has shown more results than most is the Metropolitan Washington Council of Governments, which is composed of officials from the District of Columbia and two other cities (Alexandria and Falls Church, both in Virginia) and five counties, two in Maryland (Montgomery and St. Georges) and three in Virginia (Arlington, Fairfax, and Prince William). First organized in 1957 for a more effective attack on the problem of juvenile delinquency, the council has since spawned an intergovernmental compact on transit. That compact cuts across state lines with funds and authority for the acquisition of median strips in expressways for future use exclusively by bus and perhaps ultimately by rail. The Washington Council has also embarked on a program for controlling sewage plant effluent along the Potomac. A law enforcement committee, in addition, was at work in 1962 on a uniform law for the control of firearms; strict laws to discourage their acquisition in the District were being rendered useless by more lax regulations outside it. Also under way was the creation of an areawide police communications network and central records file.

Lawyer Robert E. McLaughlin, President of the Board of Commissioners of the District of Columbia from 1956 to 1961 and a creator of the Washington Council, believes one reason that body has had more success than most lies in the District's own political peculiarities. As an area long without a voting franchise and as one that sits at the heart of government, says he, "our problems perhaps stood out in bold relief." He notes that the council was also able to get the help of Congress in knitting the grouping more closely together. Furthermore, says he, the states of Virginia and Maryland recognized "they had to work with a unique city, so they may have been more willing to do so."

The year-older, more widely known Metropolitan Regional Council, made up of the elected heads of government of 16 cities and 21 counties in three states – New York, New Jersey, and Connecticut – had no such achievements to boast of in 1962. A spokesman for the council, asked to name the body's achievements, replied recently: "We're talking with one another, that's an achievement in itself." The council in mid-1962 was pushing for authority to create a regional transportation network, a regional traffic communications system, and a regional air-pollution warning unit to at least sound an alarm when danger threatened even if it remains powerless to decree what should be done to reduce the danger.

Among smaller metropolitan areas, the mid-Willamette Valley in Oregon, which contains some 147 political subdivisions servicing some 175,000 in a 2,000-square-mile area, boasts an Intergovernmental Cooperation Council which achieved, within three years of its formation in 1958: a common parks program, pollution control of its streams, a stronger air and water port operation for the city of Salem, which lies in the heart of the area, and a pooling of government purchases. Kent Mathewson, Salem's city manager, notes that though the city of Salem and each of the counties it straddled, Polk and Marion, had park commissions of their own for years, the three never succeeded in creating a regional park. The counties failed to do so, says he, "because they were disinterested in providing facilities for city folks and the city because it could not find sufficient appropriate acreage within its boundaries." Under its highly ballyhooed "Massive Cooperation" effort, however, the city and counties agreed to combine their resources, hired a regional parks director and, shortly thereafter, began planning for the provision of their first regional park.

San Francisco, on the other hand, has demonstrated the customary difficulties of getting several municipalities together for the purpose of plotting common action. Municipalities in the area had been struggling among themselves for years over the creation of an areawide transit network before they were able to bring their first bond issue to a vote in November, 1962 – and even then two of five key counties considered essential declined to participate: Marin and San Mateo. This, despite the creation in May, 1960, of the Association of Bay Area Governments, a voluntary organization which almost immediately enlisted 6 of the area's 9 counties and 54 of its 84 cities for the purpose of studying common problems and promoting their solution. The Bay Area Association may yet prove a success, but similar endeavors have long since been wrecked on the rocks of voluntary agreements.

Noting the difficulties in fashioning solutions to the problem of metropolitan areawide government, and knowing full well the cost of such failure will fall ultimately on them, the federal government and a growing number of state governments are encouraging, cajoling, and in a few cases even coercing municipalities to take the necessary steps. Senator H. A. Williams, Jr., New Jersey Democrat, in mid-1962 cited four federal programs oriented in this direction: the "open space" program, which provides for the federal government to pay up to 30 percent of land acquisition costs for projects of a "regional character" compared with 20 percent for those purely of a local character; insistence that a transit system be planned on a metropolitan-wide basis before it can qualify for federal loans, the provision of urban renewal funds on the basis of comprehensive master plans encompassing the entire area; and the provision of federal aid for planning purposes on the basis of a master plan covering the entire region.

State governments, for their part, have begun to step up their activities along lines that might be described as "preventive metro" by making annexation and consolidation easier, for instance, and the incorporation of municipalities, particularly where the purposes of self-government are obviously not being served, more difficult. A small but increasing number of states are permitting their cities to annex unincorporated areas without getting the consent of the annexees, though there is also a tendency to require the city to produce a schedule for providing services in the area and adhere to it. The annexation laws of Texas, as will be noted shortly, are especially liberal: they permit the state's municipalities to "reserve" areas for future annexation with no attendant responsibility to speak of; the device has been used by Houston to reserve almost all of Harris County for future annexation, which makes Houston a metro-already-in-being, in a sense.

More states, too, are making it harder for municipalities to incorporate themselves, particularly near existing municipalities. Nebraska, for instance, prohibits the incorporation of any municipality within five miles of the corporate limits of an established one. County commissioners in Arizona are forbidden to act on any petition to incorporate within six miles of cities over 5,000 population unless the city or town affected authorizes the incorporation. A newly enacted statute in Idaho prohibits new incorporations within certain distances of existing cities, according to population size.

The menace of uncontrolled city incorporation is described by Stanley Scott, Assistant Director of the Bureau of Public Administration at the University of California in Berkeley: ". . . the conventional conception of a city as a balanced community, governed and served by a municipal corporation," says he, "has been modified considerably by areas attempting to cope with special problems and by interest groups trying to gain special advantage. Cities have been incorporated, not to provide urban services, but to act as zoning devices to preserve the rural nature of their areas."

There are many reasons, besides the genuine desire for self-determination, which encourage communities to attempt to incorporate themselves as independent municipalities. A kaleidoscope of such reasons can be read in histories of the Los Angeles area. Barnes City, for example, which has since been consolidated into the city of Los Angeles, was created by the owners of a circus seeking to make winter quarters safe from zoning exclusions of their animals. Dairy farmers, similarly motivated, have spawned four cities of their own in Los Angeles and neighboring Orange County in recent years: Dairyland, Dairy Valley, Artesia, and Cypress. Rockcrushers, tired of having their activities zoned into silence and cleanliness, created the city of Irwindale. The city of Gardena was formed to make draw poker safe from puritans. Cities have also been organized in the region to insulate horse racing, the liberal flow of alcohol, and the state of female undress in girlie shows.

The greatest city-creator of them all, perhaps, as it has been almost from time immemorial, is fear. However, the fear which creates cities today is not so much the fear of a bloodthirsty enemy beyond the barriers so much as it is the fear of what the big city might be planning to do with the "unprotected" land beyond its boundaries. The prospect of becoming sewage farms for neighboring municipalities has midwifed a number of cities into being in Los Angeles County, including West Covina, which did not wish to become a receptacle for the watery waste of the city of Covina, and Monterey Park, which did not relish the idea of playing that role for the cities of Alhambra, Pasadena, and South Pasadena. Once they incorporate, cities have their own zoning authority.

The fear that tends to create the greatest number of cities, of course, is the fear of a financially-desperate neighbor. High-value residential and industrial areas fearful of annexation into the big city, and therefore subjection to its tax rates, prefer to set their own public standards and levies and assume only the burdens in their own immediate vicinities rather than the welfare rolls and deterioration of the core metropolis. They may also wish to preserve a unique character which might be threatened by a less appreciative zoning czar in the bigger city. Thus wealthy San Marino, in Los Angeles County, does not let people die or suffer prolonged sickness in its environs, if it can help it; its zoning laws prohibit mortuaries and hospitals. Rolling Hills, another exclusive Los Angeles community farther to the south on the Palos Verdes Peninsula, a city which boasts more horses (for pleasure) than people, is rich in bridle paths but had yet to lay its first public street by 1963. Another peninsula municipality, the city of Palos Verdes Estates, manages through a trust indenture to require structures built in its confines to use red tile roofs in the Spanish style, wherever possible.

The insulation afforded by incorporation, whether for the preservation of the right to crush rock or the necessity to roof with red tile, is not always a permanent one. The influx of new residents, in adjoining municipalities if nowhere else, tends to restrict the performance of certain activities. Gardena and other "poker" cities are continually having to do battle with residents elsewhere in the county attempting to get higher levels of government to restrict poker-playing rights; after fighting off irate neighbors beyond its borders, the city of Irwindale now finds itself skirmishing with its own new residents over rights afforded rockcrushers.

What about the "grass roots" democracy that is assertedly being served by all this independence at the local level?

There's no question about the desirability of self-determination at the lowest level of government properly concerned with a given question – a principle that applies right down to the individual and his inherent right to decide questions of his own conscience. There is some question, however, whether these principles are served simply by size or whether the relationship of size to the job that has to be done is not **more** pertinent still. Small governmental units, in fact, may be highly deceiving in this regard, giving the appearance of serving the purposes of self-determination when, by their very size, they cannot possibly determine anything for themselves because the nature of the need is such that the cooperation of other "independent" municipalities is indispensable for their satisfaction.

Roy Sorenson, Chairman of Governor Brown's Commission on Metropolitan Area Problems in California, which recently recommended Toronto-style government for metropolitan areas in the Golden State, argues: "Democratic methods are inevitably weakened by the proliferation of government. People know what their problems are, but they can't figure out who is responsible so they simply assume they have to live with those problems because they're inevitable when, in fact, they are not at all inevitable."

The late Paul Studenski, in an article in the *National Civic Review* of October-November, 1960, insisted that "the metropolitan area problem" never would be solved "so long as politicians and civic leaders think of the region as being

362

primarily congeries of local political units and adhere to an exaggerated and bigoted view of home rule for which they find confirmation in ill-conceived constitutional provisions. Properly conceived home rule," he maintained, "does not confer a right to perpetual existence as a separate political entity."

He continued: "In the sphere of metropolitan relations, it should not be the right of any subdivision to obstruct any metropolitan development or project which does not suit its taste. The present chaos in many metropolitan areas," he said, "is a summons to a broader view and higher statesmanship than has generally been displayed."

Whatever means are devised for knitting governmental units more closely together in a given metropolitan area, they are hardly likely to eliminate unnecessary duplication, conflict, and confusion altogether. A single metropolitan-wide government, even if it were desirable, would still be capable of nurturing these unhappy phenomena even if it had no other rival in the region. Large administrative bodies almost inevitably develop a hierarchy of procedures for their functioning. Not long ago, a governmental commission detailed the mass of procedural confusion that awaited anyone who hoped to stage a street fair in New York City, a seemingly harmless undertaking.

First, the commission noted, he has to get a permit from the Police Department. If a band is to be used, he has to obtain permission from the Building Department – that is, if the band is to play on the sidewalk. If the band is to play in the road, authorization is required from the borough president's office. But the borough president's office doesn't have jurisdiction over all streets. Some, designated "marginal streets," are under the Department of Marine and Aviation, so permission for a band to play at a fair on one of these streets has to come from that unit of government. If banners are to be attached to buildings, the Buildings Department has to sanction the display; if they are to be stretched across the street, the borough president's office – or the Department of Marine and Aviation, if it is one of those "marginal streets" – has to provide the authority.

A certain amount of conflict, confusion, and duplication is inevitable, also, between various levels of government.

Highway authorities with the primary responsibility of running up their mileage in concrete roadways and cities, reflecting the outcry of citizens, have come to grips increasingly in recent years over the location of roadways and even the manner of dividing them. In 1959, when New Jersey highway authorities declined to erect median barriers to prevent center-crossing collisions on Route 17, a number of municipalities along the route – Waldick, Mahwah, Ramsey, and Allendale among them – decided to erect a few themselves. The state pointed out that the highways were state property, and promptly proceeded to tear the barriers down on the theory that they may prevent crossover collisions but they could also cause more accidents of other types. Enraged, the mayors of some 14 towns along the highway trekked to Trenton to register their complaints. As a result, cities wishing to do so were finally authorized to restore or erect the barriers pending a more permanent solution to be worked out by the state.

In Los Angeles, where a similar struggle had long been in progress between state and local authorities, the barriers are now being erected on every mile of state highway traversing the city. But the signing of those expressways continues to suffer from the conflict between state and local authorities in directing motorists to entry ramps from city streets. State highway officials for years placed the blame on the cities, contending they would not give them the sign sites they needed. City officials claimed the state was too niggardly to erect signs where they were authorized.

That big government in itself is no solution to the problem of local order has been demonstrated time and time again in regions which have been spared the problem of metropolitan multiplicity. The island of Oahu is one: for years a single government has ruled over the island's local affairs, those of Honolulu included. Yet a number of fast-growing communities on the island have been promoting home rule on the theory they can better handle their own affairs than can the relatively remote, preoccupied government that sits in Honolulu.

A more workable balance between the two – the need for metropolitan-wide government and the provision or preservation of "compact" local rule in functions that properly belong to it, or whose added costs its citizens knowingly are willing to pay – is obviously vital. It may, however, prove as difficult to achieve as the balance between state and federal government has been to achieve on the national level from the time this nation came into being.

In the burgeoning metropolitan struggle, the forces of uncompromising self-determination can hardly be over-estimated. The devotion to special privilege, to the insulation provided by one's own zoning practices and to existing institutions that perpetuate officeholders and others in jobs that might otherwise be more efficiently and effectively performed by another unit of government, to say nothing of the difficulties inherent in revising tax structures and shifting tax burdens, are likely to weigh the scales for a long time against the creation of new or stronger areawide government even where its need is imperative.

Senator Joseph Clark, the Pennsylvania Democrat who has long been active in urban affairs, is firmly convinced: "A lot of our metropolitan problems are going to have to get worse before people are prepared to take the measures necessary to make them better."

The one relatively easy course is to prevent the metropolitan area from shattering in the first place, where that happy opportunity still exists. For that purpose, the techniques and pitfalls of annexation may be worth closer study.

CHAPTER THIRTEEN

City Limits

O N E way to ensure control over outlying areas is to push one's city limits across the landscape before communities burgeoning there get a chance to incorporate themselves. The procedure makes unnecessary the accommodation to splintered government, such as metro or intergovernmental cooperation, by preventing the area from shattering into too many governmental units in the first place.

This remedy, unfortunately, is no longer open to many cities, particularly older ones where historical development has closed off all avenues to annexation. Boston, Pittsburgh, Cleveland, and Chicago are just a few examples. Cities with large populations, small geographic areas, and fast-growing suburbs are in the unhappy position of being able neither to sufficiently raise revenues nor to summon the leadership required for the solution of increasingly strenuous urban problems.

To avert such helplessness, more and more cities which can do so are taking advantage of the annexation opportunities open to them. Realizing that financially crippled cities likely will one day be their wards, more and more states are going along with the effort by improving the legal climate for city expansion.

Texas, where wide-open spaces still abound, is particularly notable in this respect. It is one of the few states – Missouri is another – which permits its cities to "reserve" territory for future expansion. The freeze is accomplished simply through a reading of the annexation ordinance in the city council. The process isn't quite so easy in Missouri, where the reservation has to be approved by the state court and may be disallowed. But the Texas law couldn't be more liberal; until recently it didn't even place a time limit on the reservation. Fort Worth, for example, which increased its land area from only 60 square miles at the end of World War II to over 153 square miles by 1961, had some 250 additional square miles reserved for future annexation going into 1961; some of its reserved area had been kept in the freezer for over three years.

The reservation plan has two distinct advantages from the central city's point of view: it prevents the reserved area from incorporating itself or being absorbed by another city. And it makes it unnecessary to pump costly city services into the territory since residents won't be able to express their dissatisfaction in city elections anyway. Hasty annexations which may prove more expensive than the city can afford are thus unnecessary. The area need not be annexed until it is sufficiently developed to turn in enough tax revenues.

As a result of liberal law and favorable geography, some Texas cities have done some rapid growing of late. Houston has gone about as far as it can go: it has reserved almost every square foot of unincorporated area in Harris County, in which it is located, for its future growth. Texas, in common with practically every other state in the Union, prohibits annexations across county lines. The land Houston had in its freezer for future annexation totaled over 1,000 square miles by 1961 – nearly three times the 349-square-mile area the city itself took in at the time and 13 times the 74 square miles it occupied as recently as 1945.

If Houston goes ahead with all its annexations, it could be the largest city in terms of area in the world. Oklahoma City snatched that title from Los Angeles with the annexation of 70 square miles in 1961, bringing its total area to 488 square miles, 31 square miles greater than Los Angeles; by mid-1962, Oklahoma City had raised its total area to

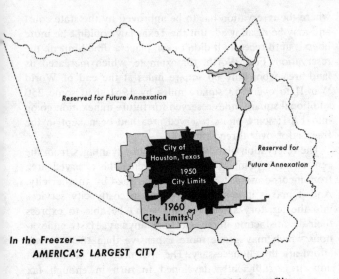

Reserved for Future Annexation

City of
Houston, Texas
1950
City Limits

Reserved for
Future Annexation

1960
City Limits

In the Freezer —
AMERICA'S LARGEST CITY

over 600 square miles. Before 1960, Oklahoma City contained only 88 square miles.

Phoenix, Arizona, increased its size tenfold in the decade to 1960 – from 17.1 square miles to over 188.4 square miles – and it hasn't stopped reaching for sagebrush yet. Norman, Oklahoma, a city of less than 35,000 people and only 10 square miles in the beginning of 1961, became one of the largest in the nation by swallowing 174 square miles that year, an area almost as large as Phoenix.

Annexation activity has been increasing in the United States practically every year since the end of World War II. In 1945 152 cities of over 5,000 population accomplished an annexation of some kind. The following year, the number rose to 259. It passed the 300 mark for the first time in 1949, the 400 mark for the first time in 1952, the 500 mark in 1955, and soared straight to 712 in 1961; it has climbed further since. The 1,083 square miles annexed in 1960 was the largest ever, 68 percent above the previous peak of 644

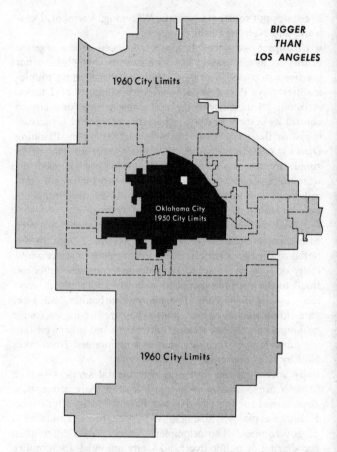

BIGGER
THAN
LOS ANGELES

1960 City Limits

Oklahoma City
1950 City Limits

1960 City Limits

square miles annexed in 1956. A survey by the American Municipal Association showed that in the seven years from 1951 through 1957 there was hardly a state in the Union whose cities did not carry through at least some significant annexation. The territory they annexed in those seven years contained more people than the 1960 census showed for five states put together: Nevada, Wyoming, Vermont, Delaware, and New Hampshire.

Champions of annexation are convinced of the urgency of this act as a lifesaving measure for cities which have not yet been strangled nearly to death by surrounding municipalities. Says Porter W. Homer, City Manager of Tucson, Arizona: "Annexation is the best single means for a city to control its destiny, and the importance of control is increasing with the growth of urbanization." The City Planning Director of Houston, Ralph S. Ellifrit, calls annexation "a simple matter of self-defense." Houston's moves, says he, were made "to end a period of hysteria in which small communities were annexing land willy-nilly in the county" – against Houston's better interests, of course.

Alfred Willoughby, Executive Director of the National Municipal League in New York, is likewise favorably disposed toward annexation: "To many regions that are physically one are being splintered into governmental units too small to perform the increasingly costly and complex services demanded of them. Too many suburbanites," says he, "are riding free on city coattails. They are driving on roads, basking in parks, researching in libraries and otherwise taking advantage of facilities built and maintained from taxes paid by city residents."

By spreading the cost of governmental services over a broader area, annexation can also lead to more economical government for the city dweller. Phoenix's City Clerk John E. Burke explains: "Size helps us reduce the per capita costs of government." The principle, he notes, is no different in the sharing of public overhead – city administration, police stations, and the like – than it is in the sharing of business overhead, which leads to cheaper products through mass production.

L. Perry Cookingham, city manager of Kansas City for nineteen years before taking the same job in Fort Worth, insists: "Cities need room to grow just like people do. Cities prevented from expanding by rigid annexation laws or encirclement by incorporated communities come to the point where they begin losing population while the periphery areas are skyrocketing. Thus they are less capable of coping with core problems such as blight and crime when the need to do so is greatest."

Such thinking has brought a good many political scientists around to the view that cities should be entitled to annex adjoining unincorporated areas as they see fit, even without the consent of those being drawn into the city. They look on the area's right to vote on annexation as a veto. They contend the city cannot zone effectively or otherwise control metropolitan growth if every segment of that region is perfectly free to devise its own rules and regulations, compete for industry, and otherwise hamper efforts of the central city to cope with regional problems.

Whatever merits may be working in its behalf, annexation is not always profitable. The immediate cost of repairing roads, providing police and fire protection, street lighting, and other public facilities may outstrip the immediate gain in property tax and other revenues. The drain lingers longest – sometimes indefinitely – where the annexed area consists mainly in low-value residential property.

Roger Freeman of the Institute for Social Science Research puts the break-even point at homes priced upward of $15,000 to $20,000, depending on tax rates and the provision of public amenities in the city concerned. Most cities are not anxious to annex low-value residential areas except for the purpose of cutting their way to more valuable areas.

Some cities, relatively indifferent to expansion, require the annexed area to help offset the cost of additional services through payment of an annexation fee. Denver for several years required areas seeking annexation to pay the city $2,000 for every acre annexed and to donate 8 percent of their land area or its financial equivalent to the city for future park, school, and other public uses. The Rocky

Mountain metropolis did precious little annexing under those provisions, but it didn't particularly care; the city's land area was deemed sufficient to accommodate growth for some time to come while the danger of encroachment from other municipalities hardly seemed excessive.

The trend toward increased state aid to local municipalities on the basis of population or other standards reflective of size is making annexation more attractive even to communities which did not have much of an annexation urge before. The annexations Phoenix accomplished in the 1950's, for instance, raised its share of the state's total sales tax revenues from 42 percent in 1950 to 46 percent in 1960. Tucson's "take" as a result of a 53-square-mile expansion during the same period boosted its share from 19 percent when the city comprised just 18 square miles to 22 percent when it had 71. Tombstone, with a moribund annexation policy, found its portion of income from this source slip from 0.28 percent to just 0.16 percent in that period.

Despite its many appeals, however, annexation can be overdone; acreage may be amassed and obligations assumed with no regard to the realities of probable future development. Personal pride and civic prestige can be misleading masters in the extension of the city as it can be in other areas of human conduct. "Growthmanship," maintains one veteran public administrator, "can be a disease in itself. It doesn't hurt land speculators and others who benefit by advertising population figures – but in reality the area may show no growth if annexation alone accounts for the increase."

Whatever the motives for annexation – and there are almost always more than one in any single instance – there's no doubt the competition between cities for unincorporated parcels is heating up. The tussle is especially notable in Arizona.

The race for annexation as it is run in the Grand Canyon State revolves around the submission of an incorporation petition or an annexation ordinance to the board of supervisors of the county involved. The board has the final authority in these questions, but Arizona law forbids any board from entertaining more than one motion at a time or stacking them up. Furthermore, no city annexation ordinance is considered valid unless it is enacted after the board has cleared the way for its consideration. The first one in to the board with his proposal after the previous one has been rejected has the advantage not only of keeping all other proposals out but also of knowing that whatever decision is reached will be reached on the merits of his own particular arguments and support and on no other. Thus annexation-anxious cities keenly poise themselves for the speedy enactment and delivery of such ordinances once the board paves the way by rejecting a previous motion.

Tucson's Mr. Homer recalls a day in 1959 when he nested himself in a telephone booth just outside the chambers of his city council awaiting a call from the city attorney hard by a conference room where supervisors of Pima County were deciding on incorporation petitions for three new cities. Tucson, which is located in Pima County, was hopeful the board would reject the motions so it could put forth a proposal for the annexation of the entire 21-square-mile area. A 25-page annexation ordinance was already written up – "the shortest we could possibly make it and still provide all the legal descriptions required," says Mr. Homer. The city clerk held it in his hands ready to read it to assembled councilmen the moment the word was given.

"As soon as the city attorney called me to report the three incorporations were denied," says Mr. Homer, "I dashed out of the booth and into the council to authorize the city clerk to start reading. He read it as quickly as he could. It took eight and a half minutes. We even timed it in advance. Then we raced it to the supervisors as fast as we could, afraid that some other city might beat us in. But they didn't. We subsequently succeeded in annexing the entire area."

Mr. Homer recalls an annexation contest between Tucson and the city of South Tucson over acreage that included a prospective airport site and some prime industrial land between the two cities. To get the final signature needed to show that the annexation proposal had the endorsement of owners of 50 percent or more of the area's assessed property, the mayor of Tucson personally flew to Dallas where the area's remaining large landowner resided. He obtained the necessary signature and streaked right back to Tucson where the city council proceeded to pass its ordinance, which was then approved by the county board of supervisors. "We thus succeeded," says Mr. Homer, "in completely encircling the city of South Tucson."

Cities may deliberately head off annexations by others. Tempe, Arizona, made no bones about its objective when, early in 1960, it tossed a loop, like a lassoing broncobuster, around an area just south of the city. The loop was only five feet wide, but its annexation was an effective means of cutting the area off from future annexation by the city of Chandler to the south or by any other cities that might have had designs upon it.

City maps betray the zeal with which the annexation process is utilized. Back in 1954, in its headlong dash for the Mexican border, San Diego annexed a strip of land three miles long and as little as 300 feet wide – most of it some 20 feet below water at mean low tide. The laws of California, like those of most states, permit annexation only of contiguous territory, and this was the only way San Diego figured it could go on growing on the other side of the bay. The move aroused opposition from a few legal purists and others, but the city was nevertheless permitted to perform the act and go on growing on the other side.

Consider the map of Houston as it looked in 1960 – like a glob flying a balloon at the end of a string. The string is

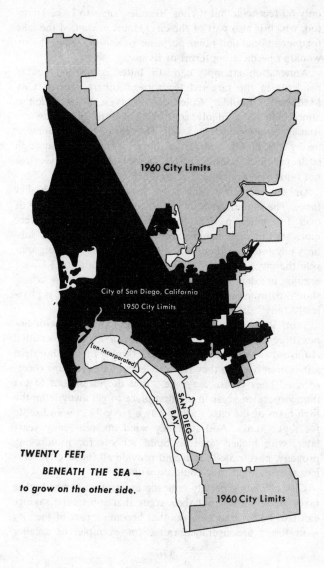

1960 City Limits

City of San Diego, California
1950 City Limits

(un-incorporated)

SAN DIEGO BAY

TWENTY FEET

BENEATH THE SEA —

to grow on the other side.

1960 City Limits

only 60 feet wide but it runs 10 miles, right to Lake Houston, which is also part of the city. Houston wanted the lake for recreational and other purposes so another municipality wouldn't be dictating terms of its use.

Annexation attempts can stir bitter opposition among residents in the targeted territories. Robert Turner, City Manager of Boulder, Colorado, observes: "Annexation is almost always a highly controversial and usually an extremely emotional issue as well. The fear of being swallowed up by a monolith and losing one's identity may outweigh such practical considerations as obtaining vital services not otherwise available at a reasonable cost."

Or the resistance may stem from the fear of higher taxes. The American Municipal Association in a survey of over 130 cities in 1957 found 63 percent of them were motivated in their annexations by the desire to make suburbs pay for what they were getting free by remaining outside the city. A slogan of the League of California Cities, arguing in much the same vein, reads: "Whatever is urban, should be municipal" – which means that whatever is physically "city" should legally be "city" as well.

John R. Kerstetter of the A.M.A., co-author with annexation consultant Robert G. Dixon of a volume entitled *Adjusting Municipal Boundaries,* thinks folks who fight annexation because they fear city encroachment dupe themselves. "They claim," says he, "that they went out to the unincorporated areas in the first place to get away from the high taxes of the city, so they buy a second car – and settle for septic tanks. And still they wind up, not many years later, with higher taxes to build schools for multiplying progeny, pave rutted roads and provide all those 'city' services they thought they could do without."

City officials generally concede annexation brings higher taxes along with it, but they argue that substantial savings can also be realized by areas that become a part of the city – in lower fire-insurance rates, for example, or smaller water bills and other charges. At any rate, they argue, the higher taxes would come inevitably, even if the area remained outside the city.

The city of Phoenix in 1960 figured the average homeowner with a house worth about $10,000 in the open market saved upwards of $39.75 a year by being a resident of the city. In a pamphlet circulated among prospective annexees it listed such economies as: $2 a month, or $24 a year, on the average, in garbage-collection services which the city provides free but which must be contracted with private collectors elsewhere; approximately $12.50 a year from lower fire-insurance rates resulting from the provision of city fire hydrants and generally improved fire protection; about $12 a year in fire-protection costs themselves (since the county levy would no longer be included in their tax bills); $5 a year from the elimination of nonresident charges on library cards; at least $30 a year through a reduction in monthly sewage charges; and at least 22 percent on water bills – all for assuming a city tax rate of $1.75 per $100 assessed valuation, or $43.75 on a $10,000 home assessed at a customary 25 percent of market value.

Phoenix's salesmanship in annexation is worth noting, as its record would suggest. Its procedure consists first in staging a series of community meetings in the area to be annexed, with the mayor and department heads in attendance. The audience is first shown a twenty-seven-minute movie depicting the advantages of being part of the city. It is followed up by a question-and-answer period. Once the entire area has been so exposed, the campaign gets down to the "block" or "neighborhood" level, with the city clerk participating in home discussions. As a final measure, petition carriers, generally part-time city employees, are put through an eight-hour indoctrination period to spread the gospel further when they go on their signature-seeking rounds. The pamphlet detailing the financial argument is distributed

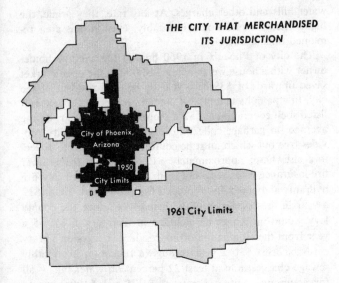

THE CITY THAT MERCHANDISED
ITS JURISDICTION

City of Phoenix,
Arizona

1950
City Limits

1961 City Limits

at every opportunity, in the "community" sessions, home meetings, and on petition-gathering rounds.

The "pitch" doesn't end with annexation. The city with continuing annexation ambitions knows there is no salesman like a satisfied "customer" and no greater obstacle to its ambitions than a dissatisfied one. To be sure the "purchasers" of its city services are satisfied, the city continues to make its officials available for community meetings to hear complaints and provide explanations. In addition, each new citizen is mailed a six-page summary of "major services" obtainable from the city. It includes more than a dozen phone numbers where additional information can be obtained on any given city service. Nothing is too incidental for note: included in the summary is a complete schedule of the city library's traveling bookmobile service.

Altogether too many cities that bemoan the magnitude of their metropolitan problems and their inability to effect annexations fail to take this first step in self-help. John C. Bollens, Director of Urban Studies at the Bureau of Governmental Affairs at the University of California in Los Angeles and author of *Exploring the Metropolitan Community,* figures only about a third of the cities engaged in annexation activities these days are circulating coveted areas with any kind of printed literature at all, and much of that, he contends, is "improvised and incomplete."

In seeking to sell their arguments for annexation, masters of the art attempt first to enlist residents of the targeted area to argue their cases for them rather than make the first overt move themselves. Those that are particularly adept at annexmanship may follow up these "home-grown" proposals with a study or two of their own. The studies invariably show, often with good cause, how much the proposed annexation would cost the city. City authorities are then likely to express disinterest in the annexation proposal on the grounds of economy. "It's like the girl chasing the boy," says a city manager who boasts of using the technique with consistent success. "She catches him by running away."

Arthur Will, Los Angeles County's County-City Coordinator, believes cities which get rebuffed in annexation attempts may be guilty of either or both of two mistakes. One, says he, lies in too carefully confining annexation attempts to lucrative commercial areas, leaving less lucrative residential "islands" to fend for themselves. The other he calls a "father knows best" attitude. Cities seeking annexations, says he, "can take more pains to research the fringe problem and particularly to find out why city residents moved out. The average outside resident, if he is aware at all," says he, "is aware of the shortcomings of his area but objects to being told he is a freeloader. He is usually suspicious of city politics and doesn't believe the power centers of the city are going to pay heed to his problems."

Mr. Will notes that taxpayers in some unincorporated areas are actually paying higher taxes than their city counterparts and getting inferior service. In addition, he figures he's contributing to the central city's costs through sales taxes on purchases there, library fees, business licenses, and in other ways, without being especially aware of the extent to which these contributions fall short of what he derives from the city.

Where gentle persuasion doesn't work in wooing unincorporated areas, other stratagems may. One particularly effective instrument for engineering consent is water – by withholding supplies or refusing to accommodate discharge. Cities that have refused or been barred from providing these services to outlying areas have relatively little difficulty lining up the joiners. The method, of coures, is more effective in some areas than in others.

Fear of insufficient water to support a growing population, in fact, has led cities to consolidate with those endowed with such supplies. It was this consideration that brought the city of Hollywood in 1910 to vote for consolidation into the city of Los Angeles. The courts had ruled earlier against permitting Los Angeles to sell water from the Owens River aqueduct to any municipality outside its boundaries, though initial deliveries were not to begin until 1913. Richard Bigger and James D. Kitchen, in their special study for Los Angeles' Haynes Foundation on the area's historical development, report the court decision was followed by "a mania for annexation" which "seemed to seize" the people living in districts contiguous to Los Angeles. "There was a general feeling," they state, "that to remain outside Los Angeles meant certain thirst."

Besides Hollywood, the cities of Sawtelle, Watts, Barnes, Eagle Rock, Hyde Park, and others promptly got in line for absorption by the city of Los Angeles. There was some criticism at the time that cities were "selling their birthright for a jug of water," but those who would today contend the move was miguided are either scarce or silent. The issue has long since ceased to stir debate in these once-independent areas.

The city of Boulder, Colorado, uses a system of "revocable permits" to soften areas up for annexation. "They don't get hooked into our water and sewer lines," explains City Manager Robert Turner, "unless they agree to petition for annexation within 90 days from the time they're deemed eligible for it."

Do cities do any better in solving their metropolitan problems, fiscal and otherwise, by pushing their boundaries outward? Professor George H. Esser, Jr., of the Department of Law and Government at the University of North Carolina, summons evidence from the Tarheel State's annals: "Of all our major cities," says he, "only Wilmington remained aloof from annexation in the years just after the war – and only Wilmington, among the state's major cities, failed to show a notable population gain." Whether or not the growth in the state's other major cities came about solely through the act of annexation or not, the point remains: the city of Wilmington, conceding the error of its ways, made its first noticeable annexation moves in a good many years in 1960, and planned to follow it up with others later.

Or one can go more deeply into history. In that case, he would find that practically all the cities which are today among the largest in the country went through vigorous annexation periods in the past – among them, New York, Chicago, Philadelphia, New Orleans, Seattle, and Denver.

Philadelphia in 1854 increased its size by legislative fiat from two square miles to nearly 130 square miles. That single act is credited with ensuring Philadelphia's position among the major cities of the nation. It has done very little growing, geographically speaking, since.

New Orleans was created in 1718 on less than half a square mile of ground. It grew gradually by annexation after 1805, but friction between the old Creole population and the American element tore the city asunder in 1833, resulting in the creation of a sister municipality known as La Fayette. The city was reunited by legislative decree in 1852 after its separate segments ran into financial difficulties. The reunited city then proceeded to absorb the cypress forests and swamplands that surrounded it until it took in all of 196 square miles by the mid-1870's; its further growth was shut off shortly thereafter by municipalities that incorporated around it.

Ballyhoo helped build Chicago to its present stature. Originally incorporated in 1830 with an area of less than half a square mile, about one-sixteenth as much as the city of Milwaukee started with, the Windy City consisted of less than 30 square miles when plans for staging the great Columbian Exposition of 1893 were put into motion. To host the fair, the city fathers of Chicago decided the city needed more room and the prestige that space could bring. Chicago then proceeded to annex 133.15 square miles of real estate, thereby assuring its status as one of the world's great cities for many years to come. Such communities as Lakeview, Hyde Park, and Jefferson thus blossomed inside the city instead of outside it.

New York City might not have been the most populous city in the world today if it had not been prodded into making the annexations it did. For nearly 200 years, from 1686 (33 years after incorporation) to 1874, all there was of New York City was Manhattan – an area which totals approximately 20 square miles. The annexation of three towns in 1874 – Morrisania, West Farms, and Kingsbridge – practically doubled the city's area, but it was accomplished only after those towns, anxious to share the city's amenities, convinced Manhattan voters to accept them over the objections of the island's political bosses. Even then, the annexed areas were treated like stepchildren for fourteen years before administration of their affairs was removed from a sort of "colonial office," under the Public Parks Commission.

The Messrs. Bigger and Kitchen credit Chicago with scaring New York into fostering and accepting the revised charter which vastly increased its area to nearly 318 square miles before the turn of the century. "Fear that Chicago (with its own consolidations in 1889 and 1890) might become the larger city," they contend, influenced adoption of the Greater New York Charter in 1898, bringing all of three counties and parts of two others into a single incorporated city. New York has done very little territorial expanding since; as a result, it is surrounded by some 300 suburban municipalities at present.

There is not much chance that many completely surrounded "core" cities will either convince or coerce their satellite municipalities to surrender their "sovereignty" to join the larger metropolis. But there are signs of stirring at the state level to compel such consolidations. Some states already do so, under rather strict conditions, but these restrictions show signs of becoming less severe as metropolitan problems multiply.

One state that allows its larger cities to gobble up smaller ones without the consent of the city being absorbed is Alaska. A state boundary commission has the final word on such proposals, which may be initiated at any time by the larger city. Recently, it permitted the city of Anchorage to consume the Public Utility District of Fairview, a one-quarter-square-mile area which Anchorage officials contended served as an "island of sin" inside the city of Anchorage. Anchorage officials claimed Fairview permitted beerhalls and brothels to operate twenty-four hours a day, seven days a week, in defiance of Anchorage's efforts to limit the hours of such activities.

"Preventive incorporation," by making the creation of new cities more difficult and annexation that much easier, is another device states are using more often to help their cities grow or, at least, prevent their metropolitan areas from shattering further. Four states in 1961 – Arizona, Idaho, Nebraska, and North Carolina – laid down laws prohibiting incorporations of new cities within specified distances from existing ones, and a fifth, New Mexico, decided to require the submission of proposed incorporations to a county commission for approval.

At the same time they have sought to make annexation easier, some states have also laid down stricter laws to make sure annexing cities don't neglect new areas once they swallow them. Tennessee, which has permitted annexation by city ordinance since 1955, amended its law in 1962 to require annexing cities to lay down a "plan of service" before absorbing any area bigger than a quarter of a square mile or containing over 500 people. The annexation plan must set forth the services and timing of their provision before the state will allow the annexation. The state of Washington has a special review board to determine whether a proposed annexation is in the public interest; the proposal may be rejected even if voters in the city and the annexed area have approved it, though this rarely happens in practice.

Joseph Robbie, chairman of the Minnesota Municipal Commission, is among an increasing number of urban authorities who believe big cities will have to be given unilateral rights to grow still bigger in the future if jurisdictions are to coincide with physical facts. A lawyer himself, he has played a leading role in the revision of Minnesota law to permit such absorptions.

No one yet is compelling municipalities to make "uneconomic" annexations, but if the cities ever get on their financial feet, such annexations may well be required. Low-value areas are being by-passed almost as avidly as high-value ones are being sought, leaving to the counties the burdens of renewal and the general provision of urban services. The problem is likely to take on considerably more significance in the future, both as unincorporated suburban areas deteriorate and as cities themselves engulf these areas, aggravating the need for added police, welfare, and other provisions that previously characterized the city core.

CHAPTER FOURTEEN

Urban Blight and Civic Foresight

"THE average building in downtown Boston is 75 to 100 years old. Our downtown streets are winding cow pastures. Traffic is so chaotic that an expressway we just built which was to have been adequate for nearly a decade was filled to capacity on the rush hour almost as soon as it was opened. It would cost us $2 billion to get the city core back into shape again and then we couldn't begin to show results for a good ten years."

This picture, painted recently by one of Boston's leading officials, has only to be altered in a few details to depict the plight of almost every large metropolis in the land today. It is becoming increasingly familiar in smaller and suburban towns as well.

A Durham, North Carolina, official estimated not long ago that he would need "five times as much money in the decade to 1970 to cope with downtown congestion and decay as we can possibly raise in that period." Walla Walla, Washington (population 25,000), would have to lay claim to the equivalent of half its budget to tackle the problems of decay in its downtown area, according to an official of that town.

The finance director of one of Chicago's leading "bedroom" suburbs, Evanston, Illinois, declares: "The biggest single problem we have is the maintenance of standards in a city that is growing older."

Despite considerable sums poured into urban renewal by public bodies and all the attendant publicity that rides every redeveloper's blueprint, efforts to contain the spread of urban deterioration have been discouraging up to now. C. A. Ripley, Mayor of Mercedes, Texas, likens the nation's urban renewal efforts to "the planting of rosebushes in a weedpatch." Author and Harvard Business School Professor Raymond Vernon calls those efforts "insignificant." He notes that though it has been at it longer than any other city in the country, New York by 1962 had succeeded in clearing less than three square miles of its 250-square mile area, a good part of which, he maintains, is in dire need of upgrading.

According to the Census Bureau, one out of every six dwellings in the nation is either dilapidated or substandard because of such basic deficiencies as the lack of plumbing facilities. More Americans, in fact, live in substandard housing than live on farms; the Census Bureau established the figures for 1960 at 22 million and 21 million, respectively. Of the 50 million homes and apartments in being in the United States at the beginning of 1960, 11.4 million were said to be in a deteriorating or deficient condition.

There's no sure way to gauge the speed of blight's spread against the rate of clearance since the concept itself varies sharply according to the beholder and his standards. The Census Bureau, which keeps figures on deficient and so-called "substandard" dwelling units, actually reported a dramatic reduction in their number, from 4.5 million in 1950 to 3 million in 1960, but the figures say nothing about commercial areas. Nor, for that matter, do they say anything about the general condition of neighborhoods which can render physically sound structures unfit, if they front on heavy truck movement, for instance, or are surrounded by factories emitting obnoxious fumes.

A good many authorities believe the only way to judge blight's spread lies simply in experienced observation. Mayors, renewal officials, and bankers have done much of that. And in city after city, from Gotham to Glendale, California, and from Bloomington, Indiana, to Birmingham,

Alabama, they agree: certainly, the spread of blight has been outpacing by a good margin the redevelopment efforts of both public agencies and private developers alike.

J. W. Dyckman and R. R. Isaacs, in their volume *Capital Requirements for Urban Development and Renewal* (published by McGraw-Hill in 1961 as one of a series of housing studies sponsored by the American Council for the Improvement of Our Neighborhods – otherwise known as ACTION), figured that if the nation were to attempt to replace all its slums and substandard structures even over a twelve-year period, it would have to spend five times as much on redevelopment annually during that span as the $4 billion worth of private and public monies it is currently devoting to the purpose. The public contribution under the Housing Act of 1961 amounted to $2 billion in federal money available over a three-year period to make up for losses suffered by municipalities in reselling land they purchased and razed for redevelopment purposes. Local governments were expected to put up one dollar for every two provided by Uncle Sam. The bulk of redevelopment expenditures, of course, is expended by private enterprise.

Approximately 3,000 acres were acquired for urban renewal projects in the United States in the year to June 30, 1961, a peak to that time. Yet, the United States urbanizes over one million acres of land every year. In other words, it would take 333 years at the present renewal rate to "restock" just one year's addition to the "urban plant." And the pace of urbanization is slated to accelerate more rapidly in the years ahead.

Urban Renewal Administrator William L. Slayton says the United States could go on spending "as much on slum clearance as it is spending today for the next twenty years and still not be within sight of completing the job." Still, the federal government spent more in the first three years of the 1961 Housing Act to help cities gouge out their slums than all public bodies put together spent for the purpose in the previous twelve years. Few expect even a bountiful national administration to vastly increase this federal outlay in the foreseeable future as long as defense continues to demand so much of the nation's resources. America's urban areas, therefore, are going to have to find some other method for coping with deterioration besides trying to hack it out after it sets in.

One device for coping with the metropolitan malignancy lies in arresting the decline as it is getting started through rehabilitation of neighborhoods that can still be saved. The federal government attempts to encourage these efforts by giving local redevelopment agencies, through the Housing Act of 1961, the power to buy, renovate, and resell up to a hundred substandard dwelling units in any designated urban renewal area. Notable progress in the reclamation of deteriorated areas of the city have been made under this provision in such places as New Haven, Connecticut, and the Society Hill section of Philadelphia, just southeast of historic Independence Hall.

Rehabilitation, however, does not provide for the accommodation of greater numbers of people. Indeed, it may result in fewer dwelling units, since housing standards often call for less crowding. Vast segments of the nation's cities, furthermore, are beyond rescue by cosmetics alone. The makeup approach, moreover, is expensive, and doomed to failure unless entire neighborhoods are inspired to improve themselves.

Because of the limitations of renewal and rehabilitation, therefore, some other approach must be sought to the problem of urban deterioration. There are some – Frank Lloyd Wright once counted himself among them – who believe civilized man should simply quit his nest after he fouls it. Close-in suburban land with roads and utilities, they argue, can generally be had for $25,000 an acre – about a tenth of the cost of cleared city land, at a rough average. The rehabilitation of existing structures frequently runs $3,000 or more per room, which is not a great deal less than what it costs to construct it new out in suburbia.

Nineteenth-century author Nathaniel Hawthorne, in *The House of the Seven Gables,* looked forward to a time of affluence that would permit such practices. Said he: "We shall live to see the day when no man shall build his house for posterity. Why should he? He might just as reasonably order a suit of clothes – leather, or gutta-percha, or whatever lasts longest – so that his great-grandchildren should have benefit of them and cut precisely the same figure in the world that he himself does. I doubt," said he, "that even our public edifices – our capitols, state houses, court houses, city halls, and churches – ought to be built of such permanent materials as stone and brick. It were better that they crumble to ruin, once in twenty years or thereabouts, as a hint to the people to examine into and reform the institutions which they symbolize."

Hawthorne's view might have been more valid today if cities had not grown so tall, largely as a result of the elevator and the development of steel construction. The taller buildings get, the costlier they are to tear down even though the technology for dismantling them is proceeding apace. To abandon existing cities, would be to scrap an investment estimated at over $500 billion, about equal to the annual national product. Much of that investment, of course, is still sound, and the strategic areas cities occupy are far too valuable to be junked even if the operation were feasible.

Thus, cities must be rebuilt, probably continuously. Public money alone cannot do it, hence the need for still greater incentives to private redevelopers by tax or other devices. Indeed, even Baron Haussmann's face-lifting of Paris over a century ago received such an assist: new structures built along the boulevards the baron created were encouraged by a lengthy period of tax exemption.

The device, of course, is not altogether unknown in the United States. It has been used to encourage the development of low-income housing and for other purposes. Boston's new 31.5-acre Prudential Center just beyond its downtown area, for example, was midwifed by the city's willingness to limit its take from property taxes to no more than 20 percent of Prudential's gross annual revenues provided the payment exceeded $3 million a year.

Ironically, cities are subsidizing blight at the same time they are seeking to uproot it. By failing to assess improved property more on the basis of land values and less on the worth of structures, they are penalizing those who keep their property up while rewarding those who allow them to run down and divide them further into slum tenements. "Taxpayers are subsidizing blight in this manner," argues the veteran Los Angeles planner Gordon Whitnall, "at the same time they are underwriting the clearance of blighted areas for redevelopment under urban renewal."

The upgrading process can be encouraged, too, by rooting out the crabgrass peculiar to a given city or segment of it. It was only after Pittsburgh's downtown area was liberated from its chronic pall of smoke and threat of flood, for example, that private financing was induced to create the city's now-famous Golden Triangle. The three aluminum and steel skyscrapers erected at the confluence of the Monongahela and Allegheny rivers were the first office buildings constructed in the area since the 1920's.

By tearing down its sun-robbing, noisy elevated railway from Third Avenue and widening that street, New York City succeeded in encouraging private capital to create a vibrant byway out of one whose degradation once stretched almost the entire length of Manhattan Island, from the derelict-haunted Bowery to the squalid tenements of East Harlem.

Neither renewal, rehabilitation, nor new housing, however, can sterilize urban ground against the seed that grows the slum. Where slums are cleared and new development takes their place, slum families often are simply scattered and offices elsewhere emptied, thus hastening the decline of other parts of the city. Where public housing is married to urban renewal, the slum family remains, and with it, its myriad of problems. Efforts to screen some of these problems from public housing by screening prospective tenants have, however, met with a certain amount of criticism despite favorable results. Richard H. Amberg, publisher of the *St. Louis Globe-Democrat*, the city's morning newspaper, notes that city's early efforts in public housing enjoyed fair success, because, he contends, "tenants were screened before they were accepted." However, he adds, there was some contention that public housing should not be selective, that those excluded were, after all, often in greatest need of decent shelter.

The St. Louis public housing authority attempted to answer the criticism by opening up one of its projects to a much broader spectrum of the underprivileged. This time, crime statistics, rather than critics, provided the commentary: Some 1,700 dwelling units housing approximately 15,000 people produced 42 robberies, 6 rapes, 42 cases of aggravated assault, and 57 burglaries in a single year. The situation was serious enough to become the subject of a grand-jury investigation, which brought measures that helped halve the crime rate the following year, though many still regarded it excessive.

Fairly or unfairly, the reputation this single experience fashioned for public housing in the city of St. Louis was not easily eradicated. A St. Louis cabdriver in 1961 voiced a widely-shared sentiment when he stated: "I'd rather live in the tenements than in the government housing. You never know when you're going to get mugged in an elevator." Says Mr. Amberg: "We succeeded only in turning a horizontal jungle into a vertical one."

In an attempt to civilize that vertical jungle, the city's housing authority hired a private protection agency to augment the services of the St. Louis Police Department.

It also reverted to greater selectivity in its screening of applicants, even to the extent of visiting the prospect's dwelling to determine his housekeeping and other habits. As a result of these and other investigative techniques, the Authority at one time was turning down as many as two-thirds of its applicants. Tenants also were more strictly supervised. Those who misbehaved were evicted, generally for "rent delinquency," since the two conveniently often go together.

The authority also is attempting to tackle the problems it has consented to house. Free X-rays and blood tests, weekly adult classes in reading to combat illiteracy, seminars in money management, and, with the help of a major utility and dairy concern, instruction in the preparation of nutritious low-cost meals comprise some of the ingredients of its "human renewal" effort. To improve housekeeping practices and stir greater civic consciousness, adults have been organized into "tenant councils" and teenagers into "junior tenant councils."

The city of Oakland, California, in 1957 organized its so-called Associated Agencies Program to bring together as many as it could of the private organizations, government agencies, educational institutions, and others interested in a more comprehensive assault on slum problems. Professors from the University of California and Stanford now sit around tables with local city officials and others in a former estate in the Oakland Hills, purchased for $500,000 with the help of a Ford Foundation grant, to plan their campaigns against such problems as the high school dropout, juvenile delinquency, and the need for effective leadership among minority groups. "We're just trying to rescue ourselves from the urban junkpile," says City Manager Wayne E. Thompson.

There are, of course, no magic methods for permanently ridding cities of slums or slum problems. Blight, of course, does not begin in buildings but in human beings. It would, however, be a mistake to look for the causes of blight solely among the residents of blighted areas. Individuals in well-manicured communities contribute significantly to the very physical and human rot they profess most to deplore when they fail to take an active role in uprooting the economic and social obstacles that breed despair among underprivileged members of minority groups and rob them of human dignity.

More than future slums are being created by the failure to achieve that "more perfect" urban union. The issue, perhaps the most serious of all problems that face a suburbanizing America, has been more fully discussed in an earlier chapter ("School Bells—and Burdens") and will be considered further in the next and concluding chapter.

. . . AND CIVIC FORESIGHT

IT took the Black Plague to get London to lay its first underground sewer system, though the need had long since been proclaimed by those anxious for the city's health. Even then, the experience failed to frighten other cities with open sewers running through their streets into similar action. Naples began confining its public filth only after suffering a cholera epidemic of its own decades later. In France, waves of the disease sowed death and dissension before housing standards finally were established to inhibit the scourge.

Civic myopia rarely takes its toll in human life in developed nations today. Modern man has conquered infectious disease in most civilized parts of the world. But he has not learned to cope with many of his other urban ills. Possibly because their alleviation is no longer a question of life or death but of lost opportunities and unvisualized benefits, civic ailments tend to be tolerated as the inevitable consequences of a more crowded urban existence.

As a result, the exercise of civic foresight in metropolitan affairs is rare. Urban giants gobble up open space with scant regard to nature's spiritual worth to man. Populations smear themselves across the landscape, but no effort is made to cultivate the lines of destiny capable of nourishing new transit systems into being and old ones back to health. City centers are strangled by thickening congestion and shattered beyond the walker's scale by ruthless expressways and land-gluttonous parking facilities, yet schemes for rescuing these strategic areas are rarely taken seriously by the populace whose support is necessary to bring them into being.

While cities in much poorer nations grow old gracefully, those in a land which boasts the highest living standard of all sacrifice their civic environment on the pyres of shortsighted self-interest. The magnitude of urban blight is mute testimony to that fact.

Instead of providing the amenities – the fountains and tree-shaded squares, the occasional statue and the luxurious boulevards – which tend to paint the patina of pride over property values and ward off the ill effects of age, American cities content themselves with public austerity in the name of practicality and free enterprise. Instead of providing a pattern of communal design to benefit the movement and living modes of its people, the city stands indifferently by as each developer pursues his own particular purpose on what is only temporarily his own particular plot of ground.

Where that plot is big enough, the private developer does not often neglect the opportunity to plan it as a whole, and a Rockefeller Center is created in the process. Unfortunately, such costly urban undertakings are not common. Where they are lacking, there is a vacuum, with almost no effort at all made to direct the inevitable piecemeal development into a sensible and attractive whole.

With the exception of the early colonial period, Americans have given almost no communal direction whatsoever to their urban development. Until the mid-1920's, in fact, exceedingly few cities had even zoning controls to prohibit the intermingling of factories and residences. Some big cities still lack them: Houston is one. As recently as 1954, only fifty American cities had housing codes to establish minimum standards in construction. Even today, a number of large cities lack these rudiments of control over urban development. Before the Wagner Housing Act was passed in 1937, there was not a city in the country with the power to condemn slum properties, clear them, and make their salvaged land available to private investors for redevelopment.

It is ironic, perhaps, that Americans, who are notorious for their nonsupport of better civic design, are nevertheless among the most ardent admirers of European cities, often those which owe their beauty most to some ambitious plan. It is true, of course, that much Old World planning was done under circumstances considerably more conducive to success than those which prevail in the United States. Well-planned cities of the past were customarily laid out by strong central governments or rulers for the relatively easily determined purpose of facilitating military movement; even Baron Haussmann's boulevarding of Paris in 1870 had the easy flow of armies largely for its purpose. It is a good deal more difficult, on the other hand, to mold a city to suit the varied tastes and needs of its populace, let alone the economic and technological changes which affect them and so rapidly alter the urban scene. When those preferences are to be interpreted, further, not by a strong central government but by a variously-composed and relatively easily-swayed democratic government, the task becomes infinitely more difficult.

Many of the most thoroughly planned cities of the past, in fact, were colonial cities created by despotic governments, often with such dispatch that even the vagaries of time had no chance to mar the scheme. Still, many of the most ancient of these cities, not only in the Mediterranean world but also in China, India, South and Central America, evidence a good deal more civic foresight than is customarily to be found among this nation's largest cities today. They exhibited orderly street systems – a sensible division of land use between residential, commercial, and civic functions, extensive water systems, and an allocation of impressive sites to the highest public purposes, in those days usually palaces.

King Philip of Spain showed solicitude for his subjects in the New World in 1573 by setting forth rules for the construction of colonial cities which called for streets to be laid out so windswept dust would create a minimum nuisance to inhabitants. He also ordered slaughtering places to be located at the outskirts of town so their odors would not waft needlessly amid the populace.

However, unless the social benefit was the will of a strong ruler, it customarily had to be purchased first by paying the wages of neglect – today, in blight, congestion, and waste; yesterday, in deadly epidemics. Even in the socially-conscious countries of Great Britain, Sweden, and Germany, it took the squalor and congestion of an Industrial Revolution to touch off wide concern for city design.

In the United States, where the old could always be left behind and the principles of individualism were not to be contained in any sphere of endeavor, what few exercises were conducted in city planning were the products of relatively halcyon periods. William Penn's gridiron pattern for the city of Philadelphia, now regarded as so wasteful of land and inefficient for traffic, was presented in 1682. Pierre L'Enfant's plan for a monument-showcasing Washington dates from 1791. And the blueprint Mormon leader Brigham Young used to lay the form for Salt Lake City in 1847 had been drawn up thirteen years earlier by Joseph Smith in envisioning "the city of Zion."

American interest in city planning (but not yet action)

was first widely stirred by the Columbian Exposition in Chicago in 1893. Daniel Burnham, architect of that world's fair, aroused the nation's imagination by expressing in visual layout a philosophy which exhorted planners to "make no little plans" because they did not have the "magic to stir men's blood" and therefore probably "would never be realized." To this day, the beauty of Chicago's lakefront development attests to the boldness of the Burnham vision. Ugly waterfronts and reviled natural assets of so many cities hold the docket for practical expediency.

Only a negative version of Burnham's brand of urban thinking ever got through to the public and their hardheaded city councils: the zoning authority to prohibit undesirable mixtures of land use. Even this principle was bitterly fought, though it had been used from time to time in the past, once to prohibit the location of storage places for gunpowder in the center of Boston. Back in the seventeenth century, there was even some attempt to "zone" the location of people, when, in an effort to fashion a more perfect democracy, the General Assembly of Massachusetts required its inhabitants to live within a half-mile of their respective Commons. The theory: they would then be more likely to participate in local government and perform their civic duties.

Walter Gropius, the German-born architect, has criticized the development of American cities as having been guided "only by zoning laws that merely forbade the worst." The American city, he maintains, "is not a product of necessity but of municipal habits. There is no lack of good planners and designers who really know what could be done to bring about a new unity of design," says he, "but they have no power."

In a democratic society, that power can come from only one source: public persuasion. Unless the planner is to be made the autocrat of city design, final decisions as to the city's form and shape must inevitably rest with the electorate or its representatives, however buffeted they may be by the political winds that happen to be blowing at the time.

The planner, to be effective, must be capable of putting across the merits of his plan while setting forth the advantages and disadvantages of alternative plans. Thus, he must also be something of a salesman. The community owes him, and itself, however, a platform for the purpose.

"Planners have been too timid up to now in presenting their ideas to the public, or else they have presented them too much on a take-it-or-leave-it basis," asserts David F. Bramhall, a Baltimore city planning consultant and a member of the faculty at Johns Hopkins University. The local citizenry, he argues, must be brought in on plans from their inception and solicited for ideas at various stages if the plan that is finally presented is to have its support.

The penalties for failing to plan are becoming less and less obtuse to read, even if the general public has yet to realize their avoidability or chance of mitigation. They are most obvious today, perhaps, in the needless ravages of blight and thickening congestion, but they exist also in all kinds of minor annoyances, confusion, and waste. The mere matter of naming streets without regard to practical considerations affords many such examples.

A homeowner of five years on Graysby Avenue in San Pedro, California, cannot recall ever having given his address over the telephone without having to spell it at least twice and, more often, three or four times. The city of Portsmouth, Virginia, recently counted among its streets six Lincolns, five Parks and Pines, and four Virginias, Elizabeths, and Pearls, not to mention a host of similar-sounding names, such as Beech and Beach; it has since renamed its streets. The Reuters news agency in 1962 reported that Moscow had 800 streets whose names were duplicated at least once; there were 22 named Sovetskaya,

11 named Gorky, and at least one Pioneer Street, Komsomolskaya Square, and School Lane in every one of several districts. Motorists dring down Cumpston Street in Van Nuys, California, can almost count the number of subdivisions its development has taken by tallying one dead end after the other, provided they are adept enough at finding the street again each time it leaves off; residents who fail to warn their guests that the street is not continuous are accustomed to having them show up as much as half to three-quarters of an hour late.

The American Society of Planning Officials defines planning as "a way of avoiding unnecessary expenditures." For good reason.

For several decades, until it was ultimately cleared and carefully planned, a strategic piece of hilly real estate near downtown Los Angeles known as Monterey Hills was rendered practically valueless through the imposition of a gridiron street pattern that made its hills almost impossible to negotiate and highly unsafe for those who tried. Its virtually inaccessible lots, sold around the turn of the century largely to absentee buyers who saw only a street plan with no idea of the terrain, for years contained only the flimsiest of structures, many of them tax-delinquent. A new street pattern is providing gently curving roads with easy grades. Marked for urban renewal under a little-used open-land provision, it will return the city substantial tax revenues when it is fully developed as a community of homes for upper-middle-income families.

The city manager of Manhattan Beach, California, reports that city, located near Los Angeles, had to lay out $75,000 per city block recently to widen one of its streets by just ten feet. "We could have saved a tidy sum," says he, "if they were built with the proper width from the beginning."

The costliness of acquiring park lands after urban development is already under way and of zoning for apartment buildings in a helter-skelter fashion without regard for the kind of alignment that might make for healthier public transport has been noted in earlier chapters.

Expressways that level newly built civic structures because their paths were not laid out sufficiently in advance, narrow sewer lines and water mains that have to be torn out because they failed to allow for the community's growth, schools doomed to underuse because their hinterlands become hospital complexes instead of residences, economies that are forgone because public facilities that can be combined to their mutual benefit are not coordinated, and substantial savings that are lost because periods of low interest rates are not used to advantage for floating municipal bond issues – these are just some of the wastes that result from the lack of civic foresight.

Danger, as well as waste, follows the failure to plan. Seldom does a summer go by that Los Angeles does not experience a serious fire in Malibu, Laurel, Mandeville, or another of its partially developed canyons. Many of those fires could be much more speedily arrested, maintains Los Angeles' Mr. Whitnall, if development had taken something other than the natural unplanned course it did take. "The roads that first went into Laurel Canyon, for instance," recalls Mr. Whitnall, with more than forty years' experience in city planning, "were short and only deep enough to reach the homes that were then being put in but they were no wider than they had to be for that purpose. Their grades were steep and their curves sharp because that was the cheapest way to build roads.

"As time went on, homes were built deeper and deeper into the canyon and its roads were lengthened until finally they broke through to the other side. Today," says he, "those roads are not only in need of costly widening to accommodate the heavy, through traffic, but they are no less fire traps than the narrow staircase in a six-floor walkup tenement. You can't get fire equipment in there and at the same time get people out."

The greater wisdom, like that of Monterey Hills, Mr. Whitnall maintains, would have been to start a major road at the canyon entrance and spiral it gently to the summit, with practically level branch roads feeding from it to residential streets. As a further bar to fire in the arid area, he would plant succulents or other water-rich flora at strategic places to act as firebreaks. And he would space homes more widely apart. "Hillsides, particularly, must be protected against thick development," says he. "A fire that starts at the bottom of a densely-developed hill will run up it as it runs up a chimney."

Water also poses a hazard in unplanned development. The uproooting of trees, the bulldozing of compacted soil, and the replacement of water-absorbing shrubbery with houses and concrete roads can result in considerable runoff in hilly areas. In 1962, one rainstorm touched off a mudslide in Los Angeles that buried a two-year-old boy alive in his bed and uprooted a tree which fell upon and killed a woman waiting for the school bus that was bringing home her child.

The chronic flooding of certain streets in Tokyo has frequently been laid to the filling-in of rivers and moats for roads without adequate provision for drainage.

Poor road planning delivers danger to the doorstep. Once commercial traffic begins crossing residential areas, children's lives are jeopardized. The trucker, too, may find such routes inefficient, but he has no choice if no provision has been made for through commercial traffic. Louis Kahn, Philadelphia architect and city planner, likens the mixture of different types of traffic on a single street to an attempt to funnel gas, hot water, cold water, sewage, and electric current all through the same tube. James Marston Fitch, Professor of Architecture at Columbia University, maintains that clearer distinctions must be drawn between streets essentially for pedestrian use and roads "meant for the speedy movement of goods and people."

Not long ago, executives of some forty companies head-quartered in Manhattan noted the impact of haphazard development on that city's circulatory system. Meeting at Harriman, New York, to discuss the problem of the city's increasing traffic paralysis, they reported the reduction in bus services to outlying areas was making commuting alto-gether too arduous and costly for many clerical employees, thereby necessitating the hiring of less qualified personnel. Employees who braved the ordeal to work, they found, were often delayed en route by breakdowns in overloaded commuter systems. Delivery trucks caught in thick traffic often arrived too late at their destinations to unload before day's end, thus having to make another trip the following day. The executives themselves were losing valuable time in congestion-wrapped taxis. The situation, they agreed, could not possibly improve unless something drastic were done. But what?

Vienna-born architect and city planner Victor Gruen came up with a solution for these and a good many other downtown ills when he drew up his plan for the city of Fort Worth in 1956. The plan called for ringing Fort Worth's downtown business district with an expressway leading to periphery garages, as well as to other road links. The garages were to be located within a two-and-a-half minute walk of the downtown core, which was to become an oasis of tree-shaded, flower-islanded malls with benches, fountains, statues, and other works of public art. Small transit vehicles were to serve weary walkers within the cen-tral area, where no other passenger vehicles were to be allowed; goods carriers were to move underground. Fort Worth never adopted the plan, which it considered too costly, though the cost of "nonplanning" may prove even greater and far less rewarding.

Undaunted, Mr. Gruen has since proposed similar auto-

"THE FORT WORTH PLAN"—
A center for walking. Two and a half minutes by foot.

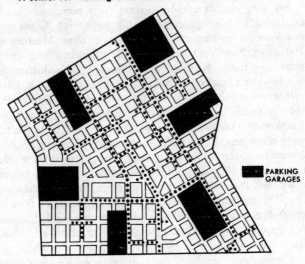

PARKING
GARAGES

limiting solutions for other cities, convinced there is no solution to the problem of re-creating vital urban cores other than to give them back to pedestrians. In 1961 he presented a plan for converting Welfare Island, a narrow strip of real estate which lies between Manhattan and Queens in the East River, into a motorless residential community. The short, narrow island was to be served by a continuous stream of trainlike individual compartments known as "carveyors." The blueprint still sits in abeyance. And Welfare Island remains a desolate piece of close-in real estate settled principally by public health institutions that might be better located elsewhere.

To remedy some of Manhattan's own ills, Mr. Gruen has proposed banning automobiles from midtown and using overhead conveyors to combat congestion in the garment district. The conveyors would link the garment center with warehouses having easy access to riverside expressways, thus speeding truck transit as well as loading and unloading operations. That plan, too, has been considered too "visionary."

Many cities, including Mr. Gruen's native Vienna, however, have begun to blow the whistle on the unrestricted flow of automobile traffic. The Austrian capital of its own accord recently scrapped plans to widen its downtown streets to accommodate more automobiles, and decided instead to prohibit parking on them and to reserve the salvaged lanes for bus traffic only.

Mr. Gruen, who believes Vienna is moving in the right direction, argues: "The time has come for us to separate human flesh and automotive metal in our downtowns. Just as we once put our sewage underground and, later, our electric wiring and our railroads, we must now take automobiles from downtown surfaces."

A few cities, notably Kalamazoo, Michigan, and Miami Beach, Florida, have attempted to effect that separation, at least in part, by turning some of their downtown streets into malls. Auto traffic is banned, and the streets are garlanded with flower beds and trees. Whether the plans are commercially successful or not remains questionable. Merchants on Miami Beach's eight-block-long Lincoln Road Mall lament the loss of buses which reminded the passing public of their existence and of the automotive "carriage trade" that occasionally stopped to shop on impulse. Even the beauty of the mall, they believe, distracts pedestrians who might otherwise be gazing into their windows. The mall's $600,000 cost, in addition, poses a financial burden on merchants along its stretch, since they must repay the city for the outlay.

The successful reshaping of downtown shopping areas, more than likely, will be executed from the ground up rather than imposed upon street patterns originally designed to accommodate automobiles along with pedestrians. Short, winding streets, narrow enough to permit the shopper to take in stores on each side while permitting a choice of return routes, broken up perhaps by pleasant plazas and other focal points of interest, cannot easily be created atop existing street patterns. Many of these efforts will not look like malls at all. It is hardly an accurate description, for instance, for Rochester's ambitious Midtown Plaza; completed in 1962 at a cost of $20 million, the area consists of a roofed-over, air-conditioned complex of more than 60 shops with wide expanses of tree-lined, bench-furnished pedestrian areas.

"First aid" for downtowns, such as promotional "dollar days" that only temporarily close off streets without solving parking and other problems, is doomed to failure from the start and cannot be considered a fair test even of the mall idea.

No section of the metropolitan area is immune to the ill effects of failing to plan for the motorcar. Vehicular approaches to the nation's greatest cities, almost without fail, are trimmed with ugliness. Known as "strip development," their strings of ramshackle enterprises with oversized signs smear the rouge of commerce over what might otherwise have been scenic or soothing vistas. Their metamorphosis, which might be accomplished through the use of setbacks and approved landscape design, could make motoring pleasanter, roadside rest more refreshing and, probably, business more profitable through improved environment. When competition runs rampant, however, the premium generally goes to the enterprise that can snatch the motorist first.

The absence of planning tends to produce a free-for-all among municipalities no less than among enterprises. Their vying for industry, subdivisions, and other development often works to the detriment of the communities involved by causing them to lower minimum standards on such features as the width and quality of roads, the type of streetlights to be provided, the width of sideyards, the number of trees to be planted on a given length of frontage, and the provision of other amenities that tend to preserve property values.

Planning might as well be nonexistent where planning agencies are too profuse. Montgomery County, Ohio, recently counted twenty-six different planning and zoning commissions operating within its confines, none of them with authority over the area as a whole. A citizens' committee from the largest city in the county, Dayton, found that little or no planning preceded the enactment of zoning ordinances even at the municipal and township levels, much less at the regional level. Frequently, cities which zone for single-family residences on one side of the line, and begin to get that type of development, suddenly find cities next door permitting commercial or even industrial development right alongside.

One reason city planning stirs more vigorous opposition than communal support, of course, is that it imposes a certain discipline on development. In instances where the developer's immediate profit is at odds with the best long-term interests of the community as a whole, it tends to pit existing interests, sometimes powerful but always very much in existence, with an amorphous mass that has yet to come into being. Planning also tends to force the resolution of problems in advance of the discomforts which might ultimately yank those decisions loose; it is a good deal easier to get the patient to take his medicine when he is writhing in pain than when he is feeling just a little uneasy. The delay may be dangerous in human beings, in fast-developing cities it is at least costly.

The dictates of planned discipline may be somewhat demanding. Homebuilders in picturesque Palos Verdes Estates, just south of Los Angeles, have been prevented for years from roofing their structures with anything but red tile, according to a trust indenture laid down to preserve

the area's Mediterranean-like character. The architectural
fidelity may be irksome to those who prefer to put their
dollars into fancier automobiles or finer china, but it is a
source of pride to its "regimented" residents and a deliverer
of character that is reflected in property values.

Communities do not have to go to such lengths for urban
conservation. The city of Beverly Hills, in California, a
good part of which is only modestly developed, goes a long
way toward keeping up appearances by outlawing billboards, junkyards, and used-car lots within its borders.
Palm Springs defends its dignity by prohibiting drive-ins,
hot-dog stands, open markets, and auction yards. Some
cities which permit these enterprises, require them to "de-
blight" themselves; thus, junkyards are frequently required
to fence themselves in, and sometimes to foreground themselves as well with pleasing shrubbery. A number of cities
prohibit the posting of advertising signs on rooftops or
hanging over streets.

More and more cities are causing unsightly power and
telephone lines to go underground. In picturesque Santa
Barbara, California, a citizens' committee has agreed to pay
half the cost of undergrounding utilities to get utility companies to go along with the project. In Oakland, California,
where utilities are having to bear the entire load, residents
must content themselves with two miles a year of new pole-
cleared streets.

Building restrictions in the Florida community of Royal
Palm, where lots are priced upward of $35,000 each, pro-
hibit the use of outside clotheslines.

The city of Evanston, Illinois, for its part, has taken to
diking itself against deterioration by planting trees on its
downtown sidewalks, bathing the surfaces of its more interesting civic and commercial buildings in light, and employing more enforcement officials to ensure the effectiveness of its housing code.

Planning has more than practical ends to serve. It has

ideals to lift aloft as well. Dr. Gulick of the Institute of Public Administration, and a lifelong missionary for better cities, puts it this way: "People who live and work in an urban area have a deep emotional need to have 'their city' stand for something worthwhile in the world and to present to themselves and to mankind a strong physical image of this spiritual ambition in the structure of the city, in its vistas and in its major monuments. Through these," says he, "men venerate the past, remember the achievements of those who have gone before, reach for the future and affirm their self-respect and idealism."

CHAPTER FIFTEEN

Conclusions

W E can leave our cities pretty much as they are and avoid radical remedies which would drastically remake them. More people in more automobiles, with more time and money to spend keeping them in motion, will speed up the conquest of urban space on earth and, notwithstanding the huge sums that will be poured into new concrete carpeting, compound congestion at critical places. Urban acreage will continue to be ravaged by blight despite vast renewal efforts. Recreational facilities will be harder to reach but more crowded. And, as the sprawling metropolis spreads its jurisdictional patchquilt of governments across the urban landscape, protection from crime, the schooling of under-privileged youth, the disposal of refuse, and a myriad of other local services will be more and more difficult to adequately finance and effectively provide.

If diversity is all that is desired from the urbanasaur of tomorrow, there need be no concern. Teeming slums and tiny commerce have always been able to flourish in free-for-all human jungles, in Manhattan no less than in Mombasa and in Brooklyn no less than in Baghdad. Those who can afford to do otherwise, however, may not choose to live their lives and raise their children in the kind of areas that make for interesting browsing. More than likely, they will continue to seek refuge, to the extent that they are able to do so, outside the central city.

Assuming maximum choice in the selection of ways of life is desirable and worthy of preservation, the phenomenon of sprawl, then, must be recognized for what it is: an attempt by a large segment of the populace to serve its environmental bent as best it can within its means. The number of families able to achieve homeownership, moreover, is bound to rise substantially as family formations and personal incomes increase. It is hardly likely this future adult populace will willingly forgo the pleasures of homeownership within their grasp. The prospect of privacy, accessible outdoors, one's own property, and the healthier environment afforded children have altogether too much appeal.

There are, of course, those who deplore sprawl and look upon the sameness in subdivisions as monotony that is evil in itself, somehow to be ended. One might ask, however, precisely what significance such an indictment might have. More distinctive housing, needless to say, is almost always desirable if one can afford individuality in the appearance of his home; but is her modern kitchen any less of an improvement over what she had before because the housewife's roof is identical to her neighbor's roof? Is the breadwinner relaxing in a garden chaise any less comfortable because his neighbor's plot is precisely of the same dimension? Is the child less safe in his backyard because his house is shaped exactly like that of his playmate next door? Is it any more difficult to find intellectual stimulation in one's living room because it resembles every other living room on the block?

The family buying mass-produced housing does so because it often cannot afford anything more individual yet wishes to live in more comfortable fashion than the way it did previously. Can one criticize that family for not affording something better – or contend that the cubbyhole it rented in an apartment house was any more different from that of its neighbor or they so much more invigorating than its neighbors in suburbia?

An observer of the sprawling urban scene today might be compelled to concede that the superficial monotony of physical similarity must be the least important of all the ailments of the squatting, modern metropolitan region whose air grows fouler and more dangerous by the day, whose water is threatened increasingly by pollution, whose mobility is undermined by accumulations of vehicles and withering transit, whose educational system reels under a growing variety of economic, social, and national urgencies, and whose entire pattern is assuming an ominous political shape and sociological form, with well-to-do whites in their suburban cities ringing poverty-ridden minority groups widening at the core. Such urban problems pose far greater challenge to human ingenuity, magnanimity, and foresight than the preoccupation with the similarity of shelter would seem to suggest.

Even if the penalties of physical monotony were as valid as sometimes is asserted, would the urban purpose be better served by preventing developers from wedding the economics of construction to the means of the buying public, as that precise taskmaster, Profit, dictates? If a social contribution is indeed to be exacted from developers, might it not be more wisely directed toward more adequate lot sizes or provisions for open space? Attempts to liberate look-alike subdivisions from the lampoonist's pen may be far costlier than they are worth.

Barring government interference with the process, therefore, sprawl is likely to continue and possibly even accelerate in the years ahead. At the same time, more than likely, cities will become more densely settled as well. The prolificacy of the species, provided it continues to be nourished by prosperity, likely will serve both types of growth, for better or for worse. Greater densities will be assured, also, not only by the increasing cost of urban realty but by technological advances that are more likely to benefit apartment-building than homebuilding, not alone in price but also in making apartment living more varied and appealing. Urban growth will thus explode, like any explosion, upward and outward.

Conclusions

It is, however, the horizontal rather than the vertical thrust which is producing so many of the urban problems of today, even those in the central city whose less fortunate inhabitants are left behind in the trek to more open living. Assuming, then, that the opportunity to live however one chooses is to be retained, the question is: How can the evils of sprawl experienced in the past be avoided or mitigated in an even more sprawling future?

Since the automobile is the principal sculptor of the modern metropolis and its ills, a goodly amount of attention must be paid to that vehicle. The principal question in this regard, then, is simply: Can the automobile be controlled or influenced in its movements without compromising the principle of maximum choice? Or does devotion to that principle mean that nothing can be done, for instance, about that vehicle running rampant in the city, cutting wider and wider swaths through valuable built-up areas, shattering strategic centers and otherwise adding to the social and economic burdens of a highly urbanized and still more highly urbanizing nation?

Granted the desirability of mass transit, it is hardly likely that the construction even of very expensive (and perhaps highly wasteful) systems will reverse the rising tide of auto use. Though polls of prospective transit riders have tended historically, sometimes disastrously, to err on the side of greater transit use, a recent survey of Chicago commuters revealed only 18 percent of them would forsake their automobiles even if the transit rides were free, and half of them still would not make the trip in a public conveyance if they were paid 35 cents every time they stepped aboard. Cities which do not even provide express lanes on their downtown streets for buses nevertheless see fit to badger Uncle Sam for millions of dollars or risky loan guarantees for the purpose of bringing rapid-transit systems into being; Uncle Sam may be fooled, but convincing the commuting motorist will be something else again. Whether they like it or not, and whether they improve their transit facilities or not, cities are going to have to cope with more automobiles.

Any effort to ban automobiles from congested downtown areas might seem inconsistent with the objective of minimizing freedom of choice. The question, however, should be posed: Is freedom to be maximized for the motorcar or the motorist as an individual? And if for the latter: Is the motorist benefited most when downtown arteries are allowed to harden with congestion and an otherwise vibrant core to fester with the kind of honkytonk development that commands the most strategic sections of some of the biggest cities in the nation, including New York? Or might the motorist's objectives be better served through the provision of close-in parking and the transformation of the city heart as a place for the uplift of culture and personal communication and the gentler pleasures of leisure which only the pedestrian scale can provide – whether the city is Paris, Venice, or Valley View?

There is nothing new in the concept of city centers spared from the automobile, of course. It is the essence of Victor Gruen's Fort Worth Plan previously described in greater detail. Nor is it unique, by any means, to Mr. Gruen. The harm done cities by unharnessed automobiles has been detailed time and time again. Lewis Mumford in *The City in History* (Harcourt, Brace & World, 1961) framed the indictment thus: "When traffic takes precedence over all other urban functions," he stated, referring to the city, "it can no longer perform its own role, that of facilitating meeting and intercourse. The assumed right of the private car to go anywhere in the city and park anywhere is nothing less than a license to destroy the city."

What are the alternatives?

One is to do nothing at all, or at least very little, and let automotive congestion choke itself. More downtown parking space and expressways, this argument runs, only generate more traffic, necessitating still more parking space and expressways which encourage still more automobiles to use them, and the dizzy cycle spins on endlessly. However, if the jam is thick enough and the parking space scarce enough, traffic will not be inclined to increase quite so rapidly. And even if it were so inclined, it could not possibly do so.

That resignation provides neither for the rescue nor the rejuvenation of the most potentially vital parts of the metropolis.

A second alternative, and one which enjoys the greatest currency at the moment because it results neither in the pain of inaction nor in the costliness of ambitious effort, is to provide parking space and expressway as and where they are needed without concern for their impact on the city itself. As traffic increases, streets are widened and, perhaps eventually, even double-decked. If need be, buildings may be reoriented to upper-level walkways so cars can have the sidewalks, too.

No one can say the concept cannot work, provided the pace of accommodation to the automobile is at least reasonably in tune with the rising need. Unfortunately, public endeavors rarely work that way. And, to the extent that they fail, some segment of the city will suffer. Up to now, it's been the downtown core. There is no reason to think it will cease to be the downtown core, and perhaps more than that, tomorrow.

Between doing all that is possible to accommodate the automobile and as little as is possible, there is another alternative: to somehow control its movement. Just as the traffic engineer decades ago learned to maximize the auto's usefulness by prescribing a discipline of motion to serve the purposes of all concerned, including the pedestrian, so the city planner of today cannot escape the necessity of circumscribing the movements of the automobile for the purpose of sparing the city as the pedestrian has known it. Cities which seek solutions to their downtown ills in any way that compromises their potential as centers of culture, commerce, and plain strolling pleasure are scrapping the greatest urban resource of all, the one asset that made for great cities in the past. To do that in the name of "realism" is to act on the basis of what is presently real, altogether too real, rather than on the basis of what, imaginatively, is both feasible and desirable.

Indeed, some cities are already making the latter choice. Kalamazoo and Miami Beach have scrapped existing roadways to create impressive downtown malls. Others, such as Rochester, New York, have recently created such urban oases from the ground up. Ultimately, if there is any validity in the plan, the fruits will be there for all to see.

But cities are going to have to do more than rescue their downtowns if they are to more fully realize the potential pleasures and reduce the penalties of urban living. They are going to have to tackle the entire problem of motion as well. In brief, they are going to have to make it easier, for those who wish to do so, to cut the length of commutation and to realize other blessings that can be available to urban dwellers.

The mere dispersal of factories has not proved enough of a lodestone to pull people closer to their places of employment. Too many other factors figure in the locating decision for that to be the case. The quality of schools, the character of neighborhoods, the convenience of attractive shopping facilities, and the access to recreational areas are some of the more important elements that enter into that decision. In other words, total communities of manageable size must be dispersed if people are to live closer to their jobs.

The dispersal of communities, moreover, should encourage industry and commerce to disperse further, since it would make labor more readily available in outlying areas, where land costs are less and parking facilities can be inexpensively provided. Air pollution, an increasingly serious problem whose solution is difficult to foresee except through the introduction of a revolutionary new engine, would likewise be given greater opportunity for diffusion if urban development were not quite so heavily concentrated in core areas.

Unless they are provided by private developers, however, self-contained communities must be planned in advance and the proper zoning and public facilities provided. They do not come into being by themselves, unfortunately, the way haphazard development does. A planned urban area has nothing whatsoever to do with a planned economy; one does not necessarily imply the necessity for the other, nor does one assure the other's success. Opposition to city planning on these grounds is wholly without foundation.

Communities will be more attractive places to live if they are reasonably accessible, as well, to a vibrant city core for the stimulation its varied opportunities might afford. Proximity to picnic areas, wooded camping grounds, refreshing vistas, and to open space generally would also seem desirable. The twin objectives are realizable in a much-maligned but almost invariably successful concept known as "the satellite city." A related concept is that of the "garden city," which does not strive for quite so much self-sufficiency in terms of encompassing its own employment opportunities. Both plans are ceaselessly attacked as nineteenth century concepts (which, along with many other worthwhile concepts, they are) – generally by those who would prefer anyway to live in the hustle and bustle of a bazaar-like core. Champions of the garden and satellite cities would not deprive them of that opportunity, but they wish also to see the creation of a true alternative.

Anyone who has ever lived or strolled in communities of this type, such as Letchworth in England (created half a century ago by the humanitarian Ebenezer Howard) or, in the United States, such as Greenbelt in Maryland, Greenhills in Ohio, or Greendale, Wisconsin, cannot help but thrill to the charm of their open spaces in contrast, for example, to so much of Manchester or Mobile.

Planned communities of this type have other features to recommend them besides their livability. They also afford means for the creation and preservation of easily identifiable, relatively manageable urban units – the kind of communities which should, with intelligence and energy, be able to foster active citizen interest in local affairs. The importance of this potential, though its realization is something else again, can hardly be exaggerated. Few, if any, worthwhile achievements by local government are ever scored without it. It is the font of all strength in a democratic society – one which can hardly go wanting in an era when that ideology is called upon to prove itself through practical results as it never has before.

Provided such communities are truly representative of the principles of the democratic system, and do not quarantine low-income or minority groups but provide the housing these people require as well, the well-planned garden or satellite city should also be infinitely more capable than the anonymous, amorphous, unwieldly central city in coping with soaring rates of crime and delinquency. Los Angeles Police Chief William H. Parker is not alone in bemoaning the "concentration of masses of humanity in urban areas" for stoking social despondency and antisocial attitudes.

Regardless of what shape the urban mass of tomorrow takes, however, the dire danger of a continuing trend toward the accumulation of low-income, minority families in the core city and wealthier whites in the suburb must be recognized for what it threatens, politically, socially, and humanely, in terms of understanding and general well-being.

There are ways to cope with that problem, of course, without changing the shape of cities. Better education and the opportunity for better-paying jobs will help, just as it has helped other low-income, minority groups in the past

– provided there is opportunity for the Negro to move where his income will take him. In addition, efforts must be made to provide housing for low-income families elsewhere than in the central city, namely in outlying areas where they might have access to open space and to jobs that are being planted increasingly there. Such housing, however, can hardly be provided if nearby residents do not understand its necessity and desirability. If such understanding is not forthcoming, the federal government, which meets much of the welfare and other costs of low-income concentrations at the core, may well consider the wisdom of withholding transit, highway, recreational, and other aid from such areas.

Such measures may seem drastic – until they are measured against the consequences of ignoring the necessity for action in this crucial area. The ostrich may roar with the jab, but its head, at least, will be yanked from its feathery hideaway.

Almost no effort to remake the urban landscape, socially or otherwise, can readily succeed, however, if it is shattered into too many uncoordinated governmental units. Some degree of closer coordination is absolutely vital if any metropolitan undertaking is to be realized, whether it is the creation of a transit system, the construction of an incinerator plant, or the provision of a more sensible housing pattern. The metropolis of today, let alone tomorrow, can no more tackle its area-wide problems on the governmental crutches of another age than it can wage war on organized crime with mounted police or fight a blaze with water buckets.

Outmoded tax systems must similarly be updated. Central cities which cannot get at outlying residents in any other way must be enabled to levy sales or income taxes, or perhaps both. Such taxes, however, will prove self-defeating if they succeed in chasing industry and commerce out of the central city. To be effective, such taxes must be instituted on a state, or at least on a county level; in any case, the state has to present the taxing opportunity.

State governments will have to assist their metropolitan areas in many other ways besides sharing more generously in the taxing power if those areas are not to become increasingly the wards of their respective state governments. State governments must, by legislative fiat if need be, make it easier for cities to annex outlying unincorporated areas where they still exist, to consolidate with county governments or other municipalities, and otherwise to create the metropolitan area-wide governments needed to rationalize the local political scene so that the metropolis can get on with its urgent tasks. State governments that fail to take these measures in behalf of their cities will succeed only in forcing their cities to look increasingly to Washington for relief from their many ills.

Index

Accident rates, 68

Accidents, cost of highway, 67; and speed, 73

Adams, Samuel, 305

Adjusting Municipal Boundaries, 376

Advertising, and public revenue, 306

AFL-CIO International Association of Fire Fighters, 196; pamphlet against unified public-safety service, 216; on unified public-safety service, 214

Agricultural chemicals, and pollution, 116

Agronsky, Martin, on air pollution, 89

Air pollution, 416-417; in Chicago, 303; cost of, 102-105; in Los Angeles, 303; in Phoenix, 303

Alabama, income tax in, 321; sales tax in, 323

Alarms, 198-200

Alaska, city annexation in, 383; sales tax in, 323

Albany, N.Y., starlings in, 280

Alexander the Great, 17

Amarillo, Tex., water shortage in, 127

Amberg, Richard H., on screening public housing, 392; on water pollution, 110

Ambulance services, in Los Angeles, 200-201

American Academy of Occupational Medicine, 93

American Colonies, population density of, 15; Stamp Act in, 305

American Council for the Improvement of Our Neighborhoods, 388

American Institute of Architects, against road network, 37-38

American Judicature Society, on contingency fees, 84-85

American Library Association, 259, 265

American Municipal Association, 369; on air pollution, 105; on annexation, 376; on commuting, 48

American Public Works Association, 285, 291, 294

American Revolution, 305

American Society of Planning Officials, 400

American Society of School Administrators, 250

American Transit Association, 54; survey, 50-51

American Water Works Association, 125

Anaheim, Calif., and fire prevention, 208

Anchorage, Alaska, annexation in, 383

Anderson, Burt L., on recreation, 145

Annexation, and city limits, 366-385; in U.S.A., 368-370

Aristotle, on cities, 19

Arizona, annexation in, 372-374; incorporation in, 359, 384; sales tax in, 323

Arizona Biochemical Company, 299-300

Arkansas River, pollution of, 111

421

Index

Index

Index

Index

Index

Index

Index

Index

Library Journal, 270
Library Services Act, 260, 270
Lie detector, use of, 180-182
Linkon, Gordon, on law-enforcement agencies in Chicago, 176
Lisbon, Portugal, subway in, 65
Living cost of, 18-19
Loeb, Henry, on "balkanized" governments, 338; on police facilities in Memphis, 176
London, air-pollution disasters in, 90; epidemics in, 394; first underground sewer system in, 394; "metro" in, 345
London School of Economics and Political Science, 334
Long, Huey, advertising tax of, 306
Long Beach, Calif., Commerce and Maritime Museum, 329
Long Island, N.Y., water pollution in, 118
Long Island Railroad, problems of, 43, 47, 56-57
Los Angeles, air pollution in, 86-87, 102-104, 303; air-pollution conference in, 108; Air Pollution Control District, 99, 100, 303; annexation in, 367, 379, 380; annual reports in, 326-327; "balkanized" government in, 337; City Traffic Department, 40; compost operations in, 299; concrete spread in, 32; consolidation in, 360, 380; control of air pollution in, 94-100; cutting costs of education in, 250-251; Department of Recreation and Parks, 141; driver training in, 246; expressways in, 36; Fire Department, 202, 203; fire hazards in, 402; firemen's pay in, 196; freeways and traffic of, 35; growth of, 14; highway problems and municipal authorities of, 364; hot-rod strips in, 187; "language laboratory" in, 249-250; local governments in area of,

Los Angeles (cont'd)
333-334; Metropolitan Transit Authority, 27-28, 45; Monterey Hills, planning in, 400, 402; motorists oppose public transit, 55; nongraded plan in, 244; "Pacific Electric" rail system, 27-30; Police Department, 165, 171; population of, 16; population growth of, 28; population percentages in, 231; public library losses, 257-258; recreational facilities, 141-142, 148; safety fencing in, 68; sanitary landfills in, 301; seeks federal transit aid, 51; service-charge opportunities in, 325; "sprawl" in, 13-14, 18; staggered work hours in, 63-64; starlings in, 280-281; as suburb, 13; traffic congestion in, 32, 34-35; transit studies in, 52-53; Unified School District double sessions, 229-230; use of helicopters in, 68. See also Los Angeles County
Los Angeles County, "balkanized" government in, 338, 351-353; beachfront problems of, 153; "creates" cities in, 360-362; and dump sites in Glendale, 287; incinerators in, 303; "Lakewood Plan" in, 353-355; municipalities multiply in, 339; patchquilt of local governments in, 331, 333; property taxes in, 308; refuse disposal in, 298, 304
Los Angeles Times, on air pollution, 108; on mass transit, 52
Louisiana, sales tax in, 323
Louisville, Ky., city income tax in, 321

McCall's, on traffic congestion, 33
McCamment, Claude, on highway safety, 75

Index

437

Index

THE OTHER AMERICA
Poverty in the United States

Michael Harrington

The book credited with sparking the government's War on Poverty. Michael Harrington gives a vivid description of America's poor – the unskilled workers, the aged, the minorities, and the other rejects of the affluent society. He analyzes the nature and causes of the Other America and warns that in the U.S. today poverty is becoming a self-perpetuating culture, a way of life. He calls for an integrated and comprehensive program to conquer it. The government has responded with the War on Poverty.

"It impressed Jack Kennedy . . . it is clear that [this] book contributed to Johnson's new drive."
—Time

"THE OTHER AMERICA has been credited with helping to open the Administration drive on poverty. . . ."
—The New York Times

"It is an excellent book – and a most important one."
—The New Yorker

THE ARMED SOCIETY
Militarism in Modern America

Tristram Coffin

"There is no evidence that we [Americans] are peace-loving or ever have been. We have taken what we wanted by force if need be, sometimes muttering a proper prayer over the vanquished." With these words Washington political writer-novelist Tristram Coffin launches a daring indictment of the American military establishment and the American spirit. In witty, hard-hitting language he describes the military hierarchy, the outmoded reactionary ideals of the military mind, the dangerous hold the military has on the public imagination as well as on the public purse strings.

"Tristram Coffin . . . pulls out the pins and flips hand grenades down the corridors of the Pentagon."
—*The New York Times*

"A serious work, well done, and somewhat frightening."
—*Houston Chronicle*

IN DEFENCE OF POLITICS

Bernard Crick

"Original and profound. It is hard to think of anyone interested in politics at any level who would not benefit by reading it."
—Max Beloff

At a time of brittle cynicism about the activities of politicians, this book makes "an attempt to justify politics in plain words by saying what it is." In a civilized community, which is no mere tribe, the establishment among rival groups and interests of political order – of agreed rules for the game – marks the birth of freedom. In spite of the compromises, deals, half-measures, and bargains which prompt impatient idealists to regard politics as a dirty word – indeed, because of them – the negotiating processes of politics remain the only tested alternative to government by outright coercion.

UNITED NATIONS
Piety, Myth, and Truth

Andrew Boyd

The UN has evolved in unforeseen ways and many people
are entirely ignorant of its true nature. This volume presents a behind-the-scenes look at its development and
present structure. The off-stage debates, the emergence of
executive power, the probable future of the organization
are among the points dealt with by Mr. Boyd, who is on
the editorial staff of the *Economist*.